ORAL AND WRITTEN
COMMUNICATION DISORDERS

Identification & Multisensory Teaching

MAUREEN K. MARTIN

THEORY AND APPLICATION
OF THE DUBARD ASSOCIATION METHOD®

Dedication

Dedicated to the children who have been enrolled in the DuBard School for Language Disorders at The University of Southern Mississippi and the teachers and staff who have so generously served them.

In Memoriam

In memory of Mildred A. McGinnis whose abilities, insights, and dedication to the educational welfare of children with severe language, speech and hearing disabilities gave guidance and inspiration to many who were privileged to study with her and to know her.

In memory of N. Etoile DuBard whose vibrant and varied life provided richness for so many who crossed her path. From a multitude of students faced with language-speech and hearing challenges, to the university students who learned under her guidance and direction, Etoile's scholarship, compassion, and generosity are reflected in the lives and work of all who had the privilege of calling her teacher, professor, mentor, and friend.

In Memory of Etoile DuBard

N. Etoile DuBard, Professor Emerita, Speech and Hearing Sciences, The University of Southern Mississippi, where she taught from 1962 to 1989, received her B.S. degree from Mary Hardin-Baylor College, her M.A. from George Peabody College, and her Ph.D. from The University of Southern Mississippi. After nine years as an elementary classroom teacher, she entered the field of speech-language pathology and deaf education, studying under Mildred McGinnis, originator of the Association Method, at Central Institute for the Deaf, St. Louis. DuBard established the School for Children with Language Disorders, The University of Southern Mississippi, in 1962 and served as director of the program until her retirement in 1989. She became full professor in the Department of Speech and Hearing Sciences and was named as Distinguished Professor of the University. In 1996, Dr. Aubrey K. Lucas, President of The University of Southern Mississippi, and the Board of Trustees of the Institutions of Higher Learning renamed the school "DuBard School for Language Disorders" in her honor. She provided professional training in a number of geographic areas of the United States, Ireland, and Canada. She was a life member of the Mississippi Speech-Language-Hearing Association and the American Speech-Language-Hearing Association and held Certificates of Clinical Competence in speech-language pathology and audiology. DuBard remained active professionally after her retirement, conducting professional training courses and special work at the DuBard School for Language Disorders. In addition, she was a founding member of the International Multisensory Structured Language Education Council (IMSLEC).

This book evolved from the work of the late Etoile DuBard, Ph.D., CCC-SLP/A, CED who authored *Teaching Aphasics and Other Language-Deficient Children* (1974, 1976, 1983), University Press of Mississippi. Subsequently, *Teaching Language-Deficient Children* (1994, 1997, 2000) was co-authored by Etoile DuBard and Maureen K. Martin. These two texts are the foundation of the current volume.

To say that Etoile DuBard was ahead of her time is a major understatement. With her initial work as a general education elementary classroom teacher and later becoming a pioneering "speech correctionist," as speech-language pathology was called in the early days, to her ultimate certification in education of the deaf and audiology, Etoile was extraordinarily gifted. Certainly, her decision to attend a summer workshop under Mildred McGinnis in 1959 changed her life and the lives of thousands to follow. Etoile subsequently made the decision to return to Washington University and Central Institute for the Deaf for two years of study under McGinnis and others. It was at the conclusion of that study that she was invited to establish a program at The University of Southern Mississippi based on the needs of a faculty member's child who had lost his language and hearing as a result of Asian flu. In the years following the opening of the school, then known as the School for Preschool Deaf and Aphasic Children, Etoile became a charter member of the faculty when the autonomous Department of Speech and Hearing Sciences was organized and degree programs were established.

It is also significant that, during the 1959 summer course under Miss McGinnis, Etoile DuBard met two Irish Dominican nuns, Sr. Mary Nicholas Griffey, O.P., and Sr. Mary Tolan, O.P., from St. Mary's School for Deaf Girls in Dublin, Ireland. Thus began a 40-year personal and professional friendship which was significant for developments in both the school in Mississippi and the school in Ireland. In honor of that rich relationship came the decision to make the cover of this text, and all previous versions, green. The collaboration and friendship among the three extraordinarily gifted women, Etoile DuBard, Sr. Nicholas and Sr. Mary, led to this author's study in Ireland during an internship at the Master's level and later during Ph.D. studies at the National University of Ireland, University College Dublin.

Etoile DuBard changed the lives of thousands of children—either through direct services that she provided or supervised or through the multitude of pre-professionals and professionals whom she taught during her 27 year tenure at The University of Southern Mississippi as well as afterwards in her retirement. Etoile's commitment to the children and university students drove her life's work. Her standards of excellence resulted in continued development and refinement of the Association Method, now known as the DuBard Association Method®, by the many staff members who served at the school over the years and by Etoile herself.

More could be said and written about Etoile's vision, innovation, and insight. Those who are interested are invited to visit and study at the DuBard School for Language Disorders at The University of Southern Mississippi where the foundation laid by Etoile DuBard continues to be the basis of the services to children, the professional development programs, and research. Extraordinarily gifted professionals continue to build on the early work in order to meet the needs of today's children, their families, and those who seek to serve them.

On a personal note, as my major professor, mentor, and dearest friend, I know that my life was richly gifted by Etoile DuBard; hopefully, her legacy lives on in the daily work at the school and in these pages. Those of us who knew her and worked with her were indeed privileged.

Maureen K. Martin, Ph.D., CCC-SLP, CED, CALT, QI
Director, DuBard School for Language Disorders
The University of Southern Mississippi

Acknowledgments

Sincere appreciation goes to all the teachers of the DuBard School for Language Disorders since its inception in 1962, to the parents of children served, and to our university colleagues and students. The encouragement, assistance, and spiritual support of innumerable persons who have known the author's intentions and hopes in writing this volume have been invaluable.

An undertaking of this nature involves many partners to bring it to successful fruition. The author acknowledges with deepest gratitude the contributions and encouragement of colleagues, friends and family. Special thanks are extended to Doris P. Bradley and Missy L. Schraeder for extensive review, proofreading, and editing; Daphne S. Cornett and Kathryn McPhail for review and formatting; Susan S. Perry and Renee Renfroe, for contributions in the area of assessment; Susan S. Perry and Edward L. Goshorn for data analysis; and Wes Brooks, Susan Sanford and Kay Severson for their support. Special thanks to Jennifer Downey for design of Fig 5.6 Essential Elements of the DuBard Association Method®.

The author is also grateful to Judy Pollard-Licklider for providing valuable case history information on use of the Association Method with children who have autism spectrum disorders.

Sincere appreciation is extended to The Fowler Group, Arlington, Texas, especially Chip Chebuhar, Chad Murphy, Jason Shupe, Kiki Thompson and Katie Goodrich for their guidance and technical support and to Rachel Weiss for the illustrations.

Contents

CHAPTER 9 **Application of Association Method/DuBard Association Method® to other Populations: Case histories 141**

Foreword

Oral or spoken language is one of the most complex tasks ever mastered by humans, yet we take for granted that most children will begin to talk somewhere around a year of age. The brain has an anatomy for oral language with centers that integrate with others to make this high level communication task possible. Humans are the only species with spoken language for communication.

Written language (reading, writing and spelling) is an even more complex neurological set of skills, which requires specific and precise visual and auditory processing at a significant processing speed. The brain does not have specific areas for these tasks but borrows from the oral language areas as well as the visual and auditory processing areas. Again, most parents and educators do not appreciate the complexity of brain processing which is required to do these tasks; rather, most just expect that a child will begin to read in kindergarten and first grade.

Many children who have average or above average intellectual ability have oral language disorders, reading, spelling and written expression disorders or a combination of these challenges. Their brains are not abnormal but do function differently. Struggling to master oral and/or written language is a frustrating and discouraging experience. Communication is a strong need for all human beings. Not being able to communicate effectively can lead to difficulty in social interactions.

The DuBard Association Method® was created to help these children improve their oral and written language skills and be able to function in a classroom learning situation. This type of instruction helps the student move from feeling that the tasks are impossible to the feeling that through hard work, success can be attained. Not only does the approach help the child attain skills previously impossible for him, but success also restores self-confidence and improves self-esteem.

I first knew of methods for helping children with hearing and/or language impairments when I met Dr. Etoile DuBard in 1960. She was leaving her position as a speech-language pathologist (SLP) in the public schools of Natchez, Mississippi, as I was coming to fill the position. She made it very clear to me that I must take good care of "her children." We kept in touch as she studied at the Central Institute for the Deaf in St. Louis with Mildred McGinnis. When she returned several years later to The University of Southern Mississippi, she began the work of setting up what is now known as the DuBard School for Language Disorders.

She found the time to train me, and another SLP, Alice Feltus, in the McGinnis Method and together we helped create the first class for children with hearing and/or language impairment in a public school in Mississippi. From that training and experience, I took her work to many schools in many locations in the U.S. and overseas. In 1990, I became Executive Director of the Shelton School and Evaluation Center in Dallas, Texas. As soon as I settled in, I contacted Etoile to help Shelton in establishing the approach, by this time expanded into the DuBard Association Method®. Always generous with their time and talent, Dr. DuBard and Dr. Maureen Martin trained selected staff at Shelton to be able to bring the approach to children in the Dallas community.

The work of Dr. Etoile DuBard and Dr. Maureen Martin, expanding on the work of Mildred McGinnis, represents over 50 years of work and the brilliance of outstanding language therapists. Their work has helped countless children to more productive lives. It is an honor to recognize the work of these dedicated individuals who have meant so much in the lives of so many and especially to mine.

Joyce S. Pickering, CCC-SLP, CALT, QI, Hum.D.
Executive Director Emeritus
Shelton School & Evaluation Center
Dallas, Texas
2012

Foreword

to
Teaching Language-Deficient Children
by N. Etoile DuBard and Maureen K. Martin

Some methodologies in speech-language pathology are destined to remain effective in every generation of professionals. Others are used almost universally, then become dormant and may or may not be rediscovered and reintroduced. A methodology that has the special destiny of being used effectively in every generation always has a few individuals who maintain the integrity of the method during periods in which others, for various reasons, discard it in favor of something else. Etoile DuBard has been such a person with regard to the Association Method for teaching children who have aphasia and other severe language disorders. During times when the Association Method was considered out-of-date by some professionals, she quietly said, "It works," and continued to use it, to apply new information to the structure of the method, to evaluate the results, and to teach the methodology to students and colleagues.

Like Mildred McGinnis, Etoile DuBard found her place and stayed there through good times and not so good times. Nearly thirty years in the same university provided the opportunity for her to form lasting relationships with children with language disorders and their families and to follow the children into young adulthood. She taught university students who graduated, established their own careers, and began extending the information they had learned from Professor DuBard. Thus, Maureen Martin, herself a student of Etoile DuBard, became co-author of this book and makes a contribution for a new generation of professionals.

A neurologist once said that research sometimes takes fifty years to explain why some clinical procedures work. Single-subject research design has finally been accepted as a viable research technique and has made case studies more creditable. This only serves to emphasize the fact that the effectiveness of teaching is measured by the changes that occur with individuals. By providing this book, DuBard and Martin have shared experiences based on multisensory association methodology, interactions with numerous children and their families, and teaching university students. Their insights regarding the process of changing methodology, curriculum, and teaching procedures, based on the learner's response to each of these will assist both experienced and beginning professionals who seek to be effective facilitators of change in the lives of those with whom they interact.

Whole-language philosophy refers to a set of beliefs about language learning in which children are encouraged to develop their ability to listen, speak, read, and write in natural environments. So beliefs have come full circle to a primary goal of the Association Method which is "to help children communicate better and more meaningfully in whatever environments make up their worlds." The cycle of scientific inquiry continues. May each generation of professionals continue to build on the heritage of previous generations to the benefit of children who do not learn language naturally.

Doris P. Bradley
Professor Emerita of Speech and Hearing Sciences
University of Southern Mississippi, Hattiesburg
1994

Original Preface

to
Teaching Aphasics and Other Language Deficient Children

by N. Etoile DuBard

I have read this book with very deep interest. Its publication is timely since so many educators today are searching—shall I say groping?—for effective teaching methods for children with severe language disorders. The characteristics of these disorders have been more fully described within recent years; fairly satisfactory diagnostic procedures are currently available and much of the confusion over the preferred terminology is gradually disappearing. The classroom teacher, however, is still faced with the problem of teaching speech and language to a growing number of children who in the learning situation differ so widely from other types of children with communication disorders.

This book describes the educational approach of a dedicated and experienced teacher of the deaf and a speech pathologist, Etoile DuBard, who selected McGinnis's Association Method of teaching aphasic children—which has been the subject of a certain amount of controversy over the years—and adapted it to suit the needs of a group of children who had been diagnosed as language disordered.

The merit of Dr. DuBard's work lies in the fact that she saw in the Association Method a remedy for the disorders in language development which stem from central nervous system dysfunction. She realized that the use of the approach suggested by McGinnis would bring about a reduction of the disorder in temporal sequencing which is characteristic of these children and which is now recognized as a highly significant dimension of oral language. The emphasis on the use of the visual modality appealed to Dr. DuBard as she worked with deaf children who are characteristically visually oriented. Then followed an analysis of the McGinnis method in relation to the motor theory. Further convinced of its effectiveness as an educational approach, Dr. DuBard used this method for many years in a self-contained classroom, and by its use succeeded in enabling her pupils to communicate. After treatment, many of them were able to benefit from education in ordinary schools. Others with established hearing losses were admitted to schools for hearing-impaired children where they made satisfactory progress.

Dr. DuBard writes with conviction, selecting issues which are pertinent for the teacher and which may have heretofore been misunderstood by students of the McGinnis method. My sincere hope is that many teachers will use this book and apply the techniques described herein to meet the needs not only of those children with an established language disorder, but also of those deaf children with average and above average intellectual functioning but who are nonachievers in school—even in schools which are fully committed to a high standard of oralism. Many of these children, as Dr. DuBard has rightly pointed out, have learning disabilities similar to those found among children with central nervous system dysfunction. With the present emphasis on early diagnosis of deafness in children, it should be possible to identify such children at an earlier age and apply diagnostic teaching which will emphasize an elemental approach and thus reduce problems associated with disorders in the perception of temporal order, dyspraxia, and dysrhythmia.

Those of us who have already been using the McGinnis method will welcome this book since it offers necessary clarification of the procedures and suggests more flexibility in the approach to the individual child.

Sister Mary Nicholas Griffey, O. P.
University College Dublin, Ireland
1974

About the Author

Maureen K. Martin received her B.S. and M.S. degrees in Speech and Hearing Sciences at The University of Southern Mississippi where she was a student of Etoile DuBard. She earned her Ph.D. at the National University of Ireland. Martin is a nationally certified speech-language pathologist and educator of students who are deaf and hard of hearing. She also holds certification in reading, learning disabilities, elementary education, and school administration. She served on the staff of the School for Children with Language Disorders (now known as the DuBard School for Language Disorders) from 1975 until 1989, when she was named director of the program. She is an adjunct faculty member of the University and has conducted numerous courses, workshops, and in-service professional training sessions in the Southeast, Southwest, in Canada, and in the Republic of Ireland. Under her leadership, the professional development program for the DuBard Association Method® has achieved accreditation from the International Multisensory Structured Language Education Council (IMSLEC) at all levels: Teaching, Instructor of Teaching, Therapy, and Instructor of Therapy. She is a member of the Board of IMSLEC and active in numerous professional organizations. Martin was the founder of the International Association Method Task Force.

Introduction

In rereading the introduction to *Teaching Aphasics and Other Language Deficient Children* (DuBard 1983) and *Teaching Language-Deficient Children (2000),* one is struck by the truth of the statement, "The more things change, the more they stay the same." Volumes such as this one often seem to have been outgrowths of authors' receipt of requests to compile various kinds of lists, outlines, and suggestions for lesson plans which they themselves had found useful and effective during their own years of teaching children. We received requests, too, but they were not the primary motivation for this volume, or the ones which preceded it, which clarifies the DuBard Association Method® for teaching children with severe language disorders and others with similar difficulties in language learning. However urgent the requests may have sounded, the principal motivation was much more personal.

The personal motivation for the earlier volumes was related initially to the task of instructing university students about the theories, principles, purposes and techniques of implementing the Association Method, later the DuBard Association Method®, teaching procedures. A need existed for a volume which contained basic information simply and concisely stated so that the students could read and question without arbitrarily concluding, " I don't believe in that method," as countless professionals have done for decades. The inexperienced teacher's need for suggestions and guidelines regarding language curricula became obvious. Inquiries from parents, mostly mothers, seeking help in teaching children who had been diagnosed with language disorders but who lived in geographic areas where no constructive help was available could not be ignored. Thus, the idea for this text took shape.

Throughout years of teaching, it became apparent that numerous teachers were experiencing considerable frustration in their best efforts to help children who were deaf or hard of hearing and who continued to fail to achieve success in language learning and in speech development. While teachers' frustrations were evident in various ways, they seemed mild compared with the frustrations and despair voiced by the children's parents. The children expressed their frustrations through various deviant behavior patterns.

Out of concern for the plight of teachers and even greater concern and compassion for the children who were the real victims, an additional motivation developed. It was hoped that a volume regarding the nature of the difficulties children with language disorders experience, and guidelines for teaching them, would enable those persons with high interest and initiative to provide differentiated teaching for these children.

This book is for teachers and clinicians who can free themselves of rigid approaches to teaching, who are innovative, and who have a genuine commitment to do more to help children learn. The book also was designed to help teachers, clinicians, and parents who believe that all children have the right to learn. Finally, it is for those who feel they have not only the job but also the privilege of teaching children with difficulties in learning, no matter what measure of differentiated teaching techniques the task may require.

The features and especially the organization of the incremental levels as McGinnis designed and taught them are described. Our own purposes, roles, modifications, and expansions are also included. More is written in chapter 5 about the transition from Association Method to DuBard Association Method®.

The Association Method procedures and modifications have been used, refined and expanded with children enrolled in the School for Preschool Deaf and Aphasic Children established in September 1962, renamed School for Children with Language Disorders in 1968 and DuBard School for Language Disorders in 1996, on the campus of The University of Southern Mississippi. The school was founded as a result of the interest and cooperative efforts of the Forrest County-Hattiesburg United Givers Fund and the University. In 1965, it became a laboratory school for the newly established Department of Speech and Hearing Sciences.

In the beginning years, the pupils enrolled were identified as having language disorders with or without established hearing losses. Many of the early students were children affected by rubella. Prior to the mid-1970s when formal tests for language and speech assessments began to be more readily available, diagnoses were based on medical histories, audiological assessments, psychological evaluations, and parent interview/case history information, and in some cases, a period of diagnostic teaching. Some children who initially and at an early age had rejected hearing aids accepted them after they attained a measure of competence in the comprehension and use of language and speech. Some who had used hearing aids from an early age did not begin to progress in language learning until the Association Method procedures were employed as the major instructional approach.

After they completed the laboratory school's educational program, the children were placed in general elementary classroom programs, in private programs with low pupil-to-teacher ratio, or in other special classroom programs appropriate to their particular needs. To date, follow-up information regarding their education indicates their satisfactory progress. Some finished high school successfully and others completed two- or four-year college or university programs. Employments vary and reflect a pattern comparable to those individuals without known disabilities.

When using multisensory teaching techniques, it is extremely tempting to take shortcuts and move ahead quickly. When we have yielded to such temptations, invariably we have regretted it. It became necessary to provide greater redundancy so as to establish the necessary **automaticity** in skills before progressing to subsequent levels of instruction. Children's "competence" is often misleading. When tempted to shortcut, delete, or reduce reinforcement and maintenance work in a child's program, one recommendation is primary: *don't do it.* Variations can be made but the foundation must be solid first.

In this volume, guidelines on curriculum and specific explanations of reinforcement activities are included. Although educators often are inclined to "toss out" the ideas and let teachers develop their own applications, teachers often ask us what to do next and how to do it. *How effective the use of the DuBard Association Method® will be is dependent on how effectively the teacher/clinician carries out its principles.* With careful ongoing monitoring of children's progress and appropriate planning and implementation, the phonetic, multisensory teaching techniques can help children learn more effectively and, thus, can make a positive difference in their lives.

This volume presents the Association Method in its original form as Mildred McGinnis developed and applied the principles to a relatively narrow-scoped population—children who were deaf who did not learn effectively if at all, even though they seemed to be only deaf. In light of the current recognition of the importance of *phonetic, multisensory, structured language instruction* for typical children who have reading deficiencies with an overlay of language disorders, additional information and suggested materials for that population are included also.

C H A P T E R

1

The Nature
of The Problem

HISTORICAL REVIEW

The expansion of knowledge in many areas has been explosive in recent decades. Too often people are tempted to discard indiscriminately the old for the new. The work of predecessors, however, provides the building blocks which succeeding generations have used in one way or another. The following is a summary of some of the background and significant findings, observations, and developments in the area of communication disorders—both past and present. While it is noted and appreciated that the currently acceptable writing style is to use person first language, i.e. referencing the person before naming a disability, in this text when references are made to professional literature of earlier decades, the terminology as used by the authors at that time was retained.

Those who have studied children's language and speech acquisition are aware of the relatively controversial ideas which exist about such learning. While being aware of differing ideas, they should view them in relation to teaching the children for whom they are responsible. Their goal is to devise an effective program of instruction. A good beginning is an examination of descriptive terms which evolved from the work of many researchers of earlier decades and which are still used by professionals in the field.

Definitions

Terms include the following:

Syntactic aphasia. Difficulties in using words in the correct order and/or forms for effective communication. Certain classes of words such as prepositions, conjunctions, and articles may be omitted. Example: "Car man hit" for "the man hit the car."

Nominal aphasia/Word-finding difficulties. The inability to know the appropriate names of things or to find categorical terms. For example: 1) "We went to that place (library) to check out books." 2) "Please do the door" for "open" or "close the door."

Semantic aphasia. Difficulty with word meanings. Example: pen for pencil.

Pragmatic. Syntax and semantic ability may be present, but they may be used inappropriately. Example: "Your birthday is May 1, 1921" repeated frequently and inappropriately in time and place. Neologisms are substituted for meaningful words. Example: "That man is clipping the kreples."

Expressive aphasia/Expressive language disorder. The individual is limited in the ability to express ideas through spoken or written language symbols.

Receptive aphasia/Receptive language disorder. The individual has difficulty comprehending language through spoken or written symbols.

Expressive-receptive aphasia. Difficulties with both types of language skills, comprehending and expressing ideas.

Global aphasia. All language forms are seriously affected to the degree that it is impossible to use one of the preceding categories. There may be an automatic expression or two which may or may not be meaningful. Example: "The puthee the puthigh" as a response to any comment or question.

Dyslexia. A developmental language disorder involving processing of phonological (sounds of the language) information resulting in a specific reading disability.

Apraxia/Dyspraxia. An inability, or limitation in the ability, to execute simple, sequential voluntary acts involving the motor system.

Dysarthria. A dysfunction in muscular control of the speech mechanism which is the result of damage to the central and/or peripheral nervous system. Characteristics include weakness, slowness, and/or incoordination.

Jargon. Intelligibility is lost because the verbal utterance is unintelligible (not understandable). All phonemes seem to be present, but they are rarely produced in understandable morphemic clusters; that is, "to do de mo ah too" (spoken with adequate speech inflection as though relating intelligible words to the listener).

Eisenson (1972) used the term *developmental aphasia* (congenital aphasia, dyslogia) to refer to a child's impaired ability to acquire the symbols of a language system. Perceptual auditory disabilities underlie the impairment. The child's disturbed ability to decode and store information is compounded by motor difficulty, either dysarthria or dyspraxia.

In earlier years, such conditions as those listed above, were identified, described, and labeled by professionals in or closely related to the medical profession. As the professional field of speech pathology, and then speech-language pathology, developed, those terms became significant in describing communication disorders in children. However, the use of the terminology with children

opened the door for considerable discord and controversies among the academicians in the field because the terms previously had been applied only to adults. For example, *aphasia* refers to 'loss of language.' Academicians contended that 'loss of' language was inappropriate for application to children because they had never developed language. Many of the differences seemed to have been based on *semantics* rather than on specific abilities/limitations of the children.

ASHA (1993) defined a language disorder as "impaired comprehension and/or use of spoken, written and/or other symbol systems. The disorder may involve (1) the *form* of language (phonology, morphology, syntax), (2) the *content* of language (semantics), and/or (3) the *function* of language in communication (pragmatics) in any combination."

These definitions provide insight into the nature of the functions and dysfunctions of individuals who are considered to be aphasic or language disordered or who seem to have central nervous system dysfunctions related to the comprehension and use of language. Definitions alone, however, do not provide sufficient information about such individuals to be especially helpful in designing effective habilitative or rehabilitative programs for them. The work and writings of Nance (1946), Myklebust (1954), McGinnis (1963), Hardy (1965), Bender (1968), Eisenson (1968, 1972, 1984), and Catts (1989, 1996, 1997), Lahey (1990), Kamhi (1998), Battle (2002), McCauley and Fey (2006), and Paul (2007) have influenced current ideas regarding the habilitation of children with language disorders. Rather than merely relying on definitions, they described children and various functions of the language.

Language Disorders-Descriptions and Characteristics

McGinnis's unpublished thesis (1939) deserves further consideration, even though her research already has exerted a far-reaching influence on children with language disorders. The influences have been both positive and negative—negative, because some professionals completely rejected her ideas regarding descriptions as well as her habilitative approach, and positive, because others in the profession have found her descriptions accurate and her procedures effective for scores of children with severe communication disorders.

In 1919, Mildred A. McGinnis, a teacher of deaf children, observed marked differences among children who had been classified as deaf because they had not learned language, appeared to have significant hearing losses, and who appeared to be at least average in intellectual ability. Although classified as deaf, and participating in an instructional program appropriate for children who were deaf, they appeared to be significantly different from other children in the groups who were deaf. Their acquisition of speech, lip-reading abilities, use of hearing and voice qualities were not like those of the other children who were deaf.

At the same time, McGinnis also was engaged in efforts to rehabilitate adults who suffered from aphasia caused by cerebral episodes (i.e., stroke, CVAs, TBIs, etc.) They had learned language and speech, but had lost the ability to communicate orally. She noticed similarities between certain children and her adult patients and speculated that the children were affected by congenital aphasia. Characteristics which were different from those exhibited by other children in her class were observed in the children who were supposedly deaf and the adults who were aphasic. These included the following:

1. A residuum of hearing (residual hearing) was not as great an aid in perfecting tone quality as one would expect.
2. Children with hearing were more difficult to teach than those who gave evidence of being totally deaf.
3. Even when impaired hearing was apparent, it was not sufficient to account for the delay in the children's acquisition of speech and language.
4. A **lack of association** in the children who were deaf or hard of hearing and children with central aphasia components prohibited an accurate measure of their hearing by audiometric tests available at the time until learning began; an "increase" in hearing was shown as their learning progressed.
5. Voice quality was unlike that typical of children who were deaf. *(Author's note: That is, they did not have the characteristic monotone voice quality typically heard in individuals who are profoundly deaf.)*
6. They had **poor attention spans** *(Author's note: poor attention spans especially for language).*
7. They showed **poor retention ability**.
8. They **lacked adequate means of monitoring** their speech **for accuracy**.
9. Their **negativism and emotional upset** indicated unused hearing.
10. They had a **poor memory** for the orderly **sequencing** of sounds that compose a word.
11. Their performance and achievement were below expectations (indicated by tests and measurements available at that time).

It has been noted that McGinnis' characteristics indicated above in boldface are also the characteristics frequently exhibited by those with dyslexia/specific learning disabilities. Eisenson (1968) focused also on the feature of 1) **poor predictability** in language skills, and 2) the premise that children with severe oral language disorders (once called developmentally aphasic) and those with specific language learning disabilities/dyslexia are on a *continuum*. That is to say, the two populations are one and the same with *similar difficulties for language learning but with varying degrees of severity*. In addition, it is evident that students with dyslexia, or disorders of written language, demonstrate poor understanding of the relationship, or association, of the language of sentences and the language of questions.

McGinnis (1963) found that, when she altered her teaching approach with her class of deaf children, the atypical deaf students responded differently and began to succeed in learning. They achieved the following goals:

Increased attention span
Increased retention
Increased ability to recall
Improved association skills
Improved listening (auditory processing) skills through use of a modified temporal (slower) rate of speech

McGinnis's children showed deficits comparable to those described for children who were deemed to be aphasic by Hardy (1965) and others mentioned earlier. She found that when they were taught according to the modified procedures, they could master functional language. Consequently, she recommended an analysis of children's learning difficulties in order to determine what teaching techniques to use. Wood (1964, 34) stated this same view: "Aphasic children cannot learn adequately in programs designed for children with other problems."

McGinnis suggested procedures which *capitalized on the abilities and strengths of the children*. She also included concerted efforts to *strengthen their deficits*. McGinnis made no serious effort to determine *why* her procedural changes in teaching were effective, nor did she attempt to establish a theory based on her methods. Her goals were to bring into focus and to direct the attention of others to the need for a revision in diagnosis and to suggest a therapeutic procedure which might result in more rapid, more effective, and more nearly complete habilitation/rehabilitation of the children. She named the procedures the Association Method (for teaching aphasic children) and offered them as one approach for helping certain children with language impairments learn language and speech.

Myklebust's descriptions of a child with aphasia (1954) included the following:

1. The child does not acquire speech naturally (162).
   a. Attempts consist of jargon.
   b. Vocalizations are not direct attempts to imitate speech of others nearby.
   c. Some words may be spoken once but are not used again or are used indiscriminately.
   d. Child may repeat words yet be unable to use them when desired.
2. Vocalizations do not have a characteristic (monotone) tonal quality (163).
   a. The child naturally uses inflections, intonation, and pitch patterns.
   b. Attempts at oral communication exhibit the presence of phonemes combined in what, linguistically, can be considered phrases, sentences, and emphasis patterns for psychological meaning.
   c. The tonal quality of the young aphasic child is quite unlike that of the deaf and/or severely hard-of-hearing child.
3. The child uses improvised sounds in a characteristic manner but does not use them projectively; they lack purpose and intent in relation to the environment (163).
4. The child does not use gestures— "Deficiency of gesture is characteristic of children with receptive aphasia" (164).
5. The child does not respond to sound consistently and does not use hearing projectively (165).
   a. There is an inability to relate and integrate experientially; reactions to stimuli, sound as well as others, vary a great deal.
   b. Inconsistent responses to intensity and to variations in pitch or frequency take place (166). Hearing and listening are quite different. One assumes that a hearing individual is able to "integrate and shift attention selectively in a sustained manner." If we hear but are unable to integrate what we hear, we will not be able to use our hearing effectively. Clinical observations are an important source of information in this context. Such observations might be more revealing and more valid than formal tests of acuity. "The aphasic child's disintegrated auditory behavior is highly observable to the experienced diagnostician" (167). Such behavior is invaluable in helping to obtain a differential diagnosis of auditory disorders.
6. The child's laughing, smiling, and crying lack intensity and reflect insecurity (167). The child displays general inadequacy related to emotions.
   a. Does not laugh or smile readily. (Why laugh if you don't know what's funny?)
   b. Laughter reflects normal tonal quality, reflecting hearing acuity for inflections and laughter tones.
7. The child is not unduly sensitive to movement or other visual clues (168). While deaf persons make a definite effort to see a speaker's face, aphasics do not (169); their utilization of movement or other visual clues prior to educational instruction is usually intermittent and limited.
8. The child is not unduly sensitive to tactile sensation (199).
9. Motor behavior is characteristic, in that motor function is rarely within limits of normal (171). Furthermore, motor development is retarded maturationally.
10. It is characteristic for the child to make little distinction between friends and strangers; child may be attracted to people because of what they are wearing rather than because of the social situation of meeting someone new. The ability to engage in typical play activities is grossly inadequate (172).
11. The child may be retarded in emotional development, emotionally immature or unable to develop and express emotions because of language deficiency (173).
12. The child shows disturbances in ability to select visual and auditory stimuli appropriate to needs (175).
13. The child is echolalic but this is not voluntary imitation (175).
    a. Parrot speech occurs.
    b. The last word or two of a sentence is echoed, which suggests the presence of some short-term memory.
14. The child is distractible and lacks the ability to maintain sustained attention (for linguistic events).

Eisenson (1968, 3–4) defined children with aphasia as those with central nervous system dysfunctions who present linguistic and behavioral manifestations that distinguish them from other children who are normal and verbally deviant. He described the aphasic children in the following manner:

1. *Developmentally,* such children give evidence of—
   a. Perceptual dysfunction in one or more sensory modalities
   b. Auditory inefficiency over and above what may be expected from audiometrically determined hearing loss
   c. Intellectual inefficiency over and above any objectively assessed intellectual limitation
2. *Linguistically,* severe language retardation for both comprehension and the production of language is characterized by—
   a. Lack of conventional grammar
   b. Reduced vocabulary, both in quantity and quality
   c. Inadequate syntactical patterns
   d. Limited sentence length
   e. Limited concepts in general
   f. Language growth which does not follow the usual incremental growth observed in other children
3. *Behavioral* characteristics include—
   a. Perseveration
   b. Inconsistency of response
   c. Emotional lability
   d. Sometimes but not always hyperactivity and/or hypoactivity

Eisenson (1968, 4) also stated the following view, "If the child could be left unimpressed, unimposed upon, and undisturbed by environmental influences so that he does not try to achieve what he is incapable of achieving at a given developmental age and stage, he might in time learn to speak." This may well be true. In fact, such children have been seen at The University of Southern Mississippi DuBard School for Language Disorders over the years. Unfortunately, however, fewer and fewer children can be "left unimpressed, unimposed upon, and undisturbed by environmental influences." Furthermore, the quality and usefulness of whatever language and speech such children achieve may be extremely limited and limiting.

The characteristics noted above are only part of the problems which affect children with language disorders. They also may have the following auditory-perceptual problems (Eisenson, 1972):

1. They give the impression of being severely hard-of-hearing or deaf or mentally retarded/deaf.
2. They may have a mild-to-moderate, measurable hearing loss.

3. Their hearing functioning varies without consideration of conditions related to the presence of otitis media, intensity, or pitch of sounds.
4. They may have some degree of difficulty in receiving sound, but more important is their functional and practical difficulty of dealing with the sounds received. Functional-practical hearing may be far more impaired than hearing tests might imply.
5. According to Eisenson, a majority of children with developmental aphasia show some neurological findings on an electroencephalogram (EEG) or otherwise. The implication is central nervous system (CNS) involvement in the child's inability to process speech signals accurately and/or adequately.
6. Children with developmental aphasia are able to discriminate between isolated speech sounds but have considerable difficulty in discriminating between contexts of two or three phonemes when they are incorporated into nonsense syllables.

If children with developmental language disorders function as just described, what are the causes of impairment? Eisenson (1972) suggested that a number of factors are involved.

Perception-Imperception. The basic impairment is with auditory perception. The child is not able to perceive or process speech at the rate it is normally used. While the child with developmental aphasia might have a slight hearing loss, conventional pure-tone audiogram would be one indicating the presence of an adequate amount of hearing to learn speech. Speech-sound or phonemic discrimination in context is, however, a major difficulty. Although such children can be trained to discriminate between isolated speech sounds (McReynolds 1966), the complexity of contextual utterances presents altogether different and more difficult tasks.

Storage Limitations (Memory). These children may achieve discrimination skills with isolated speech sounds (McReynolds 1966), but they often do not have enough short-term memory to be able to communicate. Sufficiently defective skills may make them completely incompetent for coping with the tasks of communicating. Muma (1978) cites the work of Hockett (1960) who identifies rapid fading as a general property of language. The rapid rate of speech and the rapidly fading property of oral communication compounds children's tasks for hearing, listening, discriminating, and remembering the components of speech. As Eisenson (1972) remarked: "The child does not retain what he hears very long if at all. This short-term memory for speech signals may be present or completely absent." If the storage system is somewhat adequate, language may then develop as fragmentary language, echolalia, and/or without proper syntax. (See information on Working Memory later in this chapter.)

Deficit in Comprehension/Discrimination.   Children with language disorders may be able to discriminate single sounds in isolation, such as /b/, /t/, /u/, or even /s/, but not be able to discriminate or perceive them meaningfully when they are embedded in a phonetic environment such as a word, phrase, or sentence. They experience difficulty in receiving and processing auditory signals at a rate normal to the processing of such signals. They are unable to comprehend fast speech and cannot quickly match ongoing auditory events and other events. "Unless it is possible for the child to identify the auditory signals and to keep the order of signals in mind, speech perception cannot be established" (Eisenson 1968, 6). Eisenson cited studies related to time elements of the aphasic child's understanding and likened his situation to that of "the tourist with one year of high school French trying to understand and keep up with what is going on in an argument between a French gendarme and a taxi driver on the Champs Elysees at 5:00 p.m. on a week day" (Eisenson, 1968, 8).

Impaired Ability for Sequencing. Even a person with limited clinical experience with children challenged with language disorders is aware of their impaired capacity for sequencing. While Eisenson (1968) focused attention on deficits related to the sequencing of auditory events, he also implied that visual sequencing is a deficit function. He found children with developmental aphasia to be considerably poorer in auditory sequencing when the stimuli were white noise and a complex noise, which are more distinctive than sequencing of speech sounds, and consequently considered to be more easily processed. (White noise is noise made up of all frequencies of equal intensity in the audible spectrum. Complex noise is any masking noise composed of a low fundamental frequency plus multiples of that masking noise.)

The professional literature reports several research projects related to children with language disorders and their ability to discriminate isolated phonemes more readily than when the phonemes are embedded in the phonetic environment of connected speech (McReynolds 1966; Bender 1968; Hardy 1965; Eisenson 1968; McGinnis

1963). Sequencing ability may well be of critical significance in differentiating children with language disorders from those who are deaf or developmentally delayed.

Because all linguistic events are temporal and spatial, one must have the ability to deal with events in relation to responses to linguistic events of the past and to anticipate linguistic events of the future, both immediate and not so immediate. Children must be able to deal effectively with probabilities in order to reduce the uncertainties of learning language and speech. As they acquire more and more information about any given topic, the probabilities become more predictable, thereby reducing the uncertainties which might exist. However, in children with severe language disorders frequently the information does not stay with them.

Poor Predictability. Children with developmental aphasia or language disorders have been described as "poor at guessing and gambling" (Eisenson 1968, 9), and their poor abilities in this regard only serve to increase their insecurities related to verbal behavior. Poor predictability seems to be critical to children with developmental or acquired language disorders when they are confronted with habilitation and/or rehabilitation, habilitation for those who never developed language and/or speech, rehabilitation for those with acquired conditions.

Nondisabled children become discriminative listeners and speakers of unrefined linguistic units which they gradually refine into word approximations. Single words, two- and three-word sentences, and ultimately, simple, complex, and relatively sophisticated sentences become their tools of communication. By the age of four or five, most children with hearing and intelligence within normal limits acquire the ability to communicate effectively. Because children with language disorders are unable to accomplish this feat, their situation in a highly verbal and oral society must surely become grim for them as well as for their parents and those who care for them.

Associative Skills: Representational Behavior. Eisenson (1972) addressed the issue of visual-auditory association very briefly in his recommendations related to intervention. The late Dr. Etoile DuBard and the current author observed that there are significant limitations in the ability of children with severe language disorders to *make an association*, i.e., to *establish meaning* between the linguistic event and the object, action, or event such as words related to a birthday party. This can be observed in the child who can repeat a word imitatively. For example: repeating "shoe" without having any understanding for it semantically. A similar deficit in associating and understanding relationships between linguistic and other events has been observed in children diagnosed with learning disabilities. It has been observed and countless teachers and parents have provided reports of children whose articulation was satisfactory but who did not follow directions satisfactorily and whose academic achievement at the early elementary level was poor at best. One component of the problem can be described as follows: Some children will demonstrate ability to articulate a considerable amount of spontaneous language satisfactorily but when questioned about what they have just said, they are unable to answer. **Their inability to understand the relationship between the words of question language and sentence language is a major deficit for them**. More will be said in this volume in regard to children with these kinds of challenges in chapter 8.

Hardy (1965) specifically noted the importance of not only "the incoming sensory information but also the complexity of perception and almost everything else about the behaving child—particularly attention, storage, and recall—that contribute to the relationship between individual and environment that we call intelligence."

In 1968, Bender, in writing about "a program for teaching language to young children with central auditory disorders, with or without a peripheral hearing loss," referred to children who were nonverbal as controversial children. (Author's note: This is not to be confused with the current-day term of central auditory processing disorders.) She noted that no one label seems to fit them and their classmates equally (537). Their symptoms simulate deafness though they are not necessarily deaf. They may have a hearing loss, but the hearing loss is not their major disability. While the problems of such children have been termed "central auditory disorder, aphasia, language disorder, minimal brain damage, autism, and mental retardation," they often exhibit a combination of these disorders. The one characteristic which these children have in common may well be what they cannot do. In describing the commonality, Bender stated, "They cannot use sound appropriately, whether they receive it or not,… (they) are clumsy in motor coordination to some degree,… are often faulty in perception, visually as well as auditorially… and lack the ability to retain, with consistency, the symbolism of oral language" (537). Perhaps most of all, they lack the ability to reproduce oral language by direct imitation of a whole word.

Fortunately, descriptions of children with language disorders provide some clues as to how they might learn more efficiently and effectively and, fortunately, diagnosis of children with complex profiles has advanced tremendously in recent years. Information published from the 1960s through the current day may lead to programs which can provide these children an opportunity to learn language and speech, to achieve a satisfactory academic level, and to attain a better social and emotional adjustment in society.

In discussing the nature of the problem, DuBard (1974) focused attention on a population of children who were essentially nonverbal. They were children who demonstrated little or no comprehension of spoken language and whose expressive language consisted of jargon sometimes interspersed with a few single words. They usually demonstrated little or no spontaneous meaningful use for the words they could repeat imitatively. At best they demonstrated language functions comparable to those of eighteen- to twenty-four-month-old children although their chronological ages were at least twice that. Their problem-solving abilities on nonverbal tasks were similar to those of typically developing children their ages.

Speech-language pathologists and teachers have encountered other populations with similar limitations. Many children entering kindergarten and/or first grade have been observed to be extremely deficient in language skills although they have been able to understand and use language to a certain extent. Their limitations in motivation, stimulation, opportunity, and requirement were not so severe that their school performance was diminished significantly. They had been able to "get along" at home and in the family and neighborhood environments, but "getting on" in the tasks in school was altogether more difficult, complex, and confusing. The teachers and parents were perplexed about children who were intelligent not succeeding in reading, spelling, written activities, and some aspects of math such as word problems. Remediation programs for such children are discussed in chapter 8.

In the early 1970s another population of children appeared increasingly for treatment in speech and hearing clinics, in public school programs, and at the School for Children with Language Disorders (now DuBard School for Language Disorders) at The University of Southern Mississippi (DuBard 1976). These children were mostly boys of four, five, and six years who seemed to have satisfactory comprehension of language but who had multiple misarticulations in their spontaneous speech. Sometimes the multiplicity of misarticulations made them essentially unintelligible. Some of the children responded well to speech therapy which focused on functional articulation errors or disorders. Unfortunately, the therapies used did not bring about sufficient remediation. Although some of the boys, who had only residues of subtle misarticulations, were released from therapy in the belief that classroom activities, maturity, and minimal amounts of work at home would result in complete correction of the remaining speech deviations; at later dates, they had difficulties in learning to read and spell. Their problems in pronouncing two- and three-syllable words revealed their limitations in articulating and sequencing syllables in conversational language.

There were other factors, however, which compounded the learning process for these children, including emotional stress, negative attitudes, and poor self-images in general. The children's functioning indicated that the problems were more complex than other children enrolled in speech therapy.

Careful evaluation of the receptive and expressive language skills and assessment of abilities in nonverbal tasks demonstrated that these children were experiencing the same kinds of weaknesses as those displayed by the hard-core, nonverbal children described by McGinnis (1963), Hardy (1965), Bender (1968), and Eisenson (1968, 1972). Their specific weaknesses included poor memory for sequencing and difficulty in making associations between and among auditory stimuli, objects, and written language. In addition, they demonstrated poor auditory discrimination, poor auditory closure, and sometimes difficulty in visual closure. The evaluations revealed further misleading abilities and pseudo-abilities in language functioning. In both their oral and written language, the children showed major difficulties with and/or limitations in vocabulary, concepts, verb tenses, sentence formulation, question formulation, and syntax in general. They also had a poor understanding of the relationship between the language of questions and the language of sentences.

Contemporary scholars such as Battle (2002) noted that the following criteria are useful in "determining the existence of a language disorder within the parameters established for the culture and linguistic environment of the child:"

1. Rarely initiates verbal interactions or activities with peers or family members.
2. Does not respond verbally when verbal interactions are initiated by peers or family members.
3. Has difficulty using language at the level used by her age peers.
4. Has a smaller vocabulary than expected for her age, regardless of the language used.
5. Uses shorter, less complex sentences than would be expected by her age.
6. Has difficulty communicating verbally with parents or cultural and linguistic age peers.
7. Relies heavily on gestures and nonverbal means to communicate.
8. Parents and language peers frequently repeat and rephrase instruction for the child.
9. Is inordinately slow in responding to questions or instructions.
10. Has difficulty with the noncontrastive elements of language form.
11. Peers rarely initiate verbal exchanges with the child or use a notably lower level of verbal communication with the child than with age peers.
12. Peers have difficulty understanding the child.
13. Does not attempt to repair her communication failures.
14. Does not comment on the action of others or express feelings verbally.
15. Does not take turns or maintain conversations with peers.
16. Does not ask for clarification or assistance verbally.
17. Uses false starts, self-interruptions, or revisions.
18. Makes frequent use of it, thing, this, or that.
19. Does not learn new concepts or vocabulary or forgets material assumed to be learned (375).

Source: Bernstein, Deena K.; Tiegerman-Farber, Ellenmorris. Language and Communication Disorders in Children, 5th Edition, © 2002. Reprinted by permission of Pearson Education, Inc., Upper Saddle River, NJ.

Hegde and Maul (2006) included the following in their characteristics of language disorders:

1. Limited amount of language
2. Deficient grammar
3. Inadequate or inappropriate social communication
4. Deficient nonverbal communication skills
5. Deficient literary skills (41-42)

The American Speech-Language-Hearing Association (1997-2011) noted the following characteristics of language disorders:

1. Improper use of words and their meanings
2. Inability to express ideas
3. Inappropriate grammatical patterns such as immature pronoun usage

4. Reduced vocabulary due to inability to learn new words
5. Inability to follow directions
6. Inability to understand question language
7. Problems recalling numbers in sequence
8. Difficulty with retelling a story
9. Difficulty in reading and comprehending stories
10. Problems learning words to songs
11. Problems understanding or enjoying rhymes
12. Difficulty telling left from right
13. Problems identifying letters and numbers and learning the alphabet
14. Inability to understand the sound/symbol associations needed for reading

The effectiveness of the Association Method, now DuBard Association Method®, with the hardcore, nonverbal population and the limitations and needs of those just described resulted in remediation programs utilizing selected principles and aspects of the Association Method being implemented. Modifications were made carefully to meet individual needs, making sure that such modifications did not jeopardize the children's progress. The remediation procedures of those with a history of oral communication disorders and later reading difficulties are discussed further in chapter 8.

PROBLEMS OF HEARING LOSS VS. "NORMAL" HEARING ACUITY

Parents and professionals alike usually are interested in causal factors for the problems in children, but not all factors are readily identifiable. Nevertheless, hearing ability certainly is a significant one in the case of language/speech problems. Any hearing loss is important. Time of onset and duration of hearing loss are crucial. A hearing loss prior to the age of three, that is, a prelingual loss, will be a greater detriment than one occurring at a later time. In earlier years, a hearing loss of 15-20 dB was considered non-significant. However, in more recent years, the potential negative impact of even this mild hearing loss, as well as unilateral hearing loss, has received additional attention (Ross, 2006). Northern and Downs (2002) noted that it is sometimes difficult to determine when a hearing loss becomes a handicap for a child. They proposed the following:

A handicapping hearing loss in a child is any degree of hearing that reduces the intelligibility of a speech message to a degree inadequate for accurate interpretation of speech or as to interfere with learning. Such a definition recognizes that it may not be possible to place specific measure on what precisely handicaps a child's ability to learn. Too many variables are present in the learning process of children: amount of parental stimulation, quality of parental stimulation, innate intelligence, age of onset of hearing loss, personality factors, health conditions, and socioeconomic status. These variables may so affect the learning abilities of children that a 15-dB loss may be a handicap to one child, whereas a 25-dB loss will not handicap another. (p.23)

Northern and Downs (1978) summarized the following hearing losses in relation to age as critical in a child's ability to learn: (1) hearing loss of over 15 decibels in the first two years of life, (2) serous otitis in a child under eighteen months of age for more than three months of a six-month period, and (3) fluctuating loss of from 0–15 decibels for more than half of the time during one year. Countless children who are seen clinically for language, speech, and learning problems have histories of otitis media and other types of ear infections and/or upper respiratory infections early in life. However, countless studies both supporting and dismissing the idea of an impact of otitis media on the development of communication skills have been published. It is beyond the scope of this text to review that research in depth. However, Northern and Downs (2002, 80), while acknowledging the wide variation in the quality of the research, noted that "the overall picture is that linguistic, cognitive, and behavioral effects can be documented as real sequelae of otitis media. The important factors seem to be the onset of the recurrent problem in the first few months of life and the duration of time the child has [the condition]…during the initial 2 years." Any such conditions in a child's history could have negative influences on the acquisition of skills in communicating and learning. A problem with auditory processing and/or fluctuating hearing loss may lead to delays in language development and/or language disorders, may be attributed to the infection itself or, perhaps, to the medications necessary to clear up the infections. While the answer to this may wait for decades, it is wise to keep in mind the negative and long-range influences such infections may have on learning. Although audiological assessments may indicate that a child's hearing is within normal limits at the time a problem is identified, it is reasonable to believe that there could have been deprivation and/or damage earlier, and that such factors remain part of the nature of the problem for the child.

McGinnis (1963) focused attention on children who seemed to be deaf but whose language learning, acquisition of speech, and, subsequently, academic achievements were well below what was expected. Her work focused on aspects of central nervous system dysfunction, which were considered to be the basis for deficiencies related to learning communication skills and experiencing success in academic achievement. It is now important to consider some other children who have demonstrated similar achievement records but for different and, perhaps, unknown reasons.

What about those with true hearing losses, especially those who have been poor achievers? Volumes have been written throughout the decades regarding the negative impact which deafness/hearing impairment has on a child's learning and especially the learning of language and speech. Multiple dimensions of the problems have been identified and discussed. There can be no doubt that good auditory functioning is a prerequisite to successful acquisition of language, speech, and academic achievement. There has been agreement for the last fifty years that the degree and type of hearing loss, the age at which it occurs, and the quantity and quality of educational management of children with such losses are crucial to the success of the habilitation/rehabilitation process. In addition to all of these factors, the habilitation/rehabilitation process is also influenced, either directly or indirectly, by the family members and their relationships.

Technological developments have brought vast improvements in reducing the size of individual hearing aids as well as increasing the fidelity of both hearing aids and amplification systems used in classroom settings. The advent of cochlear implants, utilized earlier and earlier and frequently bilaterally, has significantly changed the face of education of children who are deaf. Many educators have assumed, though, that if children's hearing acuity could be improved, their problems with learning and academic achievement would be solved. (Hearing acuity is used here to mean that an individual hears/detects a particular auditory signal/stimulus, that is, spoken language, at a level of intensity/loudness which makes it possible for the individual to make use of it for the appropriate purpose.) Unfortunately, this has not happened for many children. Despite the range of improvements in technology and the increase in the quantity and quality of involvement on the part of family members, the gains which have been made in professional training programs, and despite all of the improvements in early identification, early intervention, materials and methodologies introduced into the habilitative/rehabilitative process, the academic achievement levels of a significant portion of children who are deaf or hard of hear-

ing leave much to be desired.

According to Marschark and colleagues (2009) and others (Gallaudet 1996; Geers, Tobey, Moog and Brenner 2008) a fourth grade level of reading achievement has been considered the average for many years for students in the United States who are deaf. There are, perhaps, a multitude of reasons for this and research is ongoing. Certainly, in at least some of the cases, the co-existence of additional disabilities is undoubtedly to blame. Wiley and Moeller (2007) indicate the prevalence of additional disabilities in the deaf and hard of hearing population at 40%. Guardino (2008) cites research from Gallaudet Research Institute which indicates that over 50% of individuals who are deaf have at least one additional disability. Research by Shallop (In Spencer and Marschark, 2010) indicated that 39% to 54% of children with cochlear implants have another disability.

In the 1998–99 school year, there were 8 and 9-year-old children who were deaf and who were seen at the DuBard School for Language Disorders for comprehensive evaluations. Their amplification systems, including cochlear implants, boosted their hearing acuity to 30-50 dB levels. They did not demonstrate cognitive disabilities but were not progressing as expected. Their hearing acuity was adequate for better progress than they were achieving through traditional instructional programs for this population. It was for children with such difficulties that McGinnis designed and implemented the Association Method. When the children cited above were given some beginning level instruction via the Association Method, their responses were positive and they demonstrated potential for more success. As late as the 2009-10 school year, the majority of children with hearing loss in the school were diverse learners—diagnosed with multiple co-existing disabilities, including language disorders, childhood apraxia of speech, and learning disabilities, as well as other conditions. While it is a cause for celebration that a portion of children who are deaf and who are identified early, receive implants early, and receive intensive and appropriate oral-aural intervention early will be successful and independent at first grade, it behooves all professionals to continue to recognize and advocate for appropriate services for the large percentage of the population who are challenged with concomitant conditions. It is abundantly clear that improved auditory acuity *alone* cannot be counted on to solve the communication and academic problems. Conversely, in spite of the recommendations of some professionals to the contrary, it also should be noted that the successful development of oral communication skills over the decades has *not* been *solely* dependent on the degree of residual hearing. This author experienced living in St. Mary's School for Deaf Girls in Dublin, Ireland, during the mid- to late 1970s and again experienced the school in the early 1980s while pursuing Ph.D. studies. At that time, with far less sophisticated technology than is common now, with hearing aids of much less power and fidelity, it was noted that the Irish Dominican nuns and the other highly trained teaching staff in the school were very successful in developing excellent oral communication skills, aided by lipreading, in individuals who were very profoundly deaf and who had no other disabilities except hearing loss. In addition, their educational programs for students with hearing loss and concomitant conditions were models of differentiated instruction and high expectations for student achievement. The expertise and commitment of those professionals frequently led to positive results which were highly uncommon.

A significant number of children who do not have problems with hearing acuity *do* demonstrate challenges such as those described above. When the multisensory techniques of the Association Method are implemented by properly prepared professionals, significant improvement is noted. While they may learn to talk at the "normal time," their oral language may be poor in structure and content. A variety of other deficiencies may become evident through special testing. Clearly, there is more to hearing than acuity and discrimination, and in recent years, much attention been focused on the phenomenon of auditory processing.

Since the early 1970s groups of children experiencing problems in learning have been identified as having specific learning disabilities (SLD). Usually these determinations came from the fact that the children did not learn to read through the teaching techniques which were used successfully with their peers. Some were thought to be good in math. However, close analysis of their performances and skills indicated that they could achieve a measure of success in basic computation, but they could not/did not achieve the same level of ability when the task dealt with word problems. Even if they could read the words aloud, they did not demonstrate competence in solving the problems. They did not understand the linguistic components of the math. Although they could all "hear," some did not "listen" well and demonstrated behaviors which resulted in other deficiencies of various kinds which contributed to more complex problems in learning. Often they became school dropouts. Today some of these children are recognized as having auditory processing disorders/ problems, considered by some to be a subclass of language disorders.

It is thought that the problem of auditory processing may be the nucleus of many of the problems in communication disorders in children but research is inconclusive and professional opinions are diverse. The findings of Northern and Downs (1978), Tallal (1980), Levinson and Sloan (1980) support this possibility. The improvements which have been made throughout the years on behalf of children who were deaf or hard of hearing, as well as for nondisabled children, have not solved all of the problems related to their academic achievements. Perhaps a key factor and common denominator for learning for either group is yet to be determined. Therefore, there is a need to try to understand auditory processing and to use other avenues of teaching and learning.

AUDITORY PROCESSING—WHAT DOES IT MEAN?

The attention given here to auditory processing in relation to the development of language and speech and to language and speech disorders is not intended to be an all inclusive, in-depth discussion or explanation of the phenomenon. Nor is our purpose to offer theoretical models for intervention. Researchers and scholarly writers have provided a considerable amount of sophisticated material on these topics over the years and this continues to be a topic of considerable study, diverse opinions, and even controversy.

Study and analysis of the professional literature on auditory functioning, processing, and disorders confirm that the matter of how one learns, develops, and acquires specific skills/abilities for achieving competent functioning is extremely complex and still not well understood. Often, the theories offered within themselves, and, suggestions related to intervention are usually brief and too general. Specific guidelines for those who provide direct instruction are often absent from the commentaries. Nevertheless, it is important that those with the responsibility of working directly with children on a daily basis have basic knowledge about phenomena related to learning. The need to have a measure of knowledge related to what might be done to help children cope with their situations so that they may experience more success in learning is even more important.

One purpose here is to present a limited amount of information, oversimplified intentionally, about the normal processing of information/stimuli, in order to develop an awareness of the possible nature of some difficulties many children demonstrate. Another purpose is to describe symptomatic behaviors of children with auditory processing disorders. Some of these descriptions have been associated with both typically hearing children and those with hearing loss—a topic of more debate. A final purpose is to offer guidelines for remediation/intervention which have been used successfully to habilitate or rehabilitate children with these specific difficulties.

WHAT IS NORMAL PROCESSING?

To understand auditory processing disorders, one needs to have an understanding of the processes and components in place when auditory processing is adequate. The consensus of professionals regarding normal processing focuses on observing infants listening to sounds in the environment and interpreting them in relation to environmental events. This ability is essential for the development of language and of academic skills, which require the components of sensation, perception, symbolization, and conceptualization.

Sensation is defined as the activation of sensorineural structures. Failure of such activation to occur can indicate an impairment or a peripheral auditory deficit (Johnson and Myklebust 1967). Such an impairment may occur either as a solitary deficit in an otherwise intact auditory system or as one aspect of multiple auditory handicaps (Eisenson 1968).

Perception is the process of distinguishing the characteristics of stimuli (Mecham 1966). This permits children to complete a number of vital functions: (1) to recognize and attend to the differentiating properties of acoustic stimuli, (2) to screen pertinent sounds from incidental background noise on an immediate basis, (3) to discriminate among sounds and sound sequences, and (4) to recognize a word after hearing only part of it. Most of us take all of these abilities for granted. Children who have any deficits in auditory perception will be unable to make maximum use of auditory stimuli for communicating and learning.

Verbal symbolization exists when meanings are given to the sounds or sound combinations and become symbols to represent objects, experiences, concepts, or ideas (Johnson and Myklebust 1967; Bowerman 1974). Ability to achieve such symbolization is necessary for developing reasoning and to formulate concepts. Children who are unable to use sound symbolically will have deficits in understanding even the most basic language patterns of their environment and in formulating them in expressive language. While we may think of this ability as affecting only oral language, it has been observed repeatedly that children who are having difficulties with or who fail to acquire reading skills have shown marked limitations in sound-symbol relationships, and it is possible, though not proven, that their problems are related to auditory processing and/or auditory inefficiency.

Conceptualization requires that one be able to think in the abstract. This ability enables us to generalize and to make associations. Children who are unable to establish competence in conceptualizing based on symbols can be expected to have difficulties.

Integration of information calls for the ability to "get it all together." Perception, symbolization, and conceptualization are interdependent processes influenced by the integration of auditory, visual, tactile, and proprioceptive/oral motor information. Children learning to understand speech associate an auditory stimulus pattern with a visual stimulus in learning names for objects, people, letters, shapes, and actions. They learn to associate an auditory stimulus with a certain tactile sensation to understand the meaning of descriptive words such as hot, cold, soft, etc. A breakdown in sensory interpretation may result in verbal or nonverbal behaviors. A domino effect occurs when a peripheral hearing loss is present. The child with a hearing impairment who seems to be merely lacking the necessary auditory stimulation to enhance the sensation component also may have other more subtle difficulties related to hearing and the efficiency of the hearing. This is addressed further later in this chapter.

A number of skills are utilized when auditory processing is adequate: (1) awareness—*perceiving the presence or absence of acoustic stimuli;* (2) attention—*alerting to the presence of sound;* (3) sustained auditory attention—*attending to an auditory task over time;* (4) localization—*locating from what direction the sound is heard;* (5) identification—*identifying or knowing the sound heard;* (6) discrimination—*differentiating between and among sounds; suprasegmental and segmental discriminations;* (7) auditory memory/sequencing—*remembering a series of items;* (8) closure—*capacity to complete a message when part is missing;* (9) selective listening—*attending to sound in the presence of distractions;* and (10) auditory synthesis/comprehension—*restructuring/integrating/interpreting a message.* (Sanders 1977; Berry 2000). If there are weaknesses or deficits in one or more of these, difficulties in processing may be expected. The listing of these aspects of auditory processing should not be interpreted to oversimplify the complexity of the skills and their interrelatedness with one another. In effective and efficient auditory processing, these aspects are integrated and, at times, dependent one upon the other.

DEFINING, DIAGNOSING, AND TREATING AUDITORY PROCESSING PROBLEMS

Defining a problem is usually the starting point in obtaining solutions. However desirable a concise definition of auditory processing is, the professional literature of competent researchers in earlier years did not provide a refined definition per se. Sanders (1977) cited a number of critical aspects of auditory processing, including levels of segmentation, ordering of phonemic units, ordering of words, and memory processing in both short-term and long-term memory.

Tallal (1980) and Carrow-Woolfolk and Lynch (1982) provided research on auditory processing in children and some suggestions for remediation. The problems they identified and the conclusions they made were, in essence, the same as those described in a simpler manner by McGinnis (1939, 1963), Hardy (1965), and Eisenson (1965, 1972). The problems cited by Tallal on the basis of her research include the following:

1. The degree of simple peripheral hearing loss of children who are developmentally aphasic is small, if present at all, and not sufficient to affect their severe language retardation.
2. High-level deficits of auditory perception are the basis of the problem.
3. "Defective capacity for storing speech signals, impairment of phoneme recognition specifically within contextual utterances and impairment in processing sequences of speech events at the normal rate at which they occur" (Hardy 1965).
4. Lowe and Campbell (1969) concluded that disturbed temporal ordering might be a major factor in the communication of "aphasoid children."
5. Perception, storage, and reproduction of sequential auditory stimuli might be disturbed by cerebral dysfunction (Aten and Davis 1968).
6. Griffiths (1972) noted that children with developmental aphasia were markedly impaired in their ability to reproduce the more complex rhythmic patterns that were presented. From his findings, Griffiths suggested that difficulties occurred in the temporal ordering of auditory stimuli, in discrimination of relative duration, and possibly because of a reduced memory span. Van Uden (1982) reported similar findings.

Poppen (1969) and his colleagues pointed out that as well as impairments of auditory perception, "aphasic children" also have impairments in visual skills, perceptual abilities, and in memory. These weaknesses were also reported by Van Uden (1982).

As a result of their research, Tallal and Piercy (1973, 1974, 1975) concluded that children who were language delayed had difficulty responding to specific acoustic signals of short duration when they were preceded or followed by other acoustic cues, such as in a syllable, word, or sentence. They hypothesized that such children do not seem to have difficulty perceiving steady state acoustic stimuli of varying duration in isolation but do have difficulty with acoustic cues when they are presented either simultaneously or in close succession with others. The research findings of Tobey, Cullen, and Gallagher (1976) concluded: "When two stimuli were presented simultaneously, these children were unable to perceive both of them correctly as often as [typical children] did…suggesting that there is a difficulty in processing multiple acoustic cues presented either simultaneously or in rapid succession" (Levinson and Sloan 1980, 98).

Sloan (Levinson and Sloan 1980, 101–15) summarized several characteristics of auditory processing impairments in children with language disorders. These included (1) problems with sound identification and discrimination, especially when the sounds are in context rather than in isolation, (2) problems in retaining the temporal order or sequence of sounds or larger language units, (3) storage of auditory signals, and (4) problems with temporal patterns.

In addition, Liberman, Shankweiler, and their colleagues (in Levinson and Sloan 1980, 190) suggested that the process of reading is closely related to the speech system and to children's knowledge of the phonologic structure of their language. Many children who are described as having specific language disabilities have difficulties discriminating among speech sounds and associating the sounds with the letters of printed words. Sloan (Levinson and Sloan 1980, 114) concluded that "children with auditory processing disorders are potential candidates for reading disabilities when they become school age." *She identified auditory processing disorders as part of the general category of language disorders.* The problems associated with auditory processing disorders have been observed in a number of ways in preschool and school-age children by teachers and clinicians who usually describe them in less theoretical language and in words which are more specific and applicable to the tasks.

Paula Tallal, included in Levinson and Sloan (1980), wrote that evidence is readily available to document the existing problems in syntax, semantics, and conceptualization in children with language disorders. A major problem which she also cited is that of interpreting the studies which address the higher-level linguistic and cognitive abilities of such children because of the complexity and interrelatedness of the functions. Her review of the research of Rosenthal and Eisenson (1971) and Poppen et al. (1969) focused attention on the kinds of limitations which had been identified. These were summarized by Sloan (1980) and included problems with recognizing the order of two consecutive auditory sounds. According to Tallal and Piercy (1973), the children did not perceive them as being different. McReynolds' research (1966) supports this conclusion. Additional areas of difficulty included: temporal order, storage of the auditory signal, and temporal pattern.

Wood (1982) organized the language disorders in school-age children into four broad categories: (1) receptive deficiences—inadequate recognition of input (spoken or written) in terms of attaching significance to and interpreting sounds/letters, words, and word combinations and relationships, (2) expressive deficiencies—inadequate production (spoken or written) of the intended message as judged by linguistic and interactive rules of the context and the situation, (3) organizational deficiencies—inadequate planning or executing of goal-directed tasks, and (4) combinational—any combination of inadequacies in the language system or its use for interpersonal or intrapersonal service. These categories are a reorganization of a more detailed listing by Cole (1978) of behaviors of children with nonsensory auditory disorders which are considered to be diagnostically significant.

In 1992, a more sophisticated definition of central auditory processing disorders (CAPD) was proposed by an ad hoc committee of the American Speech-Language-Hearing Association (ASHA). It is as follows:

> Central auditory processing disorders are deficits in the information processing of audible signals not attributed to impaired peripheral hearing sensitivity or intellectual impairments... . Specifically, CAPD refers to limitations in the ongoing transmission, analysis, storage, retrieval, and use of information contained in audible signals.

In 2005, a technical report developed by the American Speech-Language-Hearing Association (ASHA) Working Group on Auditory Processing Disorders resulted in the following definition:

> Broadly stated, (Central) Auditory Processing [(C) AP] refers to the efficiency and effectiveness by which the central nervous system (CNS) utilizes auditory information. Narrowly defined, (C)AP refers to the perceptual processing of auditory information in the CNS and the neurobiologic activity that underlies that processing and gives rise to electrophysiologic auditory potentials. (C) AP includes the auditory mechanisms that underlie the following abilities or skills: sound localization and lateralization; auditory discrimination; auditory pattern recognition; temporal aspects of audition, including temporal integration, temporal discrimination (e.g., temporal gap detection), temporal ordering, and temporal masking; auditory performance in competing acoustic signals (including dichotic listening); and auditory performance with degraded acoustic signals (ASHA, 1996; Bellis, 2003; Chermak & Musiek, 1997). (Central) Auditory Processing Disorder [(C)APD] refers to difficulties in the perceptual processing of auditory information in the CNS as demonstrated by poor performance in one or more of the above skills. Although abilities such as phonological awareness, attention to and memory for auditory information, auditory synthesis, comprehension and interpretation of auditorily presented information, and similar skills may be reliant on or associated with intact central auditory function, they are considered higher order cognitive-communicative and/or language-related functions and, thus, are not included in the definition of (C)AP.

While the descriptions given by ASHA are related to children *without* peripheral hearing losses, they may apply to children with hearing loss as well.

The coexistence of central auditory processing disorders (CAPD) and language disorders/learning disabilities and/or attention deficit hyperactivity disorders provide a challenge to professionals and parents. Chermak, Hall and Musiek (1999) address the complexities and note that "the primacy of any one of these disorders as causal to another remains unclear." They hold the view "that CAPD and ADHD reflect two distinct clinical disorders, notwithstanding some overlap in their behavioral profiles."

DeBonis and Moncrieff (2008, 5) provide an excellent summary of the issues, as well as recommendations, for speech-language pathologists who serve school-age children with auditory processing disorders (APD). In addition to citing ASHA's 2005 technical report, they cite the work of Jerger and Musiek in 2002 who "emphasized the importance of establishing that poor performance on tests of auditory processing is due to 'an auditory-specific perceptual deficit in the processing of speech input' rather than due to some other factor(s)." Further, the report indicates that, while APD may coexist with attention, language, and reading deficits, for example, there is no research to indicate a *causative* relationship between APD and the other conditions. For example, children who struggle in reading may demonstrate good auditory processing skills; those with oral language comprehension problems may have normal auditory processing and, conversely, auditory processing deficits do not always result in language problems. However, it should be noted that other notables in the field such as Katz and colleagues (2002) are of the opinion that APDs may *cause* speech and language impairment, dyslexia, and attention deficit disorder. Clearly, additional research is needed on the topic.

What does auditory processing difficulty look like in the classroom? Those affected may: (1) demonstrate difficulty understanding directions, especially when given in noise, (2) ask for directions to be repeated, (3) misunderstand messages, (4) respond inconsistently or inappropriately, (5) delay in their responses to others' oral communications, (6) have difficulty with complex auditory directions, etc. (ASHA 2005) The less-than-optimum listening environments of typical American classrooms may intensify the problem.

Along with Sloan (1980a, b), we take the position that auditory processing disorders are a part of the general category of language disorders and therefore the problem of definitive identification is very difficult because of the complexity of speech and language development. The variability of children in specific language tasks is obvious to anyone who has dealt with children and communication disorders of any degree of seriousness. The children with the most serious disabilities will have significant difficulties learning to understand language well; they may appear to be deaf or hard of hearing to those around them. They are not likely to develop the skills of attending to or discriminating among speech sounds, of organizing them, sequencing them, or remembering them well enough to develop any conventional, age-appropriate oral communication. Other children will utilize a hodgepodge of linguistic sounds, poorly articulated, in poor syntax and with questionable meaning as a means of communicating. Still others may learn to talk relatively fluently and to be relatively adept with oral language. Their language deficiencies will not become noteworthy until they enter kindergarten or first grade where it may be observed that they do not follow the teacher's instructions well, if at all. They do not learn to read easily or to spell and to achieve academically as well as would be expected and, in general, they often show a great deal of frustration related to their unproductive efforts to learn the things that their peers seem to learn quickly, easily, and well. Some children have been observed to develop compensating strategies that gloss over their weakness and fool their teachers completely into thinking they understand. We have better ways and means of assessing children's language skills

---

Sloan (1980b, 117)	*Teacher-Clinician Comments*
1. Difficulty perceiving the accurate acoustic cues for the identification of speech sounds, especially when these are embedded in the contexts of syllables, words, or phrases.	**1.** The word in spelling was *tied*: he wrote *died*. He makes lots of errors... *bid* for *bed*, *pat* for *pad*, *screet* for *street*, etc.
2. Difficulty retaining a sequence of auditory signals.	**2.** In therapy, working to learn to say "yes" (y e s), a child could say /y/, /e/, /s/ separately slowly, though the /e/ was not of good quality. As we worked to get the whole word, she could remember the first two, or the last two or the first and last in some kind of sequence, but could not remember the three in the correct sequence.
3. Difficulty organizing phonemes into accurate sequential patterns both in perception and in production.	**3.** He says "aminals" for "animals," "efelant" for "elephant," and, in general, mixes up the syllables of words.
4. Difficulty perceiving the temporal patterns of speech and utilizing these to facilitate recognition and retention.	**4.** I have to repeat instructions to her. If I say "Put the book on the shelf" more slowly, for example, "Put ... the ... book ... on ... the ... shelf," she can follow the direction. She never does things right if I tell the children to do several things in a compound sentence, such as "Get your math book and look at the top of page fifty at the pictures and numbers."

in a more definitive manner than was possible in the past. However, frequently, a less than comprehensive assessment is conducted. In addition, the test results are not always utilized effectively for planning remediation.

Who diagnoses APD? It is well-established by ASHA (2005) that the actual diagnosis of an auditory processing disorder is within the scope of practice of the audiologist. However, both audiologists and speech-language pathologists (SLPs) may screen for the disorder. Since a diagnosis of *pure* APD precludes the presence of difficulties in hearing acuity, language, learning disabilities, etc., which could be at the core of what appears to be an auditory processing problem, the role of SLPs is paramount in making a differential diagnosis. Bellis (2003) advocated for a multidisciplinary approach to screening for APD to effectively determine strengths and weaknesses in skills which are clearly interdependent.

AUDITORY PROCESSING: RESEARCH

One needs to keep in mind that auditory processing problems are not new, but are receiving renewed interest and study. Katz (1984) cited the work of Travis and Rasmus (1931) in which they noted that pupils with articulation problems had depressed speech sound discrimination. Katz noted also that Monroe (1932) wrote that auditory synthesis skills were reduced in a large number of children who demonstrated reading difficulties.

Luria (1966) discussed auditory processing, articulation, language, reading, and spelling disorders. He suggested that the various functions are localized in certain areas or zones in the cortex, which he identified as: (1) phonemic, (2) articulation, (3) spelling, (4) reading, and (5) receptive language. Luria also focused attention on the fact that all skills are complex and are made up of a number of subskills. He stated further that "dysfunctions of the child's nervous system is not a static process," and that compensating for inadequacies may possibly be due to central nervous system plasticity. Assuming that his idea is valid, this might well offer a partial explanation of the fact that many children learn to compensate and improve enough "to get by" yet are not able to reach their maximum level of intellectual potential. They may be unable to acquire sufficient reading skills to succeed in academic educational environments, to cope with the volume of written language tasks of those environments, or to enjoy reading. Those with more severe difficulties may not be able to develop effective strategies for learning without special attention and help. The volume of material in educational programs, the rate at which it is presented, and the amount of time allowed for students to learn/master the material, in the absence of sufficient redundancy, may constitute an overwhelming task for many of them.

Katz (1984) noted that damage or immaturity of the middle and posterior portions of the superior temporal gyrus would impair discrimination, that is, the synthesizing and remembering of speech sounds. Difficult discrimination tasks would require an affected student more time to analyze, synthesize, and remember, and a depressed performance could result when such an individual listened to rapid, distorted, or less redundant speech. A logical consequence would be difficulty in processing word endings, especially in longer or more difficult words, or in dealing with words and phrases that are embedded in long and complex sentences. Katz also argued that less efficient storage systems would result in phonemic information tending to fade quickly. Since speech occurs at a relatively rapid rate, it is logical to think that difficulties could remain even after the child's central nervous system has matured and/or the child has learned to make certain compensations for his/her difficulties.

According to Luria (1970), with the articulation and phonemic zones being adjacent and somewhat overlapping, individuals with lesions to the frontoparietal and superior temporal regions demonstrated various types of articulation disorders. He speculated that limited sensory information might reach the tongue, lips, and vocal folds and suggested that a child with such limitations might benefit from articulation therapies which stressed tactile and oral-motor senses. This, then, would support a motor theory of speech perception.

The interrelatedness of spelling, sound blending, and reading has been cited by numerous researchers including Luria (1970). Although Hammill and Larsen (1978) endeavored to explain away an association between reading, auditory perception, and sound blending, they were unable to do so (Katz 1984).

As early as 1959, Penfield and Roberts determined that the receptive language zone (posterior temporoparietal areas of the left hemisphere in most people) encompasses almost completely the phonemic zone and covers a major portion of the spelling and reading zones. Being adjacent to the articulation zone, it is logical to conclude that increased interrelatedness could be expected.

All of this serves to emphasize the complexity of the entire central nervous system and its functions in relation to communication and academic tasks. However, as Katz (1984, 275) pointed out, the application of the functional-anatomical model helps one to "(1) better understand each of these individual communication and learning problems, (2) be able to conceptualize the cluster of symptoms and problems encountered in working with children who have auditory processing difficulties, (3) provide a rationale in the selection of diagnostic procedures, and (4) offer a basis from which we can understand current therapeutic procedures and develop new approaches."

Katz et al. (1992) reported on research designed to provide additional types of information about children with learning disabilities and auditory processing disorders. Four categories of information were cited. Decoding categories focused on "auditory processing that breaks down at the phonemic level" (84). Tolerance-fading memory focused on the symptoms of "auditory memory and poor figure-ground skills" (85). The children who were studied demonstrated marked limitations in these categories with the most severe limitations in decoding. Efforts were made to study two additional categories, integration and organization. The amount of information gained was limited because of the low number of case studies and the newness of the research.

The matter of *brain plasticity* has received increasing attention in recent years. Koch et al (1999) indicated that "the representation of speech sounds is plastic and that rehabilitative strategies involving enhancing speech contrasts or focused listening training may prove efficacious in some populations that exhibit speech perception deficits of central origin." Findings regarding brain plasticity suggest support for early, specific intervention for those with auditory processing disorders.

MANAGEMENT

Much of what is in the professional literature which addresses the matter of intervention/management for auditory processing disorders refers to theoretical models. Even though this information is often generalized and sometimes nebulous, it is important that those working with such children on a day-to-day basis be aware of suggestions that are available.

Katz (1984) reported his findings related to studies of a small group of children with learning disabilities, citing the therapeutic techniques of Orton (1937) and McGinnis (1963), especially their techniques incorporating sound-blending activities. He noted that the sound-blending activities described and used by McGinnis had been especially helpful to children with severe difficulties learning language and speech even though McGinnis's techniques received a great deal of criticism and caused considerable controversy because of the single pho-

neme and reduced temporal rate of presenting the auditory signals during auditory training. It is reasonable to consider that what might be unnatural for the child learning language and speech naturally would not be unnatural for a child with some kind of auditory processing disorder. The temporal rate reduction has proven to be helpful to children with unusual auditory functioning, presumed to be a central auditory processing disorder.

Sanders (1977, 236) suggested that the following considerations precede intervention:

1. Obtain a careful description of the child's language processing behavior
2. Identification of patterns derived from observation across phonetic, syntactic, and semantic contexts
3. Formation of a hypothesis as to which rule(s) is/are operant in the child's recognition and/or production of the deviant pattern
4. Identification of an appropriate intervention strategy designed to effect a modification or substitution for an incorrect rule

Carrow-Woolfolk and Lynch (1982) offered guidelines for teaching content to children with language disorders and suggested basic elements to be considered in the process.

> The basic elements of teaching have to do with (1) the type of stimulus the teacher presents to the child; (2) the type of response that is expected from the child; (3) the response of the teacher to the child's response; and (4) the amount of structure used in the interaction between the clinician and child. The first two are instructional procedures and the latter are teaching strategies. (267–68)

In addition, general procedures were given in relation to teaching cognitive thinking, semantic relations, and syntactic structures.

Wood (1982) looked at receptive and expressive disorders and discussed a number of approaches including the developmental, direct and indirect intervention, a single intervention approach, interventions which stress drill related to sets of rule-based behaviors, and behavior modification approaches. Her view as to when to start an intervention program seems significant in relation to children and their daily lives. "Intervention has to have a starting point, often before the evaluation process is completed, and sometimes in the face of numerous unanswered questions regarding the child's communication behaviors." She did not address auditory processing disorders directly but made a statement which professionals and parents need to remember: "Although the intervention process begins with the first suspicion of a language disorder," it "sometimes seems to have no end," because the deficiencies have a definite impact on the academic performance/achievements of the older child as well as problems related to basic communication observed in the younger child.

Sloan (1980a) focused attention on specific auditory processing disorders which include sound identification and discrimination, problems related to temporal order, problems with the storage of auditory signals, and problems related to temporal patterns. Sloan also discussed aspects of processing in relation to language development and perception of the phonetic code. She noted that "not all language disorders are characterized by an auditory processing disorder," but that "an auditory disorder can affect the overall development of language" (113).

Sloan (1980b, 124–128) gives the following guidelines for treating auditory processing disorders. They are similar to the seven steps of the Association Method as designed by McGinnis (1963).

1. Give the child instructions regarding what he/she is supposed to hear or do. Repetition may be necessary.
2. Don't allow guessing. It is important for the child to understand the goal. Reduced guesswork will result in greater progress in the long run.
3. Maximize signal detection. Get the message to the child by whatever means you can, regardless of the linguistic stimulus—sound, word, or phrase—to make it more perceptible. For example, prolong the signal, simplify the signal, repeat the signal keeping the rate slow, and/or associate the acoustic features with cues of other sensory modalities.
4. Gradually withdraw cues.
5. Present signals in phonetic contrasts.
6. Work until responses are automatic.
7. Make the child responsible for signal detection from the start.
8. Work on several levels of phonetic structure.
9. Use articulation as soon as possible.
10. Program in very small steps, from simple to complex.
11. Use blocks of trials, giving concrete, visual reinforcement.
12. Maintain a high success rate.
13. Use nondistracting but concrete reinforcement for correct responses.
14. Begin with a warm-up.
15. Develop a simple system to keep track of quantitative and qualitative data.

Detailed descriptions of Sloan's explanations are available in her work (124–28). The treatment which she offers is related to auditory-speech production but it should be noted that these 15 items are effective principles which may be applied to numerous therapeutic approaches. Eisenson (1984) offers similar guidelines. The auditory processing/training work is a key part of the Association Method which will be described later in this book.

Contemporary thinking regarding intervention for auditory processing disorders focuses on three areas: changing the environment, using higher order skills to compensate, and remediation of the specific deficit itself (Bellis 1997-2011). Changing the environment may include such strategies as altering the physical environment to reduce auditory distractions or techniques to enhance the delivery of the auditory information. Compensatory strategies utilizing higher order skills may include increasing attention, language, memory or problem-solving skills. Direct treatment of the deficit skills may include activities (1) to improve discrimination of sounds, words, or other language structures, (2) to improve listening in noise, (3) to improve dichotic listening skills, to name only a few (Friel-Patti 1999; Ferre 2007). To be certain, therapeutic approaches should be designed based on a specific individual's diagnosis and auditory skill profile; one size does not fit all. Listening intervention in the DuBard Association Method® includes intensive auditory training from the level of the single phoneme, to vocabulary, and through stories with language structures which gradually increase in length and complexity. One advantage of such intervention is the *relevance* it brings to the therapeutic tasks for those challenged with co-existing communication and learning disorders. Auditory skills are not remediated in isolation but rather are integrated in the context of speech, language, and reading/written language skills.

READING BY STUDENTS WHO ARE DEAF OR HARD OF HEARING: MULTIPLE CONSIDERATIONS

One has only to be somewhat aware of current criticisms leveled at many public school systems to know that there are alarming numbers of students with such poor reading skills that many of them are considered to be functionally illiterate upon completing high school. Because this is not a new situation, there are now many adults who cannot read or write. Even with the many adult education classes, the collective efforts of many professionals and volunteer forces, it is highly unrealistic to expect that a great deal of "correction" is likely to result quickly. If there are problems of such great magnitude related to teaching those with good hearing acuity to read adequately enough to meet the requirements of society, there is little wonder that the record in teaching those who are deaf or hard of hearing to read is as poor as it is.

To identify and list the volumes of the professional literature which address multiple aspects of reading, the reading process, reading skills, deficits in reading, and/or reading performance levels of various populations of individuals would be a task of unbelievable magnitude. There are, however, discussions of basic components related to the phenomenon of learning to read. Along with those basic teaching components there are equal numbers of controversies as to which is "the best" or "the way." We are reminded of a graduate professor in 1950 who, in his first lecture in a research course to his class of budding professionals, stated, "If we would make use of what we already know about teaching, there would be no need for additional research" (Drummond 1950). There is reason to think that such a statement is still appropriate. Even so, there is a need for professional literature to provide key information from the past and to provide material which might lead to additional insight into both problems and issues. The focus here will be on reading abilities of children who are deaf or hard of hearing.

King and Quigley (1985) expressed the view that there is evidence that reading performance levels of students who are deaf may well be very low. Even if one considers such variables as specific difficulties related to the language and factors (social, economic, and cultural) related to individuals, the basic problem with reading remains the same. King and Quigley describe reading as a parasitic function, based on the primarily auditory language developed in early years by hearing children. Further, they state that "reading in the narrow sense can be regarded as the decoding of print" (69) with all other prior knowledge resulting from experience and linguistic development. Since children with significant hearing loss may lack the basic knowledge of linguistic communication and linguistic development, it is little wonder that they have such difficulties. One task which nondisabled children have in learning to read is making an association between the symbols of their oral language and the symbols of the written language which ultimately they learn to write. Children with hearing loss frequently do not have command of the oral language symbols. They have little or no symbol system to associate with the symbols of the written language. It is

little wonder then that they have such difficulties and achieve so poorly.

Going still further with the reading process, King and Quigley pointed out that the "speech recoding seems to be important for hearing readers… for temporary storage of words in word memory to comprehend clauses and sentences." They also point out that coding and storage, which involve temporal-sequential memory, are deficit areas in those who are deaf. These components in learning—or failing to learn—by those who are deaf also have been described and identified in hearing children with language disorders ranging from acute/serious to subtle/mild. Hearing children with subtle/mild difficulties make up the population who demonstrate problems related to reading.

Lichtenstein (1983) confirmed Conrad's findings (1979) and those of Hanson (1982) regarding working memory: "Working memory capacity is related to the extent to which students can make efficient use of a speech-based recoding strategy in various language tasks and that this strategy is positively related to reading ability." Lichtenstein also noted the dual task of learning a language (English) and learning to read at the same time. According to him, at a time when few children who are deaf have adequate mastery of English in any form by the time reading instruction begins, large demands must be made on their working memory and recoding processes. He focused on syntax in relation to sentence structures. One must remember that while syntax is word order, single words are composed of phonemes/speech sounds uttered in a particular order also. It seems logical that memory and skills of sequential ordering would be of significant value in a child's remembering/recalling words in reading. According to King and Quigley (1985), "most deaf children do not learn English well." They suggest that the role of the speech-coding process may result in deaf children who, "unable to acquire the coding system, might simply be unable to ever learn to read well or even adequately."

Moores (1987) states that reading skills among those who are deaf show the peak grade-level achievement to be at third-, fourth-, and fifth-grade levels. The ratings were based on reading achievement levels on standardized tests with hearing norms. Although he writes that the consensus among some educators has been that "deaf individuals simply do not have the literacy skills necessary for success," he also points out that such a view "is at odds with everything known about the functioning of deaf adolescents and adults in society." It seems obvious that either the test data do not reflect the skills accurately or that at least some of those who are deaf have means of compensating for their limitations. Whatever the case, problems still exist and great effort is necessary to improve reading skills.

King and Quigley (1985) offered three suggestions: (1) Speech could be better developed with far more deaf children than is the case at present (Ling 1976; Ling and Ling 1978), presuming that improved speech skills would be a basis for improving reading skills. (2) Systems for teaching reading should be developed which do not depend on speech coding and recoding. However, they noted that use of American Sign Language (ASL) as the first and basic language of young children who are deaf "might preclude the learning of reading." (3) Videotapes in ASL should be used simultaneously with the printed word.

Steinberg (1982) proposed a plan to help children with hearing loss overcome linguistic limitations through teaching written language. Spalding and Spalding (1957, 1990) made similar suggestions on behalf of hearing children. Steinberg cited six important advantages: (1) The learning medium is appropriate. (2) Written language knowledge can facilitate speech. (3) Written language knowledge need not be acquired by instructors, only instructional methods and techniques have to be acquired. (4) Instruction can begin early. (5) All children with hearing loss can benefit. (6) Written language acquisition is compatible with other approaches. We suggest that experiences could be associated with written forms also so that such forms acquire a symbolic value, i.e., meaning.

The idea of using written language with young children who are deaf has been a practice among many professionals. Parents are often encouraged to put a label on items in the home so that the very young child will learn the names of common objects, for example, chair, bed, table, etc.

At St. Michielsgestel School for the Deaf, The Netherlands, there has long been the practice of using written language simultaneously with speech, especially for the purpose of developing and establishing principles of conversation patterns as well as the language itself (Van Uden 1968). In the division for the students with multiple disabilities at St. Michielsgestel, for students with such severe motor problems that it was not possible for the individual to learn to talk or use sign language, the teaching of written language enhanced the individual's chance to develop some written verbal skills that could be useful.

Although there always will be the tendency to view various instructional approaches from an either-or standpoint, it is unlikely that issues will be solved in absolutes. The question of whether language should be established before formal reading or whether it is feasible for a child who is deaf to learn language through the reading process has been raised (King and Quigley 1985), as has the question of whether or not reading should be focused on decoding or on meaning. Professionals need to be as well informed in as many aspects of teaching-learning as possible and to be able to draw from a variety of approaches in a systematic and consistent manner so that the child will benefit maximally.

We hold the view that learning is not based on the either-or concept. The complexity of all systems/avenues for learning is easy to acknowledge in theory, but sometimes difficult to deal with from a practical standpoint. It is vital to recognize that the systems/avenues for learning utilized by the human being are interrelated; they do not function for maximum learning as independent phenomena. Therefore, it is important that those who teach be aware of the *multisensory components* which allow learning to take place and to be able to use those systems systematically, consistently, and with competence. It is acknowledged that a segment of the population with severe to profound hearing loss is able to develop oral communication skills via auditory-verbal therapy and without multisensory cues. However there is a large segment of the population who, for a variety of reasons, will not reach optimum communication and academic skills through utilization of the auditory channel alone. It is vital that the teacher be knowledgeable about each child's capabilities and/or limitations, to be able to enhance the child's abilities and to work to reduce the limitations. It is vital that each teacher be prepared to meet the needs of all of her students with hearing loss. It is equally vital that each teacher believe in children's abilities, have faith in their abilities to achieve a particular task in learning, and have faith in his/her own abilities to teach the child. Only then will the child, whether hearing or hearing impaired, be able to begin to achieve at or near the level of his/her intellectual potential.

The multisensory aspects of teaching-learning strategies based on the principles found in the Association Method have been used systematically and consistently for several decades. Children who are severely hearing impaired, language disordered, severely speech disordered or who show auditory processing disorders have all benefited from the use of the multisensory teaching techniques. In essence, the teaching of language and speech has been achieved by helping the child develop and establish skills in semantics and syntax and to *expand the language skills simultaneously* through a balance between oral and written skills. *Each lesson is a language lesson; each lesson is a speech lesson; each lesson is a reading lesson, either oral or written or both.* In the chapters that follow we will describe, discuss, and illustrate the instructional program for this kind of balanced plan which has resulted in reading and academic achievement far beyond the fourth grade level for many students, past and present, who are deaf or hard of hearing.

CHILDHOOD APRAXIA OF SPEECH (CAS): DEFINITIONS AND CHARACTERISTICS

Wendell Johnson was one of the leading professionals of his era in the field of communication disorders. His special interest was stuttering. Curtis, a co-editor with Johnson, listed the following as causes of articulation disorders: (1) constitutional factors, (2) faulty learning, and (3) emotional maladjustments (Johnson et al. 1956). Van Riper (1972) included (1) developmental influences, (2) emotional conflicts, (3) motor incoordination, (4) organic abnormalities, and (5) perceptual deficiencies. Van Riper identified the difficulties associated with motor deficiencies as being sluggish in the use of tongue, jaw, and soft palate.

McGinnis (1939, 1963) noticed motor difficulties in some children presumed to be deaf but whom, she concluded, had congenital aphasia. Barry (1961) alluded to motor difficulties she observed as she taught children diagnosed with aphasia. However, it was not until McGinnis organized aphasia into different types that specific categories of articulatory skills were identified definitively. McGinnis gave two classifications of aphasia in children. Class I was identified as congenital motor aphasia or expressive aphasia. She referred to Class II as receptive aphasia. McGinnis described children with motor/expressive aphasia as those (1) whose intelligence was within normal range, (2) who had normal hearing and understanding of language, (3) who demonstrated inability to imitate words, and (4) who had inability or limited ability to imitate speech sounds. She also cited characteristics which included use of very short duration or staccato vowels and occasional lingua-palatal or lingua-dental consonants with vowels. Some of the children chattered constantly, reflecting perseverative patterns when trying to converse. Others communicated only to express their wants and needs. McGinnis noted that often these same children could not imitate speech sounds in isolation which could be detected in their random vocalizations. One comparison which she made was that "speech-defective children" occasionally would say some intelligible words whereas her "motor/expressive aphasic

children" did not do so. She also noted that the children with motor-aphasia demonstrated poor memory for sequences of sounds in words and poor memory for words in sentences even after they had learned the correct production of the sound in isolation or the speech for the words.

In addition to her descriptions given above, McGinnis used other specific terminology and cited conditions related to motor skills. She included the term apraxia and defined it as "a manifestation that is frequently found in one or several forms in children with aphasia: (1) limb-kinetic or innervatory apraxia… slow, awkward motor function, (2) ideokinetic apraxia. . . satisfactory complex movements, but difficulty in making a single movement, (3) ideational apraxia… faulty conception of movements as a whole with confusion as to spatial and temporal relations of the parts to a movement sequence, and (4) construction apraxia… visio-kinesthetic connections are faulty; the subject is unable to lay out sticks or blocks to form a (specific) pattern or to draw it" (McGinnis 1963, xvii). No mention was made of apraxia in relation to speech per se as it now has come to be used.

Eisenson and Ogilvie (1977) did not include the term apraxia in their organization of speech problems, but they noted that motor skills were variables in many children. They noted, too, that the component of auditory memory is related to speech learning and stated that such children "hear well" but have difficulty in retaining auditory impressions and/or in discriminating among sounds.

Van Riper (1972, 343) included the term apraxia although he expressed a reluctance to do so. The definition he gave was "an inability to command a part of the body to make a willed movement… the inability to make a voluntary movement." Eisenson (1972, 189) referred to "a very small number of children who seem to understand spoken language but who, nevertheless, are unable to acquire productive language." He noted that sometimes the children were "erroneously referred to as motor or expressive aphasics" (189) which was the classification McGinnis had used earlier. Van Riper's reluctance to use the term apraxia or apraxic and Eisenson's view that the children were erroneously being described as motor/expressive aphasic seem to have been part of some underlying controversy of the times. Eisenson (1972, 189) chose to use the definition offered by DeRenzi et al. (1966).

> Oral apraxia… an inability or a severe impairment in the individual's ability to perform voluntary movements involving muscles of the larynx, pharynx, tongue, lips, palate and cheeks… although

automatic movements of the same musculature appear to be unimpaired... an accompaniment of aphasic involvement or discrete disability observed in an adult impairment following cortical damage.

Bloodstein (1979, 301–2) cited apraxia as meaning "difficulty in the use of associative processes in order to perform purposeful acts," noting that associative processes are necessary for speech; that is, associating sound-symbol-word sequences and that purposeful acts require organization according to a plan. He stated the view that in apraxia the plan has been lost; therefore, there is a loss of skill in learned activities. He expanded the idea, noting that "apraxia of the oral structures shows itself in the failure to produce movements of the tongue, jaw, and lips on command although the patient/client can move them automatically for eating."

Eisenson (1984, 232) focused some attention on apraxia by referring to the definition of Darley, Aronson, and Brown (1975) which indicated that apraxia is a failure or impairment of a complex oral behavior to be established rather than a breakdown of previously established behavior as in acquired conditions. Basically, "the apraxia for speech is an impairment in the ability to produce a sequence of voluntary and intended movements involving the muscles of the mouth (tongue, lips, palate, cheeks) pharynx and larynx on the basis of cerebral pathology."

McGinnis (1963) classified the children who displayed a measure of understanding of language and severe motor problems as Class I Congenital Aphasia. Johnston (1980), writing about auditory processing and adult aphasics, cited apraxia as one of the complicating conditions, thus supporting the idea that the two conditions can coexist. She stated with reference to aphasia:

> Another complicating factor that can be present is apraxia, the inability to immediately assume the correct positions of tongue and lips. There is no paralysis of the speech musculature. Oral apraxia is a confusing phenomena because it usually does not exist in isolation. It is called by various names. It can be difficult to distinguish from motor aphasia. (172)

Johnston also indicated that apraxia can exist with aphasia and stated further that auditory processing disorders can be present. This idea is in agreement with those of Sanders (1977) who suggested that children with very severe articulation disorders may have an underlying language disorder masked by the unintelligible speech. Our

observations of some children substantiate that likelihood.

In his 1984 publication, Jaffe provided a comprehensive summary of characteristics of apraxia of speech. They include: history of feeding problems, little distinguishable vocal play, poor self-monitoring, reduced repertoire of phonemes, poor imitative skills for articulation, problems in phonetic synthesis for speech, highly inconsistent errors, delayed and deviant speech development, sequential sound production difficulties, connected speech more unintelligible than would be expected on the basis of single word articulation test results, groping trial-and-error behavior, oral diadochokinetic rates slower than normal and often incorrectly sequenced, typically poor response to "traditional" speech therapy.

The American Speech-Language-Hearing Association (ASHA) (2007-2011) defined childhood apraxia of speech (CAS) "as a motor speech disorder. Children with CAS have problems saying sounds, syllables, and words. This is not because of muscle weakness or paralysis. The brain has problems planning to move the body parts (e.g., lips, jaw, tongue) needed for speech. The child knows what he or she wants to say, but his/her brain has difficulty coordinating the muscle movements necessary to say those words." According to Kaufman (2008), "Apraxia of speech is a motor-speech programming disorder resulting in difficulty executing and/or coordinating (or sequencing) the oral-motor movements necessary to produce and combine speech sounds to form syllables, words, phrases and sentences on voluntary control." Characteristics of CAS include, but are not limited to, inconsistent speech errors, limited consonants and vowels in spontaneous utterances, groping trial-and-error behavior when trying to articulate sounds, difficulty imitating speech and delayed language development (DuBard and Martin, 2000; Kaufman 2008; ASHA 2007-2011).

Intervention for Apraxia

Most authors cited above do not discuss intervention approaches for children with apraxia. However, McGinnis devised teaching techniques for these children. Young and Hawk (1955) suggested an approach similar to hers. Eisenson gives some guidelines related to therapy emphasizing oral work. McGinnis's multisensory Association Method was used with Class I and Class II congenitally aphasic children at Central Institute for the Deaf, St. Louis, for several decades. Some students who studied there and who became speech-language pathologists have continued to use the techniques successfully, making modifications as necessary after it was evident that a sufficient foundation of phonemes and skills would support modifying McGinnis's sequential program without jeopardizing the child's progress.

Current treatment literature is based on two theories of motor learning, schema theory and dynamic systems theory. Schema theory (Schmidt and Lee 2005) assumes that the production of motor movements involves motor programs that are retrieved from memory and then adapted to the parameters required by particular situations. These parameters include details about the movement such as duration and force of muscle contractions (Ballard, Granier and Robin 2000). Because movements are never produced in exactly the same manner, schema theory assumes the generalization of these motor programs into a variety of contexts. That is, the movements necessary for production of phonemes for speech are retrieved from memory and adapted according to the coarticulatory features of the phonetic context. A large number of practice trials helps to automatize the activation of motor programs which enhances the stability of the production. Because speech is a motor skill that involves multiple components, it may be beneficial to divide a complex movement into its component parts for practice. This is thought to minimize the cognitive load of the task until the movement is automatic. These generalized motor programs may correspond to phonemes, syllables, words, or phrases.

Dynamic systems theory (Ballard, Granier and Robin 2000) is based on motor gestures, which are abstract representations of movements. These movement gestures emerge through interaction of the parts of the speech system with each other. This theory emphasizes the shaping of movement gestures for speech production based on the phonetic context of the phonemes. As the student receives motor-kinesthetic feedback from these productions, the accuracy of the movement gestures improves and leads to automaticity (Strand, Stoeckel, and Baas 2006). Therefore, therapy following this theory begins at the syllable, word, or phrase level. Despite current literature supporting these two theories, research in this area remains limited which underscores the importance of the need for studies of efficacy of treatment for CAS.

According to ASHA (2007), because practice in planning, programming and production are needed for the remediation of motor speech disorders, intensive treatment for apraxia should be provided on an individual basis. Hall, Jordan and Robin (1993), Strand and Skinder (1999) and Skinder-Meredith (2001) published research that supports the need for three to five individual sessions per week for children with CAS, rather than the traditional, less intensive, one to two sessions per week. The Ad Hoc Committee which developed the ASHA Technical Report on Childhood Apraxia of Speech (2007) affirmed the need for intensive therapy in order to reach a level of maximum progress in the remediation of CAS. It was stated that individualized therapy is the preferred delivery method, regardless of age.

In our experience, children with severe childhood apraxia of speech (CAS) require non-traditional, intensive, phonetic, incremental instruction in order to achieve the intelligibility that is needed. A number of children diagnosed with severe apraxia have been enrolled in the DuBard School for Language Disorders over the years. Many had had long-term, traditional speech therapy on a typical therapy schedule (30 minutes, 3x per week; 60 minutes, 2x per week, etc.). The therapy was conducted by qualified speech-language pathologists using traditional articulation therapy techniques. However, the *intensity* of therapy was inadequate for the severity of the child's needs. When placed in a specialized educational program in which speech-language therapy was provided as an integral component incorporated in all instruction, intelligibility was achieved. Use of the DuBard Association Method® in its purest form in a full-day program resulted not only in intelligible speech but the development of reading, writing, and language skills. The challenge for speech-language pathologists in public school settings, and in private practice settings which use the typical scheduling format, is to find ways to give these students more intensive services and a phonetic, multisensory incremental program. With this plan of intensive therapy, many children with childhood apraxia of speech will achieve intelligible speech and avoid a lifetime of augmentative communication devices and/or sign language.

In analyzing and using the multisensory aspects of the teaching techniques in the DuBard Association Method®, it becomes apparent that the multisensory feature itself is a key factor in the effectiveness of the techniques. The approach also provides the amount of repetition that is needed for the child to be able to establish the memory skills and master the linguistic plan necessary for meaningful communication to become well-established. Through the technique the child also learns reading skills. Clinical experience indicates that the child's speech supports his developing reading skill and his reading supports correct speech.

Johnston (1980) also noted the value of multisensory teaching techniques to develop coordination of hand, eye, and ear with movements for the speech musculature, and stated that a need to continue therapy will exist until the patient "has enough language to communicate effectively in his environment" (174). Johnston also acknowledged that the body of knowledge is not yet complete and that research, experience, and common sense are important in diagnosing auditory processing and treatment of severe language disturbance. These same components are needed for better intervention with those with childhood apraxia of speech/oral apraxia/developmental apraxia.

WORKING MEMORY—A FACTOR IN ACHIEVEMENT

Much has been written about Working Memory (WM) in recent years. While it is not the goal of this text to review all of the literature on this topic, suffice it to say that the WM literature may hold the scientific evidence which explains what makes the procedures of the Association Method as McGinnis devised it, and the DuBard Association Method® as it has evolved, effective for many children with significant communication disorders. Montgomery (2002) cited what he considered to be the two most prominent theories of working memory, Baddeley's (1998) phonological loop model and Just and Carpenter's (In Montgomery 2002, 78) model. The first model proposes that working memory is *"capacity limited"* and contains a finite amount of storage space which holds speech information in memory while processing takes place. The latter views verbal working memory (VWM) for language as a *"resource-limited* system that includes *both* storage *and* processing functions." Baddeley's model reflects one's ability to hold information in memory while simultaneously processing. Just and Carpenter describe a fluidity which exists between storage and processing implying that when less capacity is needed for storing information, such as with information that is familiar, more capacity is available for processing. Conversely, when more capacity is needed for holding information in memory, less capacity is available for the processing and, thus, comprehension of it. The memory problems that many clinicians have observed in children with language disorders may be explained by the theory that the language impairment is caused by an inadequate capacity to store phonological information and to process it. In a later work, Baddeley (2000) expanded his model to include the concept of the "episodic buffer" which emphasizes the *integration* of the previously described components of phonological loop, central executive for attentional issues, and the visuospatial sketchpad component (Baddeley and Hitch 1974).

In describing the relationship between Working Memory and Long Term Memory, Gillam (1997, 73) described "four interrelated memory phases (encoding, storage, retrieval and reporting) that occur simultaneously within long-term (relatively permanent) and working (ever-changing) memory." These processes are highly interrelated and influenced by factors including, but not limited to, motivation, world knowledge, and language skill. Alloway and colleagues (Alloway et al 2005; Alloway et al 2009; Alloway 2009) have studied working memory, including the predictive value of working memory, rather than IQ, on achievement. One finding in a study of typically developing children was that "working memory at the start of formal education is a more powerful predictor of subsequent academic success than IQ during the early years (Alloway and Alloway 2010). Future research in these areas should prove fruitful for researchers and practitioners alike. The interested reader will find multiple references on this topic in the Bibliography.

CHAPTER

2

Assessment of Students' Abilities

DuBard did not include any information in *Teaching Aphasics and Other Language Deficient Children* (1974) related to evaluating, assessing, or testing the abilities of children who are essentially nonverbal or of those with less severe language deficiencies. Perhaps the reason is that there were limited assessment tools and little agreement on what should be done. Because so many requests have been made, this chapter was written to suggest some ways and means by which skills, abilities, and limitations of children can be determined so that appropriate educational programs can be implemented.

It is important to have general and specific information related to the mother's health during pregnancy and delivery, the child's medical history, developmental history and information related to the relationship between and among family members and the child's relationship to people in the community or neighborhood. Interviewing parents is equally important. Informal techniques, as well as lengthy and detailed checklists available on the commercial market, may be used for such data gathering. Getting the parents to talk about the child in question is preferable to asking many direct questions. A preferred means of official recording and report writing by those evaluating a child has been narrative-style summarizing of the child's abilities and limitations in certain areas. Excellent guidelines and suggestions related to interviewing may be found in the research done by Kinsey on sexual behavior (1953). The effectiveness of the interviewing techniques may be of value in other kinds of data gathering.

The following comments regarding evaluating preschool and school-age children will focus attention on tests and informal assessments. It is presumed that no evaluation would be complete without data related to pre-, peri-, and post-natal history and developmental data about the child, including a current medical history. Those with special interest in detailed discussions of pediatric-neurological assessments and other medical evaluations and audiological assessments, as well as language assessments, are referred to portions of the writings of Myklebust (1954), Hardy (1965), Davis and Silverman (1970), Eisenson (1972), Irwin and Marge (1972), Carrow-Woolfolk and Lynch (1982), Bernstein and Tiegerman-Farber (2002), Northern and Downs (2002), and Shipley and McAfee (2004).

ASSESSING YOUNG CHILDREN

Many young children who are evaluated are unable to participate in a sufficiently meaningful manner to allow the examiner to get a clear picture of their abilities. Children must be able to understand the nature of the task before they can demonstrate their skill in doing it. When language and speech are significant components in administering tests to the child with language and speech deficiencies, the information obtained may not represent the child's abilities. Instead, the results may simply reflect a failure to understand the language used. Consequently, it becomes important that the means of assessing a child's abilities not be dependent on his/her understanding and use of language and speech.

With the passage of federal legislation mandating that children with disabilities from birth forward be identified and served, the need to assess younger and younger children has increased and will continue to do so. At the same time, very young children are not expected to be able to respond to standardized tests in a manner or to an extent which allows any reliable determination of their language and speech comprehension. For this reason, informal assessment plans remain viable and valuable. The development of criterion-referenced checklists appropriate for this population has been useful. Caution should be exercised, however, in determining the presence or absence of a communication deficit based on some test instruments which may have a very limited number of test items given at a particular age level.

In earlier years, prior to the development of commercially available standardized tests, evaluating young children at the DuBard School for Language Disorders consisted of assessing their skills in verbal and nonverbal tasks and informal hearing-listening tasks in less sophisticated ways. If the child's age and other circumstances indicated appropriateness of nonverbal standardized tests of learning aptitude which did not penalize the child for not understanding or using language or speech, such tests were used also.

INFORMAL ASSESSMENT

Identifying and Naming

In making assessments of school-age children's performances, tasks in the use of oral and written language were included according to need and/or desire. Verbal tasks sought to determine the child's ability to understand and identify receptive language: (1) noun language of naming things, (2) concepts of placement (prepositions), and (3) concepts of verbs, ongoing actions/present progressive language, completed actions/past tense. If receptive language ability was sufficient, expressive skills, including articulation skills, were evaluated. The linguistic assessment used a wide variety of pictorial noun items and/or objects to determine if the child's receptive language was intact. Colorful, child-oriented pictures of the child's environment were used to assess his/her understanding of and ability to identify noun items. Sometimes the objects themselves were presented if the child did not become too engrossed in playing with them.

Following Simple Directions: Placements; Prepositions

If the child was able to complete the tasks of naming and identifying, determining how well he/she could follow simple directions followed. Gestures were used initially in order to support the child in a more difficult linguistic task. Then the gestures were discontinued after the second or third direction so as to test the child's abilities to understand the language rather than gestures. Parents and teachers are often convinced that children understand certain language; close analysis, however, often reveals that it is specific situations, informal gestures, and facial expressions that the child understands rather than the linguistic symbols, language, and speech. Therefore, we use the following simple directions stated clearly and without haste:

Give me the _________. (with gesture)
Give me the _________. (with gesture)
Give me the _________. (no gesture)
Give me the _________. (no gesture)

Without making any changes other than in the linguistic material, giving directions without any gestures followed. What the child did was observed, whether he/she actually followed these directions or continued the previous pattern. This gave an indication of the actual understanding of linguistic material. Subsequent directions included the following:

Put the _________ on the floor. (one item)
Put the _________ on the floor. (another item)
Put the _________ in the chair.
Put the _________ in the cup.
Give the _________ to mama.
Give the _________ to daddy.
Give the _________ to me.
Give me the _________.
Pick up the _________
Give it to _________ or put it _________ _________ _________.

The extent to which such direction-following abilities were assessed depended on the child. If the child demonstrated that his/her responses were related to the recognition of only the noun portion of the directions, the task was discontinued earlier. If the child demonstrated acceptable understanding on the single directions, the ability to remember two directions and to carry them out in the exact order in which they were given was assessed. For example: "Put the _________ on the floor and the _________ on the chair," or "Put the _________ in the box and the _________ in the cup," and subsequently, "Put the _________ in the _________ and the _________ on the _________." Some children were able to complete the last direction only; others completed the first and were not able to complete the last. Some children demonstrated an understanding that several items or pictures were involved, but were unable to carry out instructions related to them.

When children succeeded in demonstrating understanding in the tasks just described, we then tried to assess their expressive language skills as they related to concepts by asking, "What is this?" for the noun language and by setting up arrangements of items and asking a child, "Where is the ________?" A common response was often "Here" or "There" or merely a pointing gesture to indicate the item. The examiner had the challenge of trying to determine how to get the child to indicate "in," "on," or "under," as was appropriate. The examiner had to listen for the language structure the child used as well as his/her articulation in spontaneous speech.

Ongoing Actions and Completed Actions

When a child successfully completed the earlier portions of the evaluation, assessing the understanding of the concepts of ongoing actions (present progressive language), and of completed actions (past tense language) followed. For this a variety of pictures was used. At each level of the assessment, expressive skills were evaluated by asking the child appropriate questions. It was carefully determined whether the child's expressive language consisted of the full structure of the respective verb tenses or whether the responses simply contained the root forms of the verb. The child's use of pronouns and syntactical structure in any sentence responses and/or conversational language also was noted.

The means just described for assessing a child's abilities work best with the child who shows varying degrees of success with linguistic tasks. If the child cannot identify noun vocabulary at the lowest level of the language tasks suggested, other means of determining abilities will be needed. Failure at the lowest level indicates what a child cannot do; but, there is a need to determine what can be done easily, well, or even with effort in nonlinguistic tasks. However, before judgments are made regarding the child's success or lack of success in nonverbal tasks, it should be determined whether or not the child: (1) has had the opportunity to engage in such activities and been stimulated to solve comparable problems, (2) has experienced motivation for solving such tasks, or (3) has had the opportunity and been stimulated for such problem solving but has been unable to do so because of lack of ability. Lack of opportunity, stimulation, and motivation yield one kind of profile in ability; lack of ability in the presence of these factors yields a different kind of profile.

Nonverbal Activities

Activities appropriate for assessing a young child who is nonverbal include the following:

1. Inset puzzles where only one placement of a puzzle part is accurate
2. Puzzles of three or four large pieces for which there are guidelines in the backing of the puzzle which may help children to recognize the appropriate place for the puzzle part
3. Puzzles with more pieces, smaller size, and without any guidelines to aid in proper placement
4. Puzzles dealing with various shapes fitting together as with a fit-a-space activity
5. Manipulative toys which can be used to determine children's reasoning ability and manual planning as they reassemble arrangements of items or parts of wholes in order to achieve a specific goal
6. Manipulative toys which indicate children's abilities to make judgments related to sizes, shapes, and spaces
7. Manipulative toys utilizing shape-size relationship factors ranging from simple to complex within the single activity
8. Tasks necessitating that children construct a design using cubes while looking at a model provided by the examiner
9. Matching pictures
10. Matching object to pictures
11. Organizing a selection of pictures into specific categories, such as animals, furniture, and so on

The types of tasks just described are similar to those found in the *Central Institute for the Deaf Preschool Performance Scale* (CID-PPS) (Geers and Lane, 1984). The primary disadvantage of informal assessments of children is that they do not yield the kinds of raw scores/statistical data which most departments of education and state agencies require for children to be declared eligible for specific remedial programs. However, many activities previously included only in informal, non-standardized assessments, have now been incorporated into such standardized instruments as the *Battelle Developmental Inventory - Second Edition (BDI-2)* (Newborg, 2004) and the *Learning Accomplishment Profile - Third Edition (LAP-3)* (Chapel Hill Training Outreach Project, 2003).

STANDARDIZED TESTING

The child who is deaf or hard of hearing, language-disordered, or the child with specific learning disabilities (SLD)/dyslexia can be expected to do poorly on one or more types of language skills yet be able to demonstrate good nonverbal cognitive skills. Even on the performance scale of such a test as the *Wechsler Intelligence Scale for Children®-IV* (WISC®-IV, 2003), it is necessary for the subject to understand linguistic instructions although responding may require only a motor act. Therefore, other aspects related to testing/assessing need to be given consideration. The following guidelines given by Sattler (1988, 1994) are still worth remembering today:

Psychological reports do count.
Words can be misinterpreted.
IQ's change.
Different tests may provide different IQ's.
Placement decisions must be based on more than one assessment approach.
Instruments must be appropriate.
Previous findings must be reviewed.

Categories for *comprehensive assessment* for students with dyslexia are identified later in this chapter. Some additional points to keep in mind whether for children with hearing loss, language/speech disorders, or SLD/dyslexia are:

1. Each child is unique with observable similarities and differences in abilities and limitations.
2. Findings of any given test must be considered independently and in relation to results obtained on other tests with similar subtests, and information observed and reported.
3. When a diagnosis is less than clear-cut, the input and additional assessments from competent professionals other than those who administer the tests and/or those who might be drawing conclusions should be given serious consideration.
4. Saying "I don't know" or "I'm not sure" is very difficult for many professionals. However, there are times when this is necessary. Such frankness should lead to a period of consistent and systematic diagnostic teaching for a sufficient amount of time so that the primary disability can become more evident.
5. Determining a child's status, (cognitively challenged, hearing impaired, behaviorally disordered, etc.) cannot be made on the basis of how he or she looks.

Simply administering a test to a child is quite different from testing to determine the child's abilities. Formerly, psychologists gave the tests, and few of these tests were suitable to assess abilities. Often the tests depended heavily on language to give instructions, thus making them inappropriate for children with limited language skills. Many professionals, other than psychologists, began to do alternative kinds of assessing.

Even now, audiologists, speech-language pathologists, psychologists, and any others who have the responsibility to find out about children's abilities do so under a variety of limitations. Too often children are tested in a clinical setting. Although the location may be as comfortable as possible, it remains a new and unfamiliar place. In addition, parents or some other adult will have brought the child to strangers. Often, it is not the first such experience the parents and child have had. There is hardly a satisfactory way for the examiner to know whether the child is sufficiently at ease to demonstrate his/her best performance. Yet, traditionally, professionals have viewed with skepticism parents' comments indicating that the child did at home many of the things he/she did not do for the examiner during the evaluation. Results of the tests may have limited value because they usually do not indicate whether or not the child demonstrated any ability to learn. *Too often only his/her limitations are assessed rather than his/her strengths.*

The number and type of tests to be used should be determined by several criteria. Simple guidelines for selecting tests to administer should include: (1) the child's chronological age and developmental age, (2) language function as determined through observation and in interview with parents and other adults who are around the child, (3) time available for the assessment (keeping in mind that schools do not always allot adequate time for comprehensive assessments), and (4) variables related to the test environment and situation. In addition, individual examiners may have criteria or guidelines which reflect their working philosophies and their familiarity with the tests.

Because the array of tests available today is almost endless, professionals should select them on the basis of the child's age and what seems to be appropriate to his/her needs. *It is crucial that assessments be adequately comprehensive.* In addition to a hearing screening or a complete audiological assessment, if at all possible, an evaluation should include an assessment of nonverbal abilities, receptive and expressive language skills, and articulation skills. Based on an individual child's needs, the areas of visual acuity, visual perception, visual-motor integration, auditory perception, memory, fine and gross motor skills, individual and/or group achievement tests, phonological awareness, specific reading skills of decoding, comprehension, and fluency, as well as social and self-help skills may need investigating. Contradictory or puzzling results in any area may call for more in-depth testing in that particular area. It should be remembered that the best test available, if interpreted poorly, too broadly or too narrowly, and not in relation/comparison to other tests with similarities and differences, may be of limited value.

In the past, one useful standardized test of nonverbal skills administered for children like those we have been discussing was the Hiskey-Nebraska Test of Learning Aptitude (HNTLA). The *Hiskey-Nebraska Test of Learning Aptitude* (1966) is undergoing revision and restandardization and will be re-published as the *Hiskey Test of Learning Aptitude*. While the HNTLA is under revision, we have made use of other nonverbal measures such as the Reynolds Intellectual Assessment Scales (RIAS) (Reynolds and Kamphaus, 2003) and the Universal Nonverbal Intelligence Test (UNIT) (Bracken and McCallum, 2005).

The *Test of Auditory Comprehension of Language (TACL-3)* (1999) provides rather in-depth information about a child's language abilities and is appropriate for extensive assessment of receptive language. For older students, the *Clinical Evaluation of Language Fundamentals (CELF-4)* (2003) is valuable in assessing receptive and expressive language skills as well as working memory. Other appropriate instruments, such as the *Test of Language Development-Primary:4 (TOLD-P:4)* (2008), also are available. The *CELF-4 Screening Test* (2004) is often used to rule out oral language deficits in children suspected of having dyslexia or a specific learning disability.

The *Arizona Articulation Proficiency Scale-3rd ed.* (AAPS-3) (Fudala 2000) is utilized as a sound, objective measure for articulation skills. It assesses oral production of single phonemes, including vowels, in single-word contexts and yields total and standard scores as well as an interpretation of intelligibility. The weakness of this measure can be that a child may be quite intelligible on a one-word test item with an accompanying picture cue but the intelligibility of the same phonemes in spontaneous, connected utterances may be far less intelligible. Of course children with significant speech disorders frequently need specific therapy to achieve carryover of the learned speech skills into discourse settings

There is no easy solution to the problem of assessing some children. However, the individuals, professionals or lay persons, who are in daily contact with the children can learn a great deal about them. With basic knowledge, ability to observe, and guidance in translating the findings into teaching-learning activities, the most effective evaluations of children may be obtained by the people who are working with the child daily rather than the person who sees him or her for a single-session assessment. To be more specific, the person who is frequently in a position to carry out diagnostic teaching is the one who can get the best information about the child's potential for learning language, speech, or academic tasks.

Diagnostic teaching is a method of determining abilities and limitations of a child by careful observation of the response to specific instructional intervention over time. It yields a wealth of information, though it is not standardized. The ability to recall, the rate of learning, the optimum times and avenues for learning are all subject to the observation and interpretation by the astute diagnostician.

After a number of years of assessing younger children at our school, we began to evaluate school-age children. They demonstrated similar abilities and limitations. Some had experienced speech difficulties earlier and had received speech therapy which had "corrected" the problem. Others had had speech difficulties, received speech therapy, been released, but still demonstrated difficulties in saying two-syllable and multisyllabic words. All of the children of this category were demonstrating poor achievement in school, especially in reading and spelling. Math computation skills were satisfactory, but skill in solving word problems was extremely poor.

According to every indication, the school-age children had done "fine" or "all right" at the first-grade level; however, as each year progressed, they had more and more difficulty. Parents were concerned that their children were failing in spite of their early success. Teachers identified a number of common problems. Almost without exception the children in question were said to: (1) have short attention spans, (2) be unable to follow directions, (3) be unable to remember what they were told to do, (4) be unable to remember a word when told what it was or unable to remember a word in one line when they had just been told the word in a previous line, (5) be able to copy words from the chalkboard but be unable to read what had been copied, and (6) often read and copy words and/or write words and numerals backwards. Most of the children demonstrated limitations in blending sounds and making associations between letters and sounds; most were unable to say or write the alphabet. Some of the children had been administered a version of the *Wechsler Intelligence Scale for*

Children (Wechsler, 1974, 2001, 2003) and/or the *Stanford-Binet* (Thorndike, 1986). A variety of abilities and limitations had been demonstrated on the respective tests. Those who had been administered the *Illinois Test of Psycholinguistic Abilities (ITPA)* (1968), now *ITPA-3* (2001), had demonstrated a variety of limitations and a few abilities. In spite of the information available through these tests, we felt we needed still more information in order to give teachers some guidelines for preparing instructional programs.

It should be noted that, whether conducting informal or standardized assessments, there is great value in observing *how* students respond to a task. The diagnostician's power of observation can provide much insight as to a child's thought processes and ability to learn. There is much more to an evaluation than a count of + and - responses or a score. For example, a child may be unable to complete a three-piece shapes puzzle. Child 1 picked up the circle and repeatedly tried to place it in the square space. Child 2 picked up the square and tried to place it in the circle space and then tried to place it in the square space. Child 2 never placed the square completely because it wasn't rotated to fit. However, Child 2 demonstrated to the astute observer recognition of the correct, matching shapes. As another example, in a memory task, a student may miss three items in a row because of an inability to recall gradually increasing numbers of shapes. Child 1 recalled 2 of 3 items, followed by 2 of 4 items, and then 2 of 5 items. Child 2 recalled 2 of 3 items, 3 of 4 items, and then 4 of 5 items thus demonstrating that, while unable to receive a correct score on the items, learning took place as the child increased the number of correct shapes in each subsequent test item. The late Dr. Etoile DuBard was masterful in this area and required her university students to acquire such skills of observation. Those who had the opportunity to develop their skills of observation and interpretation under her guidance were indeed privileged.

ASSESSMENT OF THOSE WITH DYSLEXIA/ SPECIFIC LEARNING DISABILITIES

Assessment and diagnosis of those with dyslexia, specific learning disabilities, reading disabilities or any similar condition confounds many teachers, school administrators, special educators, diagnosticians, and parents. While in some areas of the country dyslexia is seen as a relatively new and, perhaps, rather in vogue diagnosis, some professionals have been assessing and identifying these individuals very accurately for decades. Certainly, there are more tests available now to make precise, comprehensive assessments more readily accessible; however, the uncertainty about this diagnosis persists in many professional circles. It is in that light that the chart, *Categories for comprehensive assessment of dyslexia/specific learning disabilities,* is included here (*see following page*).

The author recalls a student some years ago who came to the DuBard School for Language Disorders at age 12 with difficulties in reading. The available reports indicated that the student had no oral language, articulation, voice or fluency disorders. This was a student whose informal social interactions in the school hallway would seem to indicate that his oral communication skills were fine. However, upon actually *evaluating* in those areas, it was determined that he was eligible for services in the areas of language, articulation and voice. He also was diagnosed with an auditory processing disorder. A surface, informal communication exchange was insufficient to identify his challenges. Services were needed in reading *and* the other areas and were implemented accordingly. Suffice it to say that the value of a *comprehensive assessment* cannot be underestimated. The influence of one skill area on another requires it. While it is recognized that the demands on schools, the numbers of children to be served, and the finite number of professionals to serve them at times makes it challenging to provide truly comprehensive assessments, the benefit to the child and the educational and therapeutic programming is valuable and necessary in order to serve the whole child.

Categories for Comprehensive Assessment of Students with Dyslexia/Specific Learning Disabilities
As used at the DuBard School for Language Disorders

Hearing and Vision Assess as appropriate	**Nonverbal Mental Ability** *Reynolds Intellectual Assessment Scales* (RIAS): 3-0 to 94-11 *Universal Nonverbal Intelligence Test* (UNIT): 5-0 to 17-11 *Primary Test of Nonverbal Intelligence (PTONI): 3-0 to 9-11* *Test of Nonverbal Intelligence-4* (TONI-4): 6-0 to 89-11

Oral and Written Language
Test of Auditory Comprehension of Language-3 (TACL-3):
   3-0 to 9-11
Test of Language Development-Primary:4 (TOLD-P:4):
   4-0 to 8-11
Clinical Evaluation of Language Fundamentals-4 (CELF-4): Lower
   5-0 to 8-11   Upper 9-0 to 21-11
Oral and Written Language Scales, 2nd edition (OWLS-II):
   Listening Comprehension and Oral Expression 3 to 21
Test of Written Language-4 (TOWL-4): 9-0 to 17-11
	Articulation
	Assess if needed
	
	Arizona Articulation Proficiency Scale-3 (AAPS-3): 1-6 to 18-11

	Auditory Processing *Test of Auditory Perceptual Skills-3* (TAPS-3): 4-0 to 18-0

Academic Skills
 	
Word Recognition
Wechsler Individual Achievement Test-III (WIAT-III): 4-0 to 50-11
Woodcock-Johnson III (WJ-III): 2-0 to 90+ (age range varies by
   subtest)
Decoding Skills Test: Age Kindergarten to adult
   Reading levels 1st–5th grades
 	
Word Analysis
Phonological Awareness Test-2 (PAT-2): 5-0 to 9-11
Decoding Skills Test: Age Kindergarten to adult
   Reading levels 1st – 5th grades
Comprehensive Test of Phonological Processing (CTOPP): 5-0 to
   24-11
 	
Phonological Skills
Phonological Awareness Test-2 (PAT-2): 5-0 to 9-11
Comprehensive Test of Phonological Processing (CTOPP): 5-0 to
   24-11
 	
Reading Comprehension
Gray Oral Reading Test-4 (GORT-4): 7-0 to 18-11
Test of Reading Comprehension-4 (TORC-4): 7-0 to 17-11
Decoding Skills Test: Age Kindergarten to adult
   Reading levels 1st –5th grades
Wechsler Individual Achievement Test-III (WIAT-III): 4-0 to 50-11
Woodcock-Johnson III (WJ-III): 2-0 to 90+ (age range varies by
   subtest)
 	
Spelling
Wechsler Individual Achievement Test-III (WIAT-III): 4-0 to 50-11
Test of Written Spelling-4 (TWS-4): Grades 1-12
Test of Written Language-4 (TOWL-4): 9-0 to 17-11
Woodcock-Johnson III (WJ-III): 2-0 to 90+ (age range varies by
   subtest)
	Visual Perception
	Motor-Free Visual Perception Test-3 (MVPT-3): 4-0 to 11-6

	Visual-Motor Integration *Beery-Buktenica Developmental Test of Visual-Motor Integration 6th edition* (Beery VMI): 2-0 to 100

	Memory
	Wide Range Assessment of Memory and Learning 2nd ed.
	   (WRAML-2): 5-0 to 90
	Test of Auditory Perceptual Skills-3 (TAPS-3): 4-0 to 18-0
	Clinical Evaluation of Language Fundamentals-4 (CELF-4):Lower
	   5-0 to 8-11 Upper 9-0 to 21-11
	Reynolds Intellectual Assessment Scales (RIAS): 3-0 to 94-11

	Rapid Automatic Naming
	Rapid Automatized Naming and Rapid Alternating Stimulus Tests
	   (RAN/RAS): 5-0 to 18-11
	Clinical Evaluation of Language Fundamentals-4 (CELF-4):
	   Lower 5-0 to 8-11 Upper 9-0 to 21-11
	Comprehensive Test of Phonological Processing (CTOPP): 5-0 to
	   24-11

CHAPTER

3

Differential Diagnosis

In the medical world, *differential diagnosis* is defined as "the determination of which of two or more diseases with similar symptoms is the one from which the patient is suffering, by a systematic comparison and contrasting of the clinical findings" (Stedman's Medical Dictionary, 2006). This concept of differential diagnosis is applicable to many fields—medicine, social work, education, and communication disorders. Why does this differential diagnosis matter? In this author's opinion, differential diagnosis implies looking at the whole; interpreting varied, extensive and, perhaps, conflicting data; in a simpler form, peeling back the onion, layer upon layer, of the various contributing factors in a child's profile. In considering a child with an articulation disorder, for example, it is a routine task for a speech-language pathologist to diagnose or rule out the existence of this communication challenge through standardized testing, observation, and informal assessment. Frequently, that is all that is needed. However, when considering the *total* educational program for children with *complex* profiles and, thus, complex needs, professionals must go deeper to uncover the profile of the *whole child* so that intervention may be designed based on the *determination of a primary disability and any secondary disabilities* which may impact the child's long term progress.

Over the years, in the DuBard School for Language Disorders at The University of Southern Mississippi, *comprehensive* evaluations of children have been a priority. As indicated in the preceding chapter, the goal when considering serving children in the full time instructional program is to know as much as possible about the child and to *continue to learn* about the child once the instructional program is underway. Only in-depth studies of children's strengths and weaknesses, based on appropriate standardized and informal data, including diagnostic teaching, can provide the important differential diagnoses necessary to address *all* of a student's needs and it must continue longitudinally. Without more extensive data, how do we determine the difference between a child who has a typical articulation problem vs. one who has childhood apraxia of speech? How do we determine which children are a little behind in reading and which ones have a specific learning disability/dyslexia? Who has a language disorder which affects attention vs. who has Attention Deficit Hyperactivity Disorder (ADHD), or both? Certainly, among the most complex differential diagnoses we have faced over the years has been determining the existence or absence of additional learning deficits in children who are deaf. The value of the differential diagnosis lies in being able to provide more precise intervention under the most optimum circumstances.

In the process, the value of the individual professional's expertise, experience, and skills of observation should not be underestimated. Likewise, parental input can be very valuable. This is where art meets science, where knowledge of the typically developing child, the typically developing young communicator, the typically developing elementary student blended with information from formal assessments allows a professional, or team of professionals, to make an accurate and valuable differential diagnosis. This is critical if we are to address the needs of the whole child.

In reviewing issues of assessment of language development, Carrow-Woolfolk and Lynch (1982) cited the 1950s as an era in which the purpose of the assessment process was to make a "differential diagnosis." It was presumed in the framework of a medical orientation that the differential diagnosis would identify pathology/condition and lead to treatment/therapy. They noted that the process met with considerable criticism because of its subjectivity and the absence of objective data. Perhaps more significant, however, was the fact that important differences within categories were ignored. The categories became exclusive without awareness of the fact that a child who was deaf could also be developmentally delayed, or have some other problem that could influence language and speech learning. Unfortunate, also, was that differential diagnosis of that decade rarely led to actual intervention. The purpose of obtaining a label remained the primary goal.

While Carrow-Woolfolk and Lynch focused primarily on assessing hearing children with language impairments, there are application differences among children who are deaf or hard of hearing. In the past, once the deaf/hard of hearing category had been assigned, no other consideration contributed to the planning of educational instruction for the child. The assumption that "deaf is deaf" and that language/speech and poor academic achievement levels were due to deafness alone continued through the years.

However, as a result of the rubella epidemics in the sixties, professionals were confronted with children whose "deafness" often proved to be only one of several obvious disabilities. The population of children diagnosed as multihandicapped hearing-impaired (MHHI) could not be overlooked. Common conditions were cognitive deficits, visual problems, motor difficulties, and heart defects. Such conditions were more easily recognized than any differences within the functioning of the central nervous system. Audiological data on children continued to be the primary basis for placement in educational/instructional programs and learning problems were presumed to be based primarily on the "deafness." From time to time there were professionals who appealed in their various ways and means for the idea of focusing on the child, not the audiogram. Unfortunately, while the world of audiology provides vastly more information now than in earlier days, there are those who continue to believe that the decision about a child's educational future should be based on the audiogram. The advent of cochlear implants and their dramatic impact on *some, but not all, children* may be beginning to change this mindset. Notable, though,

is the fact that the definition of specific learning disabilities under the Individuals with Disabilities Education Act (2004) eliminates this diagnosis if there are sensory deficits. This fact leads some to fail to realize that hearing loss and specific learning disabilities can, and do, co-exist. Likewise hearing loss may co-exist with numerous other conditions, such as ADHD, childhood apraxia of speech, autism, cognitive delay, emotional disturbance, etc.

Identification of children whose primary disability was specific to language learning has followed a similar path. There has always been a population of children who could hear, who gave evidence of understanding some basic language some of the time, who may or may not have had articulation disorders or marked delays in the refining of their articulatory skills. Many demonstrated ability in generating oral language under some circumstances and seemed to be doing satisfactorily until they entered first grade and then were not able to learn to read, despite the levels of intelligence they showed. Thought to be immature and not learning to read and spell, they might have been perceived as being lazy, stubborn, and simply refusing to learn. The boys became the behavior problems whereas the girls developed ways of compensating and pleasing others—looking neat and pretty, smiling, becoming the teacher's helper, doing well in dancing or gymnastics. After children had repeated grades, been socially promoted, or both, and after children, parents, and teachers had become sufficiently frustrated, all became aware of the population of children with specific learning disabilities (SLD)/dyslexia.

Few recognized that the specific disability was in language and in being unable *to relate oral linguistic skills to the symbols of written language* on which subsequent academic achievement would depend. The "normal" hearing acuity in some children masked the auditory processing disorders, which some considered to be a "subclass" of language disorders (Sloan 1980a). Concealed were difficulties in such central nervous system functions as memory, memory for sequencing, and association skills including sound-symbol relations required for learning word attack/decoding skills in reading. Many of those students who could say the words, ultimately demonstrated limitations in understanding what they could "read." Problems persisted after optimum time for learning had been lost. Professionals failed to develop or use teaching-learning strategies which would address the specific difficulties. All too often genuine help came too late.

The study by Powers and others (1986) reflects a similar pattern of "late identification of specific (learning) disabilities" among those with hearing loss. The data reflect a delay pattern similar to the delay noted in identifying children with learning disabilities/dyslexia in the hearing population. In a survey of 11,057 students with hearing loss who were receiving services, 3.6 percent of preschool-age children were identified as Learning Disabled Hearing Impaired (LDHI). At the middle/junior high level, 8.0 percent of the population was recognized as LDHI. At the high school level 6.9 percent were so recognized. In considering these data, several questions come to mind: Were the additional 4.4 percent of children identified at junior high school level not LDHI at preschool-age level? Were their difficulties/disabilities masked by the assumption that deafness was only part of the problem? What kind of diagnostic teaching was conducted at the earlier level in an effort to determine whether or not the children had "additional handicapping conditions," especially since tests are not considered too reliable for making clear determinations of the difficulties? What made the children LDHI at junior high school and not at preschool? What changes were made in instructional techniques as a means of reducing some of the disabilities? Clearly, additional research is needed in this area.

According to the U.S. Department of Education, National Center for Education Statistics (2010), 5.2% of all students were diagnosed with specific learning disabilities, 3% were diagnosed with speech or language impairments, and .2% were diagnosed with hearing impairments in 2007-08. All disability categories combined represented 13.4% of the population. While *combinations of disabilities are not reflected* in the national numbers, Pollack (1997) noted that the "prevalence of other disabilities in addition to hearing loss is approximately three times as large (30.2 percent) in the deaf or hard of hearing population as in the general school population." Research from Gallaudet University, Laurent Clerc National Deaf Education Center (1995-2011), estimates "that from 20% to 50% of all deaf and hard of hearing children have accompanying disabilities." Guardino (2008) suggests that 50% may be an underestimation of the incidence of multiple disabilities among those who are deaf or hard of hearing due to varying definitions and data collection differences. Samar (1999) cited Gallaudet's 1997 annual survey which indicated that the "incidence of LD in deaf children to be approximately 8.4%-11%, making LD the largest secondary disability affecting deaf people."

The rubella population of the 1960s presented special problems related to the education of children with disabilities. Some of the children were observed to have visual impairments. Many seemed to be deaf although audiological assessments available at that time were not conclusive. Many fitted with hearing aids rejected them, an atypical response of children who are deaf. Many of the children who were not thought to be deaf did not learn language and speech as expected and were sometimes considered to be developmentally delayed. Often the children had emotional outbursts, suggesting the possibility that they were emotionally disturbed. The means of testing children who were nonverbal were so limited in the 1960s it was necessary to rely on experience and clinical observations to guide decision making in determining the primary disability and in planning instruction.

Several of the children enrolled in the School for Children with Language Disorders, now DuBard School for Language Disorders, at The University of Southern Mississippi in the early 1960s were children with rubella in their medical histories. DuBard observed carefully as she began to teach them. Daily experiences and observations made it clear that they seemed to be deaf, but their tonal qualities were unlike those of deaf children. Some who had been fitted with hearing aids objected to them or rejected them completely. Prior to their enrollment in the school they had received services appropriate for young children who were deaf but by age five had not achieved success in learning language or speech. In nonverbal activities and play they demonstrated success expected of the average young child and cognitive skills indicated that they were not developmentally delayed. Their behaviors were generally like those described by McGinnis (1939, 1963), Myklebust (1954), and later by Eisenson (1965, 1972, 1984).

In an effort to make a differential diagnosis as to the children being deaf or being deaf in conjunction with other limitations such as having a pseudo-deafness with inefficiency in using whatever hearing was present, DuBard began a program of instruction with diagnostic teaching. She used the principles of the Association Method following very closely the program and teaching techniques described by McGinnis (1939, 1963). The result with those groups of children in the sixties and seventies was that they learned speech, language, reading skills, and written language. Their successes continued in academic subjects in regular schools, at a time when there were no special educational services available. All of the students finished high school; some graduated from colleges or universities and all now have respectable jobs, good incomes, and families. Diagnostic teaching, that is, determining students' abilities and limitations and then changing the instructional approach accordingly, made the difference in getting a differential diagnosis. The instructional program that was implemented was indeed effective.

CASE HISTORIES

In the 1980s, three children who were profoundly deaf were enrolled in the School for Children with Language Disorders (now DuBard School for Language Disorders). The two boys and one girl presented audiological assessment reports which left no doubt but that they were profoundly deaf. It was necessary to make a differential diagnosis. Their parents wanted to make a maximum effort for them to learn to speak, so they were enrolled in a program for children with language disorders where oral communication received emphasis and where teachers of the deaf committed to the oral philosophy were on the staff.

The audiological assessments of two of the children were not altogether satisfactory because of the young ages of the children. C., the older of the two, rejected the headsets but demonstrated detection of speech in free field at 45 decibels (dB) and 50 decibels (dB). With headsets held close to her ears, she was aware of speech at 85 dB. Efforts to obtain reliable data continued through several months in an aural rehabilitation program during which time C., at two and one half years of age, remained less than cooperative most of the time. She later received services on an outclient basis, but her progress in language growth was limited. Despite her lack of cooperation, she was fitted with aids on the basis of her responses at 60 dB for 500 Hz through 1000 Hz and localizing sound 500 Hz through 2000 Hz at 30 dB. Reliable responses at age eight indicated pure tone averages of 96 dB (left ear) and 95 dB (right ear).

T.'s hearing loss was suspected when he was eighteen months of age. Assessment through Brain Stem Evoked Response (BSER) reflected responses to warble tones of 4000 Hz at 90 dB. Possible responses to a noisemaker were noted at 70 dB and to babbling at 80 dB. His record of no response (NR) resulted in a conclusion of profound deafness. After months of assessments and trials with various aids, T. had aided responses to 250 Hz, 500 Hz, and 1000 Hz at 50 dB; to 2000 Hz at 70 dB; to 4000 Hz at 80 dB; and no responses to 8000 Hz at chronological age (CA) three years, four months. It should be noted, however, that through consistent auditory training and reduction of ear infections, T.'s later assessments at CA: 4–7 reflected aided responses of 250 Hz at 50 dB, 500 Hz at 40 dB, 1000 Hz at 30 dB, and 2000 Hz at 40 dB, which resulted in excellent voice quality. At CA: 10–7, T.'s

aided responses were at 35 dB at 250 Hz, 55 dB at 500, 50 dB at 1000, and 55 dB at 2000. T. and C. began to receive instruction when they were two and three years of age, respectively. C.'s first work, as mentioned earlier, was through the outclient services of a university speech and hearing clinic. At the same time, T., at two years of age was enrolled in a daily program for children who were deaf and hard of hearing in which the total communication philosophy prevailed. After approximately seven months, his parents withdrew him from the program and began seeking a program which would emphasize oral communication. For several months he had no special services. For two months in that summer, a home program was implemented for T. by Martin, a teacher of the deaf, who was also a speech-language pathologist and who was to be responsible for continuing services for him in the upcoming year in the school.

T. and C. both entered the program that fall. Each attended two one-hour sessions weekly for a time, then were put together for instruction. Each received additional individual sessions as appropriate. The program consisted of auditory training, activities for building receptive and expressive skills in vocabulary of CV and CVC phonetic arrangements using whole-word presentations, and speechreading. In general, the program followed the traditional whole-word approach used with young children who were deaf. When more specific work was to begin in speech, the techniques of the Association Method were used so as to develop more precise articulation and to establish a base for code-breaking, which is important in developing the reading process.

Both T. and C. demonstrated negative behaviors from time to time, with C.'s negative behaviors of earlier years well-established. These were addressed successfully through behavior modification techniques, employing both deprivations and rewards. An important part of the intervention program was to counsel parents and to gain support for carrying out instructional activities at home.

As T. and C. progressed, their program expanded to half-day attendance and ultimately to full-time daily attendance. Both made steady progress. Their speech skills, developed through McGinnis's techniques, became quite good. Their knowledge and performances in language, speech, math, and reading were gratifying. T.'s understanding of language which he had not been taught specifically was extremely good as were his speechreading skills. He is as "straightforward deaf" as one could find anywhere. Certainly C.'s hearing loss was significant and her amplification was of great benefit to her, but her progress was enhanced by her being in an instructional program which combined the traditional approach for deaf children with some features of the Association Method. Because of some differences which she demonstrated in learning skills, her teacher was led to say from time to time, "If C. had not been identified as hearing impaired, she'd certainly have been identified as learning-disabled." Both T. and C. did well in the mainstream general education environment. T. maintained high grades and excelled in math, became an Eagle Scout, and graduated from high school with a regular diploma in May, 2000. He attended college and earned a degree in accounting and has been employed consistently in the field of accounting since his graduation. C. also graduated from high school with a regular diploma in May, 2000.

R.'s situation was another matter. At age two, he did not demonstrate any understanding of language. Like T. and C., he said no words. Negative and manipulative behaviors were predominant as often is the case with two year olds. Initial audiological assessments indicated that he had detected speech at 50 dB. However, the responses were at a minimal level and were viewed as suspect. Six months later his responses unaided for pure tone testing ranged from 90 dB to no response at 500 Hz to 4000 Hz. Aided, his responses were at 60 dB in the speech range. Subsequent tests indicated the same levels of responses and were considered to be reliable. There were no reasons at that time to think that he had any disabilities in addition to the hearing loss. His one-to-one program with the same professional as C. and T. had had was implemented on a schedule of two, forty-five-minute to one-hour sessions per week. Auditory training, whole-word vocabulary activities, and efforts to elicit whole-word imitations were used.

R.'s parents were taught to do similar activities at home. His parents were given more guidance than the parents of the other two children in order to establish control of his negative and manipulative behaviors. Otherwise, the three children had essentially the same initial program, implemented at different times because of their age differences.

From the outset, although R. demonstrated good cognitive skills in numerous ways, his responses to the instructional efforts were different from those of the other two children. He took much more time to become aware of the communicative value of attending to the speaker's face. T. and C. had attended readily but R. had all but ignored it.

In the consistent, structured, speechreading activities using CV and CVC high-interest vocabulary pictures and objects, R. was unable to speechread the vocabulary on a whole-word basis, whereas

the other two children had done well. R. demonstrated essentially no progress in the activity. In auditory training using drums, music, and bells, R. responded well and, rather consistently, indicated greater hearing acuity than seemed to be present on the basis of audiometric findings. R.'s efforts to imitate speech productions of whole words were minimal; spontaneous vocalizations were few and of poor quality. A limited range of movement and placement of the articulators was noted. Although his behaviors improved, nothing related to communication improved.

After approximately ten months of such limited progress, the decision was made to change R.'s program to the beginning level of the Association Method. It was at that time that a component of apraxia was observed. It was very difficult for R. to imitate even a single phoneme. Little by little, through consistent application of the teaching-learning strategies of the Association Method, a number of changes were observed.

The behavior problems, which had been present frequently while the whole-word approach was used, diminished greatly. Although imitation of single phonemes was very difficult for R., having a written stimulus visible to associate with whatever happened at the speaker's face and his own mouth seemed to appeal to him and he became more attentive to the speaker's face. His level of motivation improved and his personal satisfaction with what he was learning increased. The more he learned, the more he was willing to work. The quality of his voice and of his imitation of phonemes improved. His program was expanded as his progress permitted.

His class time increased from periodic sessions to half days and finally to a full-day schedule, five days a week. Despite the apraxia which was a major factor in his learning, R. established the desired skills in the Association Method, i.e., reading the word and making the correct association with a picture or object, recalling the speech for the word and writing the word from memory for twenty-six CV and thirty-one CVC nouns, three colors, three numeral words, and three basic sentences (I see a/ an some, I want a/an some and I saw a/an some) with the corresponding question forms.

R. had unusual difficulty in understanding the relationship between basic sentence forms and their corresponding question forms, a trait often observed among children with developmental aphasia and of those with less severe language disorders. R.'s voice quality for words he had been taught specifically was reflective of his significant residual hearing. His skills in blending sounds in words which he had been taught were good, as were his recall skills for the written forms of words, of sentences, and of the respective question forms. In spite of his persistent resistance over the years to wearing a hearing aid, as characteristic of those with hearing loss and co-existing language disorders, R. demonstrated auditory discrimination skills for sets of known sentences and/or questions in a structured setting which were at 80–90 percent accuracy. When he had the support of written language, his speech was clear, with minimal indication of the earlier severe apraxia.

At a chronological age which corresponded with the fifth grade, he earned achievement test scores as follows: (a) reading and language, second grade, and (b) math, fourth grade. He was mainstreamed into the general education environment with appropriate support services and attended high school. Now, in adulthood, he is happily married and employed full time in the construction industry. See additional case histories in Chapter 9.

Over the years, we have seen numerous children with profiles such as these. Over her years of university teaching, the late Dr. Etoile DuBard told many of her students that "Each aphasic child is a population of one." Certainly each child is a population of one. Seeking accurate and complete differential diagnoses will help professionals better meet the children's needs. Arriving at a differential diagnosis among children may never be easy. Doing so can be time consuming and requires careful observations of a child's responses to whatever style instructional program is being used. What is of utmost importance is that the professional be a good observer, be knowledgeable about more than one teaching-learning strategy, and be able to implement an individually designed and appropriate program which will enable the child to experience success as a result of his/her efforts.

CHAPTER

4

Language Content, Skills and Principles

While most people can use language effectively and efficiently, they do not normally think of it in terms of components organized and expressed in a specific manner to achieve a particular goal in communication. They do not have to make a task analysis in order to achieve the goals. People normally learn to understand and use language more or less automatically, for they have been blessed with adequate intellectual potential, normal hearing, and a normally functioning central nervous system. As a result, their learning to communicate develops without mishap. In this section we will present a comparison of the developmental milestones of typical language development and the incremental stages of the speech and language program of the DuBard Association Method®.

Educators of those who are deaf and hard of hearing have long been familiar with the details of content to be considered when basic language has to be taught. Others confronted with the tasks involved in language teaching may not be so well informed. The content included in the DuBard Association Method® is no different from that learned more or less automatically by the child with good hearing acuity, despite the often poor models from which he or she has to learn. The organization of the content and the incremental progression through sequential stages may make the teaching procedures seem different and unusual. Nevertheless, the content itself varies little from that which the typical child masters; neither is the sequential order of development

so different from that observed in the typical child. One significant fact is that for the typically developing child the process of language acquisition is essentially completed by the time he or she is four or five years old (Eisenson, 1972; American Speech-Language-Hearing Association, 1997-2011).

To achieve such a level, children will have learned to produce, refine, manipulate, organize, store, and recall single phonemes, that is, vowel and consonant sounds. Their system will have produced and discarded many sounds not useful in our English language, while retaining the components common to our language. They will have mastered words through a process of trial, error, correction, and refining. They will have experimented with word order until they finally achieve syntax similar to the adults around them (Eisenson, 1972; American Speech-Language-Hearing Association, 1997-2011). The child with language disorders does not master these skills sufficiently for the communication process to become functional. The DuBard Association Method® procedures facilitate the teaching of these developmental stages to such children because to a large extent, the procedures follow the order observed in the learning process of typical children.

In the following list, the developmental stages of typical speech and language acquisition (as identified by Eisenson, 1972) are compared to the incremental teaching stages of the DuBard Association Method®.

A major difference between the progression of typically developing children acquiring language

Developmental Milestones of TYPICAL Language Acquisition

12–16 weeks: Coos and chuckles.

20 weeks: Consonants modify vowel-like cooing; nasals and labial fricatives are produced frequently.

12 months: Reduplicated sounds in echolalia; possible first words for identification; responds to simple commands.

18 months: A repertoire of words (3 to 50) can be expected to be in use.

24 months: Vocabulary of fifty or more words for naming and bringing about events; two-word phrases of the child's own formulation.

36 months: Vocabulary exceeds 1000 words; syntax is much like that in the child's surroundings.

48 months: Except for articulation skills, the linguistic system is essentially that of the adults in the child's surroundings.

DuBard Association Method®

Phoneme production is taught at an older age in precise articulation because the child usually will not have refined the productions in the normal fashion. Auditory training is implemented and continued through all subsequent phases of the instructional program.

Drop drills are reduplicated syllabic units. Some units are words; others are word-like. The child will have been taught at the earlier level to respond appropriately to simple, whole-word commands. Example: "Come."

Cross drills are used to teach the child early level nouns. Fifty nouns of CV/VC and CVC phonetic structure comprise the first unit of vocabulary.

Teaching of vocabulary in various phonetic arrangements continues.

Repetitive sentences and question forms are included because the language-disordered child's limited memory for sequences, poor skills of prediction and association are obvious. Because such children do not acquire language well, this stage focuses on teaching the child to use correct/complete syntactical patterns and respective question forms appropriate to the semantic content.

All subsequent stages/phases of the instructional program are designed, implemented, and expanded to include as much vocabulary and as many appropriate verb tenses, morphological structures and word classes as the child can learn to integrate and assimilate and to remember for appropriate use in spontaneous language.

---

naturally and children with severe language disorders is that with the severely impaired populations, the beginning timeline is often at four years or later. This delay is often associated with children having been in a situation in which it was presumed that they would talk when they wanted to or having been in a program of intervention which was either not appropriate to their needs or not sufficiently intensive and structured. In cases where children could speak a certain amount, adults may have presumed that the children were doing all right. Unfortunately, the presence of

some spoken language without comparable receptive abilities often added to and complicated further the hidden disability. Major problems often surface in the primary grades when multiple, varying, sequential instructions are given at a relatively rapid rate. Also, difficulties arise when children begin to learn to read and they have no system for remembering the sound-symbols in words; they develop poor or no decoding skills, and they have difficulty in semantics. Therefore, they achieve in written language as poorly as they have achieved in oral communication.

Figure 4.1 provides an overview of the elements of language which must be taught. These apply to anyone learning English. Only the means to achieve the learning will vary.

In order for the content and the structural principles of language to be meaningful and functional, certain basic skills are essential. For oral communication, children must be able to say words, attach some meaning to them, store them, and recall them for spontaneous use. With written language they must acquire the additional skills of writing words correctly and using them in a correct syntactical pattern of a sentence or question. The seven steps of McGinnis's Association Method teach these skills. Starting at the phoneme level and continuing through the advanced levels of language instruction, the seven steps are a vital part of the implementation. Initially, they constitute the core of instruction; later, they provide a great deal of repetition to help the child overcome storage and recall deficiencies. "English is consid-ered a stochastic process and is seventy-five percent redundant in the written form" (Attneave, 1959). The high redundancy of the DuBard Association Method® constitutes an appropriate approach for children who do not learn language and speech naturally.

IMSLEC CONTENT AND PRINCIPLES OF INSTRUCTION

The International Multisensory Structured Language Education Council (IMSLEC), an accrediting body for multisensory structured language (MSL) professional development programs addressed the *content* of language instruction (what is taught) and *principles* of instruction (how it is to be taught) for teachers and therapists who serve individuals with dyslexia. This is reflected in Figure 4.2.

Multisensory Structured Language: What is Taught
Phonology and Phonological Awareness: Phonology

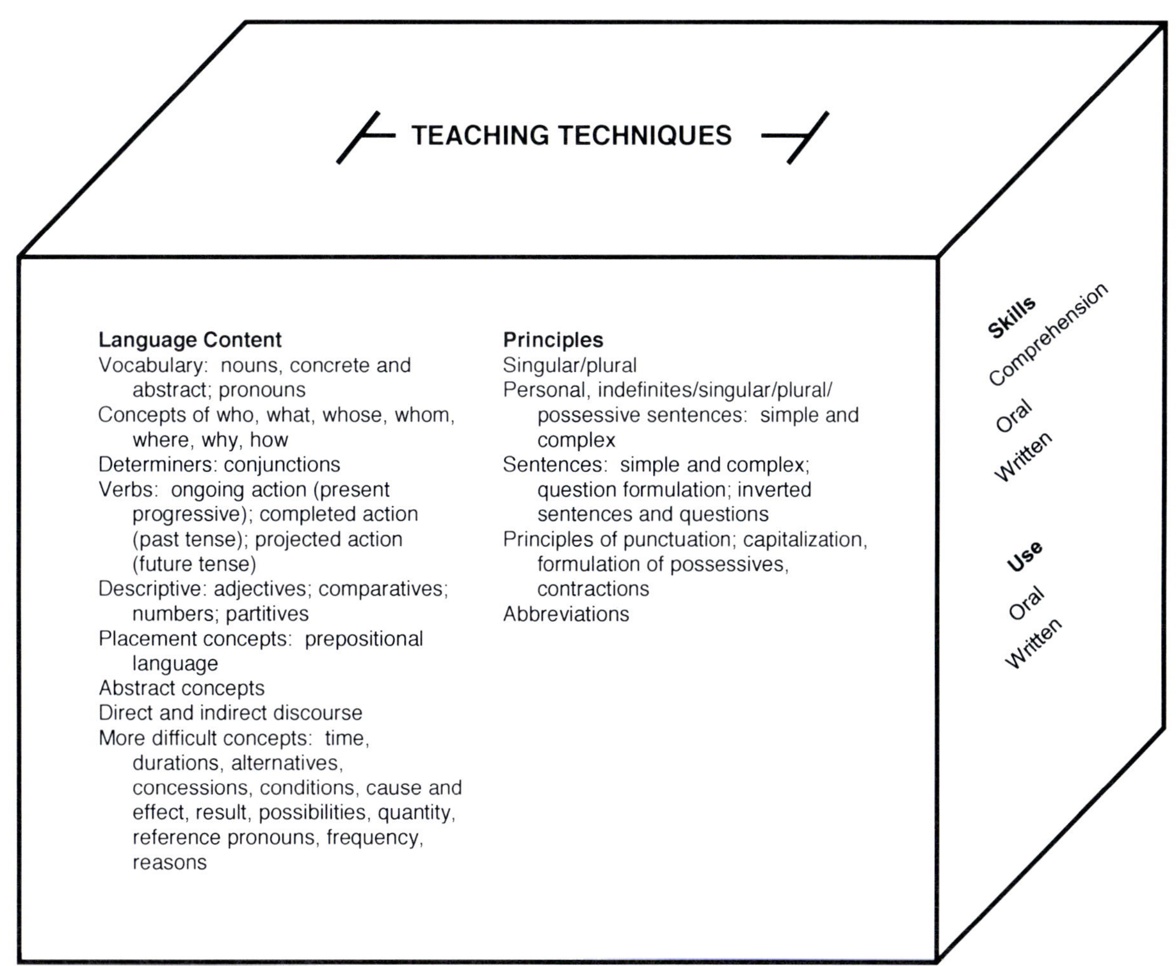

FIG. 4.1. Overview of language elements: content, principles of language structure, and skills for communicating

	Principles of Instruction				
Content: Structure of the English Language	Simultaneous Multisensory VAKT	Systematic and Cumulative	Direct Instruction	Diagnostic Teaching to Automaticity	Synthetic/ Analytic Instruction
Phonology and phonological awareness	√	√	√	√	√
Sound/symbol association: visual to auditory, auditory to visual, blending and segmenting	√	√	√	√	√
Syllables: types and patterns for division	√	√	√	√	√
Morphology: base words, roots, affixes	√	√	√	√	√
Syntax: grammar, sentence variation, mechanics of language	√	√	√	√	√
Semantics: meaning	√	√	√	√	√

FIG. 4.2. IMSLEC Content and Principles of Instruction Chart
Source: The International Multisensory Structured Language Education Council (IMSLEC) (1995). Used with permission

is the study of speech sounds and how they work within their environment. A phoneme is the smallest unit of sound in a given language that can be recognized as being distinct from other sounds in the language. Phonological awareness is the understanding of the internal linguistic structure of words. An important aspect of phonological awareness is phonemic awareness or the ability to segment words into their component sounds.

Sound-symbol Association: This is the knowledge of the various sounds in the English language and their correspondence to the letters and combinations of letters which represent those sounds. Sound-symbol association must be taught (and mastered) in two directions: visual to auditory and auditory to visual. Additionally, students must master the blending of sounds and letters into words as well as the segmenting of whole words into the individual sounds.

Syllable Instruction: A syllable is a unit of oral or written language with one vowel sound. Instruction must include the teaching of the six basic types of syllables in the English language: closed, vowel-consonant-e, open, consonant-le, r-controlled, and diphthong or vowel pair. Syllable division rules must be directly taught in relation to the word structure.

Morphology: Morphology is the study of how morphemes are combined to form words. A morpheme is the smallest unit of meaning in the language. The curriculum must include the study of base words, roots and affixes.

Syntax: Syntax is the set of principles that dictates the sequence and function of words in a sentence in order to convey meaning. This includes grammar, sentence variation and the mechanics of language.

Semantics: Semantics is that aspect of the language concerned with meaning. The curriculum (from the beginning) must include instruction in the comprehension of written language.

Multisensory Structured Language: How It Is Taught

Simultaneous, Multisensory (VAKT): Teaching is done using all learning pathways in the brain (visual, auditory, kinesthetic-tactile) simultaneously in order to enhance memory and learning.

Systematic and Cumulative: Multisensory language instruction requires that the organization of material follows the logical order of the language. The sequence must begin with the easiest and most basic elements and progress methodically to more difficult material. Each step must also be based on those already learned. Concepts taught must be systematically reviewed to strengthen memory.

Direct Instruction: The inferential learning of any concept cannot be taken for granted. Multisensory language instruction requires the direct teaching of all concepts with continuous student-teacher interaction.

Diagnostic Teaching: The teacher must be adept at prescriptive or individualized teaching. The teaching plan is based on careful and continuous assessment of the individual's needs. The content presented must be mastered to the degree of automaticity.

Synthetic and Analytic Instruction: Multisensory, structured language programs include both synthetic and analytic instruction. Synthetic instruction presents the parts of the language and then teaches how the parts work together to form a whole. Analytic instruction presents the whole and teaches how this can be broken down into its component parts.

Source: The International Multisensory Structured Language Education Council (1995) http://www.imslec.org Used with permission.

Teachers of children who are deaf or hard of hearing are familiar with the W's of language—concepts dealing with who, what, whose, where, when, and why—as well as additional concepts related to how—how much, how long, how many, how far, and so on. Verbs, verb tenses, and verb endings may cause the typical child, who learns language naturally, difficulties which may seem humorous to the listener. Such problems create major barriers for those children who must be taught language, and the difficulties they cause cannot be considered humorous. The difficulties are not likely to be corrected without direct effort. The following guidelines are offered for those whose professional training may not have included the presentation of language concepts as simply and analytically.

QUESTION LANGUAGE

key words

RESPONSE/SENTENCE LANGUAGE

requirement

QUESTION LANGUAGE key words	RESPONSE/SENTENCE LANGUAGE requirement
what	a thing (noun) a place (including proper nouns)
who	a person (proper noun)
whose	possessive for the above
where	placement concept: basic—in, on, under; more advanced—in front of, behind, in the corner, at the ________, over here, there, around the corner, in the next block, etc.
when	a time concept: clock, calendar, last, next, before, after, while, during, awhile, later, etc.
why	because is basic; also, in order to, so that, to get, to ________
what color/kind	adjectives
how many, much, far, long	basic number concepts; more abstract: few, some, many, lots of. Partitives—piece of, glass of, cup of, etc.

MORE DIFFICULT LANGUAGE CONCEPTS

A. Time
1. The rain lasted for a long time.
2. After a while, the sun came out.
3. The children played outside until supper time.
4. Tom watched TV until it was time to go to school.

B. Duration
1. The movie lasted from 1:30 until 4 o'clock.
2. The boys got to the playground at 2 o'clock and stayed until 5 o'clock.
3. Tom read from 4 o'clock until the 5:30 news started on TV.

C. Alternatives
1. We will either see a movie or play outside.
2. You may work a puzzle or play with the Lego blocks.
3. If you whine, you must go to your room.

D. Concessions
1. If you finish your work early, we will play a game.
2. You may not go to Tom's house unless you finish your homework.
3. Both of you may go to the movie if your rooms are straight.
4. Neither of us will go unless the rain stops.

E. Cause and Effect/Results
1. We will not be able to play outside because the grass is wet.
2. It is very cold outside, so we will play inside.
3. We must go to bed early because we are going fishing early tomorrow.

F. Conditions
1. The room was so noisy that we did not hear the knock on the door.
2. It was rainy most of the day.
3. It was stormy last night, but it's beautiful today.

G. Possibilities
1. We may play in the gym or see a movie if the rain continues.
2. Grandmother will come if she can get the car started.
3. It may take longer than we thought.

H. Quantity
1. Lots of people went swimming.
2. Most of the people had raincoats; fewer had umbrellas.
3. Many of the cars were red.

I. Reference Pronouns
1. Tom and Mary went to their grandmother's. They took their raincoats and boots with them. Their dog, Butch, lost his way when he tried to follow them. He went home and waited for them by the steps of their home.
2. Jon and Pete went to visit their grandparents. On the way, they realized they had forgotten their gifts for them.

J. Frequency
often   never
sometimes   usually
once in a while

K. Reasons
Because
to _________ (get, buy, see, ask)
so that

CHAPTER

5

The Association Method - Past and Present

HISTORICAL DEVELOPMENT

It is sometimes remarked that there is nothing new under the sun. Also, it is easily recognized in certain developments that what goes around, comes around. Even if the statements are only pseudo axioms, they may well apply to some aspects related to the Association Method which Mildred McGinnis devised.

As a young teacher of the deaf in the 1920s, McGinnis' after-school professional activities included working with victims of World War I who were patients of a veterans hospital in the St. Louis area. The patients demonstrated a variety of impairments to their communication abilities as a result of what would now be considered traumatic brain injuries, or from the effects of cardiovascular attacks/strokes. McGinnis noted similarities between these adults and the children who were deaf whom she was teaching and who were not learning through techniques usually effective with such children. She considered the children to have aphasia which today would be considered to be severe language disorders.

In 1979, Professor A. Loewe, University of Heidelberg, Germany, presented a paper "The historical development of oral education" at Sint-Michelsgestel, The Netherlands. He mentioned the work of Johannes Vatter and his indirect influence on the education of children in the United States who were deaf. Loewe noted that the "Association Phoneme Unit Method" of McGinnis was the "continuation of the work of Johannes Vatter" who was a well-known, well-respected, dedicated teacher of the deaf and who was a strong advocate

of the oral philosophy at the Institute for the Deaf, Frankfurt, Germany, from 1863–1874 at which time he became director of the Institute until 1916 (Van Uden 1969).

Vatter stressed the imitation of single sounds through visual, tactile, and kinesthetic senses to establish precise articulation as he himself taught children who were deaf. This approach was a major part of his initial work in his teaching. As production of single consonants and vowels was mastered, he combined two sounds into German words of two-sound phonetic construction which could be used meaningfully in the child's daily life and oral language. He did not use the written language until later in the child's educational program (Van Uden 1969). Except for the delayed use of the written symbols of language, Vatter's work was very similar to the work of McGinnis in the 1920s and 1930s as she devised and refined the Association Method at Central Institute for the Deaf, St. Louis, Missouri. Vatter's and McGinnis' approaches both utilized, in the absence of effective amplification systems, speaking the single sounds directly into the child's ear. Both consonants and vowels were established through imitation and for mastery of oral production. Precise articulation was the goal of the instruction. Both teachers utilized visual, tactile, and kinesthetic training as well as acoustic work, to establish the oral language skills. Both utilized the single phonemes expanded into two-sound combinations related to language. Both used language books developed for the child as he progressed in his work.

It is not known definitively *how* McGinnis

might have learned about Vatter's work, if in fact she did. It is known that, in the early 1900s, Max Goldstein, M.D., who founded Central Institute for the Deaf in 1914, had studied in Vienna as a post-graduate medical student, specializing in ear, nose, and throat aspects of medicine. Some personal correspondence from the late Helen Lane, an administrator at Central Institute for the Deaf in the 1950s and 1960s, stated that Dr. Goldstein sometimes spoke of the Acoustic Method in connection with Urbanschitch whom he had observed teaching children who were deaf. Whether or not the Acoustic Method was in fact the approach cited by Loewe (1979), or whether or not McGinnis adapted some of the ideas as she studied under and worked for Dr. Goldstein, is not known. However, that is a possibility.

In writing about the status of those who were deaf in post World War II in Germany, Franke (1948) cited Vatter's approach to teaching children who were deaf in the mid-1920s when Vatter was director of the school at Frankfurt-on-Main. Franke stated, "The results of the formal teaching had been good, but it was painful for the teacher and for the pupils" and, therefore, another system was introduced through which the children learned reading and speech in association with meaningful words "without excessive formal instruction." The new approach was introduced by Mr. Malisch-Ratibor.

Interestingly, somewhat simultaneously in the early 20th century years, Dr. Samuel T. Orton, a physician and researcher was working in the area of dyslexia. He, along with Anna Gillingham and Bessie Stillman (1997), devised what became known as the Orton-Gillingham method for teaching students with reading disabilities/dyslexia. While we don't know whether or not McGinnis and Orton had direct contact, we do know that McGinnis knew of Orton's work because it is referenced in her unpublished thesis (1939). Given that the principles of both the Orton-Gillingham approach and the McGinnis method/Association Method are phonetic, multisensory, incremental and systematic, it is not surprising that the approaches share many similarities. The major differences between the two approaches are 1) the Association Method was devised originally for children with significant speech, language, and/or hearing disabilities and the Orton-Gillingham approach was devised for those with reading challenges, and 2) rules are taught early in Orton-Gillingham but delayed until much later in the Association Method instructional program. The limited oral language skills of McGinnis' young students made learning rules of the English language not only impossible but inappropriate until basic language skills had been achieved. For example, why would one need to know that /bed/ is a closed syllable if one doesn't know that what we sleep in is called a bed? It is appropriate and beneficial for some students with histories of significant language/speech disorders or hearing impairments to learn the rules of the English language once adequate oral communication has been established. Over the years, many excellent derivatives of the Orton-Gillingham method have emerged including Spalding (2003), Slingerland (2008) and Alphabetic Phonics (1984).

In Subsequent Decades

In the 1980s, Monika Heising of West Germany was a student studying speech therapy at a specialized institute in Freiburg. "The director has presented us with the Association Method" (Heising 1985). During a stay at some Denver hospitals to become familiar with American developments in that field, she acquired a copy of *Teaching aphasics and other language-deficient children* (DuBard 1983). In her correspondence to DuBard regarding those experiences, she stated "as no documentation whatsoever on this method exists in German and as this method quite evidently offers a unique structure and approach to teaching these problem children, I am preparing a summarized translation of the chapters directly describing the A.M." (Association Method). Heising asked and received clarification on certain aspects of the instructional approach in specific levels of the Association Method. In January, 1986, DuBard received two copies of Heising's translation of the basic instructional program of the Association Method including DuBard's vocabulary list.

Regardless of whether or not Vatter's work became part of McGinnis' thinking, her commitment to teaching oral and written language to her population of "deaf" children who had additional problems whom she considered to be aphasic was as strong as Vatter's. Their devotion to children who were deaf and the German translation of the Association Method closed the circle for the twentieth century.

WHAT IT IS AND IS NOT

The Association Method is a phonetic, systematic, structured, incremental and cumulative multisensory approach for teaching language and speech to children with multiple difficulties in language learning. Its multidimensional aspects include concepts, language structure, sequential language, and skills for learning. The principles underlying its procedures were used decades before theories about the difficulties of nonverbal children and interventions for them were formulated. Even though the Association Method is structured, there is room for flexibility in its implementation. Maximum success with the procedures requires *intensive professional preparation* and patient work on the part of the teacher/speech-language pathologist in supporting the children's efforts and minimizing the frustrations they encounter in learning. Bolstering their confidence and supporting carryover of language and speech to the home environment are also necessary for success.

What the Association Method for teaching aphasic children is not is as important as what it is. The teaching procedures are not a panacea. They will not eliminate the aphasia, symbolic disorder, language disorder, or specific learning disability/dyslexia. Appropriately used, however, the procedures can help children learn language, speech, and academic skills in spite of the disabling conditions.

Not all children with central nervous system (CNS) dysfunction resulting in language learning differences necessarily need to proceed at the same rate through each phase of the procedures. Indeed, some children with clinical evidence of brain pathology with CNS dysfunction related to language and speech could not, would not, or did not deal effectively with certain aspects of the procedures. Those same children, however, succeeded in learning oral communication and related academic subjects when certain modifications were made to capitalize on their abilities and to minimize their limitations.

The procedures of the Association Method are *structured*. The need for structure in the instructional program and the out-of-school life of the child with severe communication difficulties is crucial and calls for maximum cooperation from those in the school environment with those in the out-of-school environment.

The Association Method procedures are *systematically organized* so that instruction consists of *incremental* units of language/speech with which a child can experience more success than failure. It requires that the child acquire *precise articulatory ability* from the very beginning and develop recall. As the child masters specific skills with phonemes (single speech sounds), the small units are organized into larger and, gradually, more complex units related to communication until he/she no longer experiences multiple uncertainties about language and speech.

Although the procedures are structured, they can be flexible. The degree and kind of flexibility

possible will depend upon the teacher's knowledge of (1) specific, general, immediate, and long-range goals, (2) the child's functional levels in numerous modalities and behavioral aspects, and (3) the role of each phase of the procedures, as well as the teacher/clinician's competence in implementing the procedures.

While it is possible and desirable to achieve flexibility in implementing the teaching procedures, too much flexibility at an inappropriate time can have a detrimental effect on the quality and quantity of the child's ultimate achievements. The progress in reducing his/her learning difficulties should not be jeopardized for the sake of flexibility. There will be plenty of time for flexibility after the child has gained a measure of ability in oral communication. In the meantime, some respite from the structure can be accomplished by using a variety of constructive activities which are significant to the learning process as a whole. An example of flexible, constructive activities might be teacher-devised worksheets appropriate for the child's level of instruction and other activities cited as reinforcement activities in chapter 6. In addition, the use of nonverbal activities with puzzles, bead patterns, or block designs provides a constructive change from the more structured teaching and may engage all senses for learning.

*It is crucial that the **intensity of services** be correlated to the **severity** of the student's disability.* For example, a student whose severe apraxia at age 5 renders him/her basically unintelligible will require intensive services. Group therapy for two 30-minute sessions per week is not likely to be sufficient to effectively remediate the motor speech disorder. *The DuBard Association Method®, a highly effective phonetic, multisensory teaching tool, is effective only to the extent that it is appropriately implemented for an individual student's particular disability by professionals who have had adequate coursework and clinical teaching experience to do so.*

One criticism of the Association Method has been that it is contrary to typical learning because we don't learn to talk by saying single sounds (phonemes). On the surface this statement may be partially true, but a closer consideration may yield a more accurate picture. While we may not learn to talk by learning single phonemes as such, typical children go through a prelinguistic stage of speech development during which they have countless experiences of uttering, monitoring, and manipulating phonemes by organizing, storing, retrieving them as word approximations, making proper associations, and refining them into words. These words are then stored, retrieved, and used in ways which represent the normal capacity for learning language. By the time children reach the age of two or three, numerous syntactical and linguistic constructions can be observed in their communications. These processes are normal for children. However, children who have severe language disorders do not exhibit such abilities. Indeed, their impaired language and speech learning give indisputable evidence that these processes are not in operation.

Teachers of these children are confronted with problems related to some dysfunction in the children's central nervous systems that results in language learning differences. A realistic view of the task includes facing the fact that unusual instructional procedures are required to cope with unusual functioning of the central nervous system. While the Association Method has been used effectively by many teachers with numerous children, one must remember that the effectiveness of any techniques or treatments depends on multiple variables, starting with the children themselves.

FACTORS RELATED TO EFFECTIVENESS OF THE ASSOCIATION METHOD

Success with children taught by the procedures discussed in this volume was influenced by certain factors in addition to the teaching procedures themselves. These factors can be expected to apply to other children and include the following:

1. Early diagnosis of difficulties and early instruction with differentiated teaching procedures
2. Innate ability of the children, i.e., their learning potential in general
3. A day-school program, or appropriately intensive therapy program, which utilizes special techniques yet permits the children to associate regularly with family and peers in their neighborhoods
4. Stability in teacher personnel over a period of several years until the children reach a level of language competence that permits them to adjust relatively easily to different teachers
5. The desire, willingness, and ability of parents to make the sacrifices necessary to provide their children with special instruction and their cooperation in reinforcing that instruction in the children's daily lives outside the special educational environment

On the other hand, certain factors will exert a negative influence on children's progress. These include:

1. Late detection of disabilities and delay in obtaining appropriate instruction
2. Low level of general intellectual ability
3. An environment which does not provide differentiated teaching instruction
4. For children who are deaf, not being with typically hearing peers in the neighborhood and family environments
5. Lack of stability in teacher personnel and lack of adequate personnel to provide continuity of instruction.
6. Inadequate or inconsistent home support.

To assume that all children with language disorders will be able to achieve the same functional level would be unrealistic. However, it is possible to believe that children with specific identified deficiencies for language learning can achieve better functioning, socially, emotionally, psychologically, and educationally.

ASSOCIATION METHOD AND DUBARD ASSOCIATION METHOD®

The careful reader of this text will, by now, have determined that while the late Dr. Etoile DuBard and the current author, Maureen K. Martin, have much appreciation for new developments in the field, there is also great appreciation for the past, for the work of pioneers in the field, and for those who have laid the foundations upon which current practitioners continue to build. It is with *great* appreciation of earlier giants and geniuses that we continue to learn and develop to meet current and future needs of those whom we seek to serve. Certainly Mildred McGinnis is one whose work we continue to respect and treasure—what she developed, even in its earliest forms, has continued to impact the lives of children, their families, and those who serve them across the decades. It was always of great importance to Etoile DuBard that Mildred McGinnis be acknowledged and that her contributions to the field continue to be studied, understood, and appreciated by the university students and professionals who have followed. The principles of the "McGinnis Method" or "Association Method" as many have named her work are as valid today as when she originally devised the approach. However, a natural evolution over the decades led Etoile DuBard and the staff at the DuBard School for Language Disorders (previously School for Children with Language Disorders founded in 1962) at The University of Southern Mississippi to create, organize, and develop a curriculum and range of tools to enhance the efficiency of the teaching, utilize available technology, and assist our own staff and colleagues with the dawn of increasing federal requirements, such as Individual Education Plans (IEPs), state standards and benchmarks, etc. To be sure, the children also have taught us a lot—and continue to do so!

In addition to the creation of organizational tools and therapy materials, the recognition of the minimal coursework and practicum needed to implement the method effectively became apparent over the years. Certainly, varied levels of training are needed depending on the population receiving the multisensory instruction of the Association Method (general education, deaf education, speech-language pathology, special education, etc.). Beginning in about 1990, an affiliation with a group which was originally a committee on teacher education through the Orton Dyslexia Society, now the International Dyslexia Association, began. The committee recognized the need to identify what is meant by phonetic, multisensory instruction and the training that is necessary to implement it effectively. Over several years, the nationwide collaborative work of specialists in numerous excellent phonetic, multisensory approaches culminated in the founding of The International Multisensory Structured Language Education Council (IMSLEC) in 1995. The mission of IMSLEC is "to accredit quality training courses for the professional preparation of multisensory structured language education specialists." (www. imslec.org) Through a rigorous process of application, self-study, and site visit, the in-depth professional development program in the Association Method developed at the DuBard School for Language Disorders at The University of Southern Mississippi was accredited in 1998 and continues to hold accreditation at all available levels.

So, from the humble beginnings of cutting pictures out of magazines, writing the stories one wanted to teach the children, and making children's books with crayons we've seen an evolving program that continually seeks to provide the highest quality of services to children. Through a standardized curriculum, organized record-keeping, and ever-developing materials to teaching university students and professionals from across the country in a manner which meets national standards and, more importantly, develops the teaching skill so desperately needed for the children, the use of the Association Method as developed, practiced, and taught at our site has become known as the DuBard Association Method®. Recognition of McGinnis' and DuBard's contributions, as well as all who have made a difference over the years, always will be acknowledged, appreciated, and celebrated. Now consumers, whether parents, professionals, school administrators, or others, will be able to recognize easily and clearly the version of the methodology that has grown through the years at The University of Southern Mississippi and is referred to as the DuBard Association Method®.

Summary of Developments and Modifications of the Association Method

As the use of the Association Method at the DuBard School for Language Disorders, The University of Southern Mississippi, evolved over the years, the late Dr. Etoile DuBard and the staff of the school implemented the following changes to the original work:

1. DuBard organized the beginning noun vocabulary so that the length of the words expanded incrementally and, thus, students' memory for longer words could develop incrementally.
2. The continued use of drop drills for students with dyslexia was implemented. McGinnis' original practice was to discontinue drop drills once cross drills had been introduced. It is now understood that continued practice of decoding nonsense syllables is useful for those with dyslexia or specific learning disabilities in reading.
3. Secondary spellings are used in all possible places (second and third columns) of cross drills.
4. The review in structure (reading, auditory-visual and acoustic work) was organized in definitive steps.
5. Three additional repetitive sentence forms and the corresponding questions were added (I have, I saw, ____has).
6. Repetitive sentences with numbers and the 'how many' questions were added as a new level of instruction. The purpose of this was to make the transition to animal stories more incremental and easier for the child to master.
7. Animal stories were organized into four levels of difficulty.
8. Expanded personal stories were organized into several levels of difficulty.
9. The use of cross drills for two syllable words was discontinued. It was determined that the organization of teaching 2-phoneme, 3-phoneme, and 4-phoneme vocabulary words developed decoding skills which made the cross drill for two syllable words unnecessary.
10. A second procedure for developing memory for sequence in stories was devised as an option.
11. Two distinct story types which emphasize prepositions, descriptive (room) stories and preposition round-up stories, which may in-

clude people, were organized.

12. A curriculum, IEP checklist, and therapy materials have been, and continue to be, developed.

13. The use of the Fitzgerald Key has been continued.

14. Experience stories are utilized at all levels of the instructional program rather than just after past tense language has been taught.

15. The systematic and incremental organization of math facts in correlative programs was developed.

16. The content, materials and procedures needed throughout the program have been clearly specified.

THEORIES

A distinctive feature of the Association Method is to require children to articulate as precisely as possible from the time they begin the instruction. The goals of establishing precise articulation and maintaining its use during the instructional program have been criticized and rejected by numerous speech-language pathologists and teachers of the deaf and hard of hearing. Two major objections are that the Association Method is not a natural approach toward developing speech because it is not the way typical children learn to talk and that this approach results in staccato, unrhythmical expressive language.

A closer examination of aspects of major deficiencies observed in children with severe problems in language learning, of their spontaneous speech in the more advanced phase of the instructional program, and of their precise articulation skills in relation to their written language may provide data which can justify placing less emphasis on the unnaturalness of the procedure. Furthermore, if critics consider the method in relation to the motor theory of speech perception, they will find that this method makes a significant contribution to children's long-range achievements in both oral and written language. Typical language development follows the pattern of comprehension preceding expression. Traditional instruction of those who are deaf has followed the same pattern. Critics should recognize at least two important factors before rejecting the requirements of the Association Method. First, in dealing with language learning and instruction for children with severe dysfunctions, one does not encounter the general learning situation which exists with typical children. Secondly, the quality of the oral and written language of the typical individual who is deaf or hard of hearing needs improvement.

Considerations of dyspraxia and dysarthria in children with developmental aphasia (Eisenson 1972) present a strong case for requiring the precise articulatory training found in the McGinnis procedures. Such training may well be the only way to establish control over components of speech on a level at which these children can succeed. In view of the general need for improved speech among the deaf, such training also may help these students.

Motor Theory of Speech Perception

Application of the Association Method requires precise articulation beginning with the phoneme level. Such articulation is unlike the speech productions acceptable from children challenged with profound deafness and those with good hearing acuity. In these cases, the usual practice is to accept approximations of phonemes in words and sentences with the idea that typically hearing children will refine the pronunciation with maturity and use, and that children who are deaf need to acquire some use of language while more attention can be given to their speech later. Both of these ideas are sound to some extent. However, confronted with the problem of children for whom such practices were apparently not successful, McGinnis adopted a different idea. She required precise articulation from the earliest levels of training, *reasoning that the motor act would provide the child with a basis for better perception and for recalling spoken and written forms of language.* Therefore, through such an approach, children's progress in language and speech acquisition would be promoted. We should recall that McGinnis' initial work was conducted during the 1920s and 1930s, when there were few theories about language and speech acquisition. We will now consider her work in the light of ideas and findings from later research in order to find a rationale to explain one of its features that appears to be unusual.

In 1965, Lane represented a speech episode as being a vocal response of the speaker providing an acoustic stimulus, which in turn results in a discriminative response by the listener (Fig. 5.1). In the same article, he represented the speech episode in a model according to the motor theory of speech perception (Fig. 5.2). *The motor theory maintains that articulatory movements and their sensory effects mediate between the acoustic stimulus and the event called perception.* According to this theory, the speech episode consists of a speaker's vocal response providing an acoustic stimulus. This stimulus results in covert vocal response by the listener. *It is appropriate to consider that at least to some extent one perceives speech through production and that the production provides a basis for recalling it for spontaneous use at a later time.*

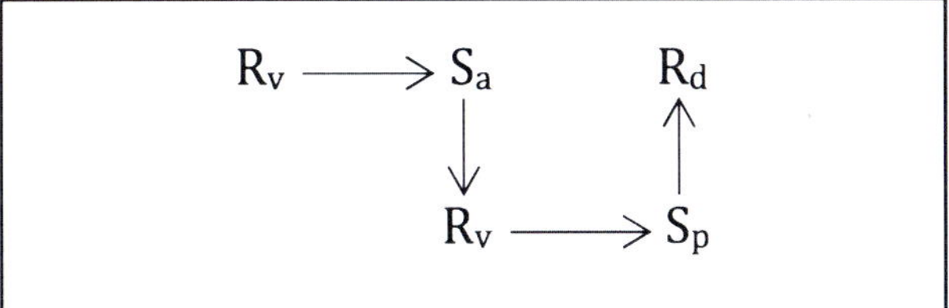

FIG. 5.1. Speech episode —A vocal response becomes an acoustic stimulus resulting in a discriminative response by the listener.

$$R_v \longrightarrow S_a \qquad R_d$$

FIG. 5.2. Speech episode according to motor theory of speech perception —A vocal response becomes an acoustic stimulus resulting in a covert vocal response; proprioceptive feedback, Sp, results in the discriminative response.

Proprioceptive feedback is the information about production of speech which results from the stimuli created by the movements of the speech mechanism such as the lips, tongue, palate, etc. The significance of the role of proprioceptive feedback as an aid to perception and recall of speech and language has become a point of interest by those teaching children with language and speech impairments. The Association Method calls for teaching children precise production of phonemes and requiring expression before expecting comprehension. Children with severe oral communication disorders are not expected to understand language which they cannot produce. McGinnis held the view that the (aphasic) child's ability to articulate language precisely before establishing comprehension served as a basis for recall and retrieval of language for spontaneous use.

Sanders (1977, 221) described the relationship between speech perception and reading in this way:

> The motor theory, as applied to reading, postulates that in processing the printed or written word we overtly or covertly articulate the speech sounds, producing either vocal or subvocal speech.

He stated further that "the evidence clearly indicates that the speech musculature is almost always involved in the act of silent reading."

Over a period of six years, twenty children diagnosed at the time with developmental aphasia, ages four to eleven years, who were enrolled in a day-school program designed for such children, were studied (DuBard). Twelve children were enrolled for weekly individual lessons. All subjects demonstrated at least average intellectual potential on nonverbal tasks. The study was conducted on a day-to-day basis in a classroom environment. Data were obtained regarding the children's abilities, limitations, and responses to the teaching empirically and through clinically oriented approaches. The observations were analyzed in relation to published research supporting the motor theory of speech perception.

The first phase of the study was modeled after one conducted by Hurst, Black, and Singh (1966). As their subjects from three racial groups practiced reading and saying the stimulus material, they became better listeners, better monitors, and better speakers. The children with language disorders also demonstrated improvement in such abilities.

Unlike subjects in other studies concerned with the role of articulation in the perception process, the children diagnosed with aphasia (language disorders) demonstrated little or no comprehension of any language. They gave no evidence that they were utilizing any system for self-monitoring. In general, they demonstrated poor listening behavior and recall, as well as severe deficiencies in language and speech.

Instructional procedures used with the children were as follows:

1. Each child was shown the cursive written pattern of the language component appropriate for him/her.
2. The child was taught to articulate the stimulus material as precisely as possible and to write the material.
3. The stimulus material was then presented visually and verbally at conversation-level intensity without instrument amplification.
4. Each child was required to repeat the stimulus material and to identify the written form. Each subject was allowed the amount of practice necessary to develop a thorough understanding of the task and the procedures.
5. After the child was familiar with the task and the procedures, the listening task was introduced. The initial distance between the speaker and the child varied according to the extent to which the child had demonstrated use of hearing in other kinds of situations. The distance was increased as the child dem-

onstrated improvement in listening.

Certain consistent changes in the subjects' responses were observed throughout the study:

1. The children who could repeat the stimulus material with precise articulation were able to identify accurately the appropriate written form. Those with less precise articulation demonstrated less proficiency in identifying the appropriate written forms.
2. Introduction of stimulus material which was unfamiliar to the children and which they did not articulate precisely resulted in more errors in identifying the written form and in writing the material. Material which they could articulate precisely, they could recall orally and write accurately.
3. The children's abilities to respond appropriately to directions improved when they were able to repeat the directions orally before responding. In unstructured settings, the children frequently repeated directions or a question before attempting to respond. Their subsequent responses were usually more accurate than when they did not repeat the directions or questions, or when their articulation was not precise.
4. As was true in the study by Hurst, Black, and Singh (1966), the children with greater facility for speech and the capacity for more precise articulation demonstrated greater improvement in listening. Recall for spontaneous use was also precise.
5. As the auditory stimulus was presented, the subjects frequently mouthed the material simultaneously with the examiner but without phonation.

The marked changes in articulation and listening support the idea that at least some of these changes were attributable to the motor function itself. Another factor could also be significant: familiarity with the stimulus material. Davis (1952) pointed out the significance of familiarity with language in one's ability to code under adverse conditions. The children with language disorders may have increased their competence with the tasks because they expanded their familiarity with language in general and the language related to the study in particular.

Liberman (1957) suggested that "when articulation and sound wave go separate ways... the perception always goes with articulation." Based on his findings in experimental studies, he stated that "the perception reflects the basic similarity in the articulatory patterns rather than the relative gross differences among the acoustic stimuli" (Liberman, Delattre, Cooper 1952). Similar patterns of response have been observed in children with language disorders. Liberman and Mattingly (1985) revised and refined their view of the motor theory of speech perception based on later studies and determined that, while perception and production are separate processes that are linked, they are "both inherently motoric."

DuBard (1967) observed a group of children diagnosed, at the time, with aphasia between 1962 and 1967 as they learned oral communication through multisensory-motor theory procedures. The significant changes noted were as follows:

1. The listening behavior of the children improved; better speakers became better listeners.
2. The ability to achieve precise articulation of an auditory stimulus resulted in more accurate identification and writing of the stimulus.
3. Self-monitoring and self-correction were developed. Children detected their errors immediately following production of speech and made accurate corrections.
4. The children improved in comprehending language when they could repeat an instruction in precise articulation.
5. Their perception and comprehension of a new speaker's communication improved after they had adequate time to adjust to the new speaker's voice.
6. Better production and perception of high front vowels were achieved through techniques which utilized increased diaphragmatic pressure and loudness during production.

Eisenson (1968) referred to the emphasis Luria (1966) placed on the "close relationship between articulation and audition in the normal development of speech." Regarding the process, Eisenson noted, "The development of ability to perceive sounds and to hear speech requires the closest participation of the articulatory apparatus and assumes its final character only in the process of active articulatory experience."

In light of the research cited and empirical data, McGinnis' point of requiring precise articulation as an aid to speech perception and the recall process was well-taken. Her process breaks down the components of the spoken word at the beginning level of instruction to such a minute level that the limitations for subtle phonetic analysis are not overtaxed in the child diagnosed with severe language disorder and/or apraxia. This is also true for children with specific learning disabilities/dyslexia who are learning to read.

While motor theory has received less attention in the field of speech science in recent years, it has received considerable focus and has been widely received in the field of cognitive science (Galantucci, Fowler and Turvey 2006). These authors noted that, for speech perception, there is now evidence that perceiving speech involves neural activity of the motor system. They cited studies by Fadiga and colleagues (2002) that demonstrated, during speech perception, the activation of speech-related muscles. Similarly, Watkins and colleagues (2003) found that while listening to speech and seeing speech-related lip movements, subjects demonstrated enhanced muscle activity in the lips. Articulatory movements influence perception according to a study by Yeung, Scott, Gick and Werker (2008).

Information Theory

Information theory deals with reducing uncertainties. Those familiar with children diagnosed with language disorders are well aware of the uncertainties the children have related to language and language learning. Weaver (1952) wrote: "…. information theory does not deal directly with information itself, but rather with representation—physical representation—of the information." Attneave (1959) observed: "We gain information only about matters in which we are to some degree ignorant or uncertain" and "information may be defined as that which removes or reduces uncertainty."

Effective communication reduces uncertainties of ideas and thoughts among human beings. A simplified version of a model for communication is shown in figure 5.3.

Using Eisenson's definition of a child with developmental aphasia as one with central nervous system dysfunction, viewing the child's central nervous system as one totally or partially limited in processing information and the speech of others, and recognizing the fact that such children have been observed to deal more effectively with very small units of "information" and phonemic components, certain facets of information theory are applicable to their difficulties in learning language and speech. The theory is applicable to the Association Method. Specific applications are given later in this chapter.

"Noise" interferes with learning and communication. Figure 5.4, adapted from Attneave, represents simple communication—either a word or a sentence. AC represents the entire communication. A1B may be thought of as the equivocation of transmission. It is the portion of the stimulus information which is lost by the subject; it represents uncertainty of the stimulus even though the response may be known. B2 and C1 may be referred to as the ambiguity of the stimulus. This is an uncertainty of the response and is considered to be the irrelevant or "noise" component of response information (DuBard 1967). Some children

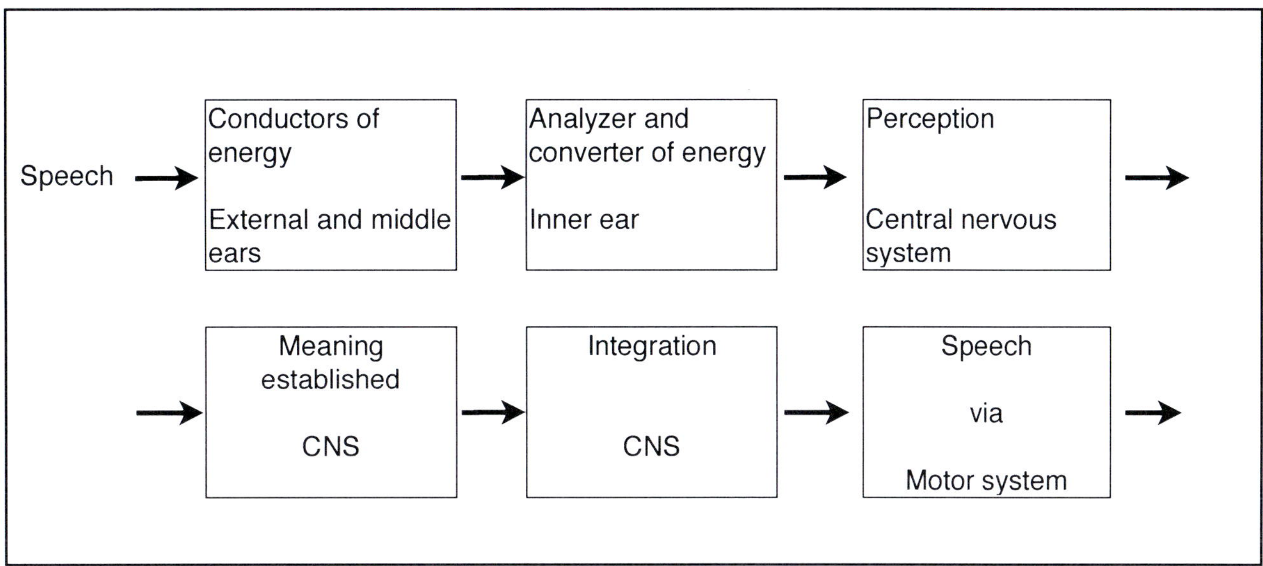

FIG. 5.3. Process leading to communication - A model for communication. Adapted from lectures given by S. Richard Silverman, Central Institute for the Deaf, St. Louis, Missouri, 1961-62.

diagnosed with language disorders can repeat after a speaker only the last portion of a word or sentence. For instance, when told, "Get me your coat," the child's attempted repetition might well be a string of jargon for all except the word coat. Thus, we might consider that for the child with language disorders, all except B2 C1 of Attneave's model is the ambiguous portion of the communication.

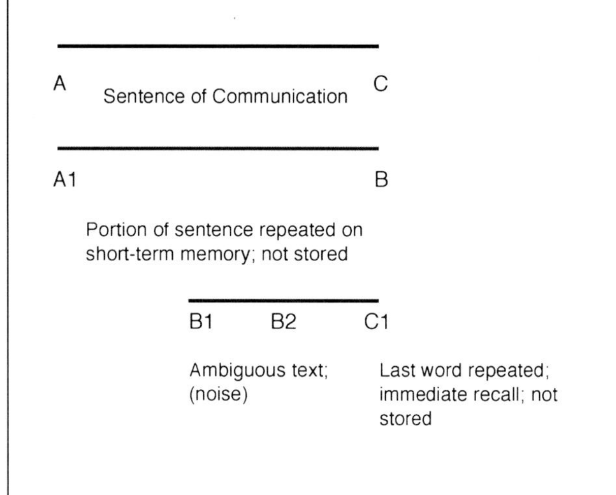

FIG. 5.4. Applied to the language learning process of certain children with aphasia and language disorders, A1 B represents the language a child may learn but then lose because of inability to store information and recall it for spontaneous use. B1 represents the first part of the message. It may or may not be stored. The balance of the language communication, represented by B2 C1, may be that which is completely ambiguous or uncertain. This portion may be referred to as the irrelevant or "noise" component.

Additional terminology basic to information theory which can also be applied to the Association Method includes the following:

The unit of selective information
Structural information
Chunks of information
Stochastic process
Ergodicity/ergodic process
Redundancy
Sequential dependencies
Surprisal of an event

Selective information is also known as a bit, a name derived from the first two letters of binary and the last letter of digit. The information involved may be defined as "that which removes or reduces uncertainty" (Weaver 1952). Selective information

of the Association Method consists initially of the single phonemes with which the child develops certain skills for learning.

Structural information deals with the degree of complexity of a representation (DuBard 1967). Sequentially, selective information constitutes the building blocks for structural information. In the Association Method, structural information consists of a particular kind of application of selective information into a more complex phonemic arrangement of sounds which are to become words. This process forms the base for the individual's learning to acquire meaning for *chunks of information* in sentences. Oversimplified, the components of chunks of information might have little or no meaning in their own right, but together they take on significant meaning for purposes of communication. In the sentence *this is some meat,* for example, the words *this, is,* and *some,* taken alone, have little to offer; used together, they function as a chunk of information expressing a basic concept in language. Gillam, in his 1997 article, describes the importance of organization of material and meaningful chunking of information as a technique to build memory/learning.

Stochastic process and *ergodicity* are basic terms dealing with relatively simple ideas. A stochastic process is one which "gives rise to a sequence of symbols to which probability laws apply" (Attneave 1959, 13). Simply stated, *a stochastic process is one which has predictability.* For example, in constructing a sentence, the sequencing of the words within the sentence contains elements of predictability. To illustrate, adjectives precede nouns as in *big cat* vs. *cat big.* This kind of feature is significant in a procedure for teaching children who, according to Eisenson (1968), are "impaired in their ability to deal with linguistic sequences." In the same article he stated:

> They are poor at the guessing and gambling which are inherent and are required for becoming proficient in verbal behavior. The developmentally aphasic child is so poor, so apt to be a born loser, that he may become apprehensive about exposing himself to situations that require him to be involved in continued tries and trials to understand and produce conventional language. (9)

For reasons described above, teaching procedures need to provide children with learning situations in which probability and predictability are built in for them. Such a feature of the stochastic process may be noted in the earliest levels of instruction and especially in the cross-drill component of instruction which McGinnis designed for teaching basic vocabulary.

One feature of a stochastic process is that there may be the presence of ergodicity or the process may be said to be ergodic. The process is ergodic if the probability laws which characterize it remain constant for all parts of the sequence. Simply stated, *the process is ergodic if the predictability continues throughout the entire process.* To illustrate, in the English language, when adjectives and nouns are used together, adjectives always precede nouns as in *slow runner, sweet tea, beautiful flowers.* The process is characterized by some degree of *redundancy*, ranging from almost zero to 100 percent. "At the 100 percent redundancy symbols are generated in an altogether lawful and regular sequence such that one can predict with complete certainty what the next symbol will be" (Attneave 1959, 13–14). Ergodicity, along with the stochastic process, is found in the early levels of the Association Method instruction and especially in the cross drill, enabling children to learn a measure of predictability through a controlled organization of selective information (phonemes). Sufficient redundancy is provided so that the information and newfound ability are useful to them later in more complex language. Careful analysis of the procedures which appears later in this chapter will show that the guaranteed predictability is embedded in stages of the procedures.

Sequential dependency may also be noted in early and later phases of the teaching procedures. Language content of the instructional program is constructed and presented in such a controlled incremental style that children have an opportunity to realize that certain phonetic arrangements are useful. They learn, too, that selection of words for word order in sentences depends on previously learned and applied information.

The *surprisal element*, as used in information theory, is related to the instructional portion of the language program dealing with teaching placement concepts, i.e., prepositional language. Whereas children with language disorders may say and understand the words *cup* and *table*, they may not be able to apply these words in some other context. The idea that the cup is *on* the table seems unimpressive to them. In the Association Method, impression is created by using bizarre representations in the initial teaching of concepts of prepositions and the language related to them. Once the concept is understood, the child can apply it in general use.

Most individuals entrusted with the responsibility of teaching children with language disorders probably give little thought to theories. They know the stresses encountered in the day-to-day managing and teaching of such children. When asked "Why… . ?", McGinnis often replied, "It doesn't matter why, (what matters is) it works." Indeed, the fact that "it works" is the most important factor at the moment in teaching the children. Understanding why a method worked and continues to work may be of greater importance in the future teaching of children with communication disorders. For this reason, the two theories formulated well after the time when McGinnis was teaching children are included herein. This information is offered as a means of helping the professional understand the relationship between the teaching procedures and information theory.

THE RELATIONSHIP BETWEEN PROCEDURES AND THEORY

How do the components of information theory relate to the stages of the linguistic program of the Association Method? Information theory deals with reducing uncertainties and calls for organization of units into a systematic program/format in order to increase predictability. For example, if one is given a square of 100 blocks (see Fig. 5.5), how could one go about identifying a single block, which another individual has selected mentally, in the most efficient way? The task is to identify the location of the block by asking questions. Binary decision making is used. By applying the rules for the game of twenty questions, a person employs binary decision making. Only a response of "yes" or "no" can be made. One could ask up to ninety-nine questions before a final determination might be made. However, by organizing the units in some manner, the amount of information (blocks) to be used can be reduced systematically and the block can be identified more readily, and with considerably fewer questions. Exactly how many questions might be needed will be determined by how one organizes the 100 squares initially.

If one divides the block of one hundred squares into two halves, either vertically or horizontally, the question might be, "Is the square in the top half?" Whether the answer is "yes" or "no," half of the total number of squares has been eliminated, thus reducing the uncertainty as to the general location of the mystery square. Organizing the remaining half into two parts allows questioning to continue. A question like "Is the mystery block in the right half?", again, regardless of the answer, automatically eliminates an additional section. By organizing information and questioning in this way, people have identified the mystery square with as few as three questions and as many as seven.

FIG. 5.5. One hundred squares.

The mystery square activity provides an example of how information was reduced then used. All of the components of the English language may be considered to be represented by the illustration of the one hundred squares. When the components of the language are organized, the information is reduced to the level of single phonemes from which language can be built and expanded. We add one new unit of information at a time and, ultimately, expand the application from single sounds in words to complete words and sentences.

We will now look at how concepts of information theory are embodied in the components of the Association Method (pages 57-58).

DISTINCTIVE FEATURES OF THE ASSOCIATION METHOD/ DUBARD ASSOCIATION METHOD®

Over the years, principles which are the same or similar to those used in the Association Method have been used in various phonetic, multisensory programs. These include The Open Court Series, first published in 1963, which was developed by Priscilla McQueen, who studied under McGinnis. Other examples are the Orton-Gillingham work (Orton, S.T., 1937 & Orton, J.L., 1966), Slingerland's *Multisensory Approach to Language Arts for Specific Language Disability Children* (1971, 2008), Spalding's *Writing Road to Reading* (1990), the Se-

quential *English Education* (SEE) (Pickering, 1997) approach based on the work of Dr. Charles Shedd and the Wilson Reading System (Wilson, 1988). All of the programs have more similarities than differences. However, certain aspects of the Association Method developed by McGinnis in the 1920s and 1930s are distinctive from other multisensory instructional programs. The distinctive features of the Association Method follow.

No Program to Buy or Sell

Perhaps one of the most distinctive features of the Association Method is that it is not a packaged program with workbooks or a series of texts. The effectiveness of the Association Method depends on the appropriate professional preparation of the teacher/speech-language pathologist and the ability to follow the method's principles sequentially and consistently. While McGinnis and her protégés had to develop materials as they taught the children, commercially published materials have been and are being developed by staff of the DuBard School for Language Disorders. However, the effectiveness of the method always will be dependent on the personnel implementing the instructional program rather than the materials used. Teachers who use it must be knowledgeable regarding phonetics, must know the Northampton Symbols developed by Caroline Yale in the early 1900s and be able to apply them to code-breaking skills, must understand sequential language development, and must possess the imagination and ingenuity required to put such knowledge to work.

Northampton Symbols

In selecting any orthographic system of symbols to be used in teaching children, certain criteria are important. There must be: (1) ease of perception, (2) freedom from ambiguity insofar as possible, (3) some means of reducing any unavoidable ambiguity, and (4) a relation between the language the child is being taught and that which he/she sees in its frequently written form. This provides an immediate application to the environment. The Northampton Symbols, also known as Yale Chart Spellings (Yale 1946), meet such criteria. While other systems or modifications of the Yale Spellings might be useful, the Northampton Symbol System is the most complete. Whatever system is chosen should be used consistently to avoid creating uncertainties for the students. (Details of the Northampton Symbols are in Appendix A.)

Cursive Script

Another distinctive feature is the use of cursive writing from the beginning level and throughout

INFORMATION THEORY	**DUBARD ASSOCIATION METHOD®**
Terminology	***Component***
Unit of Selective Information (one unit at a time)	*Phonemes* Single phonemes initially; specific skills mastered with each.
Redundancy	Practice to master desired skills.
Structural Information	*Drop Drills* Syllabic units consisting of phonemes combined into sound-symbol units and into actual CV and/or VC words.
Redundancy	Practice to master desired skills.
Chunks of Information	Syllabic units become chunks of linguistic units after the child develops skill in code-breaking of multisyllabic words through the cross-drill activities. For example, in repetitive sentences, chunking of information occurs with concept development and structure: the "object" in the sentence is "old" information applied in a new way. The carrier portion of the sentence, "I see a/an/some _______" becomes a "chunked" unit. This is similar to the way a normally developing young child begins to use some of his/her language for expansion.
Redundancy	Practice to master desired skills.
Stochastic Process Process with built-in predictability; redundancy is provided.	1. Phoneme pages, primary spellings of Northampton Symbols: predictability is 100 percent. The child learns that a given page will have one written symbol and one sound. If this child succeeds with the first unit, success can be repeated with the other units. Ex. /p/ arranged appropriately on a page, /m/, /b/, /i/, /a/, etc., on subsequent pages of phonemes. 2. Drop Drills. These consist of phonemes in primary symbols arranged in syllabic units, using "old" information in a new way. Predictability is present; redundancy provides avenues for mastery of desired skills. The child experiences a 100 percent success level. Each page, with different combinations, provides additional practice and application of previously "learned" information. An appropriate picture on the following page is a reward and the child comes to expect/know/predict that a picture will be given after success with "reading/saying" the units.

INFORMATION THEORY (CONT.)

Terminology

Ergodicity
Predictability is present throughout a given process.

Sequential Dependencies

DUBARD ASSOCIATION METHOD® (CONT.)

Component

Ergodicity is present in the process by using numerous phoneme pages. Each page of the single sound-symbol page follows the same format of repetition with the same procedures being used with each page. Drop drills follow the same type of application. Cross drills: New information consists of secondary spellings of the Northampton Symbols placed in specific sections of the drill. The child becomes conditioned to the procedures with the two previous applications. He/she reads through the procedures correctly with little or no hesitation. Ergodicity exists because each line of the cross drill is composed in a similar manner of using primary spellings which have been taught previously and now are combined and applied with new information and secondary spellings. All of these linguistic arrangements may be found in the sample child's book in Appendix B.

Words: Phonetic arrangements of words in spoken English reflect specific arrangements in simple noun vocabulary and in units which become the syllabic units of multisyllabic words. In early level vocabulary, consonants and vowels are alternated. If there is a double consonant, only one has a phonetic value in the spoken form. Ex: *apple, hammer.*

Phrases and Sentences: Word order for phrases and/or sentences follow the "sentence patterns." Ex: N+V+N (NP). Use of a given word is controlled by the word immediately preceding it. Specific rules apply for meaningful, syntactical arrangements. Knowledge of dependencies in language and word classes is essential if one is to learn to use question-sentence response patterns in conversational language or in reading material. Ultimately, knowledge of word classes and their role in sentences is essential to construct sentences successfully.

Throughout the early stages, a significant amount of operant conditioning exists. That is, a cycle of stimulus, response, reward/reinforcement, stimulus, response, reinforcement occurs. Motivational factors become significant in the learning process as more learning occurs and reinforcements become intrinsic.

the entire program (McGinnis 1963). The rationale for using cursive writing is that it gives the child a way of knowing that the letters for which he/she learned speech production can be arranged to become a word representing a thing. Manuscript does not offer such a means of informing the child that certain parts form a whole. The child with a typically developing central nervous system adequately processes information so that this awareness exists. In children with language-learning disabilities, the processing often is not adequate to the task. Almost all of the professional literature related to children with learning difficulties indicates there are common reversals, inversions, and confusions regarding such written patterns as *b/d, d/g, m/w*, and *saw/was*, etc. While cursive script may not eliminate all difficulties, it helps reduce them. The fact that some schools for the deaf have employed cursive writing from the beginning of the instructional program indicates that the merits of cursive writing over manuscript have been recognized.

Heyman (1977) promoted cursive writing in this way:

> Mastering cursive writing has many benefits for special children. It permits the child to see each word as an integral unit, helps solve spatial problems for students who run all words together, and eliminates serious letter reversal…. He learns immediately that in cursive writing letters are not isolated, but are always connected to form words. (106)

Stasio (1976) reported these results from a study on severely and profoundly retarded children:

1. Children functioning at a severely and profoundly retarded level could use cursive letters more effectively than they could manuscript.
2. When using cursive letters, less errors were made in right-to-left direction than with printed letters.
3. There were less errors made in letter reversal among cursive letters than with printed ones. (55)

In relation to his own teaching experiences, Stasio also reported:

> I noticed in printing the letter A a child must use three different motions as well as relocate the starting point of the printed letter in order to complete it. In cursive writing the A can be formed in one continuous motion. This continuous motion is related to all cursive letters except

for the letters t and x, which require the child to remove his pencil from the paper twice. But this does not involve relocating any given point to complete the letter. When writing the printed alphabet, a child has to remove his pencil from the paper and relocate the starting points no less than 55 times. (55)

In a study conducted with children who were profoundly deaf, Martin (1987) found a significant difference in the children's recognition of cursive letters and words over the same in manuscript.

Serio (1968, 67–68) promoted the use of cursive for these reasons: (1) the rhythm involved in cursive writing lends itself to a more efficient use of movement, (2) proper spacing is aided in the writing of words, (3) a single method approach eliminates the problem of retraining, and (4) the forms of individual letters in cursive writing seem to be more independent of confusion due to directionality. Early (1973, 105) suggested that with the use of cursive writing "the child more readily experiences the total form or shape of a given word as he monitors the kinesthetic feedback from his writing movements." The benefits of cursive include elimination of picking up the pencil and replacing it after each letter, letter reversal reductions, elimination of word spacing problems and the advantage of the flow and rhythm of cursive writing when learning vocabulary (Deuel 1995).

When implementing the DuBard Association Method®, the letter formations of cursive script should be as simple as the teacher is able to produce. Simple, clear letter formation which restricts the use of unnecessary loops and carefully avoids fancy letters will reduce the possibility of confusion which might stem from known or undetected visual perceptual differences. Children are taught to read print. The time at which this is begun varies according to their needs and abilities. Concern that the children may encounter difficulty in learning to read manuscript later is unjustified. Many teachers using the procedures have reported that their pupils made transitions from reading cursive to manuscript without any difficulties. Prior to 1925, it was common practice to teach cursive writing exclusively in general education classrooms (Early, Nelson, Kleber, Tregoob, Huggman and Cass 1976). This did not hinder the development of reading manuscript.

In this age of technology, computers, Smartphones, and myriad other electronic devices, much is said about the diminishing need for the skill of handwriting, particularly cursive handwriting. However, our experience has been that the use of cursive writing with students as young as three and four, as well as older students, can be a boon to their learning. The motoric aspect of writing relates to the motor theory of speech perception and is an important component of the multisensory aspect of the DuBard Association Method®. While developing keyboarding and computer skills are worthy goals, the use of writing continues to be a valued component in this approach.

Color Differentiation

Use of color in the written language is another feature of the DuBard Association Method®. At each of the early levels of the instructional program, the role of color differs. At the phoneme level, color functions primarily to attract attention. Children like color, and color variation helps to focus their attention on a given task. In teaching phonemes, the teacher may use any number of colors. In the drop drills, a transition step, and at the word level, two colors are used and these differentiate the two sound units of previously learned information, but also show that they can be used together in a sequential and meaningful way. In essence, the written form of the syllabic unit that the hearing child uttered untold times as an infant is now presented to the child with language disorders for reading purposes. The colors may be chosen by the teacher or by the child, so long as only two are employed in the three units of the drop drill. Care should be taken to avoid the use of yellow markers, fluorescent colors, and any others which may be hard on the eyes. This procedure will be discussed more fully in chapter 6. At the DuBard School for Language Disorders, black and green are used consistently in the child's book, always with the first sound/symbol written in black. At the sentence/question levels and beyond, color is used to highlight the verb and, at times, a new concept.

Phonemes

Teaching phonemes in isolation is not contradictory to the way a child with typically developing language learns to talk. To assume that a child begins to learn to speak when he/she says his/her first word ignores the fact that an infant goes through a relatively long period of prelinguistic utterances related to developing communication. According to Eisenson (1972), the child with average hearing begins phoneme level vocalization as early as twenty weeks and continues it until about eighteen months. At that time he/she may have acquired from three to fifty words, some two-word phrases, a variety of vocalizations characterized by intonational patterns, and a great increase in understanding of language. While the child with a language disorder may have experienced the coo-

ing, babbling, lalling, echolalia, and jargon speech patterns of the typically developing child, the control and associative skills related to development of speech are inadequate for those early vocalizations to be of major value to him/her. Because of presumed dysfunction of the central nervous system, the child is unable to produce phonemes easily under controlled conditions.

McGinnis (1936, 1963), Hardy (1965), McReynolds (1966), Bender (1968), and Eisenson (1968, 1972) have all called attention to the fact that children with aphasia/language disorders can deal more effectively with phonemes in isolation than in the context of words. Many of their comments focused on discrimination tasks. Continued jargon patterns, syllable reversals, and a mixture of misplaced sounds within a word approximation leave little doubt that it may be appropriate for such children to work at the level of production, storage, and recall at which they can experience success, i.e., phonemes. The previously discussed aspect of recall related to the controlled motor act of speech also supports the value of working with phonemes in isolation.

Modification of Temporal Rate

McGinnis perceived that there was a need for modification in the rate at which words were pronounced, although it is highly unlikely that research on that aspect of the problem had been conducted at that time. Discussing lipreading, one of the steps in her teaching method, she stated that the teacher says the word "first in single elements and then blended. The child repeats it in spaced form without slurring or omitting sounds." This point may be confusing to a person who has never observed this method of teaching. "Spaced form" simply means that the components of a spoken word are separated by a momentary time lapse or silence. For example, instead of pronouncing the word *boat* in the usual manner, the teacher says *b-oa-t, boa-t,* with a slight prolongation of the vowel sound. The child repeats the pattern *b-oa-t* until he/she has learned to say the word in a spaced (segmented), then blended fashion without slurring, distorting, or omitting any of the components. The practice of allowing a time lapse between components of a spoken word is continued through more advanced levels of the instructional program until the child no longer needs it to succeed in the task. Even after a child no longer needs a special instructional program, there are times when the speaker needs to slow the speech pattern to help the child understand.

Because research conducted during recent decades points out that some of the children's difficulties stem from the rate at which processing information, language, and speech occurs (Montgomery 2002), it seems reasonable to expect that the habilitative/rehabilitative program should help the child learn to develop a more nearly normal rate of processing the oral communication. McGinnis' modification of temporal rate in the Association Method provides such a feature. Faculty of the American Speech-Language-Hearing Association Workshop on Central Auditory Processing Disorders (1992) made the same recommendations for more effective habilitation/rehabilitation. In addition, the research of Merzenich et al. (1996), Nagarajan et al. (1995), Tallal et al. (1995, 1996), Ellis Weismer (1996), Gillam (1997), Boudreau and Costanza-Smith (2011) indicates that temporally modified speech may be beneficial for children with language impairments for whom the normal rate of speech has been shown to be too rapid for effective processing.

Precise Articulation

Establishing clear, precise, and controlled production of phonemes is critical to success in speech. When the child masters such production, applies it to more complex tasks, and develops automaticity in its use, his/her speech will take on the qualities of articulatory patterns evident in the speech of those who learned it naturally. The symbols also apply to written English. Thus, as the child learns to speak, he/she also learns the code-breaking skills necessary for oral reading.

Approximations of phoneme productions are accepted as adequate as a child is learning speech naturally. Likewise, speech-language pathologists frequently accept approximations of speech productions in therapy. However, for children with severe speech/language disorders, specific learning disabilities/dyslexia, and for regular education students, teaching-learning is more effective and efficient when skills of precise articulation are required, established, and maintained at each level of instruction. Consequently, it is of vital importance that the professional also use precise articulation. Thus, the child will not be producing and practicing poor speech which will need to be corrected. The importance of establishing precise articulation is supported by the motor theory of speech perception.

Child's Book

Another unique feature of the DuBard Association Method® is the individualized development of the child's speech-language book. It expands systematically as the child progresses through each level of instruction. It serves as a record book for mate-

rial which has been taught at the same time that it provides a way for the child to become aware of his/her own progress. It is also crucial for use in home reinforcement activities. The teacher writes the material into the child's book until the child is well along into the instructional program and has developed good writing skills. With current technology and with the use of a carefully selected, simple and clear font, some aspects of the child's book may be developed appropriately via computer.

Instruction in Phonetic Rules Delayed

A final distinctive feature of the DuBard Association Method® is that instruction related to phonetic *rules* in written language is delayed until the upper levels of the language program.

MCGINNIS' SKILL DEVELOPMENT PROGRAM

McGinnis organized her skill development program into seven steps. (Also see Chapter 6.) These are applied at all levels of instruction and according to the child's needs and abilities. The application of those steps as implemented at the noun level is indicated below.

1. The teacher employs syllable drills (cross drills) to teach early level nouns.
2. The teacher writes the noun below the drill and associates it with a picture of the object it names.
3. The child copies the noun as he/she pronounces each sound. If he/she is unable to write whole words when the nouns are first presented, the teacher guides the child's hand while he/she writes and says the sounds of the letters in the word. The child then turns and pronounces the noun from memory while either holding or pointing to the card.
4. The teacher demonstrates lipreading of the noun. The child watches the teacher's lips as the word is pronounced first in single elements, then blended. The child repeats it in spaced form until he/she can pronounce the blended word without slurring or omitting sounds. He/she then matches the picture to the written form.
5. The teacher shows a picture to the child, and requires him/her to say the noun without the aid of lipreading or written form as a clue, then copies the word.
6. The child writes the noun without a model.
7. The acoustic step follows the six steps outlined above. The teacher pronounces the word in a well-modulated voice close to the child's ear. The instructor says it both in bro-

ken form and blended while pointing to each sound as the child looks at the word and listens. The child repeats the word, finds the proper picture, and matches it to the written form. He/she then turns and says the word from memory. All new nouns are taught in this manner, in the first level of instruction, associating visualization and sound. As the number of learned nouns accumulates, the child, if he/she has sufficient hearing, is expected to repeat the noun without aid of the written form.

The acoustic step is given regardless of the audiometric measure of hearing…. The acoustic step should be given regardless of apathy to listening. The acoustic approach in the seventh step differs from that used with the deaf. It is given last because the child, having learned to see and to say the words, will know what he is listening for. Acoustic work of nonsense syllables and sounds disassociated with meaning do not interest an aphasic child nor encourage listening. (McGinnis 1963, 96–97)

Listening—especially associating and attaching meaning to auditory events—is a major difficulty for the child with severe language disorders. It is appropriate that he/she be thoroughly familiar with the content of the task (words, and later expanded language patterns) before he/she is expected to listen effectively and, more especially, to make some kind of identification of a word or object on the basis of an auditory stimulus alone. Studies by Harris, Bastian, and Lieberman (1961) yielded findings supporting the rationale that differentiation in discrimination was due to the subjects' long experience and familiarity with language.

In developing the Association Method, McGinnis (1963, 60) made additional differences between teaching children who were language disordered and those who were deaf. The differences for those with language disorders were as follows:

1. There is no formal lipreading of what the child cannot say.
2. There are no voice-building exercises disassociated with the words.
3. Nouns are presented sound by sound in the initial stages.

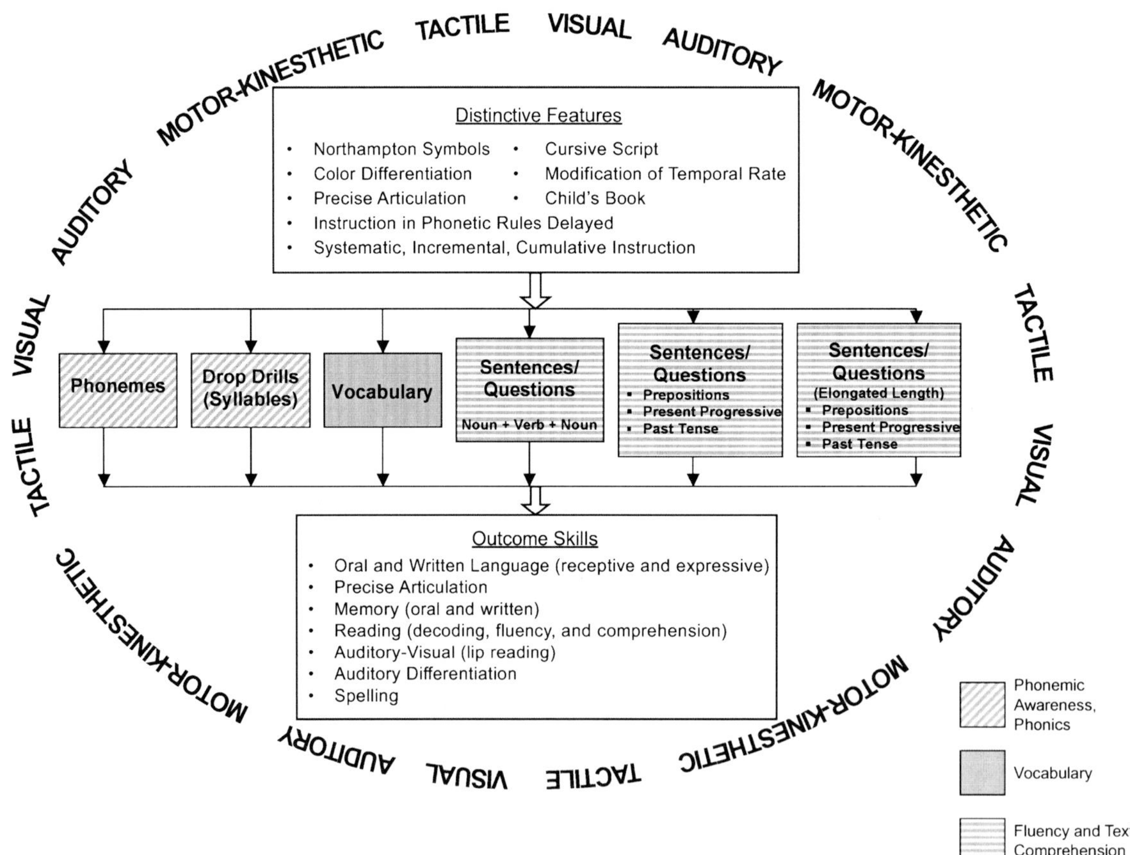

FIG. 5.6. Essential Elements of the DuBard Association Method®

4. The written form accompanies every sound that is taught.
5. The acoustic and lipreading steps are given after, not before, the child can say the nouns and associate them with the objects they symbolize.
6. After the child has learned sounds and nouns, he/she is expected to recall them without constant prompting by the teacher.

INTERVENTION: A MULTIFACETED PROCESS

Regardless of the types of language problems children demonstrate, a primary goal must be to help them communicate better and more meaningfully in their environments. Management, often through application of operant conditioning/behavior modification techniques by parents and teachers, is very important. Children learn early that they can control their environment with their behaviors whether positive or negative. Therefore, it is vital that any intervention program include parent participation and a plan for consistent management in both home and school settings.

The success of any intervention program will be determined in part by the appropriateness of the program for meeting the child's specific needs and for reducing and, if possible, eliminating specific weaknesses in his/her system for learning. However, the program alone is not the whole answer to the problem. It is important to keep in mind the other multiple factors which will have a strong influence on the child's progress. They include:

Intellectual Potential and Severity of the Problem. The degree of severity and of any reduced mental ability will have an influence on how much progress children will make, how long will be required for them to achieve specific goals, and how functional this learning will be. Even if there is a measure of cognitive limitations, this should not cause one to reduce one's efforts or to conclude that a given approach is or is not effective because of the child's slow progress. The professional's goal should be to help children develop their capabilities as far as they are able.

General Health. Children with allergies, seizure disorders, or other physical conditions, or who require some kind of medication have a more complicated situation. Their school attendance may be irregular. Even with regular attendance, their abilities to function for learning may not be up to their needs or to the teacher's expectations. The teacher-clinician must be able to determine the difference between listlessness and laziness as well as be able to identify defense mechanisms and conning

strategies of children. The professional may have to adjust the pace of instruction in the face of limited progress, but without giving up.

Since the 1990s, many children have been placed on medications related to Attention Deficit Hyperactivity Disorder (ADHD). Dosages often have to be adjusted to maintain proper balance in body chemistry and to maximize the effectiveness of the medication. The duration of their effectiveness often varies. Such factors can affect children's day-to-day functioning and general progress just as a lack of proper diagnosis and appropriate medical and behavioral intervention can.

Attendance. A child's attendance is important. Poor attendance, however, is not always caused by the child. Parents, too, are known to have problems. Therefore, the relationship between the professional responsible for the child's instruction and the parents becomes important. Parents need to understand the importance of regular attendance, provided the child is well. They may need guidance in child management for establishing good eating and sleeping patterns as part of good health and successful learning. Parents may not know how to help their child at home with school exercises. Sometimes they may need a "compassionate ear." A professional, too, needs to maintain a balance between objectivity and subjectivity in relation to the child, the parents, himself/herself, and colleagues.

Atmosphere for Learning. The way children cope with their disabilities depends largely on the manner in which significant people in their environments respond to them (DeHirsch 1967). Anxieties beget anxieties: the importance of acceptance, respect, and appreciation of one another cannot be overemphasized. This does not mean letting children rule, manipulate, con, and control at home or in school. It does mean, however, loving them enough to discipline them, establishing realistic limits for them which will enable them to become self-disciplined, and helping them achieve a level of maturity and independence appropriate for their chronological age despite whatever communication difficulties might exist.

There are times when adults know intuitively or instinctively the attitudes of others. Further, they somehow know or sense the sincerity or lack of it in those around them. Children, especially children with disabilities, are equally keen in this respect and are able to recognize the genuineness, or lack of it, of those around them. Actions of a smile, a touch, a measure of laughter at the right time for the right reason, a facial expression of approval or disapproval when needed, can go a long way in conveying to children the idea that "You and your needs are the only reason I am here."

When the atmosphere is too objective, when the teacher-clinician is less than honest or genuine, children are less likely to experience maximum benefit. They may develop negative patterns of behavior. Thus, all of those in the children's environment need to become behavior analysts. Some behavior is caused and, unfortunately, adults also can be part of the cause. The teacher-clinician and the parents need to set up controls compassionately, with love and appreciation for the children, yet positively, firmly and consistently. Cooperative efforts can pay large dividends on behalf of everyone. It also should be remembered that the child's sense of success will positively impact behavior. Therefore, it is *essential* that the professional and the parents keep in mind *that the intensity of intervention services must be matched to the severity of the child's problem.* The child's successes, however small they may seem, should be celebrated; intervention should be designed to minimize the child's frustration or failure. Small, repeated successes will develop into a long term pattern of achievement.

CHAPTER

6

Incremental Levels of the Instructional Program

BEHAVIOR-SHAPING TECHNIQUES

The importance of having children work with the teacher cannot be overemphasized. Children normally like to please the teacher. Patterns of adverse behavior which have developed as a result of permissiveness in the home, the child's frustration due to difficulty communicating or some innate tendency on the part of the child can be reshaped and corrected. Since socially acceptable behavior is the ultimate goal, it is recommended that, from the outset, a sad or happy face, a sticker, and social acceptance be used as reinforcement.

With the increased understanding of behavior and of attention deficit hyperactivity disorders, it is important to remember that, for some children, medical and/or psychological intervention is crucial to the development of appropriate behaviors. It also should be noted that some adverse behaviors are the result of medications for various bonafide physical conditions. Therefore, a careful analysis of a child's medical history and status is always necessary.

One purpose of this volume is to provide guidelines for organizing and implementing the multisensory DuBard Association Method® as a structured instructional program for children who need a more definitive, analytical, and controlled incremental teaching method. Another purpose is to give teachers some specific information to help with that task.

We do not wish to tell teachers what to say moment by moment; however, implementation requires a definite structure during early phases of the work. Especially useful at the beginning level, when there is a need for self-controlled behavior by the child, the structure can set the stage for a more effective teaching-learning situation later.

A chart with often-used instructions or commands can be helpful. What, to some, seems a measure of rigidity appears at this level. "Come, _____, stand on the line," "Read it," "Match it," "Turn around," "Sit down," are familiar phrases used during instruction. Teachers should demonstrate what they expect of children, and then require that they follow the commands. Consistent implementation will result in the procedures quickly becoming automatic for the children. A capacity for proper responses in the proper manner on the part of children is vital to their long-term success in the program.

ATTENTION-GETTING EXERCISES

One major problem of children whose language-learning problems are related to central nervous system dysfunction is short attention span. If a teacher cannot get and keep a child's attention long enough for the child to receive instruction, teaching will be difficult, if not impossible. Attention-getting devices, therefore, assume a vital role in the success of the overall teaching program.

Attention-getting exercises may be as simple as gross motor activities carried out as imitative behavior. The teacher's ingenuity in devising such activities is important. Any activity which gets the child's attention and helps the child learn to modify his/her own behavior can be useful. These activities should be based on the idea of developing a behavior-response pattern of conditioning in which the teacher does something, the child responds, and the teacher then approves or corrects the response. In essence, a simplified form of operant conditioning goes on. A teacher's stimulus is followed by a child's response, the teacher's approval or disapproval and correction, a new stimulus, the child's response, and so on.

PLANNING REMEDIATION

In addition, young children who have learned only a few phonemes and drop drills at the very beginning of the program can benefit from other constructive, developmentally appropriate activities interspersed with their DuBard Association Method® instruction. Before designing activities for improving children's skills in a given area, reviewing detailed information about their performances on subtests and levels of subtests is useful. Teachers can plan activities using colored cubes, beads of different colors and different shapes, beads of the same color but different shapes, and small cards showing geometric designs, objects, or creatively contrived symbols. The ingenuity of the teacher-clinician will determine the kinds of materials to use so as to apply a principle and work toward changing a child's performance level of any given skill. Ultimately, it is important to use letters, phonemes (sounds), and words that are directly related to academic tasks. As the child's volume of instruction and independent skills in the method increase, the need for other activities diminishes.

To improve understanding of relationships and categories as required in making associations, organizing objects or pictures into categories and implementing instruction to focus attention on the similarities and differences between and among items can be helpful. Association activities are also beneficial in building vocabulary as well as developing skills in making associations for children whose language deficiencies are related to environmental factors.

PROCEEDING TO INSTRUCTION

Skills and Procedures

The seven steps of McGinnis's Association Method are the actual skills to be taught and that the child is expected to learn. The skills and procedures for helping the child become competent in language permeate the entire linguistic content of the program. The skills the children are to learn to a level of automaticity are:

1. Recognition (reading) of the written, cursive form of each Northampton Symbol.
2. Production in precise articulation of the spoken form of the Northampton Symbols while looking at the written form. These two skills are a key aspect of children's learning to "break the code" and of establishing word attack skills for oral reading.
3. Associating the written form of the English language with the spoken form of the English language and/or an appropriate picture of an object, the object itself, or an action or placement, depending on the language being taught and used.
4. Copying correctly the written form of the language.
5. Establishing recall of both the spoken and written forms of the language.
6. Development of auditory-visual association, that is, they become able to associate the spoken form of the linguistic content with its written form. At the highest level of competence, the children will recognize and understand the linguistic content without any written form. This skill is comparable to the step which McGinnis identified as the lip-reading step.
7. Recognition of the linguistic unit from an auditory stimulus only.

The procedures followed during the instruction are simply the mechanics utilized to teach the skill. Children who are challenged with language learning differences need guidelines and structure regardless of the degree of severity of the problem. These provide the children with a measure of security by letting them know what they are to do and where and how they are to do it. As the children become older, learn more, have more success and achieve more easily, the amount of structure may be reduced unless it is required to work on specific skills. *Care should be taken to apply all seven steps at all levels of instruction.*

The procedures and structure also help the children learn social skills, such as taking turns, waiting until their turn, not interrupting when they are not the major participant in the instructional activity, and listening to others while waiting for their turn. They develop more socially acceptable behavior, in general, and are easier to live with and easier to teach. The children themselves take pride in their behaviors.

The following are specific instructions about how to teach the various levels of the Association

Method/DuBard Association Method®.

SINGLE PHONEMES—BEGINNING MCGINNIS' FIRST UNIT OF LANGUAGE

Purposes
1. To teach the child to watch the teacher's face.
2. To teach the child to imitate accurate articulation of the elements of speech (single phonemes) produced by the instructor.
3. To teach phonemes appropriate for the first vocabulary that is to be taught and thus build a foundation for teaching syllables and words.
4. To teach the child to recognize the cursive written patterns of single phonemes.
5. To teach the child to associate the spoken phonemes with their written patterns.
6. To help the child form a habit of coordinating speech and the reading of written symbols.
7. To teach the child to write the phonemes.
8. To strengthen the child's habits of attention and retention.
9. To teach the child to listen discriminatingly, especially to selective information.
10. To teach the child to lipread single phonemes.

Criteria for Selection
1. Utilization of cursive written form using *primary spellings only*, mixing consonants and vowels.
2. Knowledge of the age level at which the average child should have mastered the production.
3. Knowledge of the degree of ease in conveying information about the production of the specific sound to the child through a multisensory approach.
4. Age of the child.
5. Knowledge of the child's motor capabilities and/or limitations.
6. Appropriateness of a specific sound for application to more complex verbal tasks in the immediate future (syllables, words).

Role of Color
Color is attractive to children and will draw their attention. Any number of colors may be used initially, although we suggest avoiding yellow and fluorescent colors because they strain the eyes. In addition, it is best to use materials that do not bleed through the page.

The Child's Book: Phoneme Pages
Phonemes of a suitable size for the age of the child should be written to produce neat, uncluttered pages. They can be arranged in ways in order to attract children's attention. The sample pages reproduced in figure 6.1 may serve as a guide.

Saying the names of the colors as whole words gives the child a chance to learn whole words. Such an activity can become a part of diagnostic teaching to determine how much and at what linguistic level the child can learn through a less analytical manner. Any such learning, however, should not mislead the teacher or tempt him/her to abandon analytical work.

Reinforcement Activities: Phoneme Level
Materials: The child's book, phoneme cards, chalkboard and a pointer

Phoneme cards, four inches by six inches (or another desired size) can be used in a variety of ways, for example, as flash cards for a quick, oral recall activity. It is often helpful to have several sets available since not all children within a self-contained classroom setting will necessarily be working together at all times or at the same level. Color-coding the sets enhances organization and classroom management.

Activity 1: Reading the Child's Book
The child's book, made by the teacher, is cumulative. Children can read their books independently once they have learned the sounds well and do not need maximum monitoring. Reading is a good activity for children to do as soon as they arrive in the classroom while waiting for others to arrive. Repetitive reading is important in establishing the necessary overlearning. We have observed that being able to read their books, with or without a listener, is gratifying for children. Teachers can supervise as needed to insure accuracy, making sure that the book is read at an appropriate rate, with top-to-bottom and left-to-right orientation, and with good articulation. The child's book is also useful as a home reinforcement tool.

Activity 2: Phoneme Review
Figure 6.2 illustrates a practical arrangement for the instructional area but is not the only arrangement possible. The working space should not be crowded, but neither should it be so large that the desired structured environment cannot be

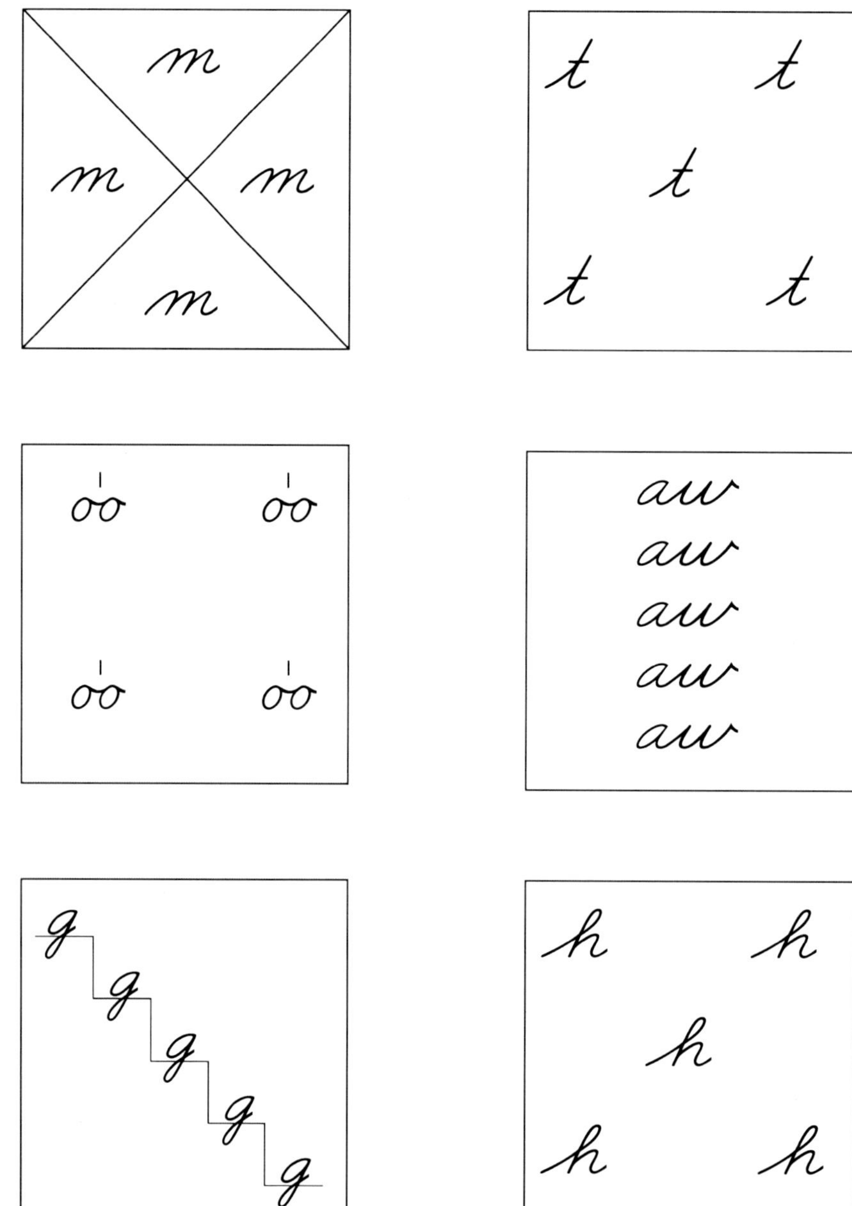

FIG. 6.1. Sample pages of the child's book at the phoneme level. Each phoneme page may employ as many different colors as the teacher wishes.

achieved.

The teacher writes selected phonemes, vowels, and consonants in a scattered fashion on the chalkboard. The number used will depend, in part, on the number of sounds children have been taught and that are in their books. In general, six should be the maximum number used at one time. As the children are taught more and more sounds, more than one phoneme review will be needed during a day's work in order to reinforce initial instruction and establish their competence with the desired skills. This activity may be done one-on-one or with a small group of children. The teacher-clinician's responsibility is to rotate instruction, reinforcement activities, and breaks in a manner that will keep children motivated and participating without overloading them. If the teacher-clinician feels bored, her expressions and manner will convey the boredom to the child who will learn to be bored and unmotivated. If the teacher is enthusiastic about the teaching and what is to be achieved, the child will be an interested participant and better and more learning will occur.

A. Linguistic Content: Selected phonemes are written on the chalkboard; phoneme cards may be used. Children like them because they provide something to manipulate.

B. Reading Step

Skills:
1. Recognizing the written symbol (reading skill)
2. Recall of speech production
3. Associating (matching) the written symbol on the card with the written symbol on the chalkboard, if phoneme cards are used
4. Saying the linguistic content from memory

Procedures:
1. Selected phonemes are written on the chalkboard as indicated above.
2. The teacher calls a child to a designated place where he/she can see the board well and other children can see his/her face easily.
3. *The teacher points to, but does not say, the phoneme.* The *child reads* using precise speech production. If cards are being used, the child matches the phoneme card to the written symbol on the board and repeats the sound.
4. Child turns around, says the speech sound from memory and sits down.

Each child has a turn reading/saying *each* phoneme, matching the card to the symbol on the board, and saying it from memory. As a concluding activity, the teacher may call on each child to read all of the phonemes again, at one standing, deleting the matching and memory skills.

The *Auditory-visual* step, which follows, should be used in close conjunction with the reading step, either immediately or later, as is appropriate. (McGinnis called this the lipreading step.)

C. Auditory-visual/Lipreading Step

Skills:
1. Recognition of the symbol from the teacher's spoken production
2. Association of spoken production with written symbol
3. Production of symbol from memory

Procedures:
1. The teacher says the phonemes selected from the board *in random order without pointing.*

2. The child is called to the board.
3. The child repeats the speech sound given as the stimulus.
4. The child points to the written symbol.
5. If the cards are being used, the child matches the phoneme card to the written symbol and repeats the sound.
6. The child turns around, says the speech sound from memory, and sits down. The teacher rotates children and sounds until each child has practiced the auditory-visual skill with each phoneme used in the activity.

The auditory/acoustic work can be implemented either immediately after reading and auditory-visual or later. The important thing to remember is that before the auditory tasks are undertaken, the child should be "saturated" with exposure, practice, and competence in the other skills of reading, saying, and writing from memory. However, if one is working with children as young as three years of age, it is not always possible to have the writing skills well-established before pursuing the auditory work. Since a major problem for many children is with the auditory processing, identifying, discriminating, and using of auditory stimuli for communicating, it is important to get the training under way as early as possible without waiting for the motor skills for writing to be acquired. The written skills can and will be achieved gradually, and they will strengthen the recall and memory skills for the linguistic content. In the meantime, auditory training needs attention. A minimal number of voiceless consonants should be included since they provide limited acoustic clues. Children will achieve accuracies in this setting by their awareness of the absence of sound.

D. Auditory training/Acoustic Step

Skills:
1. Learning to identify the auditory form without other clues. Implementing this work and establishing the skill is achieved by using additional clues at first and gradually removing them until only the acoustic signal remains.
2. Associate spoken form with written symbol.
3. Memory development.

Procedures:

Phase I.
1. The teacher, the source of the sound, stands or sits behind the child at a distance of

twelve to eighteen inches depending on the child's height and hearing function.

2. *The teacher says a speech sound while pointing to the symbols in a sequence on the chalkboard.* This lets the child, who is facing the board, know what the listening task is.

3. The child repeats each sound after the teacher's production.

Matching of cards to the board is optional in phase I or II.

Option: The teacher can complete this procedure with all of the sounds with the same child or rotate children and phonemes, always making certain that each child receives auditory work on each phoneme. The number of children in the group may determine the teacher's decision. If the children become excessively restless while waiting their turns, then rotating children is a good idea.

Phase II.

The clue of pointing to the written symbol is removed. Presenting the auditory stimuli, the speech sounds, in the same consecutive order as when the pointing was used gives the child a subtle clue, a measure of predictability.

1. *Teacher says each sound in order without pointing.*

2. The child repeats each sound after the teacher.

3. The child sits down, according to the teacher's instructions.

Phase III.

1. The teacher emphasizes to the child that he/she must listen carefully.

2. *The teacher says the phonemes in random order without pointing.*

3. The child repeats what he/she heard.

4. The child identifies the written form, matches the card to the written form on the chalk-

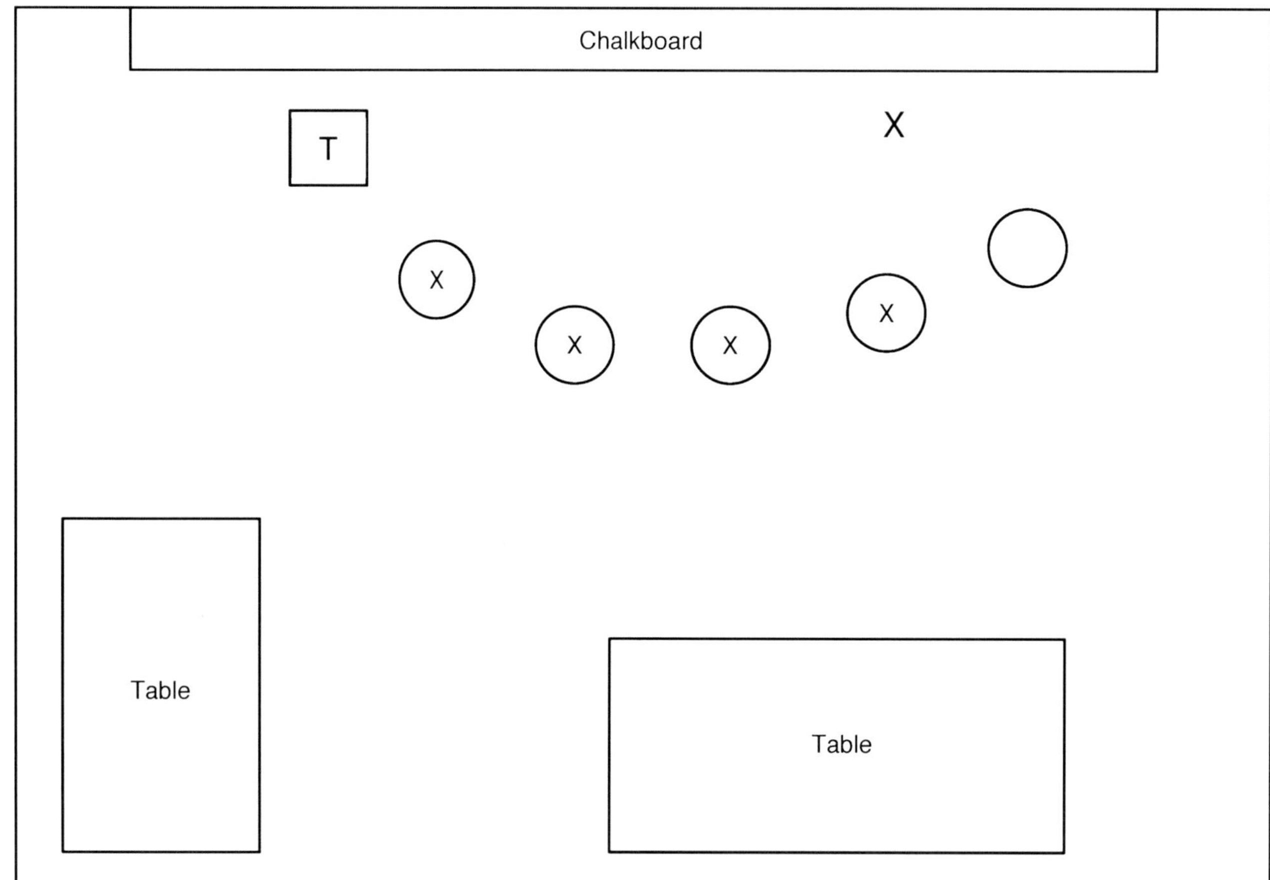

FIG. 6.2. Classroom arrangement
T = Teacher; x = Children; X = Child standing at the board

board, turns around, says it from memory and sits down.

Activity 3: Oral Recall

After arranging phoneme cards in a stack, the teacher (or a child in the role of the teacher) shows the face of one card. The teacher instructs the child on any incorrect recalls and *recycles the missed cards* so that the child has another chance to recall the sound. In the DuBard School for Language Disorders, the general goal is for the students ultimately to demonstrate *oral recall with a minimum of 90% accuracy and automaticity.* When less ability is demonstrated, a variety of other reinforcement activities indicated in this section may be used to reach the level of mastery desired.

Activity 4: Go Fishing

A variation of the "go fishing" game is useful. The child chooses one card from a group of six face-down cards; if the child can say the sound correctly, he/she keeps the card. If a classmate has to tell the child the sound, the classmate gets the card. A second variation of the game is to use two sets of phoneme cards. The children are dealt six cards and work at acquiring matching pairs. One child asks another child if he/she has *ee*, for example. If this child has it, he/she gives it to the first child. If not, child one "goes fishing" from the stack of cards in the middle of the table. This continues until the pairs have been made. This variation of the game, of course, can only be done with children whose speech and language skills will permit it.

Activity 5: Concentration Game

Pairs of phoneme cards are put out in random placements, face down. The number of pairs used will be determined by the number of children participating. Teachers should be careful that the number of tasks involved does not overtax children's abilities and lead to frustration instead of success. A child chooses two cards, turns them over, and says the sounds. If they are the same, the child keeps them. If not, they are turned face down and another child gets a turn. The game continues until all cards have been matched and removed. This activity serves as a memory task for positions of cards and as a recall of speech production using the written symbol as the visual stimulus.

Activity 6: Writing

McGinnis made few if any references to aspects of visual perception in children except for certain parts of her work. In her application of the Associa-

tion Method, she insisted on using *clear and simple cursive letter formations slanted slightly to the right.* Loops were to be deleted wherever doing so would add clarity and contrast. As an example, she used an open cursive 'p' rather than the usual cursive 'p' to avoid confusion with the cursive 'k.' In the event that the child's performance suggested possible visual perceptual differences, such as reversals, inversions, and rotations, the clear and simple cursive writing form reduced visual confusion as in b/d, p/g, n/u, m/w, etc.

The use of writing activities will vary according to the child's fine motor skills. If the skills are not developed sufficiently to require competence, they should be taught steadily and gradually with improvement as the goal. Using pencils of larger circumference, and/or using pencil grips, is sometimes helpful for young children. The size of letters also should be relatively large for the young child. As their skills improve, children can practice writing smaller letters. However, there is no reason for rushing to smaller writing. *Holding the pencil properly is a big help to a child and care should be taken to establish a correct pencil grip from the beginning.* Implementing writing activities on paper and on the chalkboard is valuable. Paper with bold black lines is beneficial. Spaces between the lines should vary according to the child's size of writing. Considerable hand-holding help with writing both on the board and on paper may be needed. *The child writes only in pencil/chalk of one color, not in two colors.*

Tracing: Some children benefit from tracing letters—on paper, with a pencil rather than on the sandpaper models sometimes used. Cursive letters of appropriate size, written in a color, are easy for the child to trace. Tracing letters which have been written on paper using a wide-tipped highlighter marker can be useful and enjoyable for the children. The colorful pages are inviting and the translucent aspect of the highlighter marker makes for a productive activity. *Teachers should be sure that children, when tracing the cursive writing, do not lift the pencil until the letter has been completed and that strokes are formed in the correct manner with the appropriate starting and stopping places noted.* Many children require help until they develop control of pencils/chalk and fingers.

Writing Practice: When independent writing skill has been acquired, writing practice *on the board and on paper* is a beneficial reinforcement activity. *Care should be taken to insure that the children say what they are writing.*

Copying: As writing skills improve and children need additional practice, lined paper with a sample of what they are to copy may be the only guidance they need. Copying from the board is a complex task. It requires distance focusing, memory of item to be copied, near focusing, recall of item to be written, fine motor skill for mechanics of writing item, distance focusing again with recognition of accurate place to begin again, and repetition of the remaining steps. A copying activity of reasonable length can provide a constructive break from oral work. *To increase their recall skills, children should say the sounds as they write the letters.*

Activity 7: Writing Phonemes from Dictation

As indicated by McGinnis (1963), *writing the letter and saying the sound simultaneously* supports and increases the recall of the linguistic content. Children can begin developing this skill during instruction at the phoneme level. Once they possess an adequate amount of control and skill, the teacher can dictate phonemes for them to write independently. Writing phonemes independently from dictation can also be combined with the auditory-visual and acoustic activities, already described. *In conducting dictation activities, the teacher says the item, the child repeats the item first and then writes it.* This insures that the child has correctly *perceived* the item prior to writing it. In the DuBard School for Language Disorders, the general goal is for the students ultimately to demonstrate *written recall /dictation with a minimum of 90% accuracy and automaticity. Thus, while all skills are important, the two skills oral recall and written recall with 90% accuracy and automaticity become the primary benchmarks for determining when to move on to new instruction.* When less ability is demonstrated, a variety of other reinforcement activities indicated in this section may be used to reach the level of mastery desired.

Delaying Writing Activities: When children have very poor motor skills because of age or poor motor development in general, participating in writing activities can be postponed and only oral work used. However, writing readiness activities of some kind should be devised and used to promote development of writing skills. Also, it should be remembered that writing and saying the material used simultaneously helps establish recall. Therefore, if writing is not used, care should be taken to use other structured activities to establish competence in recall/retrieval abilities.

DROP DRILLS

Apparently, McGinnis used the label "drop drill" for two reasons. First, the format in the child's book "drops" down the page in a left-to-right, top-to-bottom fashion. Second, *in the pure form of the Association Method,* the instruction of drop drills is deleted, or dropped, once the next stage of instruction, cross drills, is introduced. (Continuation of drop drills, or nonsense syllables, for students who have dyslexia will be addressed later.)

In selecting criteria for advancing from teaching phonemes to introducing drop drills, the teacher should give prime consideration to the composition of the drop drills. *Drop drills are syllabic units or syllables.* They constitute a transitional stage in which the goal is to apply previously taught sounds into larger units of speech. McGinnis (1963) suggested first-day, second-day, and third-day activities for teaching phonemes and beginning a child's book. Specific designations of what to do each day and how much should be accomplished in a given period of time do not take into consideration individual differences among teachers, among children, and among different types of instruction schedules. Variables may exist in all of these factors. The instructional program in which a child receives one, two, or three hours of individual instruction each week cannot be planned to achieve exactly the same goals and rate of learning as might be expected from a group of children in self-contained, half- or full-day programs. McGinnis (1963, 85) suggested, "When approximately three vowels and three consonants have been learned through the routine for teaching phonemes, a combination of consonant and vowel is presented." However, teaching of new phonemes would continue even after drop drills have been initiated.

The Child's Book: Drop Drills

A vowel-consonant or consonant-vowel combination constitutes a drop drill. Two colors are used to denote that there are two sounds. ***Only primary spellings*** *of Northampton Symbols of previously taught phonemes are used in a drop drill.* Figure 6.3 illustrates the arrangement of several drop-drill pages. The picture page which follows the drop-drill page should be one in which the sounds are the same as on the drop drill immediately preceding. Example: for a drop drill fo͞o, fo͞o, fo͞o, the appropriate picture would be food of an unidentifiable type such as a casserole. No word is written on the drop-drill picture page. When drop drills are taught to students who have specific learning disabilities/ dyslexia or to general education students whose *oral* language skills are intact, it is recommended that pictures not be used so that the total focus is on *decoding* the written syllable. Since these students are often inclined to "guess the word," the drop drill level of instruction is very valuable since it <u>requires</u> decoding and there is no word to guess. In fact, research indicates that continuation of decoding of nonsense syllables is very valuable for students with dyslexia.

The number of consonants and vowels taught prior to incorporating them into drop drills can vary from child to child. Three of each, four of each, or even five of each may be the specific number under various circumstances. For children with very severe oral motor speech disorders, or those with severe memory deficits, we recommend that approximately 15-20 phonemes be taught in isolation before applying them in drop drills. This gives the students more practice in mastering single units before requiring memory for two units. In planning for drop drills, a wise selection of phonemes can result in much more effective teaching and learning than that resulting from on-the-spot ideas and decisions. Although impromptu decisions can be useful, they should be the exception rather than the rule if one hopes to achieve consistent and continued progress.

Once drop drills are introduced, the teaching of new phonemes and the development of additional drop drills continues simultaneously. Our approach is to teach new content and apply it immediately—teach and apply.

New phonemes must be introduced until all phonemes have been taught. Drop drills should be continued until the next level—syllable drills/cross drills—is introduced, then they can be discontinued. However, teachers of students with specific learning disabilities/dyslexia or general education students often continue the drop drill beyond the level which McGinnis utilized it due to its value in decoding practice. Review and reinforcement of individual phonemes continues for as long as it is needed.

Purposes

1. To teach the child that phonemes may be organized into larger units, both in spoken and in written patterns, to form syllables.
2. To build a good foundation for teaching noun vocabulary words through the cross drill.
3. To improve memory and recall, using written forms of syllables.
4. To practice reading and writing syllables and

FIG. 6.3. The first phoneme is one color; the second is another (here underlining denotes change of color). The pages following could have a picture of a man's tie, a picture of a moon, a picture of a coke, a coat, or an ice cream cone, and a picture of a cat or a cap. The sequence of pages is a drop-drill page followed by a picture, another drop drill followed by a picture. New phoneme pages will be interspersed among drop-drill pages.

associating the spoken syllables with their written patterns.
5. To facilitate lipreading and auditory training. (Although McGinnis did not advocate this particular activity, we find it effective.)
6. To teach the child to read syllabic units from left to right. This also helps establish correct eye tracking movements, left to right for reading.

Criteria for Selection

1. Use previously taught primary spelling phonemes for composing the drop drill.
2. Use syllables the children can apply in early vocabulary learning.
3. Use sounds that can be taught and learned easily through visual, auditory, tactile, and motor-kinesthetic clues.
4. Use compositions in which the sounds can be associated with a picture placed on the next page. For children with intact oral communication skills, pictures are not used.
5. Use syllables that will be used later in teaching basic noun vocabulary of a more complex arrangement.

Role of Color

Only two colors are used in a drop drill. For example, black for the first sound and green for the second. The use of two colors focuses attention on the fact that two units of sound are used together. Color differentiation of the primary spellings written as a *connected* unit makes each unit with which the child is familiar stand out, but at the same time shows it to be part of a larger whole.

Reinforcement Activities: Drop-Drill Level

Materials: Drop drills written in two colors (indicating two sounds) on cards.

Linguistic Content: Syllabic units of a consonant-vowel or vowel-consonant arrangement. Any phonetic combinations which may, in fact, be real words should not be written as a whole word but should be written one time as they appeared on the drop-drill page, for example, to-e, not toe for a drop drill. Only primary spellings are utilized.

Skills, Procedures, and Reinforcement Activities: The same reinforcement activities to establish the same skills implemented through the same procedures given for phonemes may be used at the drop-drill level. However, it should be remembered that the drop-drill work is a transition stage from learning phonemes/single sounds to actually teaching noun vocabulary. Drop drills are not used indefinitely in the pure form of the method. Typically, as soon as phonemes and drop drills have been used and the respective skills have been established, the drop-drill work should be discontinued and the syllable drill/cross drill should be introduced and teaching of noun vocabulary should begin. However, continued use of drop drills for decoding/encoding practice may be beneficial for students with specific learning disabilities/dyslexia or for general education students.

McGinnis delayed having the children blend sounds until 50 words had been taught. In our experience, this is a good practice for children with severe oral communication problems. However, children who have established oral communication skills have a tendency to automatically blend syllabic units in the drop drills. If this occurs, the teacher should insure that the student reads the syllable in both broken/segmented (analytic) and blended (synthetic) forms to strengthen code-breaking skills.

CROSS DRILLS

The label cross drill is indicative of the technique's format. It progresses from left-to-right and uses a repetitive, or drill, format.

McGinnis recommended that about ten drop-drill combinations should be well-practiced before children begin cross drills. This means that they should be able to read the units orally, to repeat them from lipreading and from hearing them, and to write the syllabic units from the lipreading and acoustic stimuli. Some children may master these skills within the first ten combinations; others may take longer, depending on individual variables related to the children. As in establishing skills at the phoneme level, we recommend that children with very severe oral motor speech disorders, or those with severe memory deficits, master 15-20 drop drills before beginning cross drill instruction. One factor is certain: the better the child's foundation at the drop-drill level, the more easily success will be achieved at the syllable-/cross-drill level. The fact that children must be able to recall the written form of the phonemes before they proceed to the next step cannot be overemphasized. When a child or a group is allowed to advance while still demonstrating weaknesses in recalling the written form of the phonemes, usually additional time will be necessary to establish the skills related to recall of the written forms. This delay can be expected to slow the process of more complex learning for which the children may show a psychological readiness. The child's psychological readiness and a desire to give him or her a psychological boost should not take precedence over the child's actual abilities to achieve consistent success with the required skills.

The syllable drill/cross drill consists of a systematic arrangement of phonemes in order to accomplish the *primary goal of teaching a vocabulary word.* The secondary goals indicated below are also accomplished. One can observe the stochastic process and ergodicity of information theory in the cross-drill exercise. A high rate of redundancy exists in this drill also. In essence, the cross drill is an extension of the drop drill. The format of the drop drill is rearranged and secondary spellings are introduced to replace units of primary spellings of the drop drill. In the syllable drill/cross drill, *consonant sounds remain constant; vowel sounds are varied* on each line so as to become the nucleus for different words. See figure 6.4 for a sample of the simplest form of syllable/cross drill.

Purposes

1. To teach fifty or more basic vocabulary nouns. Nouns should be singular form or collective nouns. Example: cake, food, etc.

Many children need to use the cross drill until a hundred or more vocabulary words have been learned. Phonemes, drop drills, and cross drills for fifty nouns constitute the first unit of language.

2. To introduce secondary spellings (from the Northampton Symbols) of both consonants and vowels.
3. To prepare children to read orally, to write the nouns presented to them, and to associate the symbols with the objects they represent.
4. To teach the child that sounds are organized into words (symbols) which represent things.
5. To help children to increase their ability to retain and recall sequences of sounds and letters as related to oral and written language.

Criteria for Introducing Cross Drills

1. Cross drills should not be begun until children have acquired reasonably good writing skills, that is, copying skill which produces a reasonable facsimile. Exceptions, however, can be made on the basis of individual differences and circumstances.
2. Cross drills must not be introduced until children have mastered drop drills for reading and writing. An exception to this would be, for example, in the case of a child whose development of writing skills is delayed because of significant fine motor problems, but who is ready to progress in reading and speech. This type of situation would be the exception.
3. Content of the drill will be determined by the vocabulary to be taught by means of the drill; one drill may contain phoneme content and arrangements which make it applicable to several appropriate words.
4. The vowel and consonant sounds children will use in both immediate noun vocabulary and more advanced-level noun vocabulary should be considered.
5. Drills should be composed of vowels and consonants for which children have already established as good a speech production as is possible.
6. Drills should include vowels which children need to practice for better speech production.

Role of Color

Colors are used in the cross drill to indicate visually the number of sounds in the sequence which children are to learn. Only two colors are used; colors are alternated on the basis of the number of phonemes or sounds in the word, not necessarily on the basis of consonant/vowel arrangement. At the early levels, color alternating seems to be on the basis of consonant-vowel because of the specific words chosen. However, two colors are alternated on the basis of the number of sounds or phonemes in the word (see figures 6.4–6.8). For example, in the words *cow*, *bee*, and *tie*, the first sound should be indicated by one color, the second (underlined in our illustrations) by another color. In words of more phonemes, the pattern of color alternation should be as follows: *boat*, *top*, *chair*, and *milk*, and finally, an arrangement of probably maximum length in vocabulary instruction: *basket. Some children do not require the color alternation beyond the CVC level; others may.*

FIG. 6.4. Cross drill for a CV word—*bow*; *bee* and *boy* may also come from the drill. Lines of the drill go in the child's book without the word at the end. An appropriate picture is placed on the next page with the word, *bow*, written in two colors. Other pictures may be placed on the page after the words are taught. Underlining here indicates the use of another color. Numbers over letters differentiate between graphemes that are written the same but pronounced differently.

Cross-Drill Instruction for Teaching Noun Vocabulary

Linguistic Content: Primary and secondary spellings of Northampton Symbols written in two alternating colors.

Skills:
1. Oral code-breaking: word attack skill for oral reading.
2. Learning secondary spellings of Northampton Symbols.
3. Memory for sequences of sounds comprising the noun vocabulary word being taught.
4. Practice on speech sounds needing additional work but not necessarily part of the noun vocabulary word being taught.

Procedures:
1. The first two sounds of the word to be taught are written in a horizontal line on the chalkboard but in three distinct columns. *Consonant sounds remain constant. Vowel sounds vary from line to line in the drill. Primary symbols are used in the first column. Secondary symbols are written in the second and third columns. If there are no secondary symbols, primary symbols are repeated.*
2. With the horizontal line completed as indicated above, the teacher calls on one child to come to the chalkboard. The child reads the line, turns around, says it from memory, and sits down. Each child takes a turn at reading the line and saying it from memory.
3. After each child has followed the above procedure, the teacher puts up the next line and the same procedure is repeated.

Figures 6.5, 6.6, and 6.7 illustrate stages of and a completed cross drill. Other factors related to cross-drill instruction are discussed below. *Reinforcement activities are not used with the instructional drill.* Since the primary purpose of the drill is to teach noun vocabulary, that noun vocabulary is the content which is used in reinforcement activities.

The cross drill is presented at the chalkboard, one line at a time. Each unit is composed of the same phonemes (sounds), regardless of written letter forms, to give the stochastic process. Children with proper preparation at the phoneme and drop-drill stages quickly get the message: what is said/read in the first column is repeated in the other columns. Thus, the child gets three exposures to a particular arrangement that is to be expanded gradually into more than two sounds for longer words. Ergodicity may be observed because each line of the cross drill follows the same format. In other words, the predictability is repeated on each line with a high level of redundancy. Figure 6.4 gives the format of the cross drill as it should be

developed for a CV (consonant-vowel) word. How much space to leave between the lines is determined by the age of the child and by the presence of any visual perceptual problems. Figures 6.5, 6.6 and 6.7 illustrate consecutive stages for a CVC noun.

In teaching a noun containing a diphthong (i.e., *i-e*, or *a-e*), the final sound is "added at the end of the syllable rather than on the blank where they belong for proper spelling" (McGinnis 1963, 92). This is to establish in precise articulation the proper sequence of sounds for a spoken word until the child has acquired a measure of competence in memory for the spoken sequence. After the completed word has been taught at the board, the word is written correctly under the drill. Later the word is written in correct spelling under the picture in the child's book, alternating color in relation to the number of sounds. Figure 6.8 illustrates the last stage of the drill for such words.

Selecting Nouns to Teach

McGinnis (1963) suggested that "only a few words consisting of a consonant-vowel, such as *bow*, *bee*, *shoe*, should be taught. Nouns consisting of consonant-vowel and consonant, such as *boat*, *bike*, *meat*, and *fish*, seem to offer a more interesting challenge to a child." For children attending the DuBard School for Language Disorders, a specific list of CV, CVC, selected CVCC words, as well as words with other phonetic arrangements, was developed. McGinnis's thesis (1939) indicated that she chose nouns to teach in a random manner. The vocabulary list for initial instruction was *organized* by the late Dr. Etoile DuBard to consist of CV, VC, and then CVC words in order to utilize the *incremental increase for building memory for sequencing.* Vocabulary of more complex composition was taught as the child progressed. This list also helped us to accomplish other goals, which were to build a repertoire of picture cards needed for the program and to aid persons who might be less imaginative than others. The list is included in Appendix C. This vocabulary is applied and expanded through stories and experiences.

For general purposes, the nouns taught should provide a gradual increase in number of sequences the child will have to remember, should constitute a core of vocabulary that can be used easily in the next level of work, should be applicable to the child's needs and interests, and should be depicted in clear, lifelike, colorful pictures. Magazines and many reading readiness books as well as packaged programs offer a wide selection of pictures, in addi-

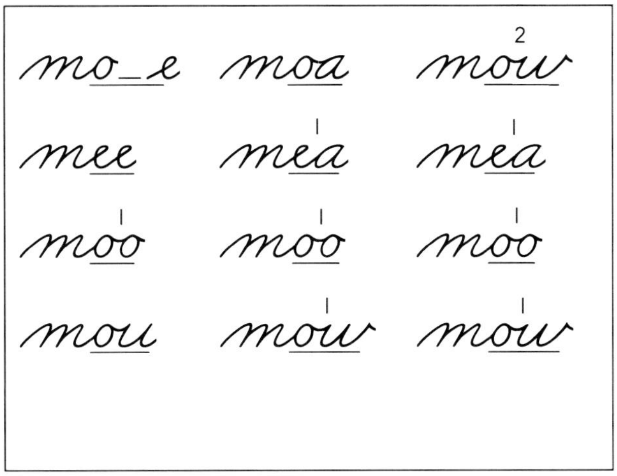

FIG. 6.5. First stage of a cross drill for CVC word. Each line is presented separately/consecutively. The child reads each line after it is written, turns around, and repeats the line from memory. Underlining indicates another color.

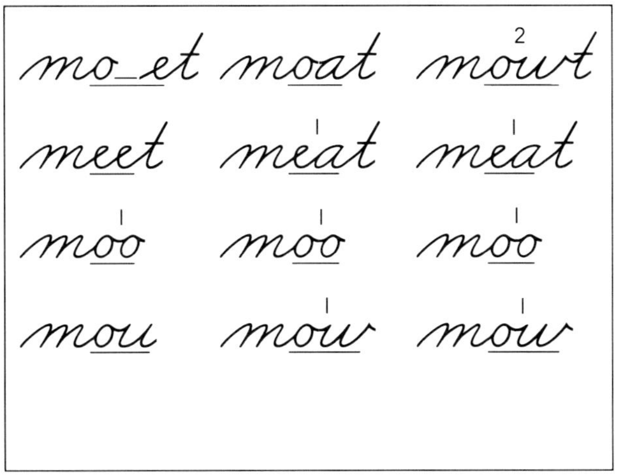

FIG. 6.6. The final sound is added to the lines in figure 6.5. Children take turns reading the line and saying it from memory as in previous drills. Construction of the drill continues until all lines contain all the sounds needed for the new word or words. The lines not appropriate for a word per se simply offer children additional practice in code-breaking, reading, increasing their memories for sequences, and producing precise speech.

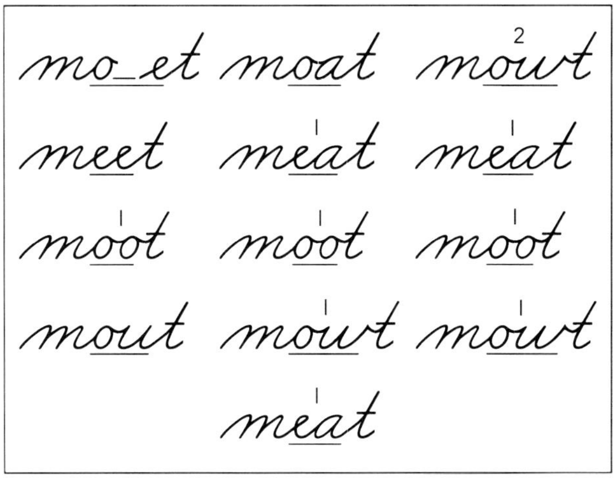

FIG. 6.7. After all lines contain all sounds of the new word being taught and each child has read them and said them from memory, the new word is written under the drill and a picture of the item is shown to the children so that they may associate the spoken and written forms with the thing itself.

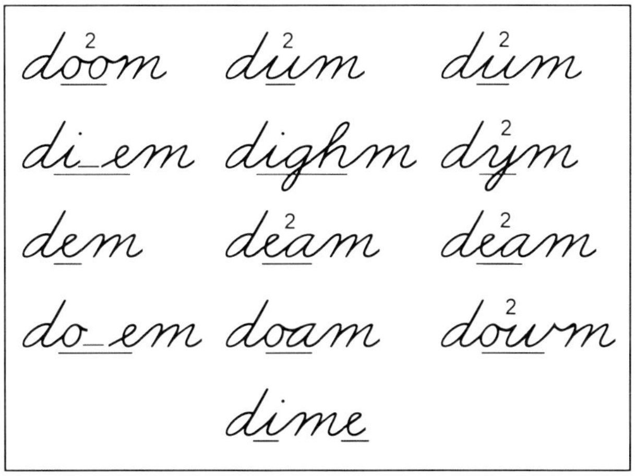

FIG. 6.8. Final stage of split pattern diphthong. All lines of the drill have been completed for a word with a "split" pattern diphthong for instruction at the chalkboard. Sequence of sounds for the spoken word is established without regard for spelling. The word is written correctly at the bottom of the drill with color differentiation indicating the diphthong symbol. Throughout cross-drill instruction, only the first two sounds are written in the child's book.

tion to endless resources available on the internet. In addition, specific materials for DuBard Association Method® instruction have been developed and are available commercially. See Appendix F.

Completing the instruction and establishing the designated skills related to most of the phonemes utilized in the English language and a vocabulary of fifty nouns constitute McGinnis's **first unit of language**. Additional vocabulary at this level may consist of basic colors and numbers to five.

Blending

McGinnis believed that children should not be blending syllables until they knew the individual sounds perfectly.

> Blending should be delayed until the sounds can be blended into a word without loss of their value. The position of each sound should be held until the position for the succeeding one is taken. There should be a timing of the voice so that it stops before the next position is taken. Care at this time will help the child to monitor his speech and produce a better voice than would be the case if smoothing were forced before kinaesthetics and memory of sequences were firmly established…. When approximately fifty nouns have been learned, the children have an easier memory for sequence and can smooth the nouns while maintaining good articulation and voice. (McGinnis 1963, 91)

We have found that for some children different guidelines for beginning blending can be followed without jeopardizing the child's progress and without losing the value of any phonetic unit in the word. However, it is vital to require automatic, precise articulation when the child is shown the written symbol. Adhering to that requirement becomes especially important if blending is initiated before the fifty nouns are known.

McGinnis did not utilize any specific criteria or guidelines in selecting nouns to teach. "Bead" and "bell" might have been taught the same day as "flower" or "radio." The child would have encountered from three to five sounds in sequence and blending would have been extremely difficult if not unsuccessful. The child would have had little or no security, elemental predictability, or opportunity to process and learn through "chunking." The DuBard Association Method®, however, establishes a systematic expansion with a controlled number of increments. Vocabulary for early instruction was organized by Etoile DuBard according to the number of sequential sounds in a given word. This permits those children who are able to blend two-sound and three-sound words before fifty have been taught or learned.

The idea is simple and logical. The abilities of most children and their performances in developing memory for sequences support this. The rationale is this: if the child learns single phonemes, then learns to put the two together, segmented and later blended, much as an average child does in developing speech normally, and if the number of increments is controlled at the CV/CVC level until skills in memory for sequences are well established for that phonetic structure, it will be easier

for the child to learn to say monosyllabic words of three and four sounds, such as *ch-a-ir* or *h-a-n-d*. Further, it has been observed that with skills firmly established at that level, the child can master the speech and spelling for multisyllabic and polysyllabic words more easily.

The idea has proven sound and effective because of the nature of word construction in the English language. Dictionaries reflect that there are few words in which a syllable contains more than three or four sounds. Therefore, if the child masters the blended speech and spelling for a specific amount of CV and CVC vocabulary and establishes comprehension for the words, much of the expansion of vocabulary and functional level for memory for sequences will be enhanced and "chunking" can then be applied to sentences as well as to words. It is imperative to remember that if blending is initiated before the fifty-noun level, it is vital that emphasis be put on the speech of the final sound until the child overlearns it and maintains it in his/her use of the word. If this emphasis is not made, the child can and will quickly begin to drop phonemes from the spoken pattern and there will be a loss of phonetic values in words. In such instances, a child might very well say something like: "de do- ha- a pa- a foo- a-su waer" for "The dog has a pan of food and some water."

While speech-language pathologists are familiar with such a pattern and would identify it as omission of sound, the primary problem is more than just omission. The major problem is likely to be poor memory for sequences. The techniques and instruction used in general in the DuBard Association Method® have proven to be very effective with such children in articulation therapy.

Learning to blend sounds into words and "chunking" words into phrases and sentences does not come easily for all children. A child's oral communication can be choppy, nonrhythmical, artificial sounding, and perhaps unpleasant for the listener. Qualitative blending of words and chunking of longer linguistic units requires that the teacher/clinician address the task specifically, systematically, and consistently until the desired quality of phonetic content and the rhythm and flow of connected spoken language has been achieved. When children possess the maximum amount of automaticity they need, their communication will flow in the same way as that of the rest of the world.

The Child's Book: Cross Drills

Typically, cross drill instruction takes place at the chalkboard. While the child practices copying the cross drill from the board, the teacher should write it in the child's book. The book provides a record of what drills have been constructed. Children can use their books for practice and review work while their mothers or fathers monitor their reading. This process helps to include parents and other family members in the educational program. The teacher should explain to the parents the goals and directions of the program. Children are proud of their new-found abilities, and the books are concrete evidence of what they are learning. Reading them gives the children a sense of success and pride. Simple as it seems, this factor is important in developing motivation from within the individual; unless children are motivated internally, their success will be limited.

The cross drill written in the child's book should not include the completed word; only the drill lines are placed in the book. The word itself is written under the appropriate picture placed on the following page. Two alternating colors are used in the word. From this point on, the child is responsible for being able to read the word. Reinforcement activities are then used to establish competence related to the skills of associating, matching, copying, lipreading, and recalling of spoken and written forms of the word with only a picture as a stimulus. An ultimate goal is that the child be able to identify the word from an acoustic stimulus alone. Such variables as hearing acuity, quality of discrimination skills, depth of instruction, and maintenance of skills will influence the child's achievement in this aspect of functioning. The child is not required to memorize the cross drill, only the word.

Once the child's book contains a wide range of cross drills **using virtually all of the phonemes,** *writing drills in the book may be discontinued.* At this stage, instruction is conducted at the board as usual. Only the picture with the corresponding word written underneath are placed in the child's book. A page may have pictures of nouns with several different beginning phonemes. This is referred to as the *noun page format.* Alternating colors may be continued if needed.

Reinforcement Activities: Noun Level

After several nouns have been taught, activities for developing skills (see pages 67-72) can be introduced. A sufficient number of nouns usually means a minimum of three; five or six give more variety. Exactly when to begin other activities is determined by the teacher.

Materials: The child's book, picture and/or word cards (four-by-six index cards work well), chalk-board, and a pointer. Picture cards consist of the noun picture under which the number of sounds in the word are represented by single horizontal lines. With children who are unable to recall the names of items, the use of picture cards is essential. For children whose primary difficulty is in code-breaking the written form, picture cards can be deleted early on and word cards are used. The words are written on four-by-six index cards, using two alternating colors to indicate the number of sounds in the word.

Activity 1: Reading the Child's Book

With supervision as needed to insure accuracy, children read their individual books. The observers will check to see that children read at an appropriate rate, with top-to-bottom and left-to-right orientation, and with good articulation.

Activity 2: Noun Review/Vocabulary Review

A. Linguistic Content: Noun words previously taught through a cross drill are written on the chalkboard in one or two colors depending on the child's needs.

B. Reading Step

   Skills:
   1. Reading the word orally.
   2. Speech work requires precise articulation. Otherwise children can be practicing poor articulation/poor speech and thereby overlearn a speech pattern of poorer quality than desired.
   3. Associating/matching the picture with the word.
   4. Memory for sequences.

Procedures:

   1. Four to six nouns are written on the chalkboard in alternating colors in a column at an eye level appropriate for the children. The corresponding picture cards are placed on the chalk tray underneath the written words.
   2. The teacher calls a child to a designated place where he/she can see the board well and other children can see this child's face easily.
   3. *The teacher points to a noun written on the board, the child gives the precise speech production ". . . in a 'spaced' or 'broken' manner"* (McGinnis 1963), matches the noun card to the written symbol on the board, and says the word again.

4. The child then turns around and says the word from memory and sits down.

Each child takes a turn going through the complete procedure. To conclude, the teacher may call on each child to read all of the words again, at one standing, deleting the matching and memory skills.

Later the teacher should use activities related to the skills of lipreading, recall of speech for the word with the picture stimulus only, recall of the written form, and finally the acoustic step. Blending of sounds is not stressed at this point because of the tendency for children to drop out the final sounds of words, transpose sounds within a word, and/or produce the sounds with poorer articulation.

C. Auditory-visual/Lipreading Step

Skills:
1. Recognition of the symbol from the teacher's spoken production
2. Association of spoken production with written symbol
3. Production of symbol from memory

Procedures:
1. *The teacher says the desired noun selected randomly, without pointing to the written symbol.*
2. The child is called to the board.
3. The child repeats the word given as the stimulus.
4. The child points to the written symbol.
5. The child matches the picture (or word) card to the written symbol and repeats the word.
6. The child turns around, says the word from memory, and sits down. Each child gets a turn as the teacher rotates children and words until each child has had the auditory-visual skill applied to each word used in the activity. As mentioned with phoneme work and for the same reasons (see pages 69-71), the auditory/acoustic work can be carried out either immediately or later.

D. Auditory training/Acoustic Step

Skills:
1. Learning to identify the auditory form without other clues. Implementing this work and establishing the skill is achieved by using additional clues at first and gradually removing them until only the acoustic signal remains.

2. Associate spoken form with written symbol.
3. Memory development.

Procedures:

Phase I.
1. The child stands with his/her back to the teacher (the source of the sound) and about twelve to eighteen inches from the teacher, depending on the hearing function of the child.
2. *The teacher says a noun while pointing to the symbols in sequence on the chalkboard.* This lets a child know what the listening task is.
3. The child repeats the word. *The teacher can complete this procedure with all of the words with the same child or can rotate children and words, always making certain that each child receives auditory work on each word.*

Phase II.
The clue of pointing to the written symbol is removed. Presenting the auditory stimulus, the word, in the same consecutive order as when the pointing was used gives the child a subtle clue, a measure of predictability.
1. *The teacher says the word without pointing; the speech stimulus is given in consecutive order as when pointing was used.*
2. The child repeats what was heard.
3. The child sits down, according to the teacher's instructions. Matching and memory tasks are optional, according to needs and/or desires.

Phase III.
1. The teacher indicates to the child that he/she must listen carefully.
2. *The teacher says a word using random selection and without pointing.*
3. The child repeats what he/she hears.
4. The child identifies the written form, matches the card to the written form on the chalkboard, turns around, says it from memory and sits down.

Activity 3: Oral recall
Using noun cards, follow the same procedure described for use of phoneme cards on page 71. *At the DuBard School for Language Disorders, the current practice is to use both noun picture cards and noun word cards. The goal is for the child to achieve 90% mastery of oral recall (and written recall) with automaticity.*

Activity 4: Writing

Skills:
1. Copying the word.
2. Recall of the written form with only a picture stimulus.
3. Recall of the written form from the spoken stimulus (dictation).

Tracing: Some children, whose independent writing skills have not yet emerged due to a young age or severe fine motor skill deficits, benefit from tracing words—on paper with a pencil. Cursive words of appropriate size, written in a color are easy for the child to trace. Tracing letters which have been written on paper by the teacher using a wide-tipped highlighter marker can be useful and enjoyable for the children. *Care should be taken to ensure that the child starts and stops the letter formation in the correct places and follows the correct sequence when tracing the letters.*

Writing Practice/Copying: As writing skills improve and children need additional practice, they can be given lined paper with a sample of what they are to copy. Such an activity of reasonable length serves as a constructive break from oral work. *Children should say each sound in the word as they write it.* This increases the recall skill. It should be remembered that copying from the board is a more complex task than writing practice from a teacher's model written on the paper. In <u>all</u> writing activities, *both saying* and *writing* the item is a crucial element of the multisensory program.

Written Recall:

Procedure:
1. The child is shown a noun vocabulary picture.
2. The child says the word, in broken and/or blended form, depending on abilities, needs, and/or teacher's desires.
3. The child then writes the word.

This activity can be carried out at the chalkboard with each child taking a turn or as a group with each child being shown and given a different picture until each child has had the desired number of words. In another activity, children are given a selected number of nouns which they then say aloud and write.

At a later level of instruction, when *written recall* is done for a *story and questions*, the procedure is:

(1) Show the child the picture and ask for the story to be written on the board or paper. (2) If accuracy on the story is at a 90% level, instruct the child to write the questions about the story. If accuracy is less than a 90% level, this indicates the need for additional reinforcement activities on the story. (3) If the child completes written recall of the story at a 90% level and completes the questions at an equivalent level, new instruction may be appropriate. If written recall of the questions is less than 90%, reinforcement activities are needed.

Dictation:
Writing the word and saying each sound simultaneously supports and increases the recall of the linguistic content. The teacher says the words in broken (segmented) and/or blended forms as appropriate for the children. The children repeat the item, precisely as the teacher said it, and then write it.

Other Activities
Two other activities that work well with noun cards are the games of "Go Fishing" and "Concentration," already described in this chapter in the section on phonemes.

Children must achieve multiple successes before the teacher can be certain they have become competent. The fact that children demonstrate competence one day does not necessarily mean they will be able to repeat their performances the next day. For this reason, a high rate of redundancy is essential in reinforcement activities. In essence, because children with language disorders have severe limitations in the storage and recall aspects of their processing, a state of *overlearning* is necessary.

A teacher needs to be only slightly imaginative to devise ways for children to demonstrate their newfound abilities in written form. The one limitation in the early work is that only nouns are available. Nevertheless, activities requiring children to recall the written form from lipreading or acoustic work will not only add variety to their participation but also offer them additional opportunities to use more than one skill at a time. Using picture cards as stimuli, children can write the learned vocabulary of nouns at their seats.

With the teacher's careful supervision, children occasionally may take on the teacher role for oral recall or dictation of nouns. An advantage is that the child assuming the teacher role must pay close attention to whether or not his classmates respond correctly. Also, when children assume the teacher role for dictation of nouns, it requires that they use their best articulation so that the other children will be able to understand the word to be written. The author recalls occasionally allowing children to be the teacher and dictate words or other material to her. When writing what the student said, including a misarticulation, the student might protest that the wrong word was written. For example, the word was *match* and the child dictated *m-a-sh, mash*. The teacher wrote what the child said, *mash*, which was a reminder to the child that a misarticulation occurred. The item was repeated and corrected. Some humor and practice on the correct speech resulted. Children enjoy playing the role of teacher, and the activity often gives insight into how the children see the teacher. They should not, however, be placed in the teacher's role for the acoustic step.

Criteria for Progressing to Sentence Level

McGinnis (1963, 98) wrote that "when approximately fifty nouns have been learned, the children have an easier memory for sequence and can smooth the nouns while maintaining good articulation and voice. The first unit is completed and the children are ready for the beginning of simple language forms and questions." Requiring the mastery of fifty nouns affords two marked advantages for introducing sentences. First, the variety of nouns and their respective determiners/articles (*a, an,* and *some,* which are to be introduced) will be substantial. Second, a vocabulary of fifty nouns allows a greater variety of material to be used with all of the basic sentence levels.

It must always be remembered that children with severe language learning disorders need to experience more success than failure in their efforts to learn. The teacher and supervisor are responsible for avoiding unnecessary difficulties which might arise from going on tangents which disregard the basic principles of the association procedures. Children will benefit more in the long run by having a high quality of code-breaking skills as related to the unblended speech form and blended speech for the fifty nouns than from having a hodgepodge of skills with words and simple sentences. Sentences are followed by questions and children can be overwhelmed easily by their learning tasks if too much is undertaken too quickly and without a lot of security.

Helping children to generalize any given noun, from the picture in their books or from pictures used during instruction, to various kinds of such items, either pictured or actual, is the teacher's responsibility. Promoting such generalizations can

be carried out in less structured settings than the instructional one. The teacher is the key person in this regard and the ability to obtain cooperation from family members to promote application of instructions is vital to obtaining carryover into daily life situations.

Maintenance: Skills and Linguistic Content

As the children learn more and more vocabulary and concepts, establish skills with the linguistic content of particular levels of instruction, and develop more efforts to communicate through the use of incidental language in the school and home environments, it is very easy for a number of things to occur which can be detrimental to their overall progress.

1. When children's communication and language expand rapidly, it is easy for a teacher-clinician to forget that it is vital that the temporal rate of instruction and general communication be kept at a slower rate than normally used. In part, it is through the reduced rate that the child begins to hear/process better and pick up language more easily. The slower temporal rate improves the auditory processing of language. A secondary benefit of using a slower rate of speech is that it provides the child with an enhanced articulatory model.

2. Because of this improved use of hearing the teacher-clinician may neglect consistent auditory training and the acoustic step of the program of skills. *However, no matter how much children's hearing seems to improve, they need the acoustic step of training.*

3. As more and more language is learned, it is easy for the program of instruction to move so rapidly that the teacher-clinician forgets that there is a need to *check, recheck, and recycle vocabulary and language taught in the early part of the program.* Even the child who learns as typically expected has a need to maintain certain skills and retain specific information on a long-term basis. Children with major communication disorders have even greater deficits in long-term memory than the typical child. Therefore, it is imperative that teachers incorporate considerable *maintenance work* into the daily program to establish more retention skills for what has been taught and is being taught. The more children learn, the more they can learn, but there is a need to help them in retaining as much as possible for recall. It

is at this point that the coordinating of the long-term goals (McGinnis' vertical program) and the short-term activities (McGinnis' horizontal program) becomes so vital.

The first unit of language consists largely of instruction of phonemes and monosyllabic words and appropriate reinforcement activities, which serve as a maintenance program for establishing and maintaining skills at the lowest level of linguistic content. Tables 1 and 2 present the beginning level of instruction with the least amount of linguistic content, organized according to vertical and horizontal programs. These are provided as guides for teachers and therapists to plan instruction. Later, similar organizations will be given for more advanced levels in which there is more linguistic content. See Appendix C for noun vocabulary lists.

Sentence Structure, Concepts, and Principles

The foundation for effective use of the multi-sensory DuBard Association Method® lies in the competence established by children during the early stage of instruction, McGinnis's "first unit of language" (1963, 79). Unless children establish a relatively strong competency for breaking the written code—that is, using phonetics for reading—achieving the more complex tasks will fall short of the desired goal. For this reason, the child's competence with just fifty nouns may not be sufficient. In such a case, a wise teacher will make haste slowly in expanding activities to sentence language. Instead, it might be wise to use additional vocabulary in reinforcing acquired competence. Such an extended vocabulary could include additional nouns, names, numbers, and colors, carefully selected so as not to overload the memory for sequence skills which have been established.

REPETITIVE SENTENCES AND QUESTION LANGUAGE—BEGINNING THE SECOND UNIT OF LANGUAGE

The basic sentences used in the DuBard Association Method® are repetitive sentences. Such a label describes these sentences well and focuses attention on the need for redundancy in solving the memory, storage, and recall problems.

McGinnis (1963, 62–99) discussed details regarding presenting the simple sentences. Some of the purposes related to this phase of the language instructional program are outlined below.

Purposes

1. To increase the child's memory span for sequences and recall of sequences expanding to the length of a simple sentence.
2. To introduce articles—*a, an,* and *some.*
3. To introduce simple verb concepts—"this is," "I see," and "I want." (Note: The number and types of sentences used has been expanded beyond McGinnis's original work. See page 49.)
4. To use previously taught vocabulary in sentences.
5. To teach the child that words are organized into sentences in a given sequential order for communicating ideas.
6. To provide practice in establishing competence related to syntax in oral and written language.
7. To strengthen the child's reading and writing abilities.
8. To teach the child to apply language which he/she has learned by rote to appropriate untaught situations.
9. To improve lipreading skills and acoustic work.
10. To introduce question language and establish ability in learning to formulate questions.
11. Punctuation is taught by example. Periods and question marks should be applied as appropriate beginning with repetitive sentences and questions.

Use of capital letters, except for *I,* which is always capitalized, and *w,* in which case both the capital and lower case forms are much alike, is delayed until the child is able to understand some explanation about the use of capitals. Depending on the child's ability in the mechanics of writing skills, the teacher may choose to introduce capital letters later in names at the personal story level. Use of capital letters at the beginning of a sentence is easily achieved in the preposition round-up stories. By that time, the children's language comprehension is sufficiently stable to enable them to deal effectively with this new aspect of written language. Trying to achieve too much too soon can easily overload the child's system for learning, however. In the case of implementing the method for students whose oral language is good (in general education or for those who have dyslexia), an appropriate *modification* may be to introduce capital letters earlier since these students have adequate oral language to understand the rules of using them.

TABLE 1

Sequential Language: Day-to-Day Activities

Typical Vertical and Horizontal Programs for the Beginning Level, Unit I

LONG-TERM GOALS

1. Child learns phonemes.
2. Drop drills reinforce learning.

SHORT-TERM ACTIVITIES

Specific short-term activities necessary to establish recall and retention skills include:

1. Instruction at chalkboard or with the child's book
2. Reading of the child's book (oral recall-precise articulation)
3. Writing readiness activities or independent writing activities as appropriate
4. Constructive free time
5. Tracing written form
6. Phoneme review (reading, auditory-visual, acoustic)
7. Instruction of new phonemes/drop drills
8. Recheck of first six skills on linguistic content
9. Writing from dictation if independent writing skills are present

Linguistic Content: Determiners *a*, *an*, and *some*. Simple sentences and corresponding questions in consecutive order; verbs are in a different color. In McGinnis's program, the three following basic sentences were used.

I see _____ _____.	What do you see?
this is _____ _____.	What is this?
I want _____ _____.	What do you want?

At the DuBard School for Language Disorders the following sentences of the same length and equal value were added without overtaxing the child's memory:

I saw _____ _____.	What did you see?
I have _____ _____.	What do you have?
_____ has _____ _____.	What does _____ have?

Materials: Picture cards of nouns which have been taught previously.

Skills: Reading, associating, increasing memory for sequences.

TABLE 2

Unit I Expanded to Begin Teaching

Noun Vocabulary via Cross Drill

LONG-TERM GOALS

1. Child learns all phonemes needed for the English language.
2. Drop drills are no longer used in the child's book.
3. Cross drills are introduced to teach noun vocabulary until at least fifty nouns are known well.

SHORT-TERM ACTIVITIES

Specific activities are rotated to achieve desired goals. They include the following:

1. Work with phonemes
   a. Previous instruction applied in phoneme reviews at chalkboard (reading, auditory-visual, acoustic)
   b. Concentration game with phoneme cards
   c. "Go Fishing" principle applied to old and new phonemes
   d. Reading books/copying phonemes
   e. Writing phonemes from dictation
   f. Oral recall of phonemes
2. Use of drop drills as board work for auditory-visual, writing, and acoustic training may be desired and serves a good purpose for some children.
3. Work with nouns
   a. Children copy cross drill from board while teacher puts a drill in a child's book. Ultimately, each child will have the drill in the book with the noun picture and word written on the following page. The word is not written under the drill because subsequent words taught with the same beginning sound, but different ending sounds, may be added on the page following the drill.
   b. Noun review (reading, auditory-visual, acoustic)
   c. Oral recall of word from picture stimulus only (precise articulation)
   d. Copying noun words
   e. Recall of written pattern from picture and/or teacher's dictation of words

Procedures:

  1. The teacher writes the sentence on the board.

  2. To demonstrate the procedure, the teacher reads the sentence, associates it with a noun and clarifies the meaning of the linguistic content related to new concepts in the sentence, primarily *I, this*, and the verb forms.

3. The teacher turns around and tries to say the sentence from memory. She may pretend to fail. If so, she reads it again and says it from memory. This is to indicate to the child that if he/she cannot remember all of it, he/she will be aided by the teacher or by turning around and reading from the board.

4. Each child then has a turn to (a) read the sentence, (b) associate the language with the picture and other concepts included, (c) turn around and try to say the sentence from memory and (d) sit down. The determiner *a* should be taught first since it is the easiest. The appropriate question form is taught only after the child can say and write the sentence without error.

Reinforcement Activities: The same reinforcement activities described for phonemes, drop drills, and noun vocabulary are appropriate for use with sentence work. It is important to remember that *the most difficult task is the acoustic task and this should not be undertaken until the child is well "saturated" with the other skills and very secure with the new linguistic form/forms.*

Procedures: When the sentence "I s[1]ee a ________" has been mastered by the child, then the question "What do you see?" is introduced and mastered. Afterwards, the "I s[1]ee s[1]ome ________" sentence form should be introduced and appropriate reinforcement activities utilized. The same question is applied. *It is essential that sentence and question forms be <u>mixed</u> prior to introducing new content in order to establish full comprehension and application skills.* Example, in reinforcement activities, mix "I see a ________" and "I see some ________" and the corresponding questions before introducing "I see an ________." This will be followed by introducing the determiner *an*. There are few words of the vowel-consonant phonetic arrangement but introducing the use of *an* without explanation of rules is appropriate. Rules can be dealt with later when the child has more understanding of language. Mastery of determiners is not easy. Even children who learn language normally have difficulty in knowing when to use *a* or *some*. They will learn the reason for using *an* at some later time in school. By teaching the child the a/an/some determiners with one sentence form and establishing a measure of competence with that limited amount of

linguistic content, the correct use of the determiners is merely reinforced as additional sentences are taught and learned. Later, mix "I see" sentences/ corresponding question with other sentence forms (this is, I want, etc.) which will have been taught individually and subsequently mastered.

As more sentences and questions are taught, using the same procedure as for "I see ________ ________," reinforcement activities can include "Go Fishing" and similar games which children enjoy. If they need a guide as to which sentences and/or questions are to get the emphasis, having the written form on the chalkboard at the beginning of the activity can be helpful. This can provide security for the child at the beginning of an activity and can be removed easily as the activity proceeds. Each child should assume the teacher's role regularly for practice in asking questions and giving answers. However, children should not be placed in the teacher's role for the acoustic step. Children enjoy playing the role of teacher, and the activity often gives insight into how the children see the teacher.

Sentences with pictures are put in each child's book as illustrated in Appendix B. The question form is written in the book only after the child demonstrates competence with the respective skills with the sentences.

Criteria for Selecting Specific Linguistic Content

McGinnis's second unit of language was based on three simple statements: (a) I s[1]ee ________, (b) t[2,1]his i[2]s ________, and (c) I want ________, and the corresponding questions: (a) What do you s[1]ee? (b) What i[2]s th[2,1]is ? (c) What do you want?

Each sentence utilizes one of three articles/determiners (*a, an,* or *some*). Use of the word *the* as a determiner is delayed until later. The specificity of *the* versus the others listed is more appropriately applied at the descriptive story level of instruction and beyond. Although McGinnis (1963, 100) suggested that the articles should all be used in the first presentation, we have found that children learn more easily if we establish the use of one before a second and a third are introduced. The decision for the change was based on the idea that, if children have poor memories as to when to use a given article/determiner, their choices will be only guesswork. Since children with severe language disorders tend to be poor guessers, they face a task with built-in uncertainty which could prove to be frustrating. Rather than arbitrarily adopting one plan or another, a teacher might be able to tell in advance which one would be more effective for a particular group. The overall goal is to teach the use of articles; how to accomplish this goal with the least possible frustration for the child is left to the teacher's discretion and skill.

Another modification which we have made has been at the simple sentence, repetitive sentence level. The decision to make the change grew out of the difficulties children experienced at a more advanced level dealing with the concepts of pronouns in personal stories. The statements, "I have a/an/some ________," and "________ has a/an/some ________" were added at the simple sentence level. Appropriate questions were also formulated. In addition, "I saw ________ ________" with the question "What did you see?" were added to expand the linguistic patterns children used while not overloading their memories for syntactical sequences.

As a result of the additions, more sentences were employed, two additional concepts were used, proper nouns were introduced, and the names of individuals were utilized more extensively. Since the length of sentence was in keeping with that suggested by McGinnis, the addition seemed to be reasonable. In addition to those cited previously, the basic simple sentence level, then, may include the following concepts in questions and statements with the appropriate article or determiner:

Who is this?   this is ________
Who has ____ ____?   ____ has ____ ____.

Introducing "who" can be achieved easily after the "I have ________ ________" and "________ has ________ ________" forms have been introduced and taught. "Who" and "whose" can be reinforced easily with classroom experiences when a stray paper is found without a name or some misdemeanor occurs which would call for the teacher to ask "Who . . . .?" or "Whose . . . .?"

Conceivably, colors might be added as modifiers if care is taken to retain the structured environment for establishing the desired level of competence. One might wonder if numbers could not also be employed. To do so would require that the comprehension and formulation of plurals be taught. The use of numbers with repetitive sentences is addressed below. Caution must be exercised in increasing the volume of new items with which the child will be dealing. Overloading the system with language symbols and principles could be a mistake.

McGinnis did not introduce the concepts of "have" and "has" in basic sentences with "I see," "I want," and "this is," neither did she advocate

teaching the past tense form of verbs in the early stage. In fact, according to her original organization (1963, 64), past tense verbs are delayed until the third unit of language. However, because of the natural application of the concept and its use in daily experiences, the concept of "I saw a/an/some" and the appropriate question language may be taught easily and systematically at the repetitive sentence stage. In implementing this level of the instructional program, one should keep in mind certain guidelines.

1. At the initial, repetitive sentence level, use noun vocabulary with which children are very familiar.
2. Use nouns based on each child's need for reinforcement work in both oral and written work if at all possible.
3. Use vocabulary and sentences that will help children associate the structured work with their daily environment.
4. Use collective nouns, such as *food, ice*, and *juice* with the article/determiner *some*, and delay using nouns with plural forms, such as "some hats," "some houses," etc.
5. The order in which the sentence forms are taught may vary according to the needs of the child. For example, with children who have severe apraxia, "this is ________ ________" may be delayed until later in the sequence of the six sentence forms because acquiring accurate speech skills may be challenging.

Use of Capital Letters

McGinnis (1963) made references to the use of capital letters. Regarding the pronoun *I*, she stated that since it is always capitalized, it should be taught as a capital letter from its initial use in sentences, "I see ________ ________" and "I want ________ ________." In her section on personal stories, McGinnis noted, "Capital letters are now used on the chart, as the children are familiar with all of the small letters" (108). At the same time, the sample instructional personal story does not use capital letters. It may well be that the presence or absence of capital letters at this early language level is not critical to a child's progress since *the use of capital letters does not change the meaning.* Nevertheless, the personal story is a logical context in which to teach the use of capital letters for personal nouns. Using capitals in other contexts, however, may present too many variables at one time. Whereas *I* and personal nouns are always written with capital letters, such words as *the, it, his, her*, and *a* are not written with capitals unless they happen to be the first word of a sentence. Using capital letters early in the language program can confuse children and cause them to make errors in written language. For example, they might produce the following:

> This is a cat.
> A cat has A tail.
> A cat has A __________.
> This is Tom.
> He is A boy.
> He Has blue eyes.
> His Hair is brown.

If teachers wish to teach capital letters from the beginning, they should be prepared to clarify for children by some simple, reliable means when a given word is to be capitalized and when that same word should not be capitalized. If, on the other hand, language learning is the major goal, instruction regarding the use of capital letters can be delayed without jeopardizing children's overall progress. In the early stages of teaching language, meaning is more important than capital letters.

The more advanced preposition round-up story provides an opportunity to introduce the use of the capital letter for the first word of each sentence. Names are not normally used in the stories, and capitalizing the first word of each sentence will get the full attention of the child without confusing him/her.

TABLE 3

Typical Program for the Beginning of the Second Unit of Language

---

LONG-TERM GOALS

1. Cross drills are used to teach new vocabulary, including numbers one through five, noun vocabulary to be used later in animal stories, and other noun vocabulary, especially foods, which can carry over from home activities to school

2. Introduction of basic sentences, determiners of *a*, *some*, and *an*, and appropriate question forms

3. Establishing competence with numbers one through five

4. Instruction related to plural forms, adding *s*, related to number concepts after the six sentence forms and questions have been taught

5. Application of numbers one through five to repetitive sentences/questions

6. Begin language math for addition (see chapter 7)

7. Maintenance of previously taught material

Specific SHORT-TERM ACTIVITIES to achieve desired goals

1. All skills (seven steps) should be rotated in activities to insure retention and recall of old and new language instruction (see short-term activities listed in table 2).

2. Establish reading recognition and dictation skills for words selected randomly from sentence and question forms.

3. Apply sentence and question forms in school and in incidental language activities; with parental help, apply same at home so as to get carryover of performance and skills from "structured" activities into life situations.

4. Develop all skills for language math as in #1 (see also, chapter 7).

5. Maintain all skills cited earlier for phonemes and noun vocabulary that have already been taught.

REPETITIVE SENTENCES WITH NUMBERS/"HOW MANY" CONCEPT

In McGinnis's work, the application of numbers and plurals began at the level of animal stories. Through the years, it became apparent that a transitional level of instruction which included numbers and the "how many" question language would be helpful. Consequently, a new level of instruction including these concepts was introduced after the basic repetitive sentence and question content had been mastered and prior to the introduction of animal stories. We will now describe this level.

Linguistic Content:

1. Number concepts, including numeral and number words in oral and written forms, one through five. See Chapter 7, Correlative Programs.
2. Principles of formulating plurals requiring the addition of voiceless *s* or voiced *s* (e.g., boot$\overset{1}{s}$, egg$\overset{2}{s}$). Instruction of other plural forms was delayed until a later level of instruction.
3. "How many" question language.

Procedures:

Number concepts one through five are applied to the previously mastered repetitive sentence concepts. When all skills have been established for the sentence material, the question language, "how many…" is introduced. Care should be taken to make certain that the children understand the association between the question language and the presence of a number word in the sentence. The following sentences provide a sample of this instructional material:

how many cat$\overset{1}{s}$ did you $\overset{1}{s}$ee?	I saw three cat$\overset{1}{s}$.
how many boot$\overset{1}{s}$ doe$\overset{2}{s}$ amber have?	amber ha$\overset{2}{s}$ one boot.
how many apple$\overset{2}{s}$ do you want?	I want two apple$\overset{2}{s}$.
how many car$\overset{2}{s}$ do you $\overset{1}{s}$ee?	I $\overset{1}{s}$ee five car$\overset{2}{s}$.
how many mop$\overset{1}{s}$ is th$\overset{2\cdot1}{is}$?	th$\overset{2\cdot1}{is}$ i$\overset{2}{s}$ one mop.
how many dog$\overset{2}{s}$ do you have?	I have four dog$\overset{2}{s}$.

It must be established that when the number is one, *s* is not added, though the question form will still be "how many…" and the plural form of the noun will appear in the question.

Once students show competence with such material, repetitive sentences with numbers are mixed with sentences without numbers. Instruction includes establishing the correct application of the "what…" or the "how many…" question with the corresponding statement. Examples:

what is th$\overset{2\cdot1}{is}$?	th$\overset{2\cdot1}{is}$ is $\overset{1}{s}$ome soup.
how many light$\overset{1}{s}$	

did you $\overset{1}{s}$ee?	I $\overset{1}{s}$aw one light.
how many toy$\overset{2}{s}$ do you want?	I want t$\overset{1}{h}$ree toy$\overset{2}{s}$.
what doe$\overset{2}{s}$ mary have?	mary ha$\overset{2}{s}$ an egg.
how many shirt$\overset{1}{s}$ do you have?	I have five shirt$\overset{1}{s}$.
what do you $\overset{1}{s}$ee?	I $\overset{1}{s}$ee a lake.

When children learned the concepts illustrated above, they were much more successful at the animal story level.

Applying the number concepts at the repetitive sentence level of instruction requires appropriate instruction on the formation of plurals. An example of a plurals chart may be found in chapter 7.

While collective nouns should be used at the initial, repetitive sentence level of instruction, they should not be used in work related to formulating plurals. Only nouns which are pluralized by adding the voiceless $\overset{1}{s}$ or the voiced $\overset{2}{s}$ (boat$\overset{1}{s}$ or dog$\overset{2}{s}$) should be used in this instruction.

To pluralize a noun ending in a voiceless consonant, a voiceless $\overset{1}{s}$ is added. To pluralize a noun ending in a voiced phoneme, a voiced $\overset{2}{s}$ is added. Special attention should be given to the linguistic rule which requires that the plural form be used in all questions regardless of the singular or plural nature of the corresponding sentence. Example: In the case of "I see one dog," it is sometimes difficult for the child to learn that the appropriate question is "how many dogs do you see?" rather than "how many dog do you see?" Reinforcement activities are important to establish competency with these rules.

In implementing the pure form of the DuBard Association Method®, rules such as the above are not to be memorized by the children. Practice in applying the principles until mastery is achieved is appropriate and necessary.

Prior to progressing to the animal story level, it is essential that children have mastered the skills for the following:

1. Basic repetitive sentences and questions
2. Repetitive sentences with numbers and corresponding "how many" questions
3. A mixture of sentences with and without numbers and the corresponding appropriate "how many" or "what" question form

Child in Teacher's Role

Placing the child in the teacher's role is important at all stages of the instructional program in which questions are applied. When stories constitute the major part of the instructional program, however, placing the child in the teacher's role is a critical factor. In playing this role, the child participates in expressing the language of questions by asking, as well as answering, questions. *At no time should the child read the sentence which answers his own question.* For example, the child does not read: "What is this? This is a boy." He reads the question and another child, or the teacher, reads the sentence and then the roles are reversed or rotated. This is important to establish the true role of question language, that of asking for information which is typically provided by another person.

Role of Color in Sentence Structure

From this stage of the instructional program, color is employed to differentiate the new verbs. An exception occurs when color is used to demonstrate prepositional language or placement concepts. The verb and the preposition are written in one color, and the remainder of the sentence in another.

Table 3 shows a relationship between new instruction and maintenance work early in the second level of the program.

INCIDENTAL LANGUAGE

Incidental language, that is, language which children use independently in the classroom, can be used for sentence patterns, too. This may be done when the children are at the cross-drill level of instruction and have developed some code-breaking skills. The teacher writes what is to be said on charts. Typical school incidental language would include such expressions as the following:

> I want… .
> May I get…. some water/paper/a pencil/a tissue?
> May I draw…. a picture?
> Will we go outside?
> May I go outside?

In this way, children begin to be required to ask for what they want and they are supported by the forms the teacher has written until they acquire the memory for sequence of the new language, both sentences and questions. Initially, the pupil reads the appropriate sentence or question as a beginning toward establishing memory for it. Certain basic purposes and criteria serve as guidelines in teaching the use of incidental language.

Purposes

1. To teach language which is applicable to children's school and home environments in a less structured way
2. To help children realize that they have some responsibility for expressing their needs and wants through spoken language; to indicate their role in daily situations and how they can function through oral communication
3. To expand their ability to read and apply their knowledge of Northampton Symbols to additional written language

Criteria Related to Incidental Language: When and What

The use of the incidental language illustrated above is new to children only in that they initiate the language rather than waiting to respond to someone else's language. The time when children should be required to take an active role in this respect will be determined by their ability to apply, even with help, their knowledge of Northampton Symbols. What to use as incidental language will be determined by each child's setting and the people in it.

Every effort should be made in both the school and home environments to help children generalize the use of language they are taught. Both teachers and parents are remiss if they allow a child to say only "apple," when he/she is capable of saying "I want an apple" or "May I have an apple?" Children should be encouraged and required to use the language that represents their maximum level of competence. Such skills as lipreading, speech, and auditory abilities should be developed to whatever level children's hearing acuity permits. If their acuity is essentially normal, or if they have only a mild acuity deficiency, auditory training should be pursued consistently. Auditory training also is implemented consistently with those who have a profound hearing loss to the maximum extent possible. After a student can generalize language of the repetitive sentence and question forms, and has mastered the skills previously identified, animal stories should be introduced.

ANIMAL STORIES

Purposes

Animal stories are highly interesting and enjoyable to children. Certain purposes of animal stories which should be kept in mind include the following:

1. To broaden the child's language and relate knowledge to it.
2. To increase the child's memory for longer

sentences and questions and to increase recall of sentences in a given sequence.

3. To teach new vocabulary, including names of animals, nouns related to body parts.

4. To apply numbers to body parts and to teach such adjectives as long, short, sharp, flat, bushy, big, and little.

5. To increase the child's proficiency in asking questions and to teach additional question language.

6. To expand lipreading and listening tasks by using more complex material and longer sentence structure.

7. To teach the language for the following and similar concepts—fly, swim, run, walk, climb, and jump—utilizing both affirmative and negative, can/cannot. Other concepts may also be used.

8. To teach such concepts as "is covered with," as a bird is covered with feathers, a bear is covered with fur.

Criteria for Selecting Linguistic Content

The following criteria are used for determining the linguistic content for animal stories. This list is more detailed than that found in McGinnis's discussion of animal stories.

1. Children must have mastered the fifty basic nouns, repetitive sentences, number concepts through four, and concepts of plurals.

2. The teacher should use nouns which have been taught previously; *new vocabulary, if children need it, should be taught by syllable/ cross drills, or on a whole-word basis if appropriate, before the story is presented.* Syllabic units perfected for speech and writing can be used for teaching new vocabulary if the children no longer need drills.

3. Animals described in the stories should be ones which interest children, lend themselves to a similar format of description, and afford opportunity for repeated use of the basic sentences. At the same time, they should be chosen to provide an opportunity to expand children's vocabulary and concepts.

4. The first stories should be about familiar animals which have no unusual characteristics.

5. The teacher should write *beginning* animal stories using *basic characteristics.* Animals appropriate for this level include dogs, cats, cows, horses. Other animals with unique characteristics are appropriate for upper lev-

el stories (for example, pig: curly tail, snout, hooves).

6. The teacher should avoid using colors to describe an animal unless the animal is always the same color. For example, an elephant is gray or a zebra has black and white stripes.

7. Any pictures used should be of an individual animal, not of one animal among others. This eliminates the chance of children becoming uncertain or confused and reduces the possibility of distracting their attention.

Although children may demonstrate a high level of competence for breaking the written code and being able to read orally what is given them, the teacher must continually make certain that they associate the words they read orally with the meanings of the written language. Requiring children to demonstrate that they understand what they read is necessary if one is to ascertain that their comprehension is as satisfactory as their ability to read or write the material. The teacher can check comprehension by asking children to identify a body part or demonstrate an action.

Composition and Manner of Presentation

The degree of complexity of any given story will be determined by the abilities and limitations of the child or group. A simple story could be used early in the program and repeated later with more recently learned concepts and a more difficult vocabulary.

Initially, stories should be no longer than four or five lines. At the previous level of instruction, children will have been responsible for committing to memory a four-word sentence for recall in oral and written forms in a structured setting. The animal story increases the number of sentences which they are to master. Even though a story is presented and mastered at the rate of one line at a time, and even though a high percentage of redundancy occurs in the story, every effort should be made to assure that children succeed with the greatest ease possible. Adhering to short stories which are gradually expanded in sentence and story length will help achieve the desired goal.

The sentence and question forms related to animal stories may seem extremely obvious to persons who acquire language in the typical manner, that is, incidentally if not accidentally. The use of "yes" or "no" as preface words for certain sentences when question language is introduced may seem both obvious and awkward to us. On the other hand, probably nothing seems obvious to children learning language through highly specialized teaching. Any element of awkwardness in language at this particular level becomes lost and is insignificant as the child masters the concepts and makes language functional.

Although McGinnis (1963) suggested teaching fifteen animal stories with corresponding question language, this is not necessarily a magic number. Some children may need more; others may master the desired skills in fewer stories. Because children like animal stories, their continued use while expanding the language content may be desirable.

Samples of animal stories developed in four incremental levels of difficulty are included in Appendix D. One should keep in mind, however, that since each group of children will differ, what is appropriate for one group may not necessarily be appropriate for all. Teachers will determine the sequence of stories based on their judgments of the children for whom the narratives are intended. In the sample stories, such adjectives of contrast as long-short and big-little are proposed for use in the same story. While McGinnis did not suggest this specifically, Van Uden, in *A World of Language, Part I* (1968), pointed out the appropriateness of *using opposites together,* to *provide contrast* as an aid to teaching.

McGinnis (1963, 105) stated, "By the time fifteen descriptions have been taught, the children will be able to answer questions about animals and birds that have not been presented in class and to write independent descriptions of them. This should be tested in class and given for seatwork." When the child has demonstrated the skills designated in previous stages, the inanimate object story and the indefinite pronoun can be added to provide variety. It should be noted, however, that McGinnis used the Association Method primarily for students who were deaf and hard of hearing with co-existing language and/or speech disorders. The method is now used effectively for additional and more diverse populations, such as those who have normal hearing acuity in the presence of language and/or speech disorders, those with autism spectrum disorders, those who have dyslexia or specific learning disabilities, as well as those who are typical learners in general education elementary classrooms. Therefore, looking at a student's ability to *apply, or generate,* language structures, rather than considering a set number of stories to teach, is preferable so that adequate instruction is provided but students are allowed to move on to new instruction as soon as they are able to do so. This is addressed in additional detail later in this chapter.

Linguistic Content:
1. Noun vocabulary, including animal names not previously taught, is taught through cross drills, if needed. Whole word vocabulary instruction may be used if the child has progressed to that level.
2. Numbers, usually two and/or four only: "a tail" is used rather than "one tail."
3. Adjectives, excluding colors, except black and white for a zebra and gray for an elephant since the color of these animals is not subject to change.
4. Plural forms related to body parts.
5. Abilities of animals: can fly, swim, run, etc.
6. Affirmation and negation concepts: yes, no; can/cannot fly, swim, climb, etc. "A _________ can _________" should be established before "a _________ cannot" is introduced.

The linguistic content is used in a selective manner and put in sentences for accurately describing a given animal. At the appropriate time, *when oral and written recall of the story has been established, appropriate question language is introduced.* The second unit of language in the child's sample book, Appendix B, contains sample animal stories. Appendix D contains an organization of linguistic content appropriate for animal stories. Early stories should have no more than four or five lines. A maximum number of lines in a story could be six or seven depending on the group and the story itself. It is a teacher's/clinician's responsibility to know the exact linguistic content that is appropriate and needed for a given group or child.

Skills:
1. Reading
2. Associating concepts to linguistic units
3. Applying good speech
4. Increasing memory for sequences for sentence length and the number of sentences in the story
5. Associating question forms to sentence forms
6. Written recall
7. Ability to *generate* stories/questions about which there has been no specific direct instruction. *Learning to generalize the application of previously taught language is of vital importance and applies to all subsequent story levels.*

It has been observed that many children with

language learning differences have a significant amount of difficulty relating question language to the language of statements. This is true also for children who fail to learn to read via teaching methods usually satisfactory for many children and who may be described as having a developmental delay and/or a specific learning disability (SLD)/dyslexia.

Procedures:

1. New vocabulary should be taught via cross drill, if the child needs the drill, or on a whole-word basis. All skills identified earlier should be well established before the vocabulary is used in a story.
2. To introduce/teach the story, the teacher writes the first sentence of the story on the chalkboard.
3. Children are called to the board individually; they read the line, make the appropriate identifications, turn around, say it from memory, and sit down.
4. Each child in the group goes through the same process until all have read the line in the manner indicated.
5. The teacher writes the second line on the board and each child goes through the procedure indicated.
6. The teacher continues adding one line to the story, having the children read it, associate the language to the proper part of the animal, and say the line from memory until the instruction related to the animal has been completed.

Reinforcement Activities

The children can copy the story on paper while the teacher begins writing the story in one child's book. It is the teacher's responsibility to write the story in each child's book. This can be completed later in the day or even the following day. Children will not be upset by waiting a day so long as they know that in due time the story, with a picture of appropriate size and clarity, will be put in their respective books.

The same reinforcement activities for specific skills cited in earlier stages are appropriate and necessary if the child is to master the semantic content, speech, and memory skills needed for syntax in oral and written language. It is very important that children not be required to attempt the acoustic step until they can say and write the entire story from memory. Likewise, questions for the story should not be introduced until all of the

skills are mastered for the story itself. *Ninety percent accuracy for oral recall and written recall should be established with automaticity before proceeding to new instruction.*

Maintaining the reduced temporal rate for both sentences and questions is vital. The children are gradually being asked to process both visually and auditorily more and more linguistic information. Therefore, a time lapse of one second between words in sentences and questions is a must if the teaching/learning process is to be effective, satisfying, and of long-term duration.

Development of Memory for Sequence in Stories

McGinnis (1963) outlined the following procedure for developing memory for sequence in *current stories*:

1. Each child in turn reads a line at a time, turns, and says it from memory.
2. Each child reads the second line, turns, and says it from memory; then, while still taking his/her turn, he/she reads both lines and says them from memory. Each child reads the newly added sentence, repeats it, then reads all of them and says them from memory. This routine is carried on until four, six, or perhaps eight lines can be remembered.

Another technique, perhaps easier for children, is as follows:

1. Each child reads the first line, turns, and says it from memory.
2. Each child reads the first and second lines, turns, and says both from memory.
3. This pattern is continued with the child reading from the first line and adding a line each time until he/she is able to either recall the entire story or until the maximum number of lines which can be recalled without frustration has been reached. When the child reaches the point of maximum recall, he/she may reread the same number of lines and attempt to recall again. If recalling that segment is still difficult, the point at which success was achieved becomes the beginning point to resume the activity during the next session.

These procedures enable those with language learning differences to improve memory for sequence skills. Committing an entire story to memory is, in a sense, a mental gymnastic for children with language disorders. There is probably a far more basic reason to have them achieve such a task than the reasons which existed in the past for requiring high school students to memorize long passages of poetry. Through the redundance of reading and saying one, then two, and eventually more and more lines, one builds up memory for the whole. How else did those of us required to memorize poetry accomplish it? The motor speech activity no doubt supports the memory for the ever-lengthening sequences. Writing the passages also aided many typical learners to memorize the assignment long enough to earn a passing grade. Although the above plan for memory work might be necessary for some children, students with less severe deficits can memorize the story in a less structured way. The teacher/clinician should be aware of each child's strengths and weaknesses and be able to make responsible decisions regarding the requirements made of a child at a given time and in a given activity. *It is important to note that the above procedures* ***are applied only to stories in current instruction***. It would be unreasonable to expect, for example, that a child learning his seventh animal story would need to remember that 'four legs' was on the third line in a previous story while it appears on the fifth line in the current story. *Maintenance* activities for previously taught stories would include an expectation for a student to write a story including *all previously learned elements* (number, can/cannot, adjectives, etc.); however, *when recalling a story for maintenance purposes, it is not necessary for the student to recall the exact story in the exact sequence that was learned at an earlier time.*

If children can master memory for the content of animal stories, that ability will support them in establishing memory for sequences which exist in longer and more complex sentences. The ability to retain memory for sequences and language formulations is the long-range goal. The early memory work included in the DuBard Association Method® is merely a means to that end. As the child's language program contains longer and longer sentences, committing an entire story to memory becomes less important. Establishing memory for longer, more complex sentence structure and question language has a higher priority than memorizing an entire story.

How Many Stories Should Be Taught at Each Level of Instruction?

It is sometimes challenging for teachers and therapists to determine when a child is ready to move from one level of story instruction to another, i.e.

from Level 2 Animal Stories to Level 3 or from Present Progressive stories/questions to Past Tense. As noted frequently in this text, a student generally should acquire *90 percent accuracy for oral recall and written recall with automaticity before proceeding to new instruction.* In this instance, we are referring to ***individual stories/questions***. To progress from one story/question *level* to another requires that the child demonstrate ability to ***generate*** *stories and questions at the* ***current level*** *of instruction.* For example, if a child has demonstrated mastery for eight individual expanded personal stories/questions, the teacher or therapist will want to determine the child's ability to carryover and apply these language structures to new material. An *unfamiliar* picture, appropriate for that level, is presented to the child who *generates* a story and the corresponding questions using the highest level of language structures taught to date. If the student is able to do so on both an oral and a written basis, progressing to a new level of instruction is indicated. If applying the current, highest level of language instruction to an unfamiliar picture is not possible, the student has indicated a need for more teacher-directed instruction at that level.

CVCC/CCVC DRILLS

In teaching monosyllabic noun vocabulary of CVCC (milk, sand) or CCVC (clock, glass) constructions, the first stage of the drill consists of the CVC portion of the word. In the second stage of the drill, the remaining consonant sound is added in its proper place. The rationale for such instruction is based on the fact that the child will have mastered CVC combinations. This method of instruction capitalizes on the strength of the child's skills with the CVC sequence and provides for ease of transition from recalling the three-sound sequence to recalling the four-sound sequence. (See Appendix C.)

By this stage, the need for using two colors for instruction at the board is rare. However, if the child demonstrates a need for it, use it.

ADVANCED DRILLS AND WHOLE-WORD VOCABULARY TEACHING

In teaching two-syllable words such as *basket*, McGinnis utilized a cross drill with two lines devoted to the first syllable and two for the second syllable. (See Fig. 6.9.) However, we have learned that children rarely need this type of drill when they are ready for two-syllable words. The reason is that, with the organization of vocabulary as discussed previously, children *overlearn* the phonetic system to such an extent that the two-syllable cross drill is unnecessary. We have found it appropriate to proceed to whole-word instruction at this point. By the time children are ready for vocabulary words with as many as six sounds in sequence, they can rely on their competence with the CV and CVC arrangements, which generally are the syllabic units. Previously learned material, practice in cross-drill reading, and memory practice will support the newer and more complex tasks.

Once a child becomes competent in code-breaking for CV and CVC words and can remember the oral and written forms and use them in sentences as indicated in the following sections, different types of drills can be used for teaching new vocabulary. Since the CV, VC, CVC words are basically syllabic units, if the child is competent in all of the skills with such a unit, two-syllable words can be taught more easily and quickly; *simply divide the word into syllables* **according to spoken rather than written form**, *spaced so that each syllable is seen clearly.* Have each of the children read each sound or syllable, depending on the individual ability; then, ask them to turn around and say it from memory and proceed from there with associating the word for meaning and applying it in the desired sentence form. It is vital to children's progress to have them master the speech and spelling of words taught in this manner and to be able to maintain the highest possible level of competence with the more advanced level of vocabulary, for example, *foot-ball; can-dle; bas-ket; car-pet.*

Procedures:

1. The teacher writes multisyllabic words on the chalkboard with slightly more space added between the syllables.
2. The child reads the *first syllable segmented, then blended three times, reads the second syllable segmented, then blended three times and, finally, says the word as a whole.* For example, for the word carpet, the child would say *c-ar, car, car, car; p-e-t, pet, pet, pet;* followed by both syllables blended *car-pet, car-pet, carpet.* If the child forgets the first syllable when going back to say both syllables, repeat the procedure from the beginning. In our experience, having the child say the blended syllable three times helps him/her to recall it after decoding the second and/or subsequent syllables.
3. For a multisyllabic word such as *calculator,* the procedures are the same in the syllable-by-syllable decoding *with the student return-*

ing to the preceding syllables before adding new syllables. For example: *c-a-l, cal, cal, cal; c-u* (pronounced k-u-e), *cu, cu, cu; cal cu l-a-e, la-e, la-e, la-e; cal cu la t-or* (pronounced t-ur) *tur, tur, tur; cal cu la tor, calculator, calculator, calculator.*

It is more challenging to describe the technique here than for the children to decode the multisyllabic word. After all, the word *calculator* is simply a combination of CVC and CV syllables which, after learning cross drills, is simple for the child *if the program's principles and techniques have been followed systematically and consistently up to this point.* The same reinforcement activities and criteria for progressing to new instruction, as described earlier, should be applied here. It should be noted that the technique described here has speech as its primary focus with decoding and encoding following. This is different from teaching syllable types and syllable division rules which may be appropriate for students at the upper levels of the DuBard Association Method®. These are taught in many multisensory structured language approaches (Alphabetic Phonics, Orton-Gillingham, etc.) to children with dyslexia without co-existing oral language and speech disorders.

FIG. 6.9. The first two lines of the drill relate to the first syllable, the second two to the second. The word as written at the end of the drill shows color alteration in relation to the number of sounds to be remembered. Use of secondary spellings may not be needed in such a drill.

INANIMATE OBJECT STORIES

Without being explicit regarding the purposes of inanimate object stories, McGinnis (1963) indicated that the stories would include the following: (1) colors, (2) numbers, (3) the pronoun *it*, and (4) adjectives as modifiers of objects in the sentences. The structure remains that of a simple sentence, noun-verb-noun or noun-verb-noun phrase. The suggested purposes and criteria given below may serve as guidelines for those composing the stories. Sample stories are included in Appendix D.

Purposes

1. To introduce the pronoun *it* and show its use.
2. To teach new vocabulary of nouns and adjectives.
3. To teach articles of clothing in a descriptive context.
4. To apply numbers to daily life.
5. To increase memory for vocabulary.
6. To increase question language.
7. To add variety and expand the language program.
8. To increase the child's memory for sequences by using longer sentences.
9. To enable the child to visualize parts of inanimate objects by associating the part with the whole object in the picture as new nouns are taught.
10. To prepare the child to learn to tell time and to distinguish the days of the week and months of the year. A clock story is appropriate and a calendar story may be used if the days of the week and the months of the year have already been taught.

Criteria for Selecting Linguistic Content

1. Inanimate object stories are best taught after the child has had a minimum of fifteen animal stories.
2. The language of the first stories should include parts that the objects always have; variables may be incorporated later.

The manner of presenting and the routine for establishing memory for the stories are the same as for animal stories. Only a few stories are needed for introducing this type of content. Reinforcement activities are the same as for previous levels of instruction.

Linguistic Content:
1. Indefinite pronoun, *it*.
2. Noun vocabulary of almost unlimited categories is available. As in animal stories, skills

with new vocabulary should be well established before it is used in a story.
3. Adjectives describing clothing or other selected nouns, such as *car, wagon, clock, bicycle, tricycle, big wheel.*

Skills:
The skills are those given previously. In fact, the seven skills permeate the entire language program.

Reinforcement Activities
The same kinds of activities which were appropriate earlier are appropriate from this point on. *Reinforcement work in the child's instructional program at this point is really a matter of maintenance. The teacher has the responsibility of recycling noun vocabulary, sentence and question work, animal story work, etc., as well as teaching new vocabulary, concepts, and language forms.* A hypothetical program of depicting a rotation of work is given later in this chapter (Tables 4-6). Use of the inanimate object story should be of limited duration while introducing a small amount of additional vocabulary. The referential aspect of *it* and other pronouns can complicate comprehension, so instruction should be carried out carefully in order to avoid letting the child become "locked into" a single meaning for *it* or the other pronouns. At the same time, providing instruction related to the linguistic forms of personal pronouns and the indefinite pronoun *it* is necessary. *As before, establishing oral recall and written recall with 90% accuracy and automaticity, as well as other skills, is essential before proceeding to new instruction. In addition, learning to generalize the application of previously taught language is of vital importance and applies to all story levels.*

PERSONAL DESCRIPTION STORIES
When children can demonstrate their comprehension of the indefinite pronoun *it* in various contexts at this early level of the instructional program, personal pronouns should be introduced. A wise teacher will check regularly and consistently on the children's comprehension and use of personal pronouns. It is easy to assume that once they demonstrate comprehension and correct use of any given concept or structure, they have mastered it. However, the teacher should not take too much for granted and needs to keep in mind that children with significant language disorders have deficiencies related to memory for storage and retrieval of language information. The teacher should continually monitor and check the child's competencies before proceeding to personal de-

scription stories.

Even though one normally thinks of self and others as more important than inanimate objects, personal stories are taught after the inanimate object story. To reinforce the child's learning, the indefinite pronoun can be incorporated easily into the personal stories. Purposes of personal description stories are given below.

Purposes

1. To introduce the pronouns, *he* and *she* and the possessive adjectives *my, his,* and *her.*
2. To instruct children about changes necessary in language and to teach them to use the proper words to refer to themselves or to others.
3. To increase children's interest in and awareness of their own and others' personal appearances.
4. To apply color names to language instruction.
5. To increase memory for sequences.
6. To continue work in question language.
7. To reinforce lipreading and auditory training.

The first personal description stories seem simple enough. Little new vocabulary, other than personal pronouns, is introduced. This seemingly easy task, however, may not be easy for children with language disorders. The fact that there are two sets of pronouns for self, two for female and two for male, results in more volume. The interchangeability of personal nouns and pronouns can create unanticipated complexity. One should, therefore, be aware of the possibility that learning the appropriate use of personal pronouns and their relationships to nouns may be more difficult for some than for others. The child with good hearing acuity and typical language development establishes competence in using pronouns through trial and error, misuse, correction, and a sorting-out process. One can hardly expect the task to be any less difficult for a child who has significant hearing loss or language disorders. Capital letters for names can be introduced with personal stories if children's writing skills are good enough for them not to be confused by the complexities of capital letters. Plural pronouns can be taught at subsequent language levels.

Criteria for Choice of Language

The teacher may use a photograph of the child, the child's picture drawn on the board, or the actual child as a model. If needed, a color chart may be used for reference. The teaching of personal stories is simplified since the concepts of *has* and *have* have been taught at the repetitive sentence level.

The simplest approach is to teach children the *two stories* about themselves first. Then, *two stories related to a boy* and *two stories related to a girl* are taught. Sample stories are given below.

About Self

Who are you?	I am ________.
What are you?	I am a ________.
What color eyes do you have?	I have ________ eyes.
What color hair do you have?	I have ________ hair.
What is your name?	my name is ________.
What are you?	I am a ________.
What color are your eyes?	my eyes are ________.
What color is your hair?	my hair is ________.

About a Boy

Who is this?	this is ________.
What is he?	he is a boy.
What color eyes does he have?	he has ________ eyes.
What color hair does he have?	he has ________ hair.
Who is this?	this is ________.
What is he?	he is a boy.
What color is his hair?	his hair is ________.
What color are his eyes?	his eyes are ________.

About a Girl

Who is this?	this is ________.
What is she?	she is a girl.
What color eyes does she have?	she has ________ eyes.
What color hair does she have?	she has ________ hair.
Who is this?	this is ________.
What is she?	she is a girl.
What color are her eyes?	her eyes are ____.
What color is her hair?	her hair is ____.

After the stories of the type illustrated above have been taught and the child can demonstrate comprehension of the pronouns and adjectives, stories reinforcing the use of personal pronouns may be used to advantage. A sample of an expanded story follows. Additional expanded stories, organized into distinct levels of difficulty, are in Appendix D.

Who is this?	this is _________.
What is he?	he is a _________.
What color hair does he have?	he has _________ hair.
What color eyes does he have?	he has _________ eyes.
What color shoes[2] does he have on?	he has on _________ shoes.[2]
What color pants[1] does he have on?	he has on _________ pants.[1]

Typically, children learn two stories for each picture. For example, after mastering the story above, another story and questions would be learned using *his. At all story levels, new vocabulary is introduced prior to introducing the story itself.* The students' familiarity with the vocabulary makes the introduction of the story proceed more smoothly and with greater success for the students. The vocabulary will be determined by the teacher who will choose new words in order to include facts about the children, others in the school environment, and/or pictorial material. The choice should be made in view of the primary goal of teaching the children the use of personal pronouns. Question forms are introduced after the child has become competent with the sentences. Likewise, children with good hearing acuity and typical language development should not be expected to answer questions before they have "learned some answers." Certainly no more should be expected of the child with language learning differences than of the typically developing child.

Skills and Procedures

Personal stories should be introduced one line at a time just as animal stories were. The same skills apply to personal descriptive stories that apply to any previous levels. Children should be able to say and write the story about themselves before any questions are introduced and all of the self story-question linguistic content should be mastered before a story about a boy or a girl is introduced. Capital letters may be used for names provided they are kept fairly simple in form and if the child's motor skills for writing are developed adequately. Previously identified reinforcement activities and criteria for progression to new instruction continue to be appropriate. *Establishing oral recall and written recall with 90% accuracy and automaticity, as well as other*

skills, is essential before proceeding to new instruction. In addition, learning to generalize the application of previously taught language is of vital importance and applies to all story levels.

PREPOSITIONS

McGinnis (1963) did not specify exactly when the teacher should introduce prepositional language, concepts, and structure to the child. An indirect guideline, however, can be useful. One should always remember that the procedures are based on the principle that children should achieve a maximum level of competence at any given stage of the instruction before new material is introduced. They should have achieved a high level of mastery of the skills related to the instruction—reading, appropriate association indicating their comprehension, lipreading, recall of spoken and written forms of the language, and identification of the stimulus language from an auditory stimulus. Children should be able to demonstrate that they comprehend and can apply all concepts and structures of language taught thus far. They should be able to demonstrate their abilities in a generalized situation as well as in structured settings of the school environment. In order to ascertain such progress, the teacher must check and double check. The imaginative teacher will devise numerous ways of making certain that their children have reached an appropriate level of competence before introducing new work.

Purposes

The primary purpose of this phase of the program is to teach the concepts and appropriate language for the placements *in, on,* and *under;* such words as *around, by/beside, above,* and *below* may be taught in the context of simple stories after the child masters the basic ones. Secondary purposes include teaching new vocabulary, expanding sentences to include more modifiers, and increasing the length of sentences. The child's book should contain *sample* pictures and sentences related to each concept—*on, in,* and *under.* The question "Where is/ are _________?" should be placed on the page facing the pictorial material.

A. Linguistic Content:
   Prepositions *on, in,* and *under* are basic placement concepts with a corresponding question form of "Where is the _________?" The preposition concepts and language are taught before the question language is introduced.

Materials:
Teacher-constructed pictorial cards using magazine advertisements which portray bizarre arrangements. For example, pictures that show "the cow is on the table" are needed. Bizarre arrangements provide a surprising element which creates a definite impression on the children and gives them enjoyment. The surprisal element concept is part of information theory.

Skills:
Reading, associating, and saying the new sentence from memory are skills involved in the introductory work.

B. Manner of Presentation:
In a previous chapter we discussed the element of surprise as a part of the terminology related to information theory. A surprise, gained through using pictures of bizarre arrangements as a way of teaching placement concepts and other prepositions, will impress the child. A unique approach can be valuable in focusing attention on concepts which are obvious to the average individual but which may be less than obvious to the child with a language disorder. McGinnis (1963, 110) pointed out, "The appropriateness of the relationship should not be considered. The unusual will attract the child's attention and emphasize the concept of the word designating relationship." The bizarre relationship, the unusual, will help the child grasp the concept. Telling, showing, or having a child read "the book is on the table" may be too obvious for him to comprehend completely because the situation is ordinary. On the other hand, since one is not likely to see a cow on a house, a picture of such a situation, accompanied by the appropriate language, will indeed make an impression on the child. In addition, these pictures add a welcome bit of humor to the whole teaching/learning process.

McGinnis (1963) suggested drawing pictures on the chalkboard to illustrate the desired concept. One need not be an accomplished artist to execute these drawings; even crude drawings usually are accepted by the students.

The above simple procedure lays the foundation for more extensive work. After the placement/prepositional concept and language are introduced, a number of unusual pictorial arrangements, accompanied by appropriate language should be presented. Finally, the concept is taught by using ordinary arrangements found in the environment. This method provides new vocabulary as well as an opportunity to apply previously taught vocabulary. Activities related to all of the skills already mentioned provide the reinforcement work.

When the child demonstrates competence in oral and written recall of the single sentences about the pictures, the question "where is/are ________?" should be introduced. The presentation of pictures and objects in both unusual and usual arrangements should be expanded until there is no doubt that the child understands and can read, say, write, lipread, recall the spoken and written forms, and demonstrate comprehension of the auditory stimulus (to the extent possible if the child has a significant hearing loss).

After a child shows mastery of one concept (i.e., on) and the corresponding question, another one, for example, in, *should be introduced. Bizarre arrangements may be followed by the common arrangements found in the daily environment.* The two concepts, *in* and *on,* should be mixed in reinforcement activities prior to teaching the new concept, *under. This practice of mixing/integrating previously taught content before proceeding to new instruction is a principle which applies throughout the DuBard Association Method®.* Presenting the concept of *under* usually requires less specific instruction than the previously taught *on* and *in.* It is important to remember that plural forms should be included also. Thorough step-by-step teaching makes subsequent tasks easier.

Procedures:
To begin with, "is on" is written on the chalkboard in a different color to call attention to the new concept.

1. The teacher shows a picture with a unique arrangement.
2. The teacher writes appropriate sentences on the chalkboard: "this is a cow," "this is a house" and identifies each noun by pointing to it.
3. The teacher then writes the sentence, "the cow is on the house," showing the relationship between the cow and the house.
4. Each child takes a turn at reading the three sentences and identifies the objects and their relationships.

After several such sentence arrangements are presented, the first two sentences can be erased and only the sentences with the preposition language are left to go along with the respective pictures.

    E.g.: the cow is on the house.
          the elephant is on the car.
          the bow is on the dog.

5. Next, the children read, associate, and turn and say the sentence from memory.

The children may then copy the sentences on paper. The teacher may use this time to begin putting in each child's book, a picture depicting the preposition concept *on*. Ultimately, each child gets at least one such picture arrangement with the proper sentence written under it. Additional groups of sentences and questions, without pictures, may be recorded in the child's book for use in reinforcement/homework activities. The pictures which correspond to these sentences remain in the classroom.

All skills of recalling spoken and written forms from the picture stimulus only should be well established before the question language, "Where is the _______?", is introduced. After children have worked with the question, the teacher writes it on the page facing the picture page, as illustrated in the child's book, Appendix B.

Role of Color

In teaching prepositions, color is used to focus attention on new concepts and sentence structure. The phrase, "is on," "is in," or "is under," should be written in a color that is different from the other words in the sentence. For example, "The books *are on* the shelf." The question language would then be "Where *are* the books?" Later, the form may be modified: "Are the books on the floor?" Each manipulation of question language is important but should not be attempted too early in the language program. It is usually best to adhere to the simple question "Where is/are the _______?" until the child is very secure in the task. Later, a different form of questioning, such as "Is the _______ on the _______?" or "What is _______ the _______?", may be used.

At this level of work, the teacher may manipulate language in a variety of ways. If the child's language is to be as nearly natural as possible, he/she must be shown how the manipulation is accomplished and told that a question can be asked in more than one way. If the child does not understand the alternatives, his/her language will be less flexible and less functional, more rigid and more stereotyped than is necessary or desirable.

Reinforcement Activities

For this more advanced level, reinforcement activities usually are limited to:

1. Chalkboard activities related to reading and recalling the spoken language from a picture stimulus
2. Auditory-visual skills
3. Work at the chalkboard on acoustic skills
4. Seatwork using picture cards requiring the child to recall the written form of language and writing it

Additional activities can include having miniature objects, making specific arrangements of them, and asking children, "where is the _______?" to which they reply, "the _______ is on the _______." Children, too, can make arrangements and ask questions of their peers, thus giving all a chance to practice asking questions which is vital to language growth.

By this time in the new language level, pictures of commonly seen arrangements depicting "is on" can be used. As children gain competence with the "is on" concept, the "is in" concept can be introduced and taught. Mixing the concepts *on* and *in* can be utilized as a check on the child's comprehension of the linguistic forms. When children show competence with comprehension and use of these with both oral and written forms, the concept of *under* should be taught and the three prepositions can then be used in activities together for reinforcement. Such placement concepts *as between, behind, in front of,* and *around* may be taught in the same manner as the more basic concepts of placement. However, the difficulty of getting pictorial material for the more advanced concepts often makes it necessary for these concepts to be taught as part of the content in a story. This makes it necessary for the teacher to find and create ways to reinforce the instruction and to monitor the child's comprehension of them.

After the use of prepositional language has been mastered and while the previous levels of instruction are being maintained through use at school and at home, it is time to introduce round-up stories. Some children may require more structured work than others, but all should have a command of the basic sentence form and the appropriate question form at the structured level before expanded application is made through the round-up story work.

Teaching New Vocabulary: Whole Word

By this stage of the language program, the child should no longer require the redundancy of the cross drill for learning new vocabulary. If the child is competent in code-breaking, the word should be written in syllabic units, in cursive writing, spaced and connected, not hyphenated. The child should practice saying the word to develop automaticity for the speech and to establish its meaning. Some children can acquire new vocabulary in this manner at earlier levels of language instruction. The extent to which the child needs "crutches" or support should be obvious to the teacher from the amount of difficulty the child experiences. If the child begins to omit sounds in words, additional help with precise articulation and memory for sequence work is probably needed. If the child demonstrates poor recall for the spoken and written forms of new words, more practice in those phases of the work may be needed. Teaching vocabulary on a whole-word basis was discussed earlier in this chapter.

The new vocabulary to be used in stories should be presented early in the day's or week's work before the new words are used in a story. Skills related to speech, association, and recall of spoken and written forms should be established so that the child will not be confronted with both the speech and memory for new vocabulary at the same time that a more complex sentence structure is used.

PREPOSITION ROUND-UP STORIES

The language level labeled round-up stories by McGinnis (1963) does just that. *The stories round-up and incorporate multiple aspects of vocabulary, concepts, sentence structures, and question language taught up to this point.* McGinnis referred to the stories as descriptive stories since she taught primarily about rooms of a house. New vocabulary, colors, and number concepts can be applied easily. The stories provide a linguistic environment through which the preposition concepts taught in structure (*is/are on, in,* and *under*) can be applied to lifelike situations. Round-up and descriptive stories may be simple or more complex depending on the level desired. As McGinnis used them, stories now known as *descriptive stories* excluded people except in carefully chosen situations. In *preposition round-up stories,* which may include people, actions (*-ing* verbs) are excluded. This language structure, present progressive verbs, is taught at the next level of instruction. (Examples conclude this section and also appear in Appendix B.)

In our application of the language sequences, we concluded that there was a need for a round-up story level which came earlier than descriptive language and as early as possible in the prepositional level of instruction. Therefore, we constructed two types of stories which emphasize prepositions, the preposition round-up story and the descriptive story. In addition, these not only incorporate vocabulary, colors, and number concepts but also focus attention on the application of personal pronouns and the indefinite pronoun, *it.* If children have adequate skill for writing clearly, in a well-formed and well-spaced manner, they can write the story and questions following their introduction, in their own books. If they are not capable of writing in the desired manner, size, and clarity, it is the teacher's responsibility to do this for them.

If enough copies of the same picture are available, each child can have one in his/her book. The linguistic material will go in the child's book with or without the picture to which it corresponds. The picture is then used only in classroom activities.

Pictures from primers or reading-readiness books may be used to good advantage with such round-up stories. They should be put in the child's book after the teacher has conducted the instruction at the chalkboard. With the story written in the child's book and all necessary skills established, it is appropriate to introduce the question language. Once the primary question, "Where is the _______?" has been mastered, alternate questions may be applied. Sample preposition round-up stories follow:

One Version

Where are the children?	The children are outside.
Where is John?	John is on his bike.
What color is it?	It is red.
Where is Mary?	Mary is on her skate board.
What color is it?	It is blue.
Where is Tim?	Tim is on his big wheel.
What color is it?	It is yellow.
How do they feel?	The children are happy.
(for incidental treatment only)	

Another Version

Where are the children?	The children are outside.
Where is John?	John is on his red bike.
What color coat does he have on?	He has on a red coat.
Where is Mary?	Mary is on her blue skateboard.

What color sweater does she have on?	She has on a blue sweater.
Where is Tim?	Tim is on his yellow big-wheel.
What color cap does he have on?	He has on a yellow cap.

Stories of variable content help the child to become aware of the interchangeable feature of language. The stories should be varied to include the use of *she, her, he* and *his*, as well as *it. The use of capital letters should be fully implemented at this level of instruction.*

Reinforcement activities as described earlier are applied. *Establishing oral and written recall with 90% accuracy and automaticity, as well as other skills, is essential before proceeding to new instruction. In addition, the child's ability to* generate *new stories/questions, which have not been taught through direct instruction, is important in determining readiness to proceed to new levels of instruction.*

DESCRIPTIVE STORIES

Initial descriptive stories about various rooms of a house should be simple; more complex language can be used later. It is appropriate, at this point, to use capital letters for the first words of the sentences. Requiring children to remember more than six to eight lines seems unrealistic since the goal should be to increase their memory for longer sentences and for more complex language constructions, such as compound subjects or compound predicates.

There are at least two disadvantages to using the descriptive story material except in a limited way for a limited time: (1) not many homes, dens, kitchens, etc., are very similar to those pictured in magazines; availability of appropriate pictures may be limited. (2) The vocabulary in use daily and names of items are both varied and basic; finding ways to reinforce certain vocabulary applicable to the use in stories based on pictures is often difficult. Nevertheless, the stories do offer an avenue for teaching placement concepts of *between, in front of, behind*, and *in the corner*, as well as additional vocabulary. Current technology, including digital cameras and cell phones with cameras, make it possible for the child to take a picture of a room at home and write a story about it thus personalizing the instructional level and the reinforcement activities.

Purposes

In general, the round-up and descriptive stories provide a multipurpose application of language. Some of their purposes are mere extensions of those associated with previously used types of stories; some are more or less new and especially applicable to this kind of language story. Specific purposes are as follows:

1. To introduce new vocabulary and familiarize the child with names for the living areas of homes—bedroom, kitchen, living room, bathroom and den. Some pictures lend themselves to teaching concepts of inside/outside by means of language stories.
2. To provide pictorial-language instruction for the concept of such determiners as "one _________," "another," "the other/others"; to apply number concepts to language work in a context not specifically related to the subject of mathematics.
3. To apply the language of ordinal numbers. For instance, "Some books are on the first shelf; a toy is on the second shelf," and "March is the third month of the year."
4. To expand the language story in two directions—by increasing the number of sentences and by using longer sentences.
5. To increase memory for sequences in longer sentences and in sentences with compound subjects and/or compound predicates.
6. To increase the use of modifiers of various kinds.
7. To provide children with opportunities to write descriptive stories of their own as well as to establish skills for the stories provided by the teacher.
8. To apply vocabulary and concepts previously taught.
9. To apply the primary question form, *Where is/are the _________?* followed by application of alternate questions.

Criteria for Selecting Pictorial Material for Preposition Round-up/Descriptive Stories

Certain criteria should be used in selecting pictorial material for round-up and descriptive stories. Simplicity and clarity of arrangement are important. Pictures selected for preposition round-up stories, which may include people, should focus only on their placements rather than their actions. Pictures of living areas which are not cluttered and busy are most appropriate. Pictures of busy living areas that are too cluttered are overstimulating to children and contain decorative objects not ordinarily found in the average home. Great care should be used in selecting illustrations for the descriptive stories related to living areas.

A. Linguistic Content:
  1. Noun vocabulary, singular and plural forms
  2. Singular and plural verb forms for subject-verb agreement
  3. Determiners for reinforcement; colors for reinforcement
  4. Types of textile patterns: striped, checkered, flowered, print, dark _________, light _________ as well as other adjectives such as long/short, big/little, etc.
  5. Compound subjects, compound predicates, and combinations of these in some instances

B. Manner of Presentation:
  As in earlier levels of the language program, the picture is visible to all; then the story is presented one line at a time on the chalkboard and attention is focused on the aspect of language that is featured. The sentences are written one under the other. The paragraph form is introduced in the imagination stories and advanced experience stories. Children take turns reading the sentence, indicating the association by identifying the proper portion of the picture, turning their backs to the board, and repeating the sentence from memory. After each child has established the specified skills from the story content, question language for the story is given. This type of story presents an excellent opportunity for the teacher to demonstrate the possibility of asking several kinds of questions about a single sentence. If children are not instructed regarding ways to manipulate language and are not given opportunities to formulate sentences and questions, their use of language will be less complete, less natural, and less effective than is desired.

Procedures and Skills

New vocabulary should be taught either as a syllabic unit and slowly combined for the whole word or as a whole word before it is used in a story. Skills of speech, auditory association, recall of spoken and written forms, of auditory-visual recognition, and auditory identification of the new vocabulary words should be established prior to their being used in a story. Teaching new vocabulary and establishing the specific skills required the day before the story is to be taught is a good procedure to follow. The same procedures already described for presenting other stories are used with these stories.

It is important that teachers help children maintain their skills for previously taught concepts, vocabulary, and structures. *Establishing oral recall and written recall with 90% accuracy and automaticity, as well as other skills, is essential before proceeding to new instruction. In addition, learning to generalize, or generate, the application of previously taught language is of vital importance and applies to all story levels.*

Story Length

Round-up and descriptive stories usually consist of six to eight sentences with corresponding questions. With these stories, children can learn that more than one question can be asked about the same sentence. Care should be taken to teach the question "Where is _________ _________?" first, however, since the *on, in, under* concepts are being stressed. The teacher should be able to determine whether or not children are capable of dealing with additional questions, such as "What is on the _________?", "What is behind the _________?", etc.

PRESENT PROGRESSIVE LANGUAGE: SENTENCES/QUESTIONS AND STORIES/QUESTIONS

Purposes

In general, the purposes of teaching the present progressive tense are the same as those described for stories at previous levels.

A. Linguistic Content:
  1. Introduction of present progressive concepts, word construction, and question language. For example, "The _________ is/are _______ing" with the primary question form, "What is/are _________ doing?"
  2. New vocabulary as may be appropriate.

Materials:
  1. Picture cards in which a single, ongoing action is obvious. The first cards used should be those illustrating only the noun+verb+ing. Example: "The boy is eating," "The man is walking." *When the concept and new construction have been learned, it is appropriate to add a direct or indirect object. Example: "The man is riding a horse" or "The boy is mowing the lawn" or "Mother is giving a cookie to Mary." Subsequently, the language would include prepositional phrases. Example: "The boys are swimming in the pool."*
  2. Pictures showing ongoing actions which can be used for a story.

Skills:

All skills identified and discussed in previous language levels are to be established with the new linguistic content.

B. Manner of Presentation:

Stable progress will be more easily achieved if the child learns some present progressive sentence and question forms in a structured manner before attempting to incorporate the concepts and structure of the language in stories. The teacher selects a concept along with a picture depicting the concept and then writes the appropriate language on the chalkboard so that the child can make the association. "By using pictures, the action remains constant while the sentence form is being learned" (McGinnis 1963, 114). Some examples are:

The baby is sleeping.
The dog is eating.

Sentences utilizing plurals and possessive pronouns are also appropriate for instruction in this manner at this time. For example:

The boy is riding his bike.
Mary is brushing her teeth.
The men are working on the car.

Color at this level is used to differentiate the verb concept; "is _______ing" should be written in a color different from the rest of the sentence. If desired for emphasis, the teacher may choose to write the linking verb, *is* or *are* and <u>only</u> the *ing* morpheme in a different color. The primary question form should be "What is _______ doing?" At a later time, other question forms should be used. For example: "Who is brushing her teeth?" in addition to "What is _______ doing?"

After children are familiar with present progressive sentences and questions, stories can be introduced. Simple pictures are recommended for the first stories utilizing present progressive forms. Pre-primer and reading-readiness illustrations may be used to good advantage at this level. The teacher should guard against overtaxing the child with stories which are too long. A sample present progressive story with questions is given below. At the chalkboard and in the child's book the verbs plus *-ing* should be written in a different color for the sake of emphasis.

Where are the children?	The children are at the playground.
What are Tom and Bob doing? (Who is seesawing?)	Tom and Bob are seesawing.
What is Bill doing? (Who is climbing a rope?)	Bill is climbing a rope.
What are Mary and Sue doing? (Who is swinging?)	Mary and Sue are swinging.
What is Father doing?	Father is playing ball with Jim and Sara.
(Who is playing ball with Jim and Sara?)	

***Procedures*:**

After the teacher writes a sample present progressive sentence on the chalkboard (e.g., "The boy is eating.") and shows a picture illustrating it, the procedures detailed in animal stories should be followed. After all skills have been established with a number of the basic sentences, the question form (e.g., "What is the boy doing?") is introduced. When children have mastered the basic sentence and question forms, a sentence using an object can be introduced, such as, "The boy is eating an apple." This permits the use of an additional question form and focuses attention on the versatility of language with either question form, "What is the boy doing?" or "What is the boy eating?", being appropriate. The second question should not be introduced until the child can demonstrate comprehension for the simpler form.

When teaching stories that are long, the process should have two parts. The child can memorize half of the story and the teacher will provide instruction in appropriate question language. The process is then repeated for the second portion of the story. This plan lessens the burden on the child's memory.

PAST TENSE LANGUAGE: SENTENCES/ QUESTIONS AND STORIES/QUESTIONS— BEGINNING THE THIRD UNIT OF LANGUAGE

Simple actions provide good examples for introducing the concept of past tense in verbs, that is, *drew, ate, drank,* and *fell*. The first and primary question for past tense language is "What did _______ do?" After children have learned this, other question forms can be introduced. For example: "What did _______ eat?" or "Who ate _______ _______?"

Procedures:

One method of introducing work on this level is as follows:

1. Have some cookies available.
2. Give one to a child to eat.
3. Write on the board, "John ate a cookie."
4. Have each of the other children read the sentence.
5. Repeat the process until each child has read the words that tell what the other child did.
6. Follow a similar procedure using other actions. Change the name to fit the child completing the action.
7. Allow the children to copy sentences describing several completed actions, such as:

> John ate a cookie.
> Debbie drew a cat.
> Ricky broke the chalk.
> Jeff fell on the floor.
> Linda cut the paper.

The teacher can decide whether or not to practice with the question forms, "What did _______ do?" and "Who _______ _______ _______?" After this introductory work has been completed, pictures depicting obvious past tense actions should be used with appropriate language. Next, the verbs should be applied to daily activities and events at home and in the neighborhood. The use of past tense stories with related pictures will enlarge the student's grasp of past tense. Pictures that depict an obvious sequence of events provide excellent opportunities for instruction. Cartoon strips can be rewritten with language that enables the child to understand the past tense and language of sequences and time, such as "first," "next," "after that," "then," and "finally."

Role of Color

McGinnis used color to show the whole verb as different from the rest of the sentence. For regular verbs, which add the suffix *-ed* to form the past tense, only the suffix needs to be written in a different color. The color focuses attention on that part of the word and reminds the child that an additional unit is required to complete the word. Using a different color can be discontinued when the child no longer needs it, but stressing the speech for the final unit may be necessary for a longer time.

One additional comment regarding color differentiation is appropriate. At no time are children required to use color differentiation in their written seat work. At the chalkboard, the teacher may require them to use color differentiation for verb forms, for prepositional language ("is on," "is in," or "is under"), or in more advanced work when various parts of speech are being emphasized. The teacher should base such decisions on each child's needs.

Past Tense Sequence Stories/Questions

One kind of past tense story is based on a sequence of actions. Two, three, or four pictures are appropriate. These can be taken from traditional reading-readiness books or from other sources. Realistic drawings rather than cartoons are usually better for the initial instruction. The following sample is based on a series of four pictures from the DuBard School for Language Disorders curriculum. An additional more advanced sample in paragraph form can be found in Appendix D.

Where did Father and Dick go?	Father and Dick went outside.
What did they do?	They played football.
What did Father do first?	First, Father took the football.
What did Dick do?	Dick watched him.
What did Father do next?	Next, Father kicked the football.
What happened to his shoe?	His shoe came off.
What did Dick do?	Dick laughed at him.

A sequence story can be developed on the basis of a single picture as well as from a series of pictures. A single picture story is likely to have fewer actions that are obvious and the actions may be more subtle or those which are "presumed" to have happened. This makes it necessary for the child to have understanding of more vocabulary, more linguistic units, as well as knowledge of various events. Such stories provide good opportunities to incorporate language of sequences, such as "first," "next," "finally," etc., and opportunities to continue to instruct the child about the relationship between and among certain word classes, especially reference pronouns. Stories of this type become the foundation for stories of greater depth which are referred to as imagination stories.

Past Tense Stories/Questions—Single Picture

After basic past tense language structures in sentence and question form have been introduced and taught, simple, past tense stories based on a single picture and written by the teacher can be used. These should be no longer than eight or ten lines and presented in the sentence-by-sentence form. Paragraphs can create difficulties for children with language learning differences if they are used too soon.

Short stories have several advantages. They provide opportunities to introduce new concepts and to review some of those previously introduced. Such reinforcement helps children establish long-term memory for the material. Using several short stories instead of one long one also reduces the chance of boredom on the part of both children and teachers. Past Tense Stories are a transition to Imagination Stories.

Multiple Questions

Children must learn that language can be very interchangeable, that often there may be more than one word to express a certain thought and that there can be more than one question for a given sentence. Some children grasp these ideas earlier than others. However, children with language disorders, at the preposition level of instruction and certainly by the present progressive and past tense levels, need to be taught that there can be multiple questions for some sentences. If the multiple question work is established with instruction on the sentence level, application of multiple question work in the story levels can be expected to proceed much more smoothly and successfully.

Some children with language disorders have great difficulty with questions at levels of instruction. They do not understand the relationship/association that exists between the language of sentences and the language of questions. Using the Fitzgerald Key format (see page 111) at a sentence level can be very helpful in showing the relationship/association between and among the concepts and words themselves although McGinnis did not use it at all with her population of children with language disorders.

The following are examples of past tense stories based on single pictures. The first uses sequencing language. The second shows the use of multiple questions.

What did Grandfather do? (What did Grandfather want to make for Ann?)	Grandfather made (wanted to make) a sack swing for Ann.
What did he do first?	First, he put some straw in a sack.
What did he do after that?	After that, he tied the rope to a tree limb.
What did he do finally?	Finally, he put Ann on the sack swing and pushed her.
What did Dan and Sue do?	Dan and Sue watched them.
What else did Dan and Sue do?	Dan and Sue laughed at them, too.
What did Ann do? (Who else laughed?)	Ann laughed, too.

What did Jack and Kim do?	Jack and Kim went outside to feed Red.
Where did Jack and Kim go?	
Who went outside to feed Red?	
(Why did Jack and Kim go outside?)	
What did Jack do?	Jack put some dog biscuits on Red's plate.
What did Jack put on Red's plate?	
Where did Jack put some dog biscuits?	
Where was a squirrel?	A squirrel was on a tree limb.
What was on a tree limb?	
What did he do?	He watched Red.
Whom did the squirrel watch?	

The next sample past tense stories are based on a sequence of four pictures. Potential questions are shown in parentheses.

What did the family do?	The family cooked hot dogs outside.
(Where did the family cook hot dogs?)	
What did Jim do?	Jim gave one hot dog to Rover.
(How many hot dogs did Jim give Rover?)	

Where did Jim put another hot dog?	Jim put another hot dog on a long fork.
(What did Jim do with another hot dog?)	
What did Father do?	Father called to Jim.
(Who called to Jim?)	
What did Jim do?	Jim turned around.
What did Rover see?	Rover saw the hot dog on the fork.
What did he do?	He took it off of the fork.
What did the family do?	The family laughed at Jim/him.

In the following expanded past tense story, multiple questions are given.

What did Beth do?	Beth called Red.
Who called Red?	
Whom did Beth call?	
What did Red do?	Red ate his dog biscuit.
What did Red eat?	
What did he leave on his plate?	He left one biscuit on his plate.
How many dog biscuits did he leave on his plate?	
What did he do after that?	After that, he fell asleep.
What did Red do?	
What did the squirrel do?	The squirrel stole the last biscuit.
Who stole the last biscuit?	
What did Red do?	Red woke up and looked at his plate.
Who woke up?	
How did he feel?	He was shocked (surprised).
Who was shocked (surprised)?	

A past tense story based on a single picture contains sequences of thoughts, but there is a greater amount of presumed previous action and, in essence, such stories are a simple form of imagination stories. The following story was based on a single picture. The events leading to the picture itself are presumed.

> Jan had a beautiful cat.
> Its name was Tabby.
> Jan wanted to enter Tabby's picture in a cat picture contest.
> First, Jan brushed Tabby's fur.
> Next, she found a cushion for Tabby to sit on.
> She put it on the floor by a big potted plant.
> After that, she put Tabby on the cushion.
> She said, "Tabby, you sit very still."
> Tabby sat very still.
> Finally, Jan took a picture of Tabby.
> She will enter it in the cat picture contest.
> Maybe Tabby's picture will win a prize.

A teacher will decide how many sentences to use and what format to put them in (e.g., a paragraph), based on knowledge of the child/group. How many and which question forms to use also will be determined by the teacher in this way.

A problem that often occurs when children use the present progressive and past tense forms of verbs is the inclination to drop the morphemes *-ing* and/or *-ed*, thus using only the root word/ verb. A teacher will need to monitor a child carefully so that he/she uses the complete spoken and written form.

More Advanced and Complex Language

Throughout the instructional program, the teacher should help the child in the following ways:

1. Teach what is needed and apply what has been taught in as many ways as possible.
2. Maintain use of language in any way appropriate.
3. Teach new material which is appropriate to the long-range language program and to meet short- and long-term goals.
4. Apply the most recently taught material in language stories in order to strengthen all of the child's language skills.
5. Ascertain that the child can retrieve the language of the instructional level, guide him/ her in expanding that language, and in generating spontaneous language of quality and quantity. For example one child wrote:

I went to the store.
Mother bought some food.
I got an ice cream cone.
Sue wanted a candy bar.
She could not find them.

The pupil employed correct, basic, and useful language. The child's instructional level, however, incorporated language of a more complex nature than she was using, so she was shown how to apply more of her language learning. The teacher guided her to reason out the expansion of her thoughts, and the child was able to generate spontaneous language of the following composition and structure:

Saturday I went to the store with Mother. While Mother bought the groceries, I got an ice cream cone. Sue, my sister, wanted a candy bar but she could not find them.

Naturally, this last goal will be the most difficult to obtain. Children with language deficiencies have a greater need for help in learning to manipulate language in order to express difficult concepts related to conditional ideas, concrete and abstract time durations, alternatives, possibilities, and concessions. When they have a command of vocabulary, concepts, and structure, however, they will be well on the way toward learning to use more complex language.

In reading the following discussions related to specific phases of language instruction, one should keep in mind that the idea of expanding a child's language from basic to complex should permeate all phases of the instruction and its application. If this is not done adequately, the child will be the loser. The teacher will have missed the opportunity to help the child experience even more success in his/her efforts to become competent in using the language skills that have been taught.

EXPERIENCE STORIES

McGinnis delayed the use of Experience Stories and direct instruction of future tense language until the students had learned past tense language. However, at the DuBard School for Language Disorders, experience stories have been applied in a different manner. *Initially*, very simple experience stories of three-four lines are used for special events. Children are *exposed* to the language, not expected to master the sentences and questions as is done in later instruction. This exposure to the language related to a special event, gives the child the opportunity to learn vocabulary and concepts without the expectation of full mastery. It also gives the parents of children who are nonverbal the information about special school events so that they may reinforce the vocabulary and concepts at home. As the children progress through the various levels of instruction in the DuBard Association Method® and their oral and written language competence increases, the expectation for their mastery of experience story/question language increases. See Sample Experience Stories written at three levels of difficulty in Appendix D.

An experience story is one which is based on an experiential activity that the teacher plans, carries out with the children, then converts the language from future tense which is used in the initial instruction to the past tense as a completed experience. Only the story related to the completed experience is copied by each child into his book.

The idea of using the experience story in language instruction is not new. Teachers of young children—both those who have profound deafness and those with good hearing acuity—have used such stories for a long time. McGinnis suggested using such stories with children challenged with language disorders only after they had an understanding of and some ability to use the past tense. Thus, she taught the future tense last. The extent to which a teacher uses the experience story for converting future tense into past tense will be determined by the child's abilities and needs. How a teacher uses experience stories will be determined by the particular situation and circumstances. For example, making a jack-o-lantern is an activity that children enjoy and which is full of language opportunities for children at a wide range of language levels. Typically, *the past tense form of the story is written in the child's book.*

Experience stories provide an easy way to teach the relationship between the future tense and past tense concepts and language structures. While such stories are used easily with young children in typical kindergartens and first grade, use of such stories with young children with language disorders can be very misleading. Theoretically, putting specific material in a child's book is an indication to the child, to the teacher, to the parents, and to subsequent teachers that the child understands the content, can read it, and can use at least some of it. This may not be the case with some children until they have had adequate foundation instruction at earlier levels of language. Nevertheless, such stories can have a limited value with children with low language competence. Putting the story in the child's book then becomes a means of letting the parents know what has happened at school.

In presenting an experience story as a part of the instructional program, the planned experience should be written on the chalkboard in the future tense. As always, new vocabulary is taught prior to the introduction of the story. Oral reading, auditory-visual work, auditory work and a measure of memory work, as well as copying the story should be completed as part of the instructional work prior to the activity. After the activity has been completed, the language should be changed on the chalkboard story so that the child will begin to understand and to see the changing of words related to incomplete action and completed actions, that is, future and past tense language. A simple experience story follows. As in all story levels of the DuBard Association Method®, the story is taught first and questions are added when the story has been mastered.

Where will we go?	We will go to the store.
What will Tom get?	Tom will get some pencils.[2]
What will Mary get?	Mary will get some paper.
What will we see?	We will see lots of things.

Sufficient work should be completed to give the children a foundation for what is expected during the experience. The story should be left on the chalkboard for use after the activity has been completed. Follow-up work will result in the story appearing in the following form, the teacher guiding the change of tenses, sentence by sentence and question by question. With a sufficient amount of instruction and similar experience stories, the children will be expected to make the tense changes.

	did		went
Where ~~will~~ we go?		We ~~will go~~ to the store.	
	did		got
What ~~will~~ Tom get?		Tom ~~will get~~ some pencils.	
	did		got
What ~~will~~ Mary get?		Mary ~~will get~~ some paper.	
	did		saw
What ~~will~~ we see?		We ~~will see~~ lots of things.	
What things did we see?		We saw a fire.	
			We saw a fire truck.	
What people did we see?		We saw some firemen and some policemen.	

Additional questions, such as "Who got some ________?", are also appropriate once the children have had some instruction related to the basic question form.

Here is another sample experience story.

This afternoon we will see a movie.
The name of the movie is ________.
It will be a funny movie.

After seeing the movie, the future tense language should be changed to the past tense so that the child can copy the completed form in his/her book. If there were events that could be commented on in the final story form, those lines should be added. Such a final form might be as follows:

When did we see the movie?	This afternoon (yesterday or ________ afternoon) we saw a movie.
What was the name of the movie?	The name of the movie was ________.
What was the movie (it) about?	The movie was about ________.
Was the movie funny or sad?	The movie was funny.
(Perhaps added to the original future tense story:)	
What happened that was special?	We had a surprise.[1][2]
What was the surprise?[1][2]	________ brought us some popcorn to eat during the movie.

A summary of the story of the movie would not be a part of the experience, per se. However, the teacher might develop a separate story which would relate more details about the movie. This would be an appropriate language lesson within its own right.

IMAGINATION STORIES

During the day-to-day, month-to-month tasks of guiding children with language deficiencies through an incremental systematic language program, the teacher may lose sight of the ultimate goal. In the beginning, language is written about a picture. *The ultimate goal is for the child to be sufficiently knowledgeable and competent in language to visualize the appropriate picture when reading the printed page.* Imagination stories aid in achieving this goal.

We cannot withdraw money from a bank unless we have first deposited some. Teaching language by means of the techniques described herein is, in essence, putting money in the bank. By the same token, developing imagination stories is taking money out. "The child must draw on his past experiences with language in telling what might have happened to bring about the result shown in the picture used for building the story" (McGinnis 1963, 123). Some children need more guidance than others. The teacher is there to help them utilize their spontaneous language to expand ideas and language structure from simple into more complex and imaginative forms.

With Imagination Story instruction, pictures are always used. Language may be used in the story which is *not obvious* in the picture, thus, one partially *imagines* what has taken place or will take place. Imagination stories can be developed in *three levels of difficulty*. (1) The teacher constructs a story about a picture and writes it on the chalkboard. The usual skills, excluding memory of the whole story, appropriate questions, and various kinds of seatwork activities are used for that particular story. (2) At a later time, the teacher asks the children to construct their own story about the same picture and gives them whatever help they need. The teacher, in effect, serves as editor. This helps children to experience the versatility of language and to understand that a number of stories can be written about a given picture. Memorizing such stories is not appropriate. However, a variety of comprehension questions/activities may be used appropriately. These may include questions regarding how characters felt, expected additional outcomes, reasoning, etc. (3) Finally, the children

are given pictures for which they have had no specific instruction and write stories about them. The ultimate goal is for the child to be able to create language about a picture and to be able to create a mental picture for language he/she reads. This level of instruction is similar to what is considered to be creative writing in general education settings.

THE CHILD'S BOOK: FROM START TO FINISH IN SUMMARY

The primary purpose of the child's book is to provide an accurate, systematically developed record of the child's progression through the incremental stages of the vertical program. At the phoneme and drop-drill stages the book should record each phoneme as it is taught. The number of drop drills included in the book will depend on the progress of the child. If the child needs additional practice to strengthen writing, speech, or memory skills, the number of drop drills in the book will be greater than for other students. Once one begins teaching words through the use of cross drills, drop drills should be discontinued. The book then becomes a record of new phonemes taught, enough syllable/cross drills to be representative of the child's vocabulary, instructions, and each new word taught. Each word should be written under the appropriate picture, alternating two colors to depict the number of sounds in the word. After the child gains competence in learning this vocabulary, especially memory for sequence, the use of two colors may be discontinued and only one color used. If the child needs a "crutch," there is no reason for not using it. On the other hand, if he/she does not need an additional clue in order to recall the spoken and written forms, there is no need to provide it.

In subsequent incremental stages, several sentence and question forms of each new language concept and construction should be included. Often a page of repetitive sentences depicting the concept of "I see a/some/an _______" a page of "this is a/some/an _______," "I want a/some/an _______," each with the appropriate question written one time on the facing page, is helpful. Each animal story, with appropriate question language on the facing page, should be placed in the child's book. *Such material can be used at home for practice and can be helpful to parents as a guideline regarding the child's instructional program, which will show how they can work with their child at home regularly, including during holidays.* The book can become part of a measuring stick to indicate the child's level in the instructional program. Since traditional grades and grade levels are not used, it is important that parents have some indication of the child's progress and what lies ahead in the instructional program.

At upper levels of the instructional program, the book may serve as a reference for the teacher in planning as well as a record of the kinds of experiences, language concepts, and sentence constructions the child has been taught. Although there is no magic in the book itself, each child seems to demonstrate a measure of pride in his/her book and the accomplishments it represents.

Appendix B provides guidelines for sequential content and style for a child's book. When the teacher writes the work in the child's book, color differentiation is used. When the child assumes responsibility for writing the work, color differentiation in the book should be discontinued. The teacher should continue its use in other instruction, however, if using two colors makes the child's learning easier.

TEACHING AIDS

Commercial Texts

Teachers may be tempted to utilize commercial texts sooner than is advisable. Although writing one's own materials in order to achieve specific goals is demanding, it is often advantageous to do so. A solid foundation in language, acquired through the incremental levels described herein, will make the use of commercial texts immeasurably easier. In the best of circumstances, one is continually confronted with the difficulties that language in commercial materials presents; solutions to the problems and explanations can require the best efforts of the most ingenious teacher. Problems in commercial texts include abstract concepts, multiplicity of meanings, idioms, reference pronouns, and too much conversational language too soon.

Choice of commercial texts will be an important factor in the most advanced level of the language instruction program. Some texts can be applied to "straight language" principles better than others. During the last few years, commercial materials have been developed to serve a multitude of needs and certain texts reflect the principles and employ the techniques described herein. At the DuBard School for Language Disorders special texts were written for internal use to emphasize language for pictorial materials which initially had only one word for the typical child to read. One advantage of writing one's own language readers is that the teacher can tailor the language material to teach or reinforce specific concepts and principles of language. In recent years a variety of good, controlled-language readers with phonetically decodable vocabulary has emerged on the commercial market. Use of these as appropriate can be a positive experience for students who like to read in a book similar to their peers in general education.

During the imagination story level of language instruction, the curriculum has been expanded to use more conventional and commercially available materials effectively. Often, we have had to simplify and clarify the instructions for our students. The benefit of such materials is that they expose the children to the kinds of academic tasks they will encounter when they enter typical schools.

Commercial materials in reading, social studies, science, and math present difficulties that are more or less expected by anyone teaching. There will be new concepts, new vocabulary, more abstract language, problems related to multiplicity of meanings, and a variety of challenges related to the language of each subject area per se. Materials related to spelling texts present special additional problems.

For the most part, the child with language learning differences taught through the multisensory techniques we have described, succeeds in learning to spell the words in such texts. It is the other activities related to the words in the spelling lists that present problems. For example, "Say *far*. Listen for the vowel + r sounds. Which letters spell the vowel + r sounds? Now say the other spelling words. Do they have the same vowel + r sounds as far? Which letters spell the vowel + r sounds in these words?" (Henderson et al. 1987a, 130).

In earlier years, texts such as *Spelling* (Henderson et al. 1987) were used in the DuBard School for Language Disorders. The text used both manuscript and cursive forms of writing and provided expanded language and vocabulary. If the teacher *uses a text to teach language*, the potential for learning is excellent. However, *if the teaching of language is not the primary goal and the teacher expects the child to read the instructions and automatically know what and how to do the activity, there can be major pitfalls.* For example, "The spelling words in the unit all have the same vowel. In which words do you hear the vowel sound at the end? In which words do you hear the vowel sound in the middle? Do all of the words have the same vowel letters?" (Henderson et al. 1987b, 62). In order to complete the exercise successfully, the child will need to have basic knowledge related to vowel sounds, vowel letters, the differentiations between and/or among them, as well as knowledge of positioning of sounds and letters in the words. This can be a lot for the child with language disorders to sort out. Comparable exercises related to consonant letters and sounds are included, too. While such work is excellent, teachers need to carefully analyze the language of the instructions/exercises and adequately prepare their children for each task. This is the key to success or frustration for the child. An alternative to spelling textbooks is instruction in syllable types and syllable division rules. This instruction is used in the DuBard School now for students for whom it is appropriate.

The Fitzgerald Key

As McGinnis altered her teaching techniques resulting in the Association Method, she deleted a number of components of instruction commonly used in teaching young children who were deaf in an oral-aural education program. She did so because of the ineffectiveness of those components with her population of children who were *presumed* to be deaf. The Fitzgerald Key was a component which she deleted. However, we have been able to apply the principles of the Fitzgerald Key effectively at a relatively early time in the second unit of language.

Edith Fitzgerald's Key for Straight Language (1963) presents language in a way that helps children understand the principles of sentence structure. In addition to placing the W-words in a structured heading to portray the syntactical patterns, she used certain symbols to reduce confusion related to word classes and constructions. An example of a modified version of the Fitzgerald Key appears in figure 6.10.

Who/ What	Verb	Whose/ What	Where	When
I	saw	a dog.		
Tom	has	a bike.		
Beth	went		to the mall	yesterday.

FIG. 6.10. A modified form of the Fitzgerald Key

Charts

McGinnis used many kinds of charts—charts for colors, commands, nouns (pictures only and noun lists), numbers, present progressive questions, and verbs (listing the verb with the future tense and past tense forms in other columns)—as a record of what the children have accomplished. She felt that children should be able to refer to them if they needed to refresh their memories. While too many charts can make a classroom with limited space appear cluttered, a few carefully selected charts can be helpful.

Sequential Language Program

McGinnis referred to a vertical program which was the complete language program, and to a horizontal program, which was the plan for day-to-day instruction. In Table 7 we give a detailed presentation of the program. The other tables provide long-term goals and day-to-day activities which are useful guides for teachers' planning needs.

TABLE 4

Expanded Second Unit of Language

LONG-TERM GOALS

1. Animal stories/questions
   Stories of gradually increasing length and complexity

2. Basic and advanced vocabulary taught through cross-drill and/or whole-word methods

3. Establish competence with numbers six through thirty. Counting by fives for clock work

4. Addition language: math and/or math facts

5. Time concepts: calendar and clock

6. Inanimate object stories/questions

7. Maintenance of previously taught material

8. Incidental language

DAY-TO-DAY ACTIVITIES (Math work, time, clock, calendar, days of week/months of year)

1. All skills for new materials must be established and maintained (see table 2)

2. Establish reading recognition for dictation skills for words selected randomly from questions.

3. Apply sentence/question form and incidental language activities

4. Teach days of week; apply in calendar story question format; teach months of year. Apply in expanded story/question format.

5. Continue language math and/or introduce traditional math facts about addition; establish all skills (see Correlative Programs)

6. Clock time: on the hour, after the hour, before the hour

7. Maintenance of skills and applications for all previously taught content

8. Instruction and application of language appropriate for spontaneous communication

---

TABLE 5

Expanded Instruction of Stories, Math and Special Concepts: Upper Level, Second Unit

---

LONG-TERM GOALS

1. Personal stories/questions
2. Advanced Vocabulary (whole-word method)
3. Numerals thirty-one to one hundred
4. Establish language and concepts for addition/subtraction math facts; apply in basic word problems
5. Maintenance of all previously taught content
6. Preposition sentences/questions
7. Round-up through preposition stories/questions
8. Descriptive stories/questions
9. Expand incidental/personal stories
10. Present progressive sentences, questions and stories

SPECIFIC SHORT-TERM ACTIVITIES TO ACHIEVE DESIRED GOALS

1. Instruction of new material at chalkboard
2. Establishing all skills for new materials: precise articulation, reading, auditory-visual, acoustic, copying, memory for sequence (both oral and written), dictation (sentences, questions, words out of context)
3. Applying language from structured instructional program to use in incidental oral and written language
4. Establishing all skills for math facts in structured activities
5. Establishing all skills for simple addition and subtraction word problems
6. Teach numerals, number words and concepts for thirty-one to one hundred; establish all skills
7. Generate new stories/questions using previously taught language concepts, principles and vocabulary without structured instruction
8. Maintain skills and application for all previously taught content

---

TABLE 6

Vocabulary Concepts for Third Unit of Language

LONG–TERM GOALS

1. Advanced vocabulary (whole-word method)

2. Establish language and concepts for multiplication/division math facts and related word problems

3. Past tense sentences/questions

4. Past tense stories/questions
   Two-to-four picture sequence
   Single picture: sequence language applied

5. Experience stories/questions

6. Imagination stories/questions
   Direct and indirect discourse and more difficult language concepts and skills (see Chapter 4)

7. Transfer to commercial texts as appropriate; establish child's ability to create mental pictures for language he/she reads

8. Maintenance of all previously taught content

SPECIFIC SHORT-TERM ACTIVITIES TO ACHIEVE DESIRED GOALS

1. Instruction of new material at chalkboard

2. Establish all skills for new materials: precise articulation, reading, auditory-visual (lipreading), association, acoustic, copying, memory for sequence (both oral and written), dictation (sentences, question, words out of context)

3. Application of language from structured instructional program to use in incidental oral and written language

4. Establish all skills for math facts in structured activities

5. Establish all skills for word problems including multiplication and division

6. Instruction of experience stories in future tense converted to past tense after instruction has been completed

7. Apply all previously learned language to child-generated/teacher-guided imagination stories

8. Child-generated imagination stories (limited teacher guidance); formulation of questions for stories

9. Maintain skills and application for all previously taught content

10. Expand instruction to include language of specific subject areas (e.g., science, social studies, physical education, spelling, etc.)

11. Careful use of commercial texts in English, math, spelling, etc.

TABLE 7

Sequential Language Program

	Phonemes Drop Drills Words Cross Drills (50 Nouns±)	**First Unit**
I have; I saw; _____ has Incidental language begins Numbers (1-5); colors	Concept Repetitive sentences/questions (I see; this is; I want) Repetitive sentences with numbers/how many questions	**Second Unit**
Language math begins Clock work begins (Cross drill may be discontinued)	Animal Stories/questions Includes expanded concepts	
	Inanimate object stories (Introduce "it")/questions	
Capitalize names	Personal stories: two each for Self; Boy; Girl/questions	
May introduce inverted question and may begin using capital letters at beginning of sentences; Behind/beside/over + others introduced in context	Preposition sentences in/on/under/questions Descriptive stories (rooms, areas of a home) may add: by/in the corner/inside/outside/questions	
	Present progressive sentences/questions	
Top/bottom/first/second/third/middle	Present progressive stories/questions	
	Past tense sentences/questions	**Third Unit**
	Past tense sequence stories/questions	
First/next/then/after	Past tense stories/questions (single picture)	
One day + other time-related phrases	*Experience stories/questions	
Direct discourse-indirect discourse; advanced and more complex concepts and grammatical constructions	Imagination stories/questions and comprehension activities	
	Texts	

Left vertical label: Vocabulary teaching—**correlative programs** of various kinds

Right vertical label: Sentences, questions, and language of **correlative program**

*Experience stories may be utilized earlier in the instructional program. See pages 107-109.

CHAPTER

7

Correlative Programs

McGinnis (1963) identified correlative programs as those related to developing attention and interest as well as skills in writing and articulation. Although programs related to numbers and calendar work are not a part of the language program which McGinnis referred to as the vertical program (long-term goals), they do indeed deal with and use a significant amount of language. By the time the children have achieved some basic language in the instructional program, it can be expected that they will have become attentive to learning and are eager to learn new concepts and apply them to daily activities.

HANDWRITING

The basic principles associated with developing writing skills are very important. First and foremost, children who are left-handed should have their paper slanted in the direction opposite to that appropriate for those who are right-handed. Throughout the decades, elementary teachers have allowed the improper slant of the paper for children who were left-handed. Countless children developed poor mechanics in penmanship because they learned to write with the paper slanted the wrong way with the left arm parallel to the body, the left hand twisted into an awkward position, and the pencil or pen at a twelve o'clock to six o'clock position. The paper should be slanted properly for the person who is left-handed to be able to learn to write correctly.

Basic strokes of penmanship include large and small ovals for such letters as the cursive *a, g, d,*

c; loops for *l, e, f, b, k*; vertical strokes for *t* and *d*, without a loop; and inverted u strokes for *m* and *n*. Letter formation should be clear and without unnecessary loops and fancy strokes. Written skills should include clear spacing between words in a sentence. *In recent years, we have found it helpful to begin all letters with an upstroke so that the child's beginning point is always on the line.*

Special paper with bold, black lines and wider than usual spaces may be very helpful to beginning writers. The spaces should become more narrow as the child's handwriting skills improve. This teacher-prepared paper may include horizontal lines as well as paper with both horizontal and two vertical lines to provide structure for use in copying cross drills, dictation, and written recall activities. *The child should always use the same type of paper for homework activities as is being used in the classroom.* See Chapter 6 for additional information regarding the development of handwriting skills.

The ultimate goal is the use of commercially prepared wide-ruled paper. Children should not be expected to write on commercially prepared paper until their writing form and size are appropriately clear and small. In the DuBard School for Language Disorders, children are taught to skip lines on commercial paper. Frequently, in the process of developing writing skills, the child will progress through a phase in which writing is too small for the commercial paper. At this time, the teacher should instruct the child regarding tall letters touching the lines above and below and short letters being written to the midpoint. This is critical in establishing long-term legibility.

TRANSFER TO READING PRINT

The matter of transferring to the reading of print is highly individualized. McGinnis's hard-core population transferred to reading print during or after instruction at the imagination story level. However, in more recent years, we have made modifications to meet the needs of more varied groups of children with language disorders, that is, those with severe developmental language disorders as well as those on the other end of the continuum who have dyslexia. These children may be viewed in three general categories.

1. Learning to read cursive and print simultaneously and with ease is generally possible for *children with good visual perceptual/visual memory skills*. This is often begun at the CV or CVC word level, if not earlier. For example, a child whose primary reason for instruction in the DuBard Association Method® is for remediation of a severe articulation disorder may have visual skills which will permit early introduction of both cursive and print for reading.

2. The typical transfer to the reading of print for children with *more severe language disorders* who are enrolled in the full time, intensive program at the DuBard School for Language Disorders is made at approximately the Personal Story level of instruction. As instruction in the DuBard Association Method® progresses in cursive at this story level, the teacher may guide the transfer to reading of print with primary and secondary phonemes, previously taught CV and CVC vocabulary, and so on, unless this has occurred spontaneously. When it is established that the child is able to read the previously taught material in print, instruction in subsequent levels of the DuBard Association Method® may *alternate between cursive and print for reading*. Children are not taught to write in print in our setting.

3. The transfer for children with *severe visual perception/visual motor integration skill* deficits may be delayed beyond the personal story level cited above. For these children, it is essential that they are thoroughly competent in reading in cursive before instruction in print begins.

PREPARING FOR MATHEMATICS

Teaching Numerals, Number Words, and Concepts

McGinnis taught the numbers up to at least four before proceeding to animal story instruction. However, with the addition of the Repetitive Sentence with Numbers level of instruction, at the DuBard School for Language Disorders it has been our practice to teach *numerals, number words, and concepts* one through five during the basic Repetitive Sentence level of instruction. This prepares children for application of the number words at the Repetitive Sentence with Numbers instructional level and beyond. The children will have developed effective reading skills through the cross-drill work, so the written language becomes the avenue/tool for teaching new material. The teacher is responsible for determining how many items can be taught as new material in one session or per day. Each child differs in tolerance for new learning. For some, one new item a day might be enough, since they also will be learning other new vocabulary. Others might be able to achieve competence on more than that during a single instructional session. In any case, once the number concepts have been taught as described below, that linguistic content should be reinforced with activities like those used for noun vocabulary. It will be helpful for the teacher to remember the basic tenet of mastery presented frequently in earlier chapters: The goal of 90% accuracy for oral and written recall with automaticity is a sound goal when making a decision to move forward with new instruction.

Linguistic Content: Numerals and words for those numerals combined with domino blocks as shown in figure 7.1.

Skills:

The same skills that were established when teaching vocabulary, sentences, questions, and stories should be developed with number concepts and the appropriate related work. The redundancy is a very important feature.

Procedures:

The number words one through five are introduced on a whole-word basis rather than through cross drills. Use the chalkboard for instruction as before and capitalize on the reading skills of the children. Keep oral communication and elaboration to a minimum as far as instruction is concerned. Teach as many new items per day as the child can learn without overloading his/her system. Present one item at a time, drawing and writing whatever is needed. Have the child read the word, associate it with the number of dots in the domino block, and then look at the numeral.

By keeping the dots in the same block of the domino, the child is able to see the organization more easily. After the concepts and words have been learned, a teacher can devise activities that present the numbers in different arrangements so that the child does not think that they are always in that particular arrangement. A page showing the numbers up to ten as dominoes should be put in the child's book as a reference, or a similar presentation may be used.

one 1 (Show the speech as wun in cursive writing.)
two 2 (Show the speech as tòo in cursive writing.)
three 3 (All words should be written in cursive form.)

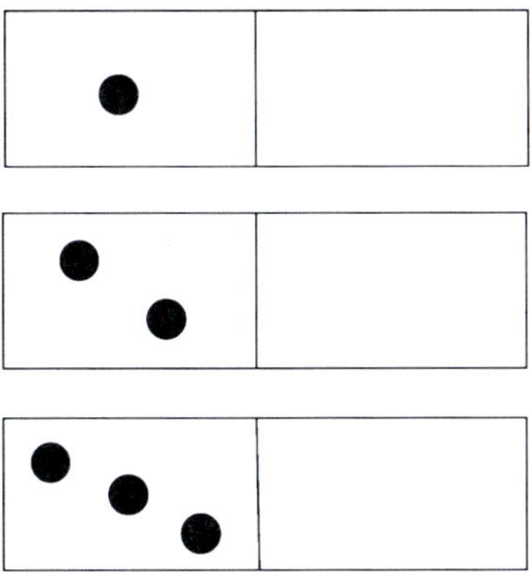

FIG. 7.1. A way to teach numbers

Teachers need to be sure that the child understands the number concepts apart from the numeral and/or number word and can demonstrate this understanding. For example, the child reads the word or numeral and is able to identify the corresponding number of objects. A number of activities can be devised to achieve this goal. All skills should be established as is done with language instruction.

Whatever commercial materials might be used, the teacher should remember that the child taught according to procedures of the DuBard Association Method® is able to learn numeral names easiest by reading them, i.e., breaking the written code through phonetics and building up his/her memory for sequence by applying these skills. Learning to associate the word with the numeral after

he/she can read is a matter of reinforcement. The amount of repetition depends on the child/group.

Plurals: Instruction

The only plural form taught in context in our setting has been *eyes;* on rare occasions with selected children, the plural form *peas* has been taught at the noun, cross-drill level because of the way it is used. Otherwise, at the noun level, the only plurals used will have been *collective nouns,* such as *food* and/or plurals which do not require adding *s* or *es,* such as *feet, fish or deer.* Plurals and numbers through four must have been taught before they can be applied in the animal story work discussed earlier. Plurals and numbers are taught as part of the short-term goals program in the early part of the sentence work of the long-term goals program. When the concepts are established adequately, they can then be applied in the linguistic content of the repetitive sentences and question work. Later, they will be applied in the animal story work.

Instruction about plurals does not have to be complicated. The most important thing to remember is that rules are *not* dealt with or incorporated into the instruction. The children's reading skills are used to maximum advantage and both words and numerals are used in the plural instruction work. Plurals requiring the changing of *y* to *i* and adding *es* and plurals requiring a complete change in spelling, such as *man* versus *men,* are not taught at the early levels of the instruction about plurals. Those forms can be taught more easily in context after the child has learned more language, is more competent with it, and can deal with variables more easily.

To teach the plural form of a word, the teacher needs only to show the appropriate kind of pictures and linguistic information on the chalkboard and apply the new linguistic unit. Showing the *s,* or the *es* later, in a different color, children are made aware of a difference between what they already know and what they are being given that is new. The new form can then be applied to pictorial material in the repetitive sentences with number concepts: "this is *(one)* _______." "I see _______ _______s," or "I saw _______ _______s." If small identical or similar objects are used, the sentence, "I want _______ _______s," associating the number of items with the linguistic form, can be used. When the child has established the skills of saying and writing the sentences and has established auditory skills on the new material, a question form, such as, "how many _______s do you have?" is used. Frequently, in observing the performance of children with language disorders at this level, it is noted that they often have considerable difficulty making an association between the linguistic units "how many . . ?" and the numeral words and concepts. As the skills are developing, it is vital that the child be put in the question-asking role as "the teacher" so that he/she can establish ability to ask questions properly.

Reinforcement activities can include picture-number cards which have varying numbers of the same items on them. Such cards can be made without great difficulty. Many math workbooks of the early levels have excellent materials for making the desired cards or they may be created easily using pictures from the internet. It should be noted that, at this time in the child's instructional program, the workbook as designed for the child in general education will be essentially useless.

After the teacher has carried out the initial instruction about the plurals, a chart with this information can be a useful reference for the children. An illustration of such a chart is given in figure 7.2. Cursive writing should be used on all charts. The number over the *s* tells the child whether the final *s* is pronounced as *voiceless* versus *voiced final*

s. See Repetitive Sentences with Numbers "How Many" Concepts in the preceding chapter for additional information on plurals instruction.

Teaching Language Math

Typically, children are ready to begin language math when they are at the animal story level of instruction. To establish the concept of addition for children with severe communication disorders, the following incremental and sequential format, known as "language math," has been utilized. When a child succeeds in understanding and establishing all skills at each given level, a subsequent level can be introduced. Initial instruction should take place at the chalkboard. The teacher should use his/her knowledge of the children's needs in making decisions as to the use of pictures drawn on the board and/or math picture cards. (See figure 7.3.) The volume of material needed and the length of time required to establish all skills at each level will vary from child to child. However, the child, when shown the math picture card, should be able to recall the entire sentence accurately in oral and written forms before proceeding to the next level. Sound knowledge at each step is essential if the child is to experience success with future use of traditional math materials.

one	two, three, four, five
I	2, 3, 4, 5
hat	hats [1]
shoe	shoes [2]
cat	cats [1]
dog	dogs [2]
book	books [2][1]
chair	chairs [2]

FIG. 7.2. A chart to help teach plurals

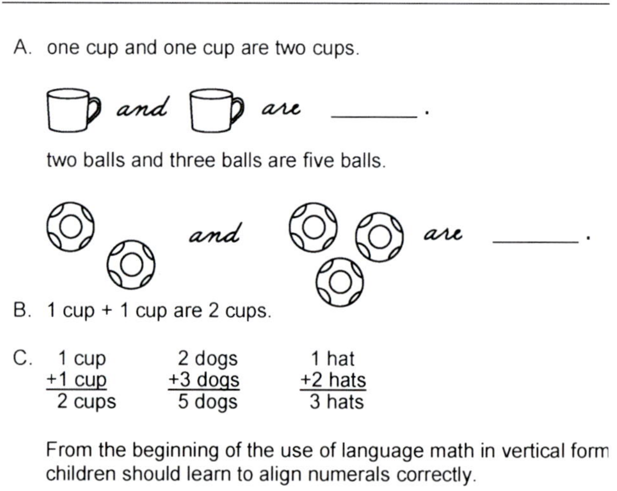

FIG. 7.3. Examples of math sentences and math pictures

Progressing from words, to pictures used with words, to the use of math symbols is a gradual process. The teacher must make sure that the child has comprehension of word-picture stages before the symbols are introduced. A simple format consisting of converting words to mathematical symbols is illustrated and can be a useful technique. The goal is to establish the child's competence with the mathematical symbols themselves; care should be taken to make sure the child understands the meanings of the symbols.

Teaching Math Facts: Addition

Children who have memory deficits have better success in establishing memory for addition and subtraction facts if they are introduced in the sequence which follows. This particular sequence is used so that children can grasp the *concept of* and *memory for* adding 1, 2, or 3 to the addend. We believe it is essential to *establish memory for the first five facts in a group* before introducing the remaining five. Oral and written recall should be established for one set of addends before proceeding to instruction for another addend. The procedure used in the noun review with words (Chapter 6) is an appropriate format to apply to establish the memory for math facts. Commercially prepared and/or teacher-made math flash cards are useful at this level of instruction.

Sequence of Instruction:

0	1	2	3	4	5	6	7	8	9
+1	+1	+1	+1	+1	+1	+1	+1	+1	+1

Specific instruction is required to establish oral, written, and conceptual skills for "zero" before it is used in computations. Based on a child's understanding of zero, teachers need to decide whether to teach plus two or plus zero next.

0	1	2	3	4	5	6	7	8	9
+2	+2	+2	+2	+2	+2	+2	+2	+2	+2

0	1	2	3	4	5	6	7	8	9
+0	+0	+0	+0	+0	+0	+0	+0	+0	+0

0	1	2	3	4	5	6	7	8	9
+3	+3	+3	+3	+3	+3	+3	+3	+3	+3

Beginning Word Problems

Simple language (word) problems should be included in the instructional program as soon as possible. Although this is more easily said than done, it is a necessity. The simplest of word problems requires that the child understand the language which gives information related to the computation process. Without that understanding, success with such problems will be lacking. It is tempting for teachers to teach more and more computation skills without giving children the opportunity to apply the computations to problem solving. Following such a practice often results in poor problem-solving skills by students.

The child with language learning differences usually has a great deal of difficulty in solving basic elementary math problems. This weakness should be kept in mind when planning and implementing each new computation and while teaching word problems and developing skills in applying the computation to the solution of problems. The language related to problems is of paramount significance even after the basic concepts have been established. Analyzing the language related to computations will help the instruction related to problem solving. Not all such language would be taught at the same time, but as skills are established in the computation per se, simple word problems using the language related to that computation should be taught. If the child is to experience success with this type of work, the words in the problem which give the "clue" to selecting the correct computation must first be taught. Some of the clue words which can be of help to any child include:

Addition	**Subtraction**
... in all; all together; altogether	left; ...more than; less than
... together; more; total	fewer than, greater, greater than

Similar analyses can be made for multiplication and division. The language of verbs and "clue" words can become very complex even at the second and third-grade levels. Therefore, a very careful foundation needs to be established before texts and/or workbooks are used by the children.

Simple addition word problems, utilizing vocabulary which has been taught previously, may be introduced when the above content has been mastered.

For example:

Tom has two apples.
Jane has one apple.
How many apples do they have in all?

    2 apples
  +1 apple
    3 apples in all

They have three apples in all.

Mary has three cookies.
John has two cookies.
How many cookies do they have all together?

3 cookies
<u>+2 cookies</u>
5 cookies all together

They have five cookies all together.

Teaching Math Facts: Subtraction

When the above addition facts and simple word problems have been well-established, subtraction facts should be introduced. It may be appropriate to do so while continuing instruction of simple addition word problems. Addition facts should be maintained while memory for subtraction facts is being established. Subtraction or the concept of "to take away" can be taught at the board or by demonstrating the idea with small objects. It is suggested that the language "take away" be used initially since it is more concrete and easier for children to understand than "minus." *Subtraction facts are taught in the same sequence as outlined for addition facts.*

E.g.:

1	2	3	4
<u>–1</u>	<u>–1</u>	<u>–1</u>	<u>–1</u>

When memory for subtraction facts through minus three has been established, simple subtraction word problems may be introduced. As with addition, clue words related to subtraction should be taught carefully (e.g., left, more/fewer...than, etc.).

Jill has five pencils.
She gave two pencils to Dan.
How many pencils does she have left/now?

5 pencils
<u>–2 pencils</u>
3 pencils left

She has three pencils left/now.

After initial instruction of several problems at the board and copying by the child, practice work should progress to the teacher providing the three-line problem for either addition or subtraction. The child should be able to set up the problem, do the computation, and answer the question with an appropriate sentence. An important goal is for the child to understand the interrelationship between addition and subtraction so that he/she will understand the "checking" process in subsequent work. For example, the child learns to check the

addition fact, 7 + 3 = 10, by subtracting the addend from the sum, 10 – 3 = 7.

After establishing competence with +0, +1, +2, +3, –0, –1, –2, –3 facts and beginning simple word problems, instruction should continue for the following math facts: +4, +5, –4, –5, +6, +7, –6, –7, +8, +9, –8, –9.

At a more advanced level of word problems, the following type of analysis can be used. It is appropriate for all children, with or without language difficulties, because it helps them to think through word problems.

Sample problem: Tom has four apples. His sister has two apples. How many apples do they have in all?

Analysis:

The problem tells:	Tom has 4 apples. His sister has 2 apples.
The problem asks:	How many apples do they have in all?
Solution:	Add to find (how many) in all.
Work:	4 apples : (Tom's) +2 apples : (his sister's) ――――――― 6 apples in all
The answer:	Tom and his sister have 6 apples in all.

Each word problem can be analyzed in a similar manner. More advanced problems requiring two and three processes will be easier for children to solve if they have first learned how to think and analyze for themselves. In essence, this is the goal of this kind of problem. The following is an example of a more advanced problem.

Sample problem: Mother sent Landon and Nathan to the store. She told them to get oranges, crackers, and a quart of milk. She gave them $10.00 for the items. The oranges cost 99 cents; the crackers cost $3.25; the milk cost $3.18. How much should they get in change?

Analysis:

The problem tells:	She gave them $10.00 for the items. The oranges cost 99 cents; the crackers cost $3.25; the milk cost $3.18.

The problem asks: How much change should they get?

First, I must find out: the total cost of the items

I will: Add

Work:

$$\begin{array}{ll} \$ \ .99 & \text{cost of oranges} \\ 3.25 & \text{cost of crackers} \\ \underline{3.18} & \text{cost of milk} \\ \$7.42 & \text{total cost of the items} \end{array}$$

Next, I will subtract the total cost from the amount of money they had.

Work:

$$\begin{array}{ll} \$10.00 & \text{the amount Mother gave them} \\ \underline{- \ 7.42} & \text{total cost of the items} \\ \$ \ 2.58 & \text{amount of change they should get} \end{array}$$

The answer is: They should get $2.58 in change.

Rote Counting

Simultaneously, while developing skills in language math, math facts, and simple word problems, the teaching of counting by rote continues. McGinnis used a chart showing columns of numbers (figure 7.4) to teach children to count to fifty in rote fashion. It should be pointed out that in the second column, a 1 is added before each number, a 2 in the next column, and so on (McGinnis, 1963). The children are taught the speech and reading for twenty, thirty, forty, and fifty, as needed, so that they can say twenty-one, thirty-five, and so on through fifty.

Counting by Fives

Counting by fives, and subsequent teaching of telling time on the hour, typically occurs simultaneously with the instruction of beginning math facts and simple word problems. The skill of counting by fives must be established before teaching the child to tell time after and before the hour by the traditional analog clock. So that the child may visualize the process, numbers may be written on the board as shown in figure 7.5. The teacher should explain to the child that he/she will not read every number, but only those which are circled. Memory for counting 5, 10, 15, 20, 25, 30 in sequence may be established by the use of the same teaching

1	1	1	1	1
2	2	2	2	2
3	3	3	3	3
4	4	4	4	4
5	5	5	5	5
6	6	6	6	6
7	7	7	7	7
8	8	8	8	8
9	9	9	9	9
10	10	10	10	10

1	11	21	31	41
2	12	22	32	42
3	13	23	33	43
4	14	24	34	44
5	15	25	35	45
6	16	26	36	46
7	17	27	37	47
8	18	28	38	48
9	19	29	39	49
10	20	30	40	50

FIG. 7.4. A chart for practicing the numbers one through fifty

techniques which are used in establishing memory for nouns, etc. At a later time, the same procedure may be used for teaching counting by twos, tens, etc.

Numeral work can be incorporated in the short-term goals in a number of ways, including repetitive sentences, rote counting, clock work, and calendar work. Rather than using a commercial calendar, the teacher and students can make a calendar for each new month. Ultimately, this information can be used to teach ordinal numbers (first, second, third, etc.).

Because children with language disorders have difficulty storing and retrieving information, the same kinds of redundancy and reinforcement activities are often needed for math concepts as for other aspects of the instructional program. The teacher who recognizes this fact can provide adequate supportive work until extensive drill is no longer necessary. The overlearning which may result from repetitive reinforcement pays dividends when the child enters general education classroom programs.

Transferring to Math Texts

When the teacher has the desire or need to use traditional math texts and accompanying workbooks, the commercial materials should be analyzed and selected carefully. Those which provide a maximum amount of repetition on any mathematical processes on consecutive pages are more appropriate for children with language challenges than those which change math concepts and processes from page to page. Initially, the goals of transferring to a math text/workbook should be to *apply previously learned math skills successfully and to read and follow the directions in a new format.* Teachers should make sure that they *teach* the child the mathematical process in the structured format *before* using commercial workbooks. Children should be able to add and subtract up to four before beginning a first-grade workbook. Teaching of the remaining math facts as described earlier may be continued simultaneously with the use of the text/workbooks and simple word problems. However, if the child is not well-grounded in the respective processes, use of the workbook pages can become frustrating and unproductive.

Subsequently, children with language disorders will need to learn multiplication and division computation. It is important for them to know the relationship between the two processes, so that they can succeed with advanced-level word problems. Care should be taken to insure that the child understands the principles of multiplying and dividing, as well as recalling the facts from memory. Remember that children can say things that they have learned and not fully understand them. For example, a child can say/read and write *two times two is four,* but if he/she does not thoroughly understand what that word *times* means in this application, this child will only be learning some information by rote and will not be able to apply the process in word problems. The same is true with the words *divided by* for division. Children need very concrete applications for these processes before they can use them in math problems. Other concepts, such as measurements, should be treated as new language and introduced on an incremental and sequential basis.

TASK ANALYSIS FOR TEACHING SPECIAL SKILLS: TIME CONCEPTS

Difficulties can develop in teaching certain con-

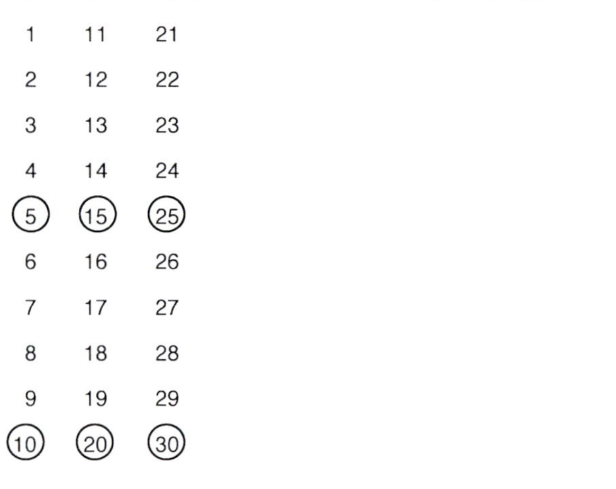

1	11	21
2	12	22
3	13	23
4	14	24
(5)	(15)	(25)
6	16	26
7	17	27
8	18	28
9	19	29
(10)	(20)	(30)

FIG. 7.5. Arrangement of numbers for teaching counting by fives

cepts or skills if the instructor makes too many assumptions of what background knowledge a child has. Teaching can be immeasurably easier if the instructor *analyzes the task* and makes special preparation for it.

Learning how to tell time can be a big boost to a child's ego and also can be of value in the home environment. Rushing into teaching such a skill before students know certain necessary information, however, can result in frustrating experiences for everyone concerned.

A. *For telling time on the hour by the clock, an understanding of the following information is necessary:*

> Numbers to 12
> Concepts of long hand/short hand
> Concept of *on*: The ______ hand is on ______.

A simple format for teaching time and for providing independent seat work as reinforcement is to draw a clock face on the chalkboard with the hands pointing to a specific time. (See figure 7.6.) Sentences describing what the child sees can be written next to it.

A related activity can be to require a child to read the words and then to draw the hands in their appropriate places on the clock.

B. *When telling time by minutes after the hour, children should be familiar with the following:*

> Concepts before and after
> Ability to count by fives to 30
> Ability to associate numbers with the appropriate numerals on the face of the clock.
> Relationship between the 30-minute mark and the concepts of before and after.

Even though the hands of the clock may be between specific numerals, it will be easier initially to teach as if the hands are on a specific number for teaching the number of minutes after/before the hour. The teaching of *30 minutes after the hour* is included in the teaching of time after the hour in 5 minute increments. Although the language of the last sentence in figure 7.7. is used less frequently, it is an appropriate concept for children to know. Teaching the expression "half past" should be delayed because of its abstractness.

C. *When teaching the concept of so many minutes before the hour,* the child will have to learn to count by fives from the twelve down the left side of the clock. Shading the right and left halves of the clock face in different pastel colors to aid visualization of before and after is helpful. (See figure 7.8.)

D. *When telling time by specific single incremental minutes before and after the hour, children will apply:*

> Counting by fives and by single digits intermittently

For example, to correctly determine "17 minutes after the hour," the child will need to count by 5's on the 1, 2, and 3 of the clock to reach 15 minutes after the hour, and then count by single digits to reach 16 and 17.

In the four stages of learning to tell time on the analog clock, A-D above, it is crucial that the student: (1) learn a new task, (2) mix the new task with the previously learned task, (3) proceed to a new stage of instruction. For example, the student masters telling time on the hour, learns to tell time after the hour, and integrates the two before learning to tell time before the hour. As in the various levels of DuBard Association Method® language instruction, all skills should be established through the reinforcement activities described in the preceding chapter. *Establishing oral recall and written recall with 90% accuracy and automaticity continue to be good benchmarks for determining a child's readiness to proceed to new instruction.*

Digital Clocks

The advent of and exposure to digital clocks does not eliminate the need for children to have an understanding of the concepts just discussed. In fact, a child's ability to read digital clocks and watches can be very misleading. The child who can look at a digital clock and say, "It's two one zero or two ten," does not necessarily understand what the correct time is. Digital clocks should not be used for teaching a child, especially one with language

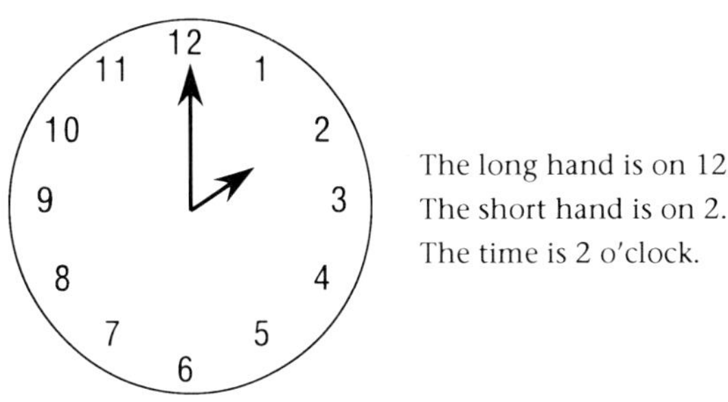

FIG. 7.6. An example of a way to teach time on the hour

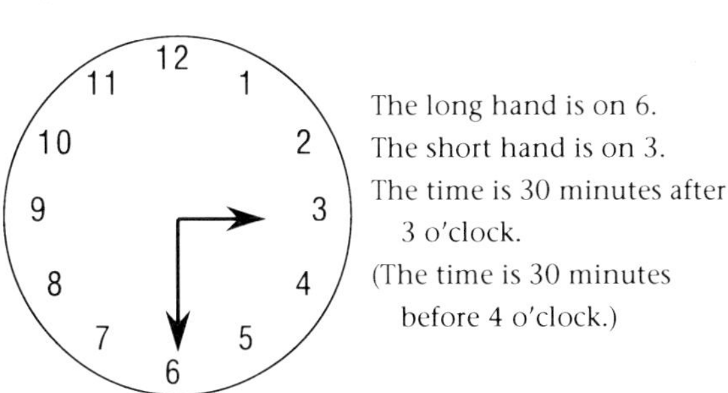

FIG. 7.7. An example of how to teach time on the half hour

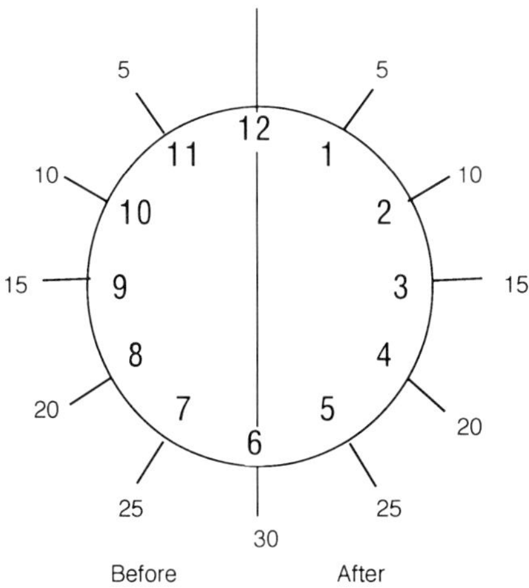

FIG. 7.8. An example of how to teach time before and after the hour

disorders, how to tell time if he/she is to have any competent understanding of it. Later, the teacher can help the child to understand the use of digital clocks and similar items. After all, such items are a reality, are here to stay, and one goal in teaching children is to help them to function in their present and future environments.

Calendar Time

Time concepts are not easily understood or easily mastered by any child. Additional difficulties arise for children with hearing and language differences. The teacher determines the aspect of time he/she wishes to introduce, establish, and reinforce. Undertaking and mastering a single aspect at a time seems advisable. A sequence similar to that observed in the development of time concepts by children who do not have language learning differences is appropriate. The use of concrete, visible representations related to time is vital.

Learning to say and write the names of the days, then applying this knowledge to a calendar, may be the first phase of organized teaching/learning related to time concepts. Seeing the sequential order of days on a calendar can help a child become aware that there is an orderly pattern to the dynamic process of time. Relating today, yesterday, and tomorrow to the same information in a visible form on a calendar expands both vocabulary and concepts.

Teaching the names of the months, perhaps incidentally at first but ultimately in a structured format involving all the months of the year, provides an expansion of time concepts which can be useful in teaching concepts of this week/month, last week/month, and next week/month. These concepts can then be incorporated into a story. A story format also can be employed to teach the concepts of weather conditions.

Sample "Today Story"

A. Simple Use

Today is ________.

Questions are introduced at each level when the sentence forms have been mastered.

B. Basic 3-line story:

Yesterday was _____.
Today is ______.
Tomorrow will be _____.

C. Expanded Application

Last month was ________.
This month is ________.
Next month will be ________.
Yesterday was ________.
Today is ________.
The date is ________. (Optional)
Tomorrow will be ________.
The sky is ________.
The sun is/is not shining.
The wind is/is not blowing.
It is/is not raining.

The language level of the group may permit use of special events of the week or month, such as "_______ is _______'s birthday" or "Tomorrow we will go to _______." Appropriate questions should be applied in A., B., and C. above.

CALENDAR/MONTH STORIES

Calendar/month stories are based on facts related to a given month. Such stories may be very simple and short or more complex and up to eight or nine lines long, depending on the level of the students.

A teacher can use these stories to reinforce and apply previously taught concepts, such as ordinal numbers, months, and seasons. These stories may contain vocabulary related to seasons, holidays, events, and personalities related to the present, past, and future. Initially, explanations of these items must be simple and in keeping with the group's language level. At a more advanced language level, explanations may become more elaborate.

The child is not expected to commit such stories to memory indefinitely. Reexposure to similar content during consecutive months and years will result in the child's absorbing the material and developing a more complete comprehension of concepts and facts as well as the ability to apply the facts to his/her independent use of language.

Question forms for language concepts in the stories may be varied. If the child's language level is sufficiently advanced, two question forms for a single sentence may be appropriate. A variety of question forms will reduce the chances of a child's question language becoming limited and stereotyped. It will broaden his/her comprehension of question language in relation to sentence structure. The language of questions can be extremely awkward if the question form adheres too closely to the sentence language. For the sentence, "New Year's Day is January 1," the appropriate questions would be "When is New Year's Day?" or "What special day is January 1?" "What is January 1?" would be acceptable although somewhat awkward. In addition, this form would require that the child be advanced enough to reverse the order of the sentence to January 1 is New Year's Day. Children without language disorders somehow learn to generate language involving inverted constructions. Children with hearing/language disorders need to be (1) informed that such a process is possible, (2) instructed how to change the language structure, and (3) given practice in doing so in oral and written language activities.

Suggested Calendar/Month Stories (Factual)

The content of such stories will vary from region to region. The length of such stories will be determined by the child's level of instruction. The instruction of these stories generally begins when the child is at the Preposition Round-Up Story level of instruction. Weather/climate descriptions should be appropriate to the local geographic area. Here are some samples.

January

January is the first month of the year.
It is a winter month.
It has thirty-one days.
The weather is usually wet and cold.
January has two holidays.
One holiday is New Year's Day.
New Year's Day is January 1.
The other holiday is Martin Luther King's birthday.
It is celebrated on the third Monday in January.

February

February is a winter month.
February is the second month of the year.
Some years it has twenty-nine days.
Other years it has twenty-eight days.
There are three special days in February.
February 12 is Abraham Lincoln's birthday.
February 14 is Valentine's Day.
February 22 is George Washington's birthday.
Abraham Lincoln and George Washington were Presidents of the United States a long time ago.
George Washington was the first President of the United States.
(Words for ordinal numbers may be equally appropriate.)

March

March is a spring month.
It is the third month of the year.
March has thirty-one days.
There is one special day in March.
March seventeenth is St. Patrick's Day.
St. Patrick lived in Ireland a long time ago.
He was a good man.

April

April is a spring month.
It is the fourth month of the year.
April has thirty days.
April first is called April Fool's Day.

Sometimes we have tornadoes in April and other spring months.

May

May is a spring month.
It is the fifth month of the year.
May has thirty-one days.
There are three special days in May.
May first is called May Day.
The second Sunday in May is Mother's Day.
May thirtieth is Memorial Day.
People put flowers on the soldiers' graves on Memorial Day.

June

June is a summer month.
It is the sixth month of the year.
It has thirty days.
In June the weather is hot.
The third Sunday in June is Father's Day.
Some children go to school in June.
Others do not go to school in June.

July

July is another summer month.
It has thirty-one days.
Our weather is hot in July.
Sometimes it rains a lot in July.
Sometimes it is very dry.
July fourth is a holiday.
It is called Independence Day.
Sometimes there are parades on July 4.
Lots of families and friends have picnics on July 4.
Some children go to camp in July.
Some do not go to camp at all.

August

August is another summer month.
It has 31 days.
The weather is usually hot in August.
Sometimes we have storms in August.
Sometimes we have hurricanes in August.
Some people have vacations in August.
We will return to school August ________.

September

September is an autumn month.
It is the ninth month of the year.
It has 30 days.
The weather is hot.
Sometimes we have storms in September.
September has one holiday.
It is called Labor Day.
Labor Day is the first Monday in September.

October
October is an autumn month.
It has 31 days.
It is the tenth month of the year.
In October the weather is cooler than in summer.
October has two special days.
October 12 is called Columbus Day.
Columbus was a famous man.
Columbus arrived in America on October 12, 1492.
October 31 is Halloween.
On Halloween night children play "Trick or Treat."
Neighbors give them cookies, candy, and other goodies.

November
November is an autumn month.
It is the eleventh month of the year.
It has thirty days.
Some days are cold.
Other days are warm.
November has two special days.
One special day is Armistice Day or Veteran's Day.
Another day is Thanksgiving Day.
It is the fourth Thursday of November.
It is a holiday.

December
December is the first winter month.
It is the twelfth month of the year.
It has thirty-one days.
The first day of winter is December 21.
Santa Claus comes on Christmas Eve.
Christmas Eve is December 24.
Christmas Day is December 25.

Additional sample stories related to seasons and holidays may be found in the appendix.

TEMPERATURE STORIES
The ability to count by twos is a prerequisite to children's comprehension of stories regarding temperature. They must also be able to speak, write, and understand the following vocabulary words: thermometer, degrees, temperature, tube, mercury, Fahrenheit, and Centigrade/Celsius.

Sample Story
This is a thermometer. A thermometer measures the temperature. Temperature means how cold or how hot something is.

A thermometer has a glass tube. Special material is in the tube. The special material is called mercury. When the temperature of something becomes warm or hot the mercury rises in the tube. When the temperature of something becomes cool or cold the mercury goes down in the tube. The temperature is measured in degrees. The symbol for degrees is a small circle by the number. The comfortable temperature inside is usually 70 degrees Fahrenheit (or 22 degrees Centigrade/Celsius). The temperature outside varies. When the temperature becomes 32 degrees Fahrenheit (or 0 degrees Centigrade/Celsius), water freezes and makes ice. When it becomes warmer, the ice melts and becomes water.

Teaching will be easier and more effective if the instructor analyzes the task, predetermines needs and probable difficulties, and prepares a foundation to support the child in his/her efforts to learn something new. Such activities as clock reading, calendar reading, and thermometer reading intrigue children and give them a psychological boost in their learning efforts. The activities illustrated herein are merely suggestions regarding specific skills. The approach can be varied according to the teacher's ingenuity, so long as basic information has been taught to the child first. As use of the metric system becomes a reality in Americans' lives, certain changes in teaching liquid and dry measurements and temperature will become necessary. One reminder: the child's ability to read, that is break the code, can be very misleading. Clarification of vocabulary for stories at the upper level becomes crucial. The teacher must check and double check to be sure the child understands the material.

Instruction in science and social studies topics also may be implemented very effectively by determining the most pertinent vocabulary, introducing it and teaching the content written in story format at a level that is appropriate for the students. As those with special needs are moving through the general education curriculum, the techniques which have been so successful for them at the various DuBard Association Method® story levels may also be used as tools to gain success in subject area content.

COMPARATIVE AND PARTITIVE CONCEPTS
This section is included as a reminder that both comparative and partitive concepts and language are an integral part of communication. The need for instruction about these ideas may be overlooked by those who learned language naturally. After a specified amount of work has been accomplished by applying the principles and procedures of the DuBard Association Method®, teaching chil-

dren with severe language disorders is not greatly different from teaching children who are deaf or hard of hearing. All children have a common need to learn multiple concepts and oral and written expressive language skills. Some examples of comparative and partitive language are listed below.

Comparative Language

_______ _______ is smaller than a _______.
_______ _______ is bigger than a _______.
_______ _______ is taller than a _______.
_______ _______ is shorter than a _______.
_______ _______ is fatter than a _______.
_______ _______ is thinner than a _______.
_______ _______ is smoother than a _______.
_______ _______ is rougher than a _______.
_______ _______ is higher than a _______.
_______ _______ is lower than a _______.
a _______ is different from a _______. . . . . . .

Forms of adjectives for other applications: *-er, -est.*

Which is _______er, a _______ or a _______?
Which is _______est, a _______, a _______, or a _______?

Partitive Language

a piece of _______
a box of _______
a glass of _______
a cup of _______
a bowl of _______
a handful* of _______
a bucket of _______
a sack of _______
a sack full of _______

DEFINITIONS VERSUS FUNCTIONS

People familiar with the spoken language of European students and those of the United States are aware of the fact that the vocabulary level of the average American is not especially high. Even decades ago, newspapers and similar publications were written in language that a sixth grader could understand. Teachers have observed similar limitations regarding defining words and objects among children and adults. While the child's notion of function of the item might have been accurate, the ability to construct definitions was lacking. This kind of inability to use language is especially true of children and adults who have aphasia, as well as those who have hearing loss and/or language disorders, as well as those with learning disabilities or dyslexia. Many of the last group can tell all about something without being able to tell what it is or to answer questions about what they have just said about it. The following are typical responses of some children with language disorders who were asked to define items which they "knew" very well.

Instruction question: What is a table?
Responses:

a table, that a person to write on a book.
a table that person take the paper to the table.
a table is one you can put forks, knife and plates on it.

for pencil:

a pencil, that person use it to write.
a pencil, the people that write by hand.
a pencil is with the eraser.

The children's responses reflected their understanding of the items in general and in terms of function. However, the academic task of defining had to be taught. Once there were a few clarifications, they were able to complete specific tasks of that type successfully and were able to apply the skill to other experiences in which there had not been specific instruction.

The instruction for establishing the desired ability was achieved by incorporating categories of various types and associating them with the proper item. At the earliest/easiest level, the instruction question can be a simple, "What is a _______?" At a more advanced level, the instruction should be: "Define a _______." Elaborate comments might be optional later.

The instruction question should be simple. The teacher asks the question and gives the correct information. For example:

What is a dog?	A dog is an animal.
What is a table?	A table is a piece of furniture.
What is a knife?	A knife is a tool.
What is a lawn mower?	A lawn mower is a machine.
What is a fly?	A fly is an insect.

It is the teacher's responsibility to determine through various means that the children comprehend the information.

Teaching concepts related to the composition of things is also an important aspect of defining things. This would include information such as: _______ is made of wood/glass/metal/plastic/paper/and any other appropriate materials.

* handfuls: handsful (for use by those who choose to be ultra-precise in a world of imprecise language which remains functional and communicative).

CHAPTER

8

DuBard Association Method® for Students with Specific Learning Disabilities/Dyslexia and General Education Students

In the 1920s and '30s, the years in which Mildred McGinnis began to design and refine what became the Association Method, her focus was on some children who were presumed to be deaf. Her experiences in teaching them led her to believe that they had aphasia. This was controversial in itself in the ideas of many professionals. The controversy seems to have been based on semantics as much as anything else. That is, aphasia—meaning loss of communication skills—was considered an inappropriate diagnosis because the children had never learned communication skills. Consequently, they could not be considered aphasic. Whether or not McGinnis had any experience or awareness of typically developing children who were unable to learn to read in the ways of instruction in that era is, as far as we know, an unknown. The children she worked with learned to read via the Association Method.

During the same decades in which McGinnis was observing and working with her narrow scope population, other professionals, especially neurologists and ophthalmologists elsewhere, were making their observations of children with good hearing acuity, many of whom had speech/articulation difficulties. Those children also were unable to learn to read or had not established reading skills comparable to their intellectual potential. One of those professionals was Samuel T. Orton, a neurologist. He and his colleagues categorized conditions of disorders of spoken language as aphasia. Difficulties related to the written language were called dyslexia. They also were aware of perceptual–motor disorders. Unfortunately, throughout decades, the controversies regarding semantics/nomenclature existed; the controversies will prevail in all probability and there will be doubting Thomases for time immemorial.

Because of Orton's beliefs and work, and that of some of his family members, the Orton Dyslexia Society, now known as the International Dyslexia Association, was formed. One early teaching-learning approach was/is known as the Orton-Gillingham approach. A number of other approaches were spin-off systems for teaching-learning techniques. The programs have various names and share more similarities than differences. The details of those multisensory systems for teaching children with reading disorders/dyslexia are identified and described in Clinical Studies of Multisensory Structured Language Education (McIntyre and Pickering), a 1995 publication of the International Multisensory Structured Language Education Council (IMSLEC). The Association Method is not a spin-off of any other teaching-learning system. Rather, it is a phonetic, multisensory structured language approach for learning language and speech devised by McGinnis for children with significant hearing loss and additional learning problems. It has been expanded and refined since 1962 at the now DuBard School for Language Disorders, The University of Southern Mississippi. Its use, modified appropriately, for instruction with children who have oral and written language disorders, speech disorders, and those in the general education environment is well-established. While the Association Method is not an outgrowth of the Orton-Gillingham method, the phonetic, multisensory principles are more similar than different.

READING AND DYSLEXIA DEFINED

Myklebust and Johnson (1962, 14) defined reading as "a symbol system, a means whereby man internalizes, integrates and organizes experience. It is related to the other principal verbal system which he uses, the spoken word. These two verbal systems, the read and spoken word, constitute man's language and each can be understood only in relation to each other." Reading is ". . . extracting and constructing meaning from written language. Writing, conversely, is expressing one's thoughts and ideas using the written language as a medium" (Aaron, Joshi, Quatroche 2008, 4).

The definition of dyslexia as a language-based disorder has led to enhanced awareness of it by speech-language pathologists as well as by educators of general and special-needs students. Catts (1989, 58-59) offered the following as a definition of language-based dyslexia:

> Dyslexia is a developmental language disorder that involves a specific deficit(s) in the processing of phonological information. The disorder is generally present at birth and persists into adulthood. A prominent characteristic of the disorder is a specific reading disability. Preceding, accompanying, and following this reading disability, the disorder manifests itself in various difficulties in phonological coding, including problems in encoding, retrieving, and using phonological codes in memory. In addition, difficulties may be observed in speech production and in the metalinguistic awareness of speech sound segments.

A formal definition adopted by the International Dyslexia Association in 2002, and also used by the National Institutes of Child Health and Human Development (NICHD) states:

Dyslexia is a specific learning disability that is neurological in origin. It is characterized by difficulties with accurate and/or fluent word recognition and by poor spelling and decoding abilities. These difficulties typically result from a deficit in the phonological component of language that is often unexpected in relation to other cognitive abilities and the provision of effective classroom instruction. Secondary consequences may include problems in reading comprehension and reduced reading experience that can impede growth of vocabulary and background knowledge.

The International Dyslexia Association also provides the following description (2011):

> Dyslexia is a language-based learning disability. Dyslexia refers to a cluster of symptoms, which result in people having difficulties with specific language skills, particularly reading. Students with dyslexia usually experience difficulties with other language skills such as spelling, writing, and pronouncing words. Dyslexia affects individuals throughout their lives; however, its impact can change at different stages in a person's life. It is referred to as a learning disability because dyslexia can make it very difficult for a student to succeed academically in the typical instructional environment, and in its more severe forms, will qualify a student for special education, special accommodations, or extra support services.

The American Speech-Language-Hearing Association describes dyslexia as follows (1997-2011):

> *Dyslexia* has been used to refer to the specific learning problem of reading. The term *language-based learning disability*, or just *learning disabilities*, is better because of the relationship between spoken and written language. Many children with reading problems have spoken language problems.
>
> The child with dyslexia has trouble almost exclusively with the written (or printed) word. The child who has dyslexia as part of a larger language learning disability has trouble with both the spoken and the written word.

Neurological Research and Reading

Extensive brain-imaging research in recent years has provided critical information about the brain's function in fluent and in struggling readers. According to Shaywitz and Shaywitz (2007), for example, "Studies indicate that younger children without dyslexia demonstrate significantly greater activation in the three left-hemisphere neural systems than do children with dyslexia." In 2008, they reported on the relationship between attention and dyslexia and focus on the role of attention in reading, specifically in the development of fluent and automatic reading (Shaywitz and Shaywitz). Other studies explore whether or not specific language impairment and developmental dyslexia share similar brain anatomical structures (Leonard, Eckert, Given, Berninger, and Eden 2006).

It is far beyond the scope of this text to provide a comprehensive review of the current state of knowledge in this area. Suffice it to say that the knowledge forthcoming in this area holds great promise for future understanding, and even potentially for future identification, of reading disabilities. Veteran teachers and therapists have for decades had clinical assumptions and suppositions about the central nervous system's perceived role in language learning disabilities. The ever-increasing technological means to study the brain and its function may verify many of those clinical assumptions. The interested reader will find numerous sources for additional information including work by Maisog, Einbinder, Flowers, Turkeltaub, and Eden (2008) which provides a meta-analysis of functional neuroimaging studies on dyslexia and other resources available through The International Dyslexia Association.

ORAL LANGUAGE DISORDERS: RELATIONSHIPS TO DYSLEXIA

Similarities and differences between children who fail to learn to read although they have acquired oral language for communication, possess adequate intellectual potential, have attended quality traditional instructional programs, and have stable environmental and emotional factors and children who fail to acquire oral communication are evident. At the risk of oversimplification, the nature of the difficulties of children with dyslexia appears to be the same as that of children with receptive language disorders, but with a different set of language symbols involved. The latter struggle to process oral stimuli, the spoken word. Their specific problems are with decoding, encoding, attaching meaning, storing, and retrieving oral symbols for spontaneous use. Children about whom the primary complaint is poor reading ability or inability to read reveal the same kinds of limitations. They have poor or limited means of breaking the written code—no word attack skills, limited ability to attach meaning to the words they can read, and poor ability to recall a word they have repeated after the teacher, parent, or peer.

Aaron, Joshi and Quatroche (2008, 72) purport that "Written language and spoken language are not separate entities but manifestations of an inner language expressed through different modalities; they are two sides of the same coin. Therefore, it should not be surprising that children who have difficulty with spoken language also, more often than not, have difficulty with written language." Keeping in mind that oral and written language are closely interrelated and integrated, it is important to recognize that deficits in speech or language can impede progress in reading. Between 40 and 75 percent of preschoolers with early language impairment develop reading difficulties later, often in conjunction with broader academic achievement problems (Aram and Hall 1989; Bashir and Scavuzzo 1992). Children with severe speech disorders may be at risk for reading difficulties because they may have poor auditory, phonologic and verbal memory skills (Sices, Taylor, Freebairn, Hansen, and Lewis 2007). According to the National Institutes of Health (1998), deficits in the ability to articulate the speech sounds create barriers to learning phonemic awareness, the alphabetic principle, and application of these skills to phonics.

In comparing the characteristics of children with learning disabilities/dyslexia with the characteristics of speech/language disorders, and the interrelatedness of spoken and written language skills, the parallels are obvious. Because of these, it seems only logical that remediation measures for the two groups also would contain similarities.

COMMON INSTRUCTIONAL PRACTICES

For as long as phonics have been taught, one feature of the approach has been instructing the child in a manner similar to the following: "When a word ends in the letter e, that letter is silent and the other vowel says its name, or if there are two vowels in a word and the last letter is e, the e is silent and the other says its name. For example, home, cake, and bike. Such an explanation discounts the phonetic value of the letter e. It is the glide component of the phonetic production of the diphthong and this gives it a definite phonetic value. This is one example of how the partial information of teachers about phonics affects their teaching of reading.

Certain consonant arrangements, that is, consonant blends, have been misunderstood by some speech-language pathologists as well as by classroom teachers. They have referred to words containing consonant arrangements of sk, sp, and st as blends. These errors probably were not intentional but were based on inadequate information about phonetics—the production of sounds in speech. The Merriam-Webster Dictionary (2011) defines *blend* as "to combine or associate so that the separate constituents or the line of demarcation cannot be distinguished." The fact is that when a person says the sk as in skate, sl as in slow, sp as in spot, st as in stop, the first sound, s, and the following sounds, k, l, p, or t, respectively, are separated in both time and place; that is, they are separate as they are pronounced. Therefore, these letter combinations are not true blends. In contrast, the bl in blue, and the br in brown are. An analysis of the correct phonetic production in spontaneous speech reveals that the tongue is actually in position for the production of the second component before the production of the first component is initiated. This action results in a true blending of the two sounds.

It is not the fault of classroom teachers that they have not had full knowledge about phonetic productions to apply in teaching phonics. University teacher-training programs have not necessarily provided a background in this area. However, classroom teachers have a responsibility to go beyond the knowledge which their instructors imparted so as to be better informed and more effective.

Another subject related to phonics and the teaching of reading is a common characteristic observed in children who experience difficulties in learning to read. This behavior is often described in this way by teachers and parents: "He looks at the first part of the word, then the last, paying no attention to what is in the middle. He will look at the last letter and say it as the first letter of the word." One is hardly able to determine whether this characteristic is an innate tendency or a learned behavior. If it is an innate tendency, it may be that the instructional program is possibly strengthening the weakness rather than reducing it. Some reading techniques call for the child to learn initial consonants and then to make substitution of initial consonants in order to formulate new words. Next, the child is instructed to focus on final consonants and again to make substitutions to formulate new words. Ultimately, the vowel in the middle of the word receives some attention. But this process is counter to what is required for good reading, that is, consistent left-to-

right eye movement. It may be that the erratic eye movements of some children may be reinforced by this practice in teaching. However, it is well-established, and previously noted in this chapter, that *language* rather than eye movements is the key common denominator in dyslexia. It also is noted that there can be some benefit for developing phonological awareness through the manipulation of sounds in their various positions.

Fortunately, with the national focus on scientifically-based reading instruction, emphasis on providing high quality professional development focused on specific skills needed by teachers and therapists is growing.

CORE ELEMENTS OF EFFECTIVE TEACHER PREPARATION

Those who are experienced in the teaching of reading to students both with and without language learning differences would certainly concur that developing fluent decoding skills with comprehension is a complex task. While the complexities of the task and the related needs for adequate teacher preparation to accomplish the desired goals are addressed in-depth in many other publications, it is pertinent here to keep in mind some of the core elements which should be included. According to a position paper of The Orton Dyslexia Society, now The International Dyslexia Association, (1997), three recommended components are:

(1) Conceptual Foundations–The Reading Process: Teachers must be provided with a solid foundation regarding the theoretical and scientific underpinnings of understanding literacy development.

(2) Knowledge of the Structure of Language: In order to teach reading, writing, and spelling, teachers need to understand thoroughly the content of instruction—linguistic units of both speech and print.

    A. Knowledge of English speech sound system and its production (phonetics and phonology)

    B. Knowledge of the structure of English orthography and its relationship to sounds and meaning (phonics and morphology)

    C. Knowledge of grammatical structure (syntax, text structure)

(3) Supervised practice in teaching reading

The National Reading Panel Report (NRP) of 2000 identified five areas that must be included in effective reading programs. They are: 1) phonemic awareness, 2) phonics, 3) fluency, 4) vocabulary and 5) text comprehension. Moats (1999), in a paper prepared for the American Federation of Teachers, stated that research supports these components in reading instruction: 1) direct teaching of decoding, comprehension, and literature appreciation; 2) phoneme awareness instruction; 3) systematic and explicit instruction in the code system of written English; 4) daily exposure to a variety of texts, as well as incentives for children to read independently and with others; 5) vocabulary instruction that includes. . . the relationships among word structure, origin, and meaning; 6) comprehension strategies; and 7) frequent writing of prose.

There is much to be done to prepare teachers and therapists with the knowledge and practical skills required to implement these recommendations fully and effectively. A study by the National Center for Teacher Quality, authored by Walsh, Glaser and Wilcox (2006) found that only 15% of teacher-training programs trained their students in the basics of scientifically-based reading research strategies (those highlighted in the NRP report). Joshi and colleagues (2009) found that the textbooks used in university reading courses were very inadequate in their attention to instruction in the five components identified in the National Reading Panel Report (2000). The content of adequate teacher preparation programs is addressed in more depth in the references cited and in Chapter 4.

PROFESSIONALS' INTERRELATED ROLES IN INSTRUCTION

Kessler (1966, 147) noted that speech pathologists were increasingly interested in the reading process because "reading difficulties are frequently associated with speech difficulties. Many of the principles of diagnosis and treatment of childhood aphasia are pertinent to the diagnosis and treatment of dyslexia." Fey (1999) noted "The evidence suggests that children who are slow to acquire speech and language skills are at significant risk for problems in reading." The valuable role of the speech-language pathologist (SLP) in the early identification of children with oral language disorders who may be at-risk for later reading problems/dyslexia was addressed by Snow, Scarborough, and Burns (1999). We agree that SLPs have a significant role and responsibility in monitoring early reading development of children receiving language-speech services. The American Speech-Language-Hearing Association (1997-2011) noted that SLPs contribute to literacy in the areas of prevention; identifying at-risk children; assessing; providing intervention; documenting outcomes; program development; advocating for effective literacy practices; and advancing the knowledge base.

In our experience, the speech-language pathologist (SLP) can have an even more direct role when he/she has had in-depth professional preparation in a phonetic, multisensory structured language approach which incorporates both oral and written language forms. The DuBard Association Method® is one such approach. By the same token, classroom teachers, reading specialists, etc., need to be knowledgeable about and able to implement phonetic, multisensory structured language teaching techniques. This allows for the delivery of carefully coordinated services to the child with reading deficits by all professionals involved in the child's education, i.e., the general education teacher, the special educator, the reading specialist, and the speech-language pathologist. This coordinated approach may enhance the child's learning due to the fact that *similar strategies* may be implemented by all professionals, modified as appropriate for that specific professional's role. A collaborative approach, such as described here, also follows national trends and federal requirements for the implementation of varied intervention strategies, through such models as the tier process, which may be implemented in the general education environment. In addition, it also may allow the student to have increased access to the general education curriculum with success.

EYE MOVEMENTS, VISION AND READING DISABILITIES

As part of a symposium, Eisenson (1970) cited some research (without providing detailed references) related to eye-movement patterns of young children who demonstrated difficulties in learning to read versus a group of children making normal progress. The patterns of eye movements of the two populations varied significantly.

The experimental task was as follows: Incomplete sentences were given to the children. (For example: The ________ ran home. The man ________ a big snake. Tom has a ________ bike, and Mary has a new ________.) Word lists arranged in appropriate word classes in columns were made available to the children. Their task was to find an appropriate word in a column and write it in the space in the sentences. Any one of several words in each word class could have been correct for any given sentence. The eye movements of both groups were observed. The children who had no problems with reading exhibited eye-movement patterns that were systematic and consistent. They looked at the stimulus sentences and read them, looked at the columns of words to find the type of word wanted/needed, read down the column of words to find an appropriate word, wrote the chosen word in the space in the sentence, and repeated the process until all of the sentences had been completed. The children demonstrating difficulties learning to read did not exhibit any systematic or consistent pattern/patterns. Their eye-movement patterns were erratic and jerky, moving from the sentences to a column, left-to-right, up-and-down, right-to-left and varying combinations of such movements. Many were unable to complete the task.

More research and information are needed regarding eye-movement patterns of children carrying out specific tasks. However, Eisenson's report suggests that the techniques used by many educators to teach reading may be part of the problem. Teaching children to read by looking at initial and final consonant sounds, by having them carry out substitution exercises for these sounds, and by teaching the vowel, which is the nucleus of the word, later may be reinforcing an undesired learning behavior. This is not likely to help children develop code-breaking skills, apply phonics in a left-to-right progression, and experience success in their efforts. Correct phonetics need to be taught. Following that, the knowledge needs to be applied systematically and consistently so that children can learn to help themselves rather than to rely on their weak memory for sight words. Reinforcing a nonsequential approach for determining new words will not be to the benefit of these children.

While Eisenson's research reported erratic eye movements in some children, it is believed that *the broader problem of specific learning disabilities/dyslexia is language,* rather than eye movements and vision. According to the Policy Statement, Learning Disabilities, Dyslexia, and Vision (American Academy of Ophthalmology 1992), "Although it is obvious some children do not read well because they have trouble seeing, research has shown that the majority of children and adults with reading difficulties experience a variety of language defects that stem from complex, altered brain morphology and function, and that the reading difficulty is not due to altered visual function per se." A similar policy was published in 2009. Hoyt (1999) described normal eye movement function involved in reading. He noted, though, that "No evidence at the present time conclusively indicates that there are any unique ocular motor abnormalities in the learning disabled student with the exception of prolonged fixation and increased number of regression saccades. With the exception of convergence insufficiency . . . the case has not been scientifically made for ocular motor training in the student with learning disability."

THE ROLE OF MOTOR ACTIVITY IN READING

Earlier in this volume, we pointed out that studies related to the motor theory of speech perception suggested that proprioceptive feedback (the result of the act of saying something) may well have major significance for perception of speech. Children learning to read also may benefit from proprioceptive feedback in perceiving written language. McGinnis believed that saying a word or sentence enabled the child to establish recall for the language more easily. In the case of children with reading problems, saying the words (i.e., oral reading) may well have merit other than enabling the teacher to know whether the child recognizes the printed words on the page. In the past, teachers of the early grades indicated that oral reading was discontinued as soon as possible and children were discouraged from reading aloud when they were reading independently. However, recent trends have recognized the value of increased oral reading. If a child needs to say the word aloud in order to gain skill in reading, this should be encouraged. When children want to read aloud, this suggests confidence. Reluctance to read aloud may indicate insecurity. Regardless, reading aloud has benefits in terms of hearing the language and the motor feedback of saying the words, etc.

Some children whose language disorders dealt primarily with written language (i.e., reading, spelling, and writing) have been enrolled in the DuBard School for Language Disorders. They were taught by the DuBard Association Method® and achieved success in academic experiences; their parents enjoyed a measure of peace and assurance. Details on those children can be found in chapter 10.

GUIDELINES FOR IMPLEMENTING THE DUBARD ASSOCIATION METHOD® WITH INDIVIDUALS WITH DYSLEXIA

Appendix E provides a detailed program of instruction for a child with specific learning disabilities/dyslexia. His case history is included in Chapter 9. Additional suggested guidelines include:

1. In some instances manuscript and cursive writing may be taught simultaneously. This

has been done with children served on an outclient basis for therapy who were enrolled in general education classrooms. Since they were already in typical schools and familiar with manuscript, and because the major portion of their education was implemented in manuscript, the DuBard Association Method® was presented in manuscript as well as in cursive. In some school settings, with the services of resource teachers and/or speech-language pathologists, it has been implemented in manuscript only. We believe that the ideal in such settings, however, is to implement cursive and manuscript simultaneously for reading.

2. Teach phonemes to build up skill in analytical word attack—code-breaking. Primary and secondary spellings may be introduced simultaneously, depending on the age of the child and the extent to which the teacher intends to use the cross drill. A working knowledge of the Northampton Symbols is necessary for success.

3. The use of drop drills (nonsense syllables) for this population can be very beneficial. They require true code-breaking, rather than attempts at "guessing" real words. Countless CV and VC combinations should be used. Initially, primary spellings only are used. Later, after cross drills have been introduced, a combination of primary and secondary spellings may be used followed by drop drills with only secondary spellings. ***Unlike the original form of the Association Method in which drop drills were eliminated once cross drills began, the use of drop drills for decoding practice may be continued for the individual with specific learning disabilities/dyslexia indefinitely.*** It may also be useful to expand the drills to CVC combinations. Pictures are not associated with the drop drill for this population so a wide range of phonetic combinations is possible. See Appendix F for materials useful for developing this skill.

4. Apply phonemes to simple words (CV, VC, and CVC), which can be used in simple sentence structures as soon as possible. For vocabulary: pictures should not be shown until after the child has broken the code analytically, smoothed/blended the units together into the whole word, and indicated that the appropriate meaning has been attached to it. Breaking the code analytically (segment-

ing) and blending the units together into the word synthetically will not necessarily prove that a child actually understands the word. How can the teacher be sure the child understands the word? Some suggestions to be used in judging the matter include the following: (a) Listen to the child's vocal inflection as the units are put together into a word. The inflection in pronouncing it can be a significant, telltale sign. (b) Watch for a change in a child's facial expression as he/she works through breaking the code of the word. Facial expression changes when one really understands something; it loses that feigned look of comprehension. (c) Without saying the word, ask the child a question to elicit the specific word. This checking device might include such questions as "Do you have one of those?", "What can you do with that?", "Have you ever seen one?", "Tell me something about it," and "Make a sentence with that word." Pictures and word cards are used in instruction in the classroom. Only the written words, not the pictures, are placed in the child's book because the focus for this population is learning to read.

5. After some vocabulary code-breaking has been accomplished, simple sentences can be used easily. All of the repetitive sentences and questions discussed earlier would be appropriate. After the child has mastered simple sentences, introduce appropriate question forms. Pictures are not placed in the child's book but may be used in the classroom for reinforcement work to elicit vocabulary for inclusion in sentences.

   The above sentences are suggestions only. By the time a child has a foundation in the sound-symbol relationships and can use them for decoding, it is imperative that he/she begin to arrange words into simple sentences. The question forms are suggested simply because these children are weak in formulating questions when a specific idea is concerned or when it is not their idea to ask a question. When fluent decoding for CVC vocabulary has been established through cross drills and applied through repetitive sentences, the use of beginning level "Sam Stories" (Appendix E) may be appropriate.

6. Use animal stories to expand code-breaking. They provide a high-interest level while utilizing relatively simple vocabulary. The stories can be more complex than those used in

teaching children with language disorders because the students may not necessarily need to memorize them.

7. Compose sentences from a wide range of vocabulary to be sure the child is breaking the code analytically rather than using auditory memory. For the same reasons, construct questions appropriate to the sentences.

8. Determine the proper time for teaching writing skills. Writing is one sense modality utilized in the multisensory approach. Whether or not one waits for these skills to be developed naturally must be determined by the teacher. Each child's abilities and limitations in this modality must be evaluated. Formal evaluation is not necessarily required. Astute observation by the teacher can form the basis for making decisions. For the younger child, if the teacher decides to proceed with oral work, such as reading, before the child has equal functional ability in writing, he/she needs also to continue to develop the child's writing skills.

9. ***Avoid using traditional reading texts too soon.*** This mistake can defeat earlier success. Teachers need to consider carefully the size and type of vocabulary and the structure of the language in the texts when making selections. A wide range of decodable, language-controlled materials has become available commercially. Lengthy stories are often too difficult for these children; they do not become competent overnight. Stories of paragraph length, which are teacher-constructed or adapted from materials written for use in teaching children who have profound hearing loss, are often much more successful than "regular" texts. In time, regular texts constructed in "straight language" can be used to the child's benefit. "Straight language" (Fitzgerald 1963) is language that is free of inference and of reference pronouns.

Children who have difficulty comprehending language demonstrate many of the difficulties observed in children who are deaf or hard-of-hearing and often can be helped by the same techniques that have worked well with them. Indeed, if the truth were known, the typical population might achieve better reading skills if some of the problems were identified more clearly so that instruction could be suited to the needs. For too long we have acknowledged the existence of individual differences among children in relation to learning but have continued to teach children as if they were all the same. The title of one volume suggests this idea: *The Geranium on the Window Sill Just Died, But Teacher, You Went Right On* (Cullum 1972). We should try to save more geraniums from the outset. If we recognize the needs of children in relation to their learning patterns, we can help them. If a "geranium" shows signs of dying, let us do something before it is too late. Let us not merely "go right on."

GOING RIGHT ON

Unfortunately, even in the new millennium, "geraniums" are still dying and many teachers continue to go right on, that is, to teach in the same ways. Some of the children are still surviving and/or even "overcoming," depending on the severity of their limitations. However, the percentage of dropouts from schools all across the nation is still too high. The number of high school graduates who are basically illiterate for reading and writing skills is alarming.

Playing "catch-up" in any endeavor is almost always a losing undertaking. The public school systems, private schools, teachers in general education classes and special education teachers alike who happen to have open minds and are willing to change their game plans of instruction have been unable to make an impressive dent in salvaging that "difficult-to-teach" population of children. However, the fact that there are more schools and teachers that are willing to try is important.

The national outcry about the high rate of illiteracy is genuine. Adult literacy programs have come into existence with funding coming from various sources. Interested citizens have become volunteers. But the training for these potential teachers has varied. For some, it sometimes seemed to have been less than was needed.

In the late 1980s, the computer age reached the school room. Some concepts proposed in earlier decades, such as those presented in The Writing Road to Reading (Spalding and Spalding 1957, 1990) began to receive attention. It is still not clear, however, how effective the electronic/computerized work will be in teaching a child to read. While the use of technology can be an avenue for appropriate reinforcement activities, a knowledgeable teacher or therapist is still key to a child's progress.

The old maxim, "what goes around comes around," seems to hold true in educational theory too. In 1968, in New Orleans, Louisiana, the National Institute of Neurological Diseases and

Stroke (NINDS) sponsored a conference, Communicating by Language, The Reading Process, for the Health Education Welfare Advisory Committee on Dyslexia and Related Disorders. The papers which resulted from that conference were judged to have been interesting and, in some cases, controversial. Monograph No. 11, Reading Forum, presented the work of the committee. The members agreed that to learn to read children must:

- know the language that they are going to learn to read
- learn to dissect spoken words into component sounds
- learn to recognize and discriminate the letters of the alphabet in various forms
- learn to use the left-to-right principle
- learn the high probability of correspondence between letters and sounds so as to recognize words they know in their spoken language and to determine the pronunciation of unfamiliar words
- learn to recognize printed words from whatever cues they can use
- learn that printed words are signals, that meanings are analogous to the spoken words and that they must understand the meaning of the total message
- learn to reason and think within the limits of their talents and experience, that is, be able to interpret abstract concepts and relationships between and among linguistic units—sounds, words, sentences, and questions

In a more current development, the California Reading Initiative (Moats, 1997) emphasized the following as necessary for reading success: (1) phoneme awareness, (2) systematic, explicit phonics instruction, (3) sound-symbol relationships, (4) decoding, (5) word attack skills, (6) spelling instruction, (7) comprehension instruction, and (8) independent reading of high quality books.

Three buzzwords of this decade are disorder, abuse, and syndrome. There is increased recognition of the fact that reading disorders, called by any name one chooses, are, in essence, language-learning disorders. Indeed, the reports of the NINDS study and the California Reading Initiative we just cited support this idea indirectly.

Abuse has become associated with numerous problems, such as physical, mental, or emotional difficulties. One other abuse seems to be obvious: educational abuse which will lead to economic abuse in later years, both of which can be expected to become realities unless some changes in the teaching-learning strategies are made for some "normal" children and those with not-so-normal deficiencies. How much better it will be for all concerned if energies and efforts can be put to use in prevention of illiteracy rather than waiting until the child has developed the failure syndrome.

As a multisensory teaching/learning process, the DuBard Association Method® as presented here addresses problems related to reading and written language skills of children. Its use has been effective with many such children for several decades. Its use also complies with the statement of a professor of educational research in 1950: "If we would use what knowledge we have, there would be little or no need for additional research in education" (Drummond). The skills an individual needs to be able to learn to read efficiently have been known for a long time. The need for those responsible for teaching children to apply what is known is long overdue. The use of the principles of the DuBard Association Method®, a multisensory system, can be helpful in achieving the desired goals for decoding and encoding the written language and helping the child acquire the other necessary skills cited in the NINDS study, the California Reading Initiative, and in current research. It is crucial that the intensity of intervention services be matched to the severity of the child's problem.

APPLICATION IN GENERAL ELEMENTARY EDUCATION

In the mid-1990s, the DuBard School for Language Disorders was involved in a three-year general education pilot project for kindergarten, first, and second grades at Petal Elementary School in Petal, Mississippi. The project was funded through the Mississippi Power Foundation and a venture grant from United Way of Southeast Mississippi. Following an intensive professional development course in the Association Method, the teachers utilized a modified version of the approach on a large group basis. *While techniques for implementation were modified, the principles remained the same* as for small group and individualized instruction for children with severe communication disorders. The general education students began with instruction in single phonemes, syllables, and progressed to cross drill instruction for teaching vocabulary. This was followed by sentence and question work, and stories/questions. For grade levels in which basal readers were utilized, vocabulary for cross drill instruction was selected from the basal texts as well as from the usual Association Method noun vocabulary. The results of the pilot project indicated that the use of a modified version of the Association Method for a cumulative total of approximately one hour per day resulted in a statistically significantly lower retention rate and fewer referrals to special education. Teachers used Association Method principles for instruction in sound-symbol relationships, handwriting, oral and written language development, etc.

Since the initial pilot project was conducted, implementation in general education settings, as well as in special services, has continued successfully in a number of school districts. Similar modifications as indicated earlier in this chapter for those with specific learning disabilities/dyslexia are applied. Teachers have found that implementation of the DuBard Association Method® story levels is beneficial for coordinating with the goals and objectives for language arts, such as identification of nouns, verbs, adjectives, creation of question language, development of auditory-visual and acoustic skills, etc. It also has been used as a basis for creative writing and coordinated with science, social studies, math, and other curricula.

CHAPTER

9

Application of Association Method/ DuBard Association Method® to Other Populations: Case Histories

CASE HISTORY DATA

Case histories are included because frequently there are inquiries about the probable future of children with such significant disabilities. While the professional literature may give prognoses for individuals who are deaf or hard of hearing and those with varying kinds of disabilities, case histories in the literature are limited. There are logical reasons for this: (1) differential diagnosis is difficult and sometimes controversial. Clear-cut profiles of children considered to have language disorders, without other co-existing conditions, are limited. A child who is nonverbal may simulate children who are challenged with deafness, developmentally disabilities, apraxia, or autism. Selecting subjects to include in such a study would be difficult at best. (2) Individuals diagnosed with language disorders, whom numerous professionals have taught, have been moved into the general population and may no longer be singled out as having language disorders. (3) Follow-up studies are time-consuming and costly in a variety of ways. Few professionals have the time and finances for or the interest in studying such a small and not too clearly defined group. (4) By the time a follow-up study could be made on a selected population large enough to be considered significant, the purposes and motivations related to the original study could become irrelevant or obscure.

Offering case history data has other hazards. Relating "what became of Bob, an individual with language disorders" might or might not be a typical story. As with all individuals, there are similarities, but existing differences make each one of us, including those with language disorders, almost a population of one. The tendency to draw broad generalizations is great; doing so can be dangerous and unfair. If a particular case has a happy ending, happy endings for others may be projected too easily. When such endings do not materialize, disappointments result. Unhappy endings could cause generalizing about poor prognoses for all such children and would be equally unfair.

These case histories are offered: (1) to suggest appropriate treatment for a specific kind of need, (2) to focus attention on some unusual factors related to the kind of condition in question, and (3) to make a plea for changes which might result in more stories with better endings.

Case histories with happy endings may offer encouragement to parents and professionals alike. However, they should not be the basis for viewing conditions and situations through rose-colored glasses. Even the most positive, productive, encouraging case history will have experienced innumerable trials, near failures, heartaches, and difficulties. The case history data and stories included here represent a population of children whose difficulties in learning language and speech clustered around the kinds of limitations described by McGinnis (1963), Hardy (1965), and Eisenson (1968, 1972). Children with these challenges still exist today. Most of the children's specific limitations, abilities, and needs were identified relatively early in their lives; for the others, there had been varying and less appropriate placements and less effective learning.

Factors Influencing Success

Countless factors influence the success or lack of success for anyone. The variables related to achievement or lack of achievement are not always clear. Most of us would be incapable of singling out the most important factor contributing to our achievement level. Solving this puzzle is not unlike trying to answer the proverbial question about the chicken and the egg. Children with limitations are influenced by all of the factors anyone else encounters. Also, they must cope with the aspects of their particular kinds of difficulties. The following general factors influencing a child's progress are considered critical to the prognosis of children with the kinds of learning problems discussed in this volume:

1. Innate intellectual potential
2. Severity of the disability
3. Presence of co-existing conditions and medical management of those conditions if needed and appropriate
4. Onset of the condition/conditions and whether or not the early years, optimum time for learning, were utilized well for learning activities and instruction
5. General health of the individual and his/her family
6. Personality aspects and motivational factors of the individual and of those with the responsibility of his/her education and guidance
7. Appropriateness of the educational placement and instructional program
8. Stability and quality of the program and of the personnel responsible for the instructional program
9. Parent attitudes, child management practices, interpersonal family relationships, and factors related primarily to the home environment

In addition, certain factors related to situations and individuals in the educational and social environments after the child has been mainstreamed must be considered. Multiple variables strongly influence the individual's prognosis; often these variables add to the problems rather than help to solve them. In such instances, the child's adjustment is more difficult, as will be his/her achievement. Some of the factors relate to teacher personalities, attitudes toward teaching, degree of compassion or absence of same as far as the child in the mainstream/general education environment is concerned.

The majority of these case histories has come from among the files of over several hundred children who were evaluated and/or enrolled in the DuBard School for Language Disorders at The University of Southern Mississippi between 1962 and 2009. Most of them are now adults, some with families of their own, working in various kinds of employment ranging from agriculture and light industry to banking, computer science, information technology and dentistry. Many of those who have left for other school placements are reported to be doing well in middle-, secondary-, or college-level studies or in vocational training programs.

Medical histories of the children varied. In the early days, some factors which may have influenced the condition included Rh factor, rubella, post-convulsive high fever disorders/seizure disorders, otitis media, Traumatic Brain Injuries (TBI) resulting in aphasia/language disorders and suspected auditory processing disorders. In one instance, there were known developmental disabilities. In several cases, the medical histories did not indicate any causal factors. Current factors include seizure disorders, autism spectrum disorders, histories of substance abuse, various genetic conditions, and chronic otitis media. There are increased numbers of children diagnosed with anxiety disorders, oppositional defiant disorder, and obsessive compulsive disorder. It is unknown whether these conditions have increased or are diagnosed more accurately than was possible in earlier years.

CHILDHOOD APRAXIA OF SPEECH

Childhood Apraxia of Speech (Severe Developmental Apraxia): More Than Just Delayed Expressive Language

Anyone who has been involved clinically will have said at one time or another, "I have this child/client/patient who has. . ." Usually, the sentence is completed by descriptions such as, "fun to work with," "difficult," "interesting," or perhaps even "trying." However, for almost any clinician, there will be one or a few who will have been outstanding for one reason or another. Adam Langston, whose parents requested that his full name be used, was such a child.

Adam was born February 24, 1983, into a well-adjusted, successful, and happy family. His mother's pregnancy with him had been no different from her previous pregnancies. Except for one report which stated that the mother was Rh negative, the mother's pregnancy and Adam's history were considered to be unremarkable. Delivery had been normal. Adam's birth weight was six pounds, twelve ounces. One series of blood tests on Adam as a newborn was reported to be abnormal. The records we received showed no evidence that the tests had been repeated. Adam achieved the early developmental milestones at the expected ages except for toilet training which he achieved very slowly. His medical history included one ear infection at twelve months of age which cleared in ten days with medication. He had frequent colds and had chicken pox at three years, four months. As far as the parents and other members of the extended family could determine, Adam's understanding of what was said to him was satisfactory. He responded to his name, responded appropriately to others' names, followed instructions appropriately, and seemed to be like any other average child except that he just did not talk. His efforts to communicate consisted of gestures and consistent use of inflectional/intonation patterns of uh, uh, uh, uhuhuh, for sentences and questions. He did not open his mouth with his utterances. He got along well with family members and friends.

At eighteen months of age, a thorough evaluation was scheduled for Adam at a comprehensive center in his home state. The reports reflected the following findings:

Hearing: Adam would not tolerate the earphones. Sound field techniques reflected speech reception threshold at 5 dB. Tympanometry was within normal limits. Acoustic reflexes were present contralaterally and ipsilaterally.

Speech and language: The Zimmerman Preschool Language Scale was attempted. The Auditory Comprehension Scale reflected a fifteen-month level of performance. Verbal ability score was at or below the twelve-month level. The judgment was that Adam's receptive language skills were delayed mildly and that expressive skills were delayed significantly.

The results from the Sequenced Inventory of Communication Development for the Receptive Scale were "grossly within normal limits." No

expressive communication could be computed. Adam was unable to imitate speech sounds or produce a consonant or consonant-vowel combination. He did not use any vocalizations suggestive of trying to use his articulators. He "would not" imitate the examiner stacking blocks. Judgment: five-to sixteen-month level with severe delay in the development of expressive language skills.

The Bzoch League Receptive-Emergent Language Scale: With the mother as the informant, it was judged that Adam had "a possible mild delay in the development of receptive language skills with severe delay in expressive language skills."

Preschool achievement record: Using observations and interview information, Adam was judged to have strengths in rapport, creativity, and responsibility. His weakness was in oral communication.

Oral peripheral examination: Vegetative movements during eating and drinking were judged to be within normal limits. Oral structures were judged to be within normal limits as well. Velar function could not be assessed because of a "lack of cooperation" from Adam. Voice quality was considered to be unremarkable. Fluency could not be measured.

Behavioral observations: Adam would not separate from his mother. He played meaningfully with building logs. His vocal output consisted of a neutral vowel, /m/, and a neutral vowel with an approximation of the vowel in book. All of the sounds were considered to have been accidental productions.

Medical examinations: Adam seemed to be small for his age. His EKG and EEG were normal; a CT scan of the head was normal; his bone age was judged to be like that of a seventeen month old versus his chronological age of twenty-six months. Growth potential was evident according to the report. Endocrinologists' examinations yielded no positive findings.

Recommendations: Speech and language intervention.

Adam was enrolled in an intensive preschool language development program at the evaluation center in his home state. For eleven months he attended two-and-one-half-hour sessions, four days a week, participating in large and small group activities. Both parents participated in weekly parent meetings. Reports available did not indicate that any particular intervention approach was used. Graduate students from one of the universities in the region were assigned to work with Adam. Goals with rationales were stated according to the patterns of the times; that is, "Adam will be able to...." The goals included linguistic and nonlinguistic activities. After three months, Adam's progress was judged to have been "limited." He "did not achieve any of the goals/objectives set up for him." It was recommended that he continue in the program and he did so.

While he was still in the intensive intervention program, Adam was evaluated by a speech pathologist of the center who also had a private practice. Because of his age (twenty-six months), formal testing was limited. "No basal for expressive language skills could be obtained." He demonstrated ability "to follow one, two, and three stage commands." It was determined, through the use of gestures, that he could categorize objects, colors, and some numerals. His gross and fine motor skills were judged to be within normal limits, and he was able to assemble relatively complicated puzzles without difficulty. Referral was made to another agency. Reevaluations were completed; the results follow.

On the Sequenced Inventory of Communication, at a chronological age of thirty-two months, Adam obtained 100 percent accuracy at that level, 75 percent accuracy at the thirty-six-month level, and 54 percent accuracy at the forty-month level. Receptive language skills were slightly below expectancy for his age and rated as "grossly within normal limits." The report also stated: "He did not demonstrate that he understood ... fast and slow." It was judged that Adam's "profile may represent severe developmental apraxia." Recommendations at the conclusion of the second evaluation included individual speech therapy three times weekly and an "alternate means of communication." A reevaluation in six months was recommended also.

Because of Adam's poor progress by age three years, four months, a friend recommended an evaluation by personnel in our setting. Sessions were held mornings and afternoons over a three-day period. Cognitive, communicative, and linguistic skills were assessed. Videotapes were made of the sessions at the request of the parents. The parents were asked to participate in some of the activities for evaluating gross motor skills, in particular for assessing limb apraxia which the examiner had observed.

Adam demonstrated severe difficulty imitating gross movements as well as those related directly to the production of speech. Efforts to imitate speech sounds were extremely poor or nonexistent. Even after some instruction, his productions for /p/ and /m/ were poor. There was little or no tension in the lip closure. Adam's efforts consisted primarily of opening the lips rather than creating any pressure that could result in a plosive component. Trying to imitate /m/ was equally difficult.

Adam could not imitate the gross movements related to the activity requiring him to roll a ball. After carrying out the activity with the examiner or one of his parents holding his arm while creating a "roll the ball" movement, there was minimal improvement. Overnight practice, however, resulted in significant improvement. The results of other tests are described in what follows.

Test of Auditory Comprehension of Language (TACL): Periodic breaks improved Adam's attention for the test items. Ten of his accurate responses on the TACL were highly suspect. Allowing credit for the items considered to have been chance accuracies, he achieved a raw score of 48 and an age rating of three years, one month, three months below his CA. All accuracies were on single word stimuli and included noun, verb, and adjective word classes. His responses to preposition concepts were inconsistent.

Hiskey-Nebraska Test of Learning Aptitude (HNTLA): At a chronological age of three years, six months, Adam earned the following age ratings on the respective subtests administered: Bead Patterns, 3–0; Memory for Color, 3–0; Picture Identification, 3–0; Picture Association, 4–6. A more realistic rating might have been 3–0 because of some suspect accuracies. On Paper Folding, he earned a rating of 3–6, and on Visual Attention Span, he earned an age rating of 5–6. Adam's overall rating was 3–6 based on administration of six of the eight subtests. His Derived Intelligence Quotient (DIQ) was 100. His ability in visual sequencing skill was judged to be promising for planning an intervention program.

Adam was communicative throughout the evaluation. He used natural gestures, nodding to communicate his desires and interests. He would point to the nonverbal activity which he wanted. His oral-expressive language skills were at less than the 12-month level.

Conclusions: On the basis of information obtained during the evaluation, it was concluded that Adam's receptive language skills were close to expectations for his age. His expressive skills were much below expectations and his communicative efforts were those indicative of expressing his needs and desires. His cognitive skills were considered to be in the normal range and the skills needed for successful learning seemed to be adequate.

Diagnosis: A diagnosis of severe apraxia/oral

apraxia/apraxia for speech without other complicating problems was made. A description of his status was comparable to the Class I, Expressive Aphasia as used by McGinnis (1963) and those of other professionals in subsequent years.

Diagnostic Teaching: Following the evaluation, sessions of diagnostic teaching began using the Association Method. Adam's abilities on the Visual Attention Span of the HNTLA indicated that he had a skill which could be utilized. Videotapes of the sessions were made for the parents' use after they returned home.

Teaching Adam was a challenge of the greatest magnitude. His fear of failure resulted in manipulative and negative behaviors which added to the severe problems related to the apraxia per se. Rewards were required to even get him to open his mouth imitatively. Ultimately, tactile clues such as the teacher/clinician shaping his mouth for /oo/, and the clinician literally opening his mouth for him resulted in enough success on which to build some abilities. Operant conditioning was a major component in the teaching-learning process. It was extremely difficult for Adam to learn the sequences of events which could lead to the production of a sound, for example, closing his lips and then phonating to produce the /m/ sound.

Three days of diagnostic teaching led to the conclusion that Adam's manipulative behaviors could be changed, that he could learn to produce speech sounds, that the incremental, sequential aspects and use of written symbols of the Association Method could be an effective means of teaching him to talk as well as to break the code for reading.

Unfortunately, only traditional speech therapy was available in Adam's home area. No improvement in his speech was observed during the following year. A reevaluation was requested. Test results during the reevaluation reflected minimal changes in receptive language skills and no changes in his expressive skills. His manipulative behaviors were a greater impairment than during the first evaluation in our setting.

Outclient therapy through our services was recommended and implemented. Because of the 650-mile distance to his home, Adam attended therapy approximately three consecutive half-days per month. His mother observed, made videotapes of the sessions, and reinforced the new skills during the intervening times. Following a year of the outclient program, Adam's family moved to within commuting distance of the program, and he was enrolled on a full-time basis.

Enrollment was discontinued after one school year due to the development of serious kidney problems which required a kidney transplant. However, by that time, Adam's speech was intelligible, though there were noticeable errors. Adam continued to receive speech therapy in his home state. He returned for another evaluation when he was seven years, eight months. Test data from the evaluation at five years, four months are included here with his final evaluation.

Case History:
Diagnosis: Severe apraxia
Chronological age at beginning of enrollment: 5–6

	Pretest CA: 5–4	Posttest CA: 7–8
Hiskey-Nebraska Test *of Learning Aptitude*		
DIQ	86	88
Arizona Articulation *Proficiency Scale-Revised*		
Picture Test Total Score	11.5%	75.5%
% Improvement		556.5%
Sentence Test	——	62.5%

At almost nine years of age, Adam was participating in and progressing satisfactorily in a small, special language-arts class for children with auditory processing disorders and normal intellectual abilities. He was in a comparable size class for science and math. He received thirty to forty-five minutes of traditional speech therapy daily. In a phone conversation, his speech for what he said was 90 percent intelligible, although his mother stated that his speech had deteriorated during the summer months when no special help was available.

Speech-language pathologists working with children with apraxia in public school settings have found the teaching techniques of the Association Method equally effective for these students. The principles selected in Adam's case were those which would: (1) develop auditory discrimination, (2) enable the child to control volitional production, i.e., drop-drill and cross-drill/syllable-drill work, and (3) enable the child to develop automaticity of production in single-syllable words and in multisyllable words in isolation and within sentence and question language forms. The material utilized with Adam to achieve the goals varied once there was a measure of controlled production and memory for sequences established (word level). Using language content appropriate for the child's age and interests merely made the process more enjoyable to him. In some instances, however, the format of the sequential language/long-range goals language program of McGinnis's work was followed closely. A relatively rapid progression through the language levels of the Association Method proved to be useful and appropriate.

Although numerous speech-language pathologists familiar with the Association Method procedures have used them successfully with children with severe articulation disorders, there will be some who may be reluctant to use the ideas because they are "old." Then, too, they may not accept the idea of beginning with such small increments of speech and may reject the redundancy aspects of the approach. In light of this possibility, it should be noted that Costello (1984, 130–52) presented some significant ideas related to motor learning, which is a major component of how speech is taught through the Association Method. Costello pointed out the following:

> The salient features among theories (of motor programs) center on the variables of practice, stages of motor skill development, cognitive analysis, and feedback processes.

> The use of practice for developing improvement and subsequent refinement of a particular motor skill is a universal notion. As the learner practices a particular motor skill, modifications from internal or external sources are received and processed for the purpose of establishing performance at a high level of accuracy . . . practice is the key variable thought necessary for mastery of skilled motor behavior.

> Teaching phonetic production skills may be conceptualized as the motor learning phenomenon.

> The motor skill model provides an organizational structure and a set of guiding principles to the treatment of persons with articulatory disorders.

To the speech-language pathologist who has mastered the application of the Association Method, Costello's ideas may not be new. To some others they might be viewed as too structured. However, it seems appropriate for all speech-language pathologists working with individuals with severe articulation disorders, oral-motor disorders, or apraxia to learn and to use intervention techniques that have been effective for a long time.

Flawed Diagnoses

The reader should note that some of the terminology in this case history is not only outdated but highly offensive by current standards. After careful consideration, the author chose to leave the original language as a reminder to professionals of the power of words/terminology that is used with parents. While, hopefully, these terms would never be used today, it is a cautionary reminder that the words we *do* choose to use need to be selected carefully.

By the time he was five years old, H. had undergone several evaluations. His intelligible communication consisted of a limited number of single words. Professionals were not in agreement about the nature of his problem. Diagnoses based on observations and standardized tests such as the WISC and Stanford Binet included: dull normal intelligence, borderline ability, borderline moron, and expressive language problem; IQ scores which became a part of the case history data included an "IQ of 66" and an "IQ of 74." EEG's yielded tracings which gave the impression of "abnormal EEG compatible with diffuse brain damage." All who were responsible for evaluations of him reported "unsatisfactory cooperation" during the assessments. Responses in hearing evaluations varied but were accepted as being within normal limits. His speech was unintelligible.

H.'s mother observed him in the home and neighborhood and was aware of his abilities as well as his limitations. Because of her awareness of H.'s abilities which the professionals did not see, she rejected the diagnosis suggesting mental retardation and borderline moron. Only an audiologist held the opinion that H. was not severely retarded. On the basis of the audiologist's opinion and her own beliefs, H.'s mother sought other evaluations and opinions, the last of which described H. as "seeming to have adequate understanding of basic language concepts," and using "fragmentary replies to questions" in largely unintelligible articulation, which might be intelligible to the professional accustomed to analyzing speech of children with articulation errors.

H. received a limited amount of instruction in the Association Method at the institute where an additional evaluation had been made. Prognosis was considered to be guarded. Following that work, his ongoing educational management began with a summer of private tutoring using the Association Method. The precise articulation requirements addressed his severe articulation disorder. Altering the temporal rate of all communications with him addressed problems which since the 1990s would be viewed as auditory processing disorders. Following an eleven-month enrollment in the school, H. left the program with intelligible speech and early first-grade reading skills at age seven. He entered a private first-grade class with twelve pupils and a retired first-grade teacher. Following that successful year, H. attended a private military academy as a day student. The low pupil-teacher ratio gave him the individualized instruction he needed. At the junior high school level, he entered the regular public school system. There were the same kinds of difficulties for H. as for other high school peers; many of his peers who had no histories of limitations had similar difficulties in their academic pursuits.

H. was popular, well-liked by both boys and girls, and, in general, accepted by his teachers. There were few traces of speech difficulties. Until a knee injury made surgery necessary, H. played high school football successfully. He graduated from high school at the age of nineteen years and entered a university.

At the end of the first term at the university, term records showed that H. had maintained a 3.0 grade point average on a 4.0 scale while also holding a part-time job. H. entered the workforce full-time. He did well in management and planning. In anticipating difficulty with three semester hours of calculus, he delayed completing his undergraduate degree. For a time, he lost motivation for doing so because of his success in business. In 1989, however, he completed the undergraduate degree and, in 1990, he completed his MBA degree. In 1993 he became manager of an international ethnic cosmetic company.

A.'s Case

A.'s medical history showed only low birth weight. Developmental milestones were achieved at expected times. The first word emerged at 18 months. There were no sentences at the chronological age of 5 years, 5 months. An evaluation at chronological age 5–10 revealed the following: Peabody Picture Vocabulary Test (PPVT) rating of 3–11, Arizona Articulation Proficiency Scale-Revised (AAPS-R) score of 65.5. A. was enrolled in therapy using Programmed Conditioning Language (Gray and Ryan 1973) to which Multi-Phonemic Articulation Therapy (Bradley and McCabe 1975) was added. Because of limited gains, the supervisor requested that the Hiskey-Nebraska Test of Learning Aptitude (HNTLA) be administered. The results indicated a hearing mental age of 3–6 (DIQ: 58) with a range of subtest scores from 3–0 to 5–0. On the Test of Language Development-Primary (TOLD-P),

she was unable to complete two subtests. Standard scores for the remaining subtests ranged from 1 to 5. The two quotients which could be derived were 61 and 64. Spontaneous utterances consisted of the first two sounds of words with up to three-word combinations. Because progress was limited, the supervisor requested that A. be placed in the DuBard School for Language Disorders.

In the new placement, A.'s instructional program consisted of the Association Method so as to focus on small incremental progression in speech, to establish memory for sequences, and to address language and early academic skills. She was enrolled full-time for four years. Near the end of her enrollment, she earned an AAPS-R score of 97. Her TOLD-P standard scores ranged from 1 to 13 and quotients ranged from 72 to 94. Her HNTLA HMA was 10–0 (DIQ: 87) at chronological age 11–2. She subsequently entered regular public school classes and as a teenager demonstrated articulation and oral language skills comparable to those of her peers. She is currently employed in a local hospital as a medical technologist and continues to have excellent oral communication skills.

CHILDHOOD APRAXIA OF SPEECH AND LANGUAGE DISORDER

Too Soon, Too Young--Childhood Apraxia of Speech/Language Disorder

In the case of Webb Warren II, whose mother asked that he be identified fully, there were mixed opinions regarding what should be done and when to start. Because he was only three years old, "It's too early—he's too young," was a common view of many professionals. A medical history of Hyaline's Membrane raised the question of possible mental limitations. However, the mother observed measures of intelligence and except for communication skills, Webb achieved other developmental milestones at the expected ages. By age three, language comprehension seemed to be satisfactory but Webb's efforts to use spoken language resulted in unintelligible sequences of sounds, consisting primarily of vowel and vowel-like expressions. His articulation was so poor that there was no way for the listener to know whether word meanings and word order were appropriate and correct. He demonstrated severe apraxia.

At this time, Webb was evaluated at the University Speech Clinic and in our school. His evaluation was an ongoing process, consisting of several weekly sessions of diagnostic teaching which gradually led to intervention procedures. He was enrolled for language/speech intervention at the age of three years, six months. He attended four days a week, three hours daily.

Webb's formal instruction of language and speech consisted of procedures and techniques of the Association Method. Two modifications of the procedures were made. Because of his young age, writing skills were not required for proceeding from one stage to the next. The second modification was that when he reached the animal story level, he was not required to remember the story in the exact order as in the instructional story. The formal program was supplemented by unstructured language activities, activities designed for developmental learning, and other activities appropriate for young children.

Progress was steady and impressive. His use of spontaneous language mushroomed. As good articulation skills became well-established, the disordered language could be observed relatively easily. Incorrect word order and saying things "funny ways" were obvious. Articulation for multisyllable words reflected reversals of sounds and syllables. Writing skills were taught by the time Webb was five years of age. Although written recall of work was not required of him on all levels of work, he was able to write words, sentences, and stories, with appropriate corresponding questions, in cursive from memory. The content of a story became the determining factor for deciding whether or not Webb would have to recall a story in exact sequence in which it was presented in instruction.

Webb left the program in 1981 at age five years, seven months. A special placement continued for a year. Some of his instruction was along the lines of the Association Method, utilizing and strengthening his excellent code-breaking skills, expanding his language skills, and making a transfer to reading and writing of manuscript which he would encounter upon entering first grade.

When Webb was six years, five months, videotapes recorded his language and speech following the termination of all special instruction. The only articulation error noted was a poor vowelized r, as in bird, work, etc., and a substitution of w for r as in red. Those errors were corrected with a minimum amount of special work the following year.

Webb entered first grade at the age of six years, eight months with second-grade reading skills. After entering first grade, Webb's teacher instructed the children to write a Halloween story. Webb's story is given below.

the Hallaween godalens
(me and my brother) went in this creepy house. I opned the door. there was a godalen. "I want to go home," he said. The godalen went away. they went inside. they saw a gost so they ran in to PP (qq) doors. then aother gost. they were trapt. the tuo gohts put them in a room. they forgot to lock the doors.

For several years in the elementary grades, Webb was in a program for children who were gifted. When the academic demands became stressful, he asked to return to a regular placement. As a tenth grader in 1991–92, he made A's and B's. His articulatory difficulties, for which he has developed compensatory measures, were observable only in multi- and polysyllabic words. Webb graduated from a public high school in 1994. His ACT score, taken prior to his senior year, was 26. One month after graduation he entered Louisiana State University with an academic scholarship. He graduated in May 2000 with majors in business and management information systems. He is employed as an Information Systems Manager.

ACQUIRED PROFOUND HEARING LOSS AND LANGUAGE DISORDER

At the Opposite End of the Continuum–Acquired Hearing Loss/Language Disorder

The story of Richard (Ricky) Alan Hurst is quite different from that of K. described later in this chapter. Ricky acquired the conditions of aphasia and profound hearing loss at thirty months as a result of a post-convulsive disorder related to rapidly rising fever and Asian flu in 1960. He had been a bright, loquacious child, the youngest of four children. By the age of three years, eight months, Ricky was enrolled in a daily program suitable to his needs as an "aphasic and deaf" child.

Ricky's mother learned the techniques of the Association Method by which he was being taught. This gave her the capability of reinforcing the school's instruction at home and supplementing his language learning. At the end of the eighteen months, Ricky had mastered the desired skills related to a wide variety of noun vocabulary and the first three basic sentences and questions of the Association Method; by age six he understood number concepts through ten and could count to and write numerals to ten. He had learned in a structured setting a few four-line animal stories with the corresponding questions. There were major difficulties with memory and memory for sequences. None of his achievements came easily; trials, frustrations, and sacrifices from all who were a part of his daily life had been a major part of his gains.

Ricky was enrolled in the School for Children with Language Disorders (SCLD) (later renamed DuBard School for Language Disorders) program in 1962 and remained there for six years. He completed the language and correlative programs. When he was mainstreamed into general education local schools in the fourth grade at age twelve, he had fourth- and fifth-grade skills in reading, language, spelling, and math. His greatest difficulties in that first year in school were related to: (1) a natural measure of shyness, accentuated by the feelings of uncertainty and insecurity of entering a school environment so different from that in which he had been enrolled—more children per class, more teachers, more subjects, (2) being in a school environment which called on him to do his best, to utilize maximum efforts—which were excellent, but not always as rewarding in successes as he had experienced in earlier years, and (3) his naive expression of pleasure and satisfaction with his successes. Upon receiving his first report card, he recognized his high marks and showed his card to his peers, for this he was teased, and he did not understand. Coping with peer jealousies was difficult for him.

During that first year of regular school, Ricky received two hours of differentiative instruction weekly in vocabulary of subject areas and any other additional help which seemed appropriate. One language assignment he was given was to write a story using a farm picture showing children collecting something from under a tree. The story Ricky wrote follows:

> At 1:00 Richard, John and Joe took their basket to the pasture because they wanted to pick up some nuts. About an hour later the boys were so tired that they went home. They drank some water. They decided to ask their uncle if they could ride his horses. He said, "Of course you may ride." They rode their horses. About 4:30, they went to their uncle's house. They put the horse in the field and said to their uncle, "Thank you." That night they went to bed. Richard dreamed that he wanted to be President. He wished it would come true!

In 1950, Richard ran for the senate. In 1968, the people of the United States voted for him. He remembered when he was about 12 that he wanted to be president and now he is. Pat and Richard have 2 daughters. One daughter is Julie Nixon. Her boy friend thought she was beautiful, so he married her. He is the grandson of President Eisenhower.

Ricky was a perfectionist in his earliest years in school; this trait continued to be a part of his basic nature. He spent unusually long hours preparing certain school assignments. In high school, part of the curriculum was a study of the inner struggles of individuals. The students examined how these struggles had been expressed in poetry, short stories, novels, and art. The study culminated in each student being assigned the task of expressing his/her own inner struggle or struggles. Ricky's expression of his struggles follows. The work appears as he wrote it. He received help in two places. Searching for the words he wanted to use, he described his feelings; his mother gave him the words appropriate for his thoughts. Those words appear in parentheses.

Carousel

> My world is a carousel.
> The calliope begins to play
> as the carousel slowly starts.
> Then the music grows louder and louder,
> And the merry-go-round goes round,
> faster, faster and faster.
> The brass ring I've gripped so tightly
> Grows smoother and slicker,
> Until my hold is almost lost.
> Wilder and wilder the horses churn!
> Up and down, up and down,
> Until I want to yell, "Stop world!
> And let me get off."
> Then I think, not now, not now,
> Let me finish the ride—
> God, please?

"Carousel" is my interpretation of my inner struggle (psychological and physical) to prove myself normal in a hearing society. The slow start of the carousel represents the very (protective environment) in which my early education took place. Then as I started to public school, each year the demands and stresses have increased. Now as a teenager in high school, the demands, desires and pressures almost become too much for me at times and for a fleeting moment I think the answer is to quit. Then I have second thoughts. I have come too far to turn back now. I want an education, a profession, a family and a place in the community. So for my own self respect, "let me finish the ride. God, Please?"

Ricky entered the University of Southern Mississippi. During his first three semesters, he maintained a 3.5 grade point average on a 4.0 scale. As the language of specialized subjects became more technical and/or abstract, as he encountered lecturers who were unfamiliar with the problems associated with language disorders, and as he encountered more and more professors with mustaches and beards, which created difficulties in lipreading for Ricky, his problems increased. The specialized vocabularies in such courses as marketing and advertising were especially troublesome for him. Nevertheless, he managed to stay on the dean's list. In May 1982, he received his bachelor of fine arts degree in graphics with a minor in photography. He worked a few years as an illustrator for an architectural firm. At last report, he was a supervisor in a large regional office of the Internal Revenue Service and was pursuing a Masters in Business Administration (MBA) degree.

CONGENITAL PROFOUND HEARING LOSS WITH AND WITHOUT CO-EXISTING CONDITIONS

See Chapter 3, Differential Diagnosis, for three additional case histories for individuals with severe to profound hearing loss.

DYSLEXIA AND SPECIFIC LEARNING DISABILITIES/DISORDERS OF WRITTEN LANGUAGE

Children with Disabilities in Written Language/ Dyslexia

Over the years, a number of children with problems related to reading, spelling, and written language in general have been enrolled in our school. Their instructional program was based on the Association Method. The gains the children made in achievement and the changes observed in their overall response to teaching-learning situations as they began experiencing success in reading was significant.

The children had been poor achievers from their first enrollments in school. In some instances, their difficulties were identified as early as the kindergarten level. In other cases, their difficulties were observed and the achievement levels remained poor,

but no action had been taken to determine causes for which some change in instruction might be appropriate. Some of the children had been placed in remedial instructional programs in their respective schools; the major change in such cases was an increase in frustrations for the children, their parents, and the teachers involved. The instructional efforts were based on the idea of increasing and repeating the same types of instructional strategies as used in the general education setting even though those strategies had not benefitted the child. No differentiative teaching techniques had been used in the remedial teaching.

Initially, children enrolled in the now DuBard School for Language Disorders for problems solely in the area of written language received individual instruction only until it was possible for the child to participate in group instruction with a measure of success. When the child with reading, spelling, and writing difficulties established skill in code-breaking, he/she was able to become a part of group instruction with children diagnosed with severe language and speech-disorders.

Because children with the limitations in skills using written language had no difficulty understanding vocabulary meaning and basic concepts of oral language, they were able to progress through the language program more rapidly than the children diagnosed with developmental aphasia or language disorders. For the most part, these kinds of children were able to complete the designated program appropriate to their needs in a shorter period of time. Such enrollments usually began in a summer term and concluded twenty-six months later, at which time the child was able to reenter a typical school program. With the development of programs for children with specific learning difficulties, those children who were unable to participate successfully in general education classes had benefit of resource teacher assistance. In a very few instances, the children were placed in self-contained class settings for children with learning disabilities.

Each child was different but all had the threads of similarity: average or above average intellectual potential, subtle language and speech differences, poor achievement records, frustration to the point of borderline emotional or behavioral disturbances, frustrated and bewildered parents who were convinced that their child was intelligent but who certainly was not learning to read, spell, and write. One case history follows.

The story of J.G. demonstrates what can be accomplished when a child has a high rating in factors influencing achievement cited earlier. J.G.'s inability to learn the academic skills normally achieved easily at the five-year level were recognized by the fifth month of his enrollment in kindergarten. At four years of age, he had been enrolled in speech therapy for minor misarticulations. His progress was good. He had been released after nine months of twice weekly instruction. When he had difficulties in kindergarten, he was given hearing tests. No hearing difficulties were found. By the fourth month of kindergarten, J.G. had begun to demonstrate his awareness of the fact that he was unable to learn what the other children were learning. He developed a very negative attitude about going to school and a negative self-image.

An evaluation through the university program revealed these facts. Although J.G. engaged in conversation readily and his articulation was good, if asked a question requiring that he use information he had just stated spontaneously, he was unable to answer the question. He did not understand the relationship between language of questions and language of answers; he could not demonstrate the understanding by using language properly in a dialogue pattern.

J.G.'s performance on the Hiskey-Nebraska Test of Learning Aptitude earned him a five year, six-month functional level when his actual age was five years, nine months. There were depressed ratings earned in picture matching and some of the memory for sequence tasks. He reversed numbers and letters in written language. He had poor command of his pencil when he tried to write. He had not learned enough sight vocabulary to merit measuring in a standardized way.

J.G. was enrolled in the program on a trial basis for the summer term. At six years of age he attended one-and-one-half-hour sessions, four days a week. His program was designed around two kinds of activities: (1) nonacademic activities to increase memory for sequences, and (2) the beginning levels of the Association Method for children with language disorders. Pretesting and post testing revealed that, while his improved attention span resulted in a somewhat better overall performance, his memory for sequences did not improve. Most important, however, he achieved a measure of skill in code-breaking of words of two and three sound units. He acquired a measure of skill in writing the phonemes and words. In order to give him a psychological advantage, one sentence and question form was introduced at an earlier level than McGinnis' guidelines. While J.G. had marked difficulty in blending any two sounds into a syllabic

unit, he had no difficulty with word meanings. His basic understanding of word meanings enabled his teacher to advance him more easily.

J.G.'s trial enrollment was based on the question of whether or not the program might be to his benefit. As it turned out, the trials involved him, his teacher, supervisor, and mother. There were J.G.'s continuing comments of "I'm the dumbest boy at school, I don't want to go, I can't learn" balanced by those of his teacher, "I believe you can, let me help you, see you did learn that" and those of his anxious parents, "You have to learn."

J.G.'s success during the summer instruction had been on an individual basis. The trials cited above were accompanied with his deliberately falling out of the chair and various other behavioral antics. Those behaviors disappeared as he became successful in learning. The continued enrollment for a regular nine-month session had to be on a three-month trial basis because his tolerance for a full day of instruction and his ability to participate in a group were not known. However, the trial aspect ended within three months because J.G. became more aware of his abilities than of his limitations; he understood, too, that the single goal of the teachers was to teach him to read and use written language. While his parents were worried that science and geography were not being emphasized and that math was given secondary emphasis compared to reading, spelling, and writing, their concerns were not sufficiently severe to cause long-lasting difficulties.

At the time that J.G. completed the program at the chronological age of seven years, nine months and the family was preparing to move away, he had achieved the following levels of functioning as measured by the American School Achievement Test, Form E, Primary Battery II, Part II:

	Grade Equiv.	Age Equiv.
Reading		
Sentence and Word Meaning	3.1	8–4
Paragraph Meaning	2.8	7–11
Spelling	2.6	7–9
Language (grammar)	3.2	8–5
Arithmetic		
Computation	2.5	7–8
Problems	3.6	8–9

J.G.'s performance on the standardized tests and performances in reading the curricula used in the program supported the recommendation of placement in a typical school program at the second-grade level. It was theorized that a home program during the summer months would help him hold onto his gains and that such a placement would put him in the top of his regular class rather than at the bottom of third grade, the age appropriate placement. Although his brother was at the same grade level in a different group and some sibling problems could be anticipated, the teachers, J.G.'s parents, and the principal of his new school were in agreement about the placement. J.G. progressed steadily. He completed high school and obtained a university undergraduate degree in business administration. His only academic difficulties were from lecturers who talked too fast for his auditory processing rate and vocabulary. Since 1992, he was a bank executive and ultimately earned a Masters degree. (See Appendix E for related information regarding this student's instructional program.)

Preliminary data from the Language Enhancement and Achievement Program (LEAP) and the outclient therapy program at the DuBard School for Language Disorders
These preliminary data on one aspect of reading, decoding—in real and nonsense words and in context—are provided to illustrate the efficacy of the scientifically-based DuBard Association Method® which meets all of the requirements of the National Reading Panel report. Data analysis is ongoing.

<table>
<tr><td colspan="2">Statistical Analysis of Pre- and Post-test
Phonic Transfer Scores on a
Criterion-Referenced Test of Reading Skills
Decoding Skills Test - PTI Scores Derived from Subtest II Raw Scores</td></tr>
<tr><td colspan="2">POPULATION - Students aged 5-10 to 9-11 (average age 7-10), with the primary diagnosis of dyslexia.</td></tr>
<tr><td colspan="2">THERAPY MODEL - After-school program (LEAP - Learning Enhancement and Achievement Program) delivered by paraprofessionals and graduate students and supervised by certified speech-language pathologists in a resource schedule of service delivery for 48 contact hours over the course of a semester.</td></tr>
<tr><td colspan="2">TEST MEASUREMENT - Decoding Skills Test (DST) (Richardson & Dibenedetto, 1985).
The DST was developed to serve two specific research purposes:
<ul>
<li>To accurately measure levels of decoding (i.e., word recognition) in subject populations involved in the study of developmental dyslexia, and</li>
<li>To measure various aspects of decoding and decoding skills development that may be useful in the study of reading disorders.</li>
</ul>
Phonic Transfer Index (PTI) Scores were analyzed.
<ul>
<li>PTIs yield information regarding the rate of application of known phonic patterns (i.e., those contained in Real Words) to the decoding of unknown (i.e., Nonsense) words.</li>
<li>Good application of phonic knowledge can be inferred when the PTI's are .70 or above.</li>
<li>PTIs below .60 indicate weak application of phonic knowledge when decoding.</li>
</ul>
</td></tr>
<tr><td colspan="2">STATISTICAL MEASURE - Paired sample t-test</td></tr>
</table>

ANALYSIS OF DECODING SKILLS for Monosyllabic Words	
N =	13
Pre-test Phonic Transfer Index for Monosyllabic Words (PTIms) Mean	0.39
Post-test Phonic Transfer Index for Monosyllabic Words (PTIms) Mean	0.63
t =	-2.666
df =	12
SIGNIFICANCE	0.021

ANALYSIS OF DECODING SKILLS for Polysyllabic Words	
N =	13
Pre-test Phonic Transfer Index for Polysyllabic Words (PTIps) Mean	0.23
Post-test Phonic Transfer Index for Polysyllabic Words (PTIps) Mean	0.33
t =	-1.653
df =	12
SIGNIFICANCE	0.124

RESULTS – Pre-test and post-test PTI scores on the DST indicated that

- Students challenged with dyslexia made statistically significant improvement in decoding monosyllabic words at 48 hours of therapy.
- Statistically significant improvement was not found for polysyllabic words in this group at 48 hours of therapy. However, it should be noted that the LEAP curriculum does not include instruction in polysyllabic decoding during the first 40 hours of therapy. Thus, the lack of significant improvement for this group is probably due to lack of instruction in polysyllabic decoding in this stage of the curriculum.

The following preliminary data is a result of two one-hour sessions of therapy per week with students diagnosed with dyslexia.

Statistical Analysis of Pre- and Post-test Phonic Transfer Scores on a Criterion-Referenced Test of Reading Skills Decoding Skills Test - PTI Scores Derived from Subtest II Raw Scores
POPULATION - Students aged 7-1 to 13-4 (average age 9-3), with the primary diagnosis of dyslexia (some with coexisting ADHD).
THERAPY MODEL - Resource therapy program delivered by certified speech-language pathologists in a resource schedule of service delivery (one hour of therapy twice weekly) for a range of 21 to 315 sessions (average # of one-hour sessions: 91.23).
TEST MEASUREMENT - Decoding Skills Test (DST) (Richardson & Dibenedetto, 1985). • The DST was developed to serve two specific research purposes: To accurately measure levels of decoding (i.e., word recognition) in subject populations involved in the study of developmental dyslexia, and • To measure various aspects of decoding and decoding skills development that may be useful in the study of reading disorders. **Phonic Transfer Index (PTI)** Scores were analyzed. • PTIs yield information regarding the rate of application of known phonic patterns (i.e., those contained in Real Words) to the decoding of unknown (i.e., Nonsense) words. • Good application of phonic knowledge can be inferred when the PTI's are .70 or above. • PTIs below .60 indicate weak application of phonic knowledge when decoding.
STATISTICAL MEASURE - Paired sample t-test

ANALYSIS OF DECODING SKILLS for Monosyllabic Words	
N =	13
Pre-test Phonic Transfer Index for Monosyllabic Words (PTIms) Mean	0.53
Post-test Phonic Transfer Index for Monosyllabic Words (PTIms) Mean	0.85
t =	-4.309
df =	12
SIGNIFICANCE	0.001

ANALYSIS OF DECODING SKILLS for Polysyllabic Words	
N =	13
Pre-test Phonic Transfer Index for Polysyllabic Words (PTIps) Mean	0.37
Post-test Phonic Transfer Index for Polysyllabic Words (PTIps) Mean	0.68
t =	-5.022
df =	12
SIGNIFICANCE	<0.001

RESULTS – Pre-test and post-test PTI scores on the DST indicated that

- Students challenged with dyslexia made statistically significant improvement in decoding both monosyllabic and polysyllabic words following a course of resource therapy.

The service providers for both the LEAP and outclient therapy programs had received a minimum of two 45-hour courses in the DuBard Association Method® and extensive clinical teaching experience in the approach.

AUTISM (WITH LANGUAGE/SPEECH DEFICITS)

Language Deficiency/Disorder and Autism

Q. was enrolled in The University of Southern Mississippi Speech and Hearing Clinic for an ongoing diagnostic evaluation at age four years, four months. He did not demonstrate any comprehension of language. His only vocalizations were screaming and yelling. Onset of the screaming and yelling was unpredictable and those behaviors stopped equally as unpredictably. Unless he was restrained in some way, he would run through the building uncontrollably. He regularly attended two, fifty-minute sessions per week. These concentrated primarily on behavior modification in an effort to help him learn to control his erratic and potentially destructive behavior. At the end of each session of work with Q., there was a parent conference. Parent cooperation was excellent and influenced Q.'s progress greatly.

Nonverbal tasks and operant conditioning techniques were used in the sessions with Q. After forty-two sessions, the decision was made to begin Association Method procedures at the phoneme level, in a highly structured manner, and on a one-to-one basis without including any written activities. Also, his schedule was altered so that he attended one-hour sessions, five days a week. The teaching-learning environment was broadened gradually to include more environmental stimuli, more individuals in and out of the sessions and a program to help him learn to take some responsibility for his behavior. This included learning to walk instead of running and learning to go to the water fountain and restroom unattended.

At five years, one month, Q. was enrolled in the group program on a half-day basis. Initially, he was unable to work well, if at all, in a group. Use of the Association Method continued largely on a one-to-one basis. Periodically, for unknown reasons, he would scream, shriek, and overturn desks and chairs unless he was restrained.

Four months later, he was still very echolalic at times, but demonstrated ability to read and write some words that were beyond the expectations of an average five year old, demonstrating hyperlexia. Through the echolalic language, he demonstrated memory for long sequences of words. At times, he did not demonstrate understanding of what he was repeating. Spontaneous language included such utterances as "get Gulf," "get Exxon," "get ________" in good articulation. This was interpreted to mean that he wanted the teacher to write Gulf or Exxon on the board or to get the person whom he had named to come in the room. He also demonstrated a desire to write the words himself.

Although echolalic language persisted for a time, sometimes Q. initiated or tried to engage in dialogue representative of conversation. His language structure was comparable to that of a two and a half year old in unrefined articulation.

Improvements came slowly with periodic regressions into behaviors of shrieking and turning over desks and chairs, but his response to the Association Method procedures was positive. Q. had a considerable amount of difficulty in understanding the relationship between question forms and sentences in the repetitive sentence work. However, by the time work in the animal story level was introduced, he had improved significantly. He achieved success in developing receptive and expressive skills using preposition concepts in a structured setting with relative ease. By this time, also, he was able to carry out two consecutive instructions satisfactorily.

During the following sixteen months, Q. attended on a half-day basis, five days per week, after which he began attending all day (8:30–2:30). Attendance was regular. In general, Q.'s behavior became more settled. There was a marked decrease in the frequency and severity of temper tantrums. The echolalia disappeared and eye contact increased. He became able to work in a group with three other children for part of each day's instruction. During such group work, he sometimes interacted with other children if they initiated the conversation. On the playground, he played with others occasionally if they initiated the play activity. Running skills and skills requiring running and throwing a ball held little interest for him. Most of the time he preferred to swing and to do it alone. In social activities, Q. objected to hearing the happy birthday song. He clamped his hands over his ears repeatedly. By the time he left the program, however, he participated appropriately in such activities.

Q. progressed through the past tense story level of the Association Method. He required a variety of reinforcement activities to establish competence for new material. However, he achieved competence for some new material at a faster rate than the children with more typical developmental language disorders. Some tasks, such as memory for math facts, were more difficult for him than for the other children. Gradually, Q. generalized language which had been taught in structure to new situations. He used grammar incorrectly at times. Errors of substituting is/are, has/have, and she/her were common. He often got words out of order and was unable to understand and use language and vocabulary which was more complex than what he had been taught. Formulation of question language had been very difficult for Q., but by the past tense level of instruction, he was able to generate a variety of question forms spontaneously if they had been taught previously in structure.

As inappropriate spontaneous language decreased, it frequently reflected errors in grammar. The quality of his articulation improved. Q.'s voice became more natural in inflection and rhythm but it remained noticeably different in prosody, mechanical, and somewhat like a talking computer. His laughter became more appropriate to situations than it had been earlier.

Q. was allowed periodic breaks from the teaching-learning situation as reinforcement for completing his work satisfactorily. During the breaks, he sometimes chose to draw on the board rather than play with toys. Usually, his drawings were very detailed, accurate reproductions of movie advertisements or road signs. Another of his rewards was receiving a copy of the university student newspaper which he read.

Despite his obvious deficiencies in language performance, it was the consensus of those who provided his instruction at that time that emotional disturbance was a primary component in his failure to develop language and speech naturally. As understanding of various disabilities has progressed in the ensuing years, it is believed that, in current terminology, a diagnosis of autism likely would have been appropriate for Q. The high degree of structure in his instruction is believed to have been a key factor in his acquisition of communication skills.

Q. progressed to the upper past tense story level of the Association Method. He worked in a first-grade reader and a reading-language workbook. He had little or no difficulty reading the words, but demonstrated difficulty in answering questions about material he read. Memory and understanding of math facts remained a weak area.

Q. soon generalized language taught in structure to new situations. In addition, he used vocabulary and verb forms which had not been taught

in structure. The number of grammatical errors became fewer. His spontaneous language structures remained simpler than those which he generated in a classroom activity and simpler than those that would be expected of a typically developing child of his age. The majority of his spontaneous language consisted of questions, and he frequently demonstrated his fixation on a given topic, such as the addresses of various people. His inflectional patterns for all situations remained high-pitched and had a robot-like quality; although he was aware of inflection and attempted to use it, the result was often inappropriate for the situation and linguistic composition. The following data reflect progress over time. Considerable intervention had to take place prior to the administration of the first tests to Q. Data are somewhat limited due to the rather small number of appropriate standardized measures available at the time. Nevertheless, the results are worth noting.

	Pretest	Posttest
Chronological Age	5–1	7–7

	Age Equiv.	Age Equiv.
Test for Auditory Comprehension of Language	3–0	6–7
Hiskey-Nebraska Test of Learning Aptitude (Hearing Mental Age)	4–0	7–7

	Posttest Grade Equiv.	Age Equiv.
American School Achievement Test Primary Battery II		
Sentence and Word Meaning	2.0	7–3
Paragraph Meaning	1.6	6–9
Language	2.2	7–5
Spelling	2.7	7–10

Q. entered a typical school at the age of seven years, eight months at the third-grade level. On any given day his behaviors at home and at school reflected those of a child with autism, a child who was gifted, and/or a child with language disorders. His performances and achievements in the new educational setting varied and remained inconsistent. Nevertheless, he was able to continue to expand his use of language and, at last report, was attending a local community college and had written a novel about a high school prom.

The use of the Association Method might be

helpful with some children with autism but not necessarily for all such children. It has been known to be of value with certain children diagnosed with autism at an early age. Some children with autism spectrum disorders, especially those with Asperger's Syndrome, have benefited from the phonetic, structured language approach. Since many have hyperlexia, the written component of the Association Method can be used as a foundation for enhancing the development of oral language as well as written language/reading.

Implementation of Association Method with Autism: Two Case Histories

Even though Mildred McGinnis did not enroll children with autism in her "aphasic language" classrooms, she did refer those children for Association Method teaching. Most notably, Ms. McGinnis referred a boy who had severe autism and deafness to a very capable graduate from her program, Barbara Baker Hull, M.A., CCC-SLP. As a result of her expert modifications and implementation of the method, this boy achieved a very positive outcome.

In the years to come, Ms. Hull modified the method for successful teaching with many more children with autism. Astounded by the superior success her daughter with autism had experienced with Ms. Hull and the Association Method, Judy Pollard-Licklider, M.A., CCC-SLP was determined to make this multisensory training available for more children with multiple disabilities. She founded Erin Is Hope Foundation in Wichita, Kansas where both modified and "pure" Association Method instruction are provided for children whose severe language impairments are complicated by autism.

Erin Is Hope (EIH) admits young children who are new to the therapy experience. The most common admissions, however, are children who have been "in-the-system" for over two years and who have gained little from conventional speech-language services. EIH also admits children for instruction who would not meet enrollment criteria in most other Association Method programs. A typical intake profile reveals a child who hits and hurts others, screams and disrupts, has no functional speech, is not toilet trained, does not point or give on request, and who uses tantrums to communicate. Some display echolalia, but do not use words meaningfully. These are children with no native language. They are isolated and anxious. No learning skills have been established.

Modifications of the Association Method (now DuBard Association Method®) vary with each child but may include:

1. Colorful icons, inspired by the McGinnis "baby book," are used when teaching the first 18 phonemes. These help to enhance both attention and memory and are faded before drop drill instruction begins.
2. Because of significant limitations in the child's ability to imitate phonemes and tolerate motor-kinesthetic development of new phonemes, the noun vocabulary groups typically used (see Appendix C) are sometimes abandoned in favor of other meaningful vocabulary. A small repertoire of sounds (e.g., /m/; /-o-/; /-a-/; /b/; /t/; /p/; /ee/; /o-e/) may result in teaching memory for both CV and CVC words (bee; mop; map; bat; pot; top). The vocabulary groups as organized by DuBard are used when possible.
3. The drop drill format is used more extensively and may be used to introduce nouns.
4. Primary spellings may be used (penciled in) to clarify pronunciation and enhance success with CV vocabulary on noun cards and during board instruction. These are faded as soon as possible.
5. The introduction of handwriting may be delayed.
6. "I see a..." repetitive sentence drills may occur earlier (before 50 nouns have been learned).

Case Histories:
Both of the children profiled in this account had received a minimum of three years of speech-language intervention prior to admission at Erin Is Hope (EIH). Both were functionally nonverbal and both exhibited extreme behavior disruptions.

Subject #1, male

This 4-9 year old boy enrolled with Erin Is Hope after over three years of specialized intervention through private programs. The parents reported training with ABA (Applied Behavior Analysis) professionals and expert speech-language pathologists specializing in apraxia. He was admitted with a co-morbid diagnosis of severe autism, severe apraxia and global aphasia. He showed no ability to understand speech or to verbally express himself, name or imitate.

Even though he was almost 5 years old, this student was not toilet trained and continued to drink from a bottle. When moving freely in the teaching area, he bolted around the room, dumped containers, threw toys, jumped and wildly laughed. He continuously vocalized a loud, monotonous "-a-" sound followed by a loud tongue clicking/grinding noise. Even when not agitated, he repeatedly slapped and punched his upper legs, aggressively clapped his hands and rocked with high velocity. When brought to the table for instruction, he engaged in fierce biting of his wrists and hands, both bruised, chapped and calloused from biting. He hit, kicked and fought to leave his chair. Lunging to swipe items from the table, this strong boy broke, threw and destroyed materials.

When admitted, this little boy was clearly familiar with ABA "do this" routines, and imitated clapping and patting. He matched colors and noun pictures in a field of two. He could not, however, point or give on request in a field of one. He did not point to even one body part. He required hand-over-hand assistance to assemble toddler pop beads, a five-piece matched puzzle and shape sorter.

This child put everything he touched into his mouth. He continuously produced the "-a-" sound, and could not imitate other phonemes. No imitation, echo or spontaneous word attempts were observed. His primary form of communication was screaming, pulling and tantrums. The following documentation demonstrates this child's progress from Association Method teaching:

Chart A: Progress achieved in first 18 months with intensive, modified Association Method strategies.

Progress Report	Phonemes Oral Recall with spoken model and icon cues	Phonemes Oral Recall without spoken model (icon cues still visible)	CV Words Oral Recall of picture and written word with *spoken model *primary spelling cues as needed	CV Words Listens, repeats, identifies both picture and written word. *primary spelling cues still visible on card	CV Words Oral recall of picture and written words *with no spoken model or primary spelling cues
Admission	0	0	0	0	0
12 months	15	12	10	5 (field of 2)	5
1.5 years	22	15	12	12 (field of 3)	8

Chart B: After 18 months, Subject #1 was ready to transition to a classic Association Method teaching format. This was initiated with the teaching of nouns through the cross drill format:

Progress Note	DuBard Grp 1	DuBard Grp 2	DuBard Grp 3	DuBard Grp 4	DuBard Grp 5	I see a...	a, an, some	what do you see?	I have a, an, some and ques.	I want a, an, some and ques.	I saw a, an, some and ques.	...has a, an some and ques.
1.5 years	7	6	0	0	0	0	0	0	0	0	0	0
2.5 years	23	16	0	0	0	0	0	0	0	0	0	0
3.5 years	23	25	22	12	10	90%	70%	70%	80%	60%	---	----
4 years	23	28	26	15	10	90%	90%	90%	90%	90%	80%	60%

After 48 months of Association Method services, Subject #1 demonstrated high accuracy in all structured skills for 102 nouns and 5 repetitive sentences with their corresponding questions. He also was able to name, identify and read 12 colors, digits and their written words to 20, 30 descriptors, 30 noun functions, and 25 action pictures/words.

Subject #2, female

Admitted at EIH at 4-8 years of age, this little girl had been enrolled in public special services for 3 years. Diagnosed with severe autism, her language impairment manifested as mixed transcortical aphasia. While she echoed word approximations, she had no ability to name items, had very poor comprehension, and could not spontaneously express herself in even single words.

Subject #2 was toilet trained, but other behaviors were dysfunctional. When brought to the table for instruction, she slapped, scratched and attempted to bite staff members. Repeatedly fighting to leave her chair, she engaged in loud screaming and shouting protests intermittently throughout procedures. She grabbed at materials, threw them or destroyed them.

At the time of admission, this child showed ability to imitate sounds as isolated phonemes were written on the page. If immediately presented with the same phoneme, however, she could not orally recall that sound without another imitation model. She was admitted for daily service in EIH's full day program. The following data showed her progress:

Chart A: Subject #2 progress during the first year of intensive, modified Association Method program:

Progress Report (months since admission)	Number of Phonemes (oral production) with spoken model		Number of Phonemes (oral recall) no spoken model		Oral Recall phonemes, drop drills, CV/VC nouns	Writes (21) primary phonemes (dictation format with trace or copy cues needed for success)	DuBard Grp 1 (22 CV/VC nouns) oral recall of pictures and of written word	DuBard Grp 1 Listens/ repeats identifies pictures or written words (field of 5)	DuBard Grp 1 Writes words dictation written recall (tracing cues needed for success)
Admission	21	90%	0		0	0	0	0	0
6 months	21	90%	21	90%	70%	80% tracing cues	57%	64%	70% tracing cues
12 months	28	90%	28	90%	90%	100% copy cues	90%	90%	100% tracing cues

When trace or copy cues are used when writing nouns, the child must listen-and-repeat, as in classic dictation. Then, after finding the target word in a group of 5, she says and traces or says and copies the word. Similarly, during written recall, tracing cues are provided as the child names the picture and then locates the target word in a group of 5. She says and traces the word.

Chart B: Subject #2 transitions to more classic presentation of Association Method systematic training:

Progress Report (months since admission)	Writes (21) primary phonemes (classic dictation format)		Number of phonemes oral recall no spoken model		Reads and matches primary to secondary spellings	DuBard Grp1 Writes word dictation written recall (no cues; classic format)	DuBard Grp 2 (34 CVC nouns) oral recall for picture and word review in structure (RIS) *trace/copy	I see a… DuBard Grps 1 and 2 reads repeats generates review in structure (RIS) (no writing)	What do you see? reads repeats generates review in structure (no writing)
24 months	21	90%	32	90%	70%	70%	78%	80%	80%

Chart C and Chart D show accelerating progress

Progress Report (months since admission)	Phonemes (42) Primary/ secondary All skills oral recall (OR) Dictation (Dict) Review in structure (RIS)	DuBard Group 1 All skills (OR) (WR) (Dict) (RIS)	DuBard Group 2 All skills (OR) (WR) (Dict) (RIS)	DuBard Group 3 All skills (OR) (WR) (Dict) (RIS)	DuBard Group 4 All skills (OR) (WR) (Dict) (RIS)	Mixed Sentences I see a, an, some... I want a, an, some.. I have a, an, some... this is a, an, some... I saw a, an, some... All skills (OR) (WR) (Dict) (RIS) generate	Mixed Questions What do you see? What do you want? What do you have? What is this? What did you see? All skills (OR) 60% (WR) 20% (Dict) 20% (RIS) generate
36 months	42 phonemes 90% Mastered	22 nouns 90% Mastered	34 nouns 90% Mastered	35 nouns 90% Mastered	31 nouns 90% Mastered	5 repetitive sentences 90% Mastered	5 repetitive questions 90% Mastered

Chart D

Progress Report (months since admission)	...has a, an, some.. what does... have? (OR) (WR) (Dict) (RIS) generate	Group 5 All skills (OR) (WR) (Dict) (RIS)	Group 6 All skills (OR) all (WR) 67% (Dict) 59% (RIS) 80%	Sentences with and without #s I see... I want... I have... this is... ...has... I saw... (OR) (WR) (Dict) (RIS)	How many do you...see/ want/have/ does...have/ did you see/is this? (OR) (WR) (Dict) (RIS) generate	Animal Stories Level 1 (4 stories) Level 2 (4 stories) Level 3 (4 stories) (OR) (WR) (Dict) (RIS) generate	Lang. Math (1-10) +1, +2, +3, +4, +5
48 months	90% Mastered	90% Mastered	---	90% Mastered	90% Mastered	90% Mastered	Mastered

Note: OR = Oral Recall; WR = Written Recall; Dict = Dictation; RIS = Review in Structure

Conclusion:

These case histories described two children who had failed to learn. They derived no benefit from conventional speech-language intervention; they had failed to learn behavior skills and had gained no ability to interact. After years of training, these students had not learned-to-learn. Certainly, they were amongst the group "most unlikely to succeed" from any method. Yet, through their Association Method success, they learned not only to speak, read, write and understand, they also learned to organize their behavior around the structure of their language.

While this review focuses upon the first 48 months of training for each subject, these children continued to progress in the method. Subject #1 has left the Wichita area, but Subject #2 was mastering "Prepositional Round-up Stories" at the time of this writing. The achievement of these children is remarkable.

As the medical and educational communities try to better understand autism, it is important that the benefits of systematic, incremental, multisensory training be studied. The success of these two children says much about what the "autistic brain" needs to form and integrate language pathways. Perhaps it says even more about the important role of language in regard to behavior.

The author acknowledges with gratitude the contribution of of the EIH data by Judy Pollard-Licklider.

DEVELOPMENTAL DISABILITY AND SEVERE CHILDHOOD APRAXIA OF SPEECH (CAS)

Developmental Disability Complicated by Severe Apraxia

Although work with J.S. was not part of a control/experimental project, it deserves mentioning in relation to the use of the Association Method with children with developmental disabilities. All of J.S.'s developmental milestones were recognized as being delayed. At two years of age, following an evaluation, he was placed in a nursery program and was in two, one-hour special sessions each week which focused on behavior management and language and speech development. Social skills also were stressed. The presence of hearing loss was ruled out soon after his enrollment.

At CA 4–6, J.S.'s vocal output was described as "communicating in a babbling manner." At CA 5–0 an evaluation was begun. At CA 5–7, the evaluation was completed and "mild mental retardation" was determined; MA was 3–4. J.S. was essentially nonverbal, but he had become more cooperative. During this evaluation, characteristics of developmental apraxia were observed. At CA 6–0, the results of the Stanford-Binet Test indicated that the mental limitations were moderate to severe. His communication was basically unintelligible. According to reports, J.S. had benefitted minimally from a computer program for teaching speech. He demonstrated a limited ability to imitate signs. The psychologist recommended that J.S. receive "extensive intervention" in an all-day program emphasizing speech and language. Also, J.S.'s parents were very eager for him to have the best opportunity to learn to talk. Their beliefs and desires led to an evaluation at the DuBard School for Language Disorders.

At the time of the evaluation, J.S. was seven years old. He was unable to achieve ratings on the Test of Auditory Comprehension of Language-Revised (TACL-R). His speech was unintelligible. No inventory of his articulatory skills could be measured through a formal articulation test. J.S.'s abilities on nonverbal tasks as measured by the Hiskey-Nebraska Test of Learning Aptitude (HNTLA), yielded earned ratings ranging from three years, six months to four years, six months, with an overall Hearing Mental Age (HMA) of three years, six months. Since children with developmental disabilities could be expected to have some speech ability by that mental age, the possibility of developmental apraxia, suspected earlier, was confirmed and was considered to be a major factor interfering with speech development, although the mental limitations were never questioned.

In diagnostic teaching, using the Association Method, J.S. demonstrated extreme difficulty imitating speech sounds. He had difficulty closing his lips voluntarily to produce /m/; it was difficult for him to add voice to achieve the proper acoustic properties once he had his lips together. The same was true for producing /p/ and releasing for the plosive component of the sound. Once his lips were closed, he had difficulty adding voice and releasing lip closure to produce /b/. He was unable to round his lips or imitate lip and tongue movements. His efforts consisted of unusual movements of his articulators.

J.S. was unable to produce approximations of acoustic properties of some vowel sounds because of lack of control of his articulators. This was especially noticeable in his efforts to produce /oi/ as in boy. Once he mastered the lip movements for the sound, he demonstrated his new found ability repeatedly and joyfully to anyone he happened to see.

J.S. received thirty-six hours of individualized instruction. The first goal was to determine if the Association Method would be a valid speech/language intervention for him. A secondary goal was to explore the quality of speech that he could produce spontaneously. Attending tasks and behavior management were ongoing goals in the expanded diagnostic work. During the eighteen days of work, J.S. learned to produce twenty-seven speech sounds; he established oral recall for producing the sounds with the visual cursive Northampton symbols as a stimulus. He was equally successful with ten syllabic units, that is, drop drills, so long as he was not required to blend the sounds. J.S. learned seven CV words through cross-drill instruction. He was not able to blend the two speech sounds and was not required to make the effort to do so. Through the work, however, he demonstrated that he could learn to say some words, read the words, and make proper associations between the two sets of symbols.

Following the instruction described, J.S. was enrolled in the program. He received individual and small group instruction. At the end of three months he was able to read, say, and use appropriately in the basic sentences of the sequential language program a wide variety of vocabulary with controlled phonetic sequences. He was able to use incidental language, such as "I want to go to the bathroom," in intelligible speech. The following data are related to J.S.

Diagnosis: Developmental Disability/Apraxia
Chronological age at beginning of therapy: 7–5

	Pretest CA: 7–1	Posttest CA: 8–11	Posttest CA: 10–4
Hiskey-Nebraska Test of Learning Aptitude DIQ*	52	43	
Test of Nonverbal Intelligence Quotient		57	
Arizona Articulation Proficiency Scale-Revised Picture Test			
Total Score	25%	69.5%	85.5%
% Improvement		178%	16%
Sentence Test	—	69.5%	72.5%

*Based on Subtests given

Articulation intelligibility began to emerge for monosyllabic words after fewer than six months of therapy. Receptive and expressive language quotients on the Test of Language Development—2–Primary were commensurate with measured mental ability. In spite of fine motor deficiencies which affected writing development, J.S. was able to write legible cursive writing. Intelligibility was good for one- and two-syllable words. Quality of articulation decreased somewhat on polysyllabic words. J.S. received instruction at the animal story, upper level of the Association Method. He became able to read and spell all materials which had been taught and he demonstrated transfer to other content. Enrollment in the intensive, full-time program was for approximately three years. In September of 1993 he entered school in his home state and continued to receive support services in language and speech daily. In June of 1994 he was reevaluated at the DuBard School. Test results and conversational dialogue reflected that J.S. was continuing to improve his communication skills. He demonstrated four percent improvement on the Arizona Articulation Proficiency Scale, Revised, ten percent improvement on the Test of Nonverbal Intelligence-2 (TONI–2), and ten to fifteen percent improvement on the Test of Language Development Primary-2 (TOLD P–2). These are gains one can expect with children challenged with developmental disabilities, and it is encouraging that there were no areas of skills which reflected regression.

J.S.'s cognitive limitations will not be eliminated. However, his use of intelligible speech in basic language has enriched his own life and that of his family.

ENGLISH AS A SECOND LANGUAGE (ESL)/ ENGLISH LANGUAGE LEARNERS (ELL)

Our initial awareness regarding use of the principles of the Association Method in relation to teaching English as a Second Language (ESL) came in the late 1960s and 1970s. An application of the teaching techniques was being made with a population of children in Mexico who were not necessarily learning their native language effectively; neither were they learning any other language. The McGinnis work was translated into Spanish for use in Mexico and has been used effectively there since that time. That translation has not been found in any American publications which have been reviewed. Another similar use of the techniques was applied by associates in Norway. Not until recent years, however, has serious thought been given to using the approach with children of various ethnic groups in the United States.

During the 1980s a wide variety of ethnic groups immigrated to the United States. Schools have needed to develop programs to teach growing numbers of children who had English language deficiencies. A child of a refugee family was brought to our attention in 1980. P. was the four-year-old son of an immigrant Cambodian family. The family desired to enroll him in a kindergarten-nursery program. Difficulties existed because of the language barrier. The university's speech and hearing clinic was contacted for placing P. in the preschool language program. P. could not be enrolled in that university program because of funding requirements. Only children with language disorders were eligible to enroll. The alternative was to serve P. through private speech/language instruction in the university speech clinic. One of the clinic's staff began instruction. After some discussion, the teacher decided to use some techniques of the Association Method.

The initial work of P.'s sessions focused on establishing appropriate behaviors and trying to extinguish his crying and fears. The desired interactions with the staff clinician were achieved through the use of play therapy. Within three sessions, P. was using some English utterances such as "uh-ohm," "oio," with reference to bubbles, "loo" for look, and "bye-bye." P. also spoke Cambodian intermittently. Within one week he began learning verbal imitation through a variety of play activities. During the second week, regression occurred because of a family crisis. However, it was noted that P. was trying to imitate two words, much as a very young child might do in developing expressive skills. For example, "no bubbles" "boy" "good" and "boy pop" would be uttered under specific situations. The articulation for the utterances was unrefined. By the third week, P. was responding appropriately to such commands as "sit down," "close (the door)," and "light out." P.'s whole-word vocabulary was expanded to include words associated with some immediate needs, such as "soup," "water," "flush," and "dry hands." Also in the third week, P. said, "My name P.," "no cookie," "water," and "good water" appropriately and spontaneously.

Aspects of the Association Method were incorporated into the sessions systematically. A notebook similar to a beginning book as used in the Association Method was begun. Only enough sounds and words to constitute a sample of his program were placed in his book. As more sounds and vocabulary were taught and used in oral sentences and question forms, more language patterns emerged, and P. began to use various kinds of responses spontaneously. Responding to the question, "What is this?", he said occasionally, "Me don't know what it is" or "me I don't know" and "that i(s) man." Another pattern which emerged was "give me ball."

At the beginning of the following semester, the clinician recognized a need for more organization/ structure for P.'s program. At this point instruction for speech production of phonemes was given. Precise production of the speech phonemes became a goal and an application of those phonemes was made into vocabulary of CV, VC, and CVC composition. When the desired speech skills had been established with an adequate volume of vocabulary, the format of the sequential language program was added to P.'s program. Simple sentence and question forms and appropriate determiners were introduced. Specific drill work was carried out in plurals. P. was placed in the teacher role in an informal manner so that he could establish skills in asking questions.

P.'s program of instruction expanded rapidly. As he established skill with one area of language, progression was made to a higher level and aspects of personal pronouns and verb forms became part of the instruction. A variety of reinforcement activities were used throughout his program.

There was no one in P.'s family who could work on carry-over activities with him at home. However, the family members observed each of P.'s instructional sessions. As he learned and progressed in language and speech, his family members learned as well. At the end of the semester, the family moved to California. Prior to their depar-

ture, however, it was possible to give P. a Peabody Picture Vocabulary Test (PPVT). During the instruction of approximately six months, beginning at a no language-no speech level in English, P., at CA 5-6, earned a PPVT age rating of 2 years-5 months. This amount of gain through a carefully planned and implemented instructional program suggests that use of some aspects of the Association Method for part of a program of teaching English as a second language was justifiable.

Choctaw Population

Use of aspects of the Association Method with a population of Choctaw children has been implemented, but has not been reported prior to this writing. Using the articulation work which permeates the Association Method for speech purposes was complicated by the fact that the language of the Mississippi Choctaw people has two alphabets or orthographic systems currently in use, whereas English is based on only one. The bilingual orthography is known primarily by younger Choctaw students. Neither orthographic system was developed by the Choctaws themselves. The Choctaw "bible" was developed in the 1800s by missionaries; the bilingual system was developed by the Choctaws, but under the direction of non-Choctaws. Just how much influence the non-Choctaw group had on the development of the system is not clear (Trigg 1990). In any case, it seems obvious that to use still a third orthographic system in an effort to establish knowledge of written English could present a number of difficulties.

Given the need and/or the desire to teach spoken and/or written English to a population of children whose native language and speech patterns are so different, it seems obvious that the professional would need to have a strong commitment to the task. There also would be a need for the professional to have a significant degree of academic freedom to plan and implement a highly specialized program.

The sequential/incremental language program presented in the Association Method follows the same incremental levels of language which the average child learns systematically, incrementally, and naturally. One major difference, of course, is that with the normally developing child, many language forms may be learned and/or emerge simultaneously. The fact that language forms may be used interchangeably and even incorrectly without losing the meaning can result in errors on the part of young children which they later straighten out on their own. Whether or not young Choctaw children experience the same kinds of differences is open to question. The marked differences between English and Choctaw would have to be solved/overcome by a professional planning and implementing work very carefully. If there were no means of involving all family members in the instructional program, the level of success could be limited. At best, the rate of progress would be expected to be slower than desired.

According to information provided by Trigg (1990), principles and techniques of the Association Method are being used with a population of Choctaw children who speak English as a second language with Choctaw as their primary language. The ages of the children range from four to twelve years. The language abilities of the children have been determined to be at least eighteen months below their mental ages. The children have been assigned a number of eligibility rulings according to the guidelines of the Mississippi Department of Education, Bureau of Special Services. The rulings include language impaired, hearing impaired, learning disabled, educable mentally retarded (EMR), and trainable mentally retarded (TMR).

Trigg suggests using the sequential language guidelines for the following purposes in the respective language areas:

Repetitive sentences: word sequencing, teaching the use of the articles/determiners *a* and *an*, memory skills and reinforcement activity for new vocabulary.

Animal stories: for reinforcing sequencing skills, sentence/question generation and recognition, memory for sequences, and reinforcement of new vocabulary.

Personal stories: to reinforce the correct use of pronouns in reference to gender in addition to the purposes stated in relation to the animal story work. This area of language and the focusing of attention on the pronouns is considered to be significant since the Choctaw language does not have any pronouns.

Other professionals have reported that they have used the Association Method in teaching speech and language to young Hispanic and Haitian children. However, no details have been given about the outcomes. There is a need for research about teaching methods with such populations, and detailed records of the results need to be reported. This is a research area for which there is vast potential among the young professionals. Determining the value of any approach is important. However, determining the value alone without reporting the results will not enable children of the present and future to benefit from this research, whether it is a success or a failure.

MULTIPLE DISABILITIES

Case Histories from the Early Years--Variables Influence Outcome--Multiple Diagnoses

S.W.'s educational management lacked the continuity reflected in the management of other children. There were multiple factors in his medical history. The Rh incompatibility was a medical factor. There were multiple neonatal problems including seizures during the first three and one-half years of his life. Clinical pathology indicated brain injury. Hearing loss and aphasia were indicated in the earliest diagnosis.

Educational placements varied because of the father's profession, but instructional management remained relatively consistent. He was first instructed as a child who had profound deafness. At the end of six months, at age four, instructional procedures were changed to those of the Association Method which was continued for several years. S.W. was enrolled on a trial basis in the university program. Emotional disturbances were obvious. During the trial enrollment, behaviors were modified, and he continued in that school's program for two full years. S.W. progressed well and reached good performance level. His speech and written language for what he was taught specifically were good. His spontaneous language was good; speech for that language was unrefined. Updated information in 1992 indicated that S.W. had good communication skills and got along satisfactorily with his friends. According to his father, hearing aids are helpful to him when he will wear them. S.W.'s difficulties with conforming to rules and regulations and his poor social adjustment made it difficult for him to maintain steady employment.

Genuine Head Starts

The cases just described share the common denominator of getting a late start in effective educational management. The next two cases we shall describe had the advantage of experiencing an unusually early start. Neither child was diagnosed officially as aphasic, language disordered, learning disabled, or as having a learning disability. It was perhaps too early for any team to agree on a diagnosis. The children were simply recognized as having special problems and were taught by what were known to be effective techniques with other children with similar difficulties.

The first child had cerebral palsy and was able to use only his right hand. He was able to walk, but, later, he was placed in a body cast to correct one of his hip anomalies. When first seen he was three-and-one-half years old. His expressive language consisted of guttural noises and shrieks; he demonstrated limited receptive language. The procedures of the Association Method were initiated during a home teaching program. Specific objectives were written for the babysitter to carry out in cooperation with the teacher of an early childhood class, who provided additional instruction as well as guidance for the home program. After one and one-half years, the child was able to be integrated into a class for children with physical disabilities engaging in regular academic work appropriate for their chronological ages. He acquired reading skills, and his spontaneous communication became clear and easily understood.

The second child demonstrated no spontaneous speech or expressive language at age three. He appeared to understand spoken language at the appropriate age level. He, too, began learning through the Association Method procedures in an early childhood education class. Aided by demonstrations, the mother became able to carry out the necessary teaching activities at home. At age five, the child was placed in a typical kindergarten. He spoke single words and three-word sentences clearly. He needed to read more complex language and commit it to memory prior to being able to use language of comparable complexity spontaneously.

These two children benefitted from head starts toward reaching their intellectual potentials. They are believed to be representative of many such children; their levels of achievement can be matched by other children with similar limitations and they should not be viewed as exceptions.

An Unfortunate Ending

It is impossible to determine whether there are more stories with happy endings than with unhappy endings. Needless to say, there are both kinds. The following one has to be viewed as an unfortunate ending.

K. had seemed to be a different kind of child since early after birth. Born in the early 1950s when few professionals were aware of the possibility of making differential diagnoses on children who did not learn to talk in the typical manner, and even fewer

professionals were undertaking the task of trying to habilitate them through differentiative teaching, it is little wonder that her parents found themselves spending unbelievable amounts of time, money, and emotion trying to find out what was wrong and, more importantly, what to do.

Conflicting opinions of medical personnel and other professionals added to the frustrations of the parents. The child's frustrations mounted. Trial teaching with the Association Method was implemented when K. was six years old. A major portion of the time was used in trying to shape her behaviors into patterns which would permit her to be taught and to learn. Her parents' efforts to manage her in the home were not very successful. Trial teaching with the Association Method procedures yielded enough success to give rise to optimism about what might be accomplished. The optimism increased when, over a period of several weeks following an interruption in the trial teaching, K. demonstrated that she (1) was able to recall the single phonemes she was taught during the trial work, (2) was able to produce them with good articulation, and (3) was able to write them relatively well. Even more encouraging, K. demonstrated a desire and willingness to learn new material. Also, she was very talented in drawing and designing and making doll clothes.

K.'s multiple audiological evaluations yielded audiograms which, when plotted on a single graph, looked like a spider web. The only consistency noted was her inconsistency in responding to pure tone and other sound stimuli used in clinical audiological assessments. Her voice inflections and jargon vocalizations were of tonal qualities comparable to those of a child with normal hearing acuity. K. never tolerated amplification. Given the opportunity to play with a stopwatch, K. would smile brightly when it was held to her ear and she would hold the watch to her ear for a minute or more at a time. Her fascination with hearing it was obvious from her facial expressions.

The family moved, and K. was placed in a program where professionals were said to use the Association Method but, in fact, did not. K. regressed. Following that school year, use of the Association Method was resumed through private tutoring on a daily basis. Within eight weeks of individualized and differentiative teaching, K. showed remarkable progress in learning new nouns. Her writing skills were good; her articulation for what she was taught was good. When she wanted to do well, she did. If she chose not to do something, it was extremely difficult to con her into doing it. Behavior modification was an ongoing component of the instruction.

At almost eight years of age, K. had no spontaneous language, but everyone involved felt that with effective teaching procedures she would make greater gains. Instruction continued on an outclient basis, two hours on consecutive days because of the distance between her home and the place for her instruction. Her mother was asked to carry out similar work at home. The long travel requirements, family illnesses, and a variety of unavoidable problems resulted in limited progress. K.'s behaviors regressed.

The following academic year the parents maintained homes in two areas so that K. could have access to daily instruction. She progressed to sentence and question work in which she did well in the structured school environment and, if required to do so, in the home setting as well. However, in time, the strains of living separately took their toll on all concerned, especially K. She was able to achieve specific goals in the instructional program if she wanted to, but when she had negative attitudes, she did not achieve. Her behavior at these times had negative influences on other children in the program. Emotional aspects of the double-home situation, ineffective management by the parents, and K.'s inconsistent willingness created difficulties related both to learning and teaching. Because of the multiple problems, her enrollment had to be terminated midyear.

Later, K. was placed in a state school for deaf students in her home state, but she was dismissed within six weeks because the school could not handle her. For about fifteen months she stayed at home. She attended a playschool with other children for two hours daily to give her mother an opportunity to be free from the direct responsibility for K. During this time, selected medical tests were conducted. The results showed considerable atrophy of the brain stem and other brain abnormalities.

Ultimately, K. was placed in another state school for deaf students, in a class of children who were difficult to teach. Differentiative teaching techniques were not utilized.

When she was twenty-one, K. was "graduated" from that school after attending eight or nine years. At the time of her graduation, her communicating consisted of natural gestures, jargon, and some word approximations. The only words for which she had acceptable speech were some she remembered from her early efforts at learning through the Association Method. She was

not able to say, write, fingerspell, or sign through other means of manual communication her needs or other basic thoughts, although the school she attended was one which emphasized manual communication skills. As an adult she was placed in a program for developing life skills without communication skills.

K. never achieved much in the way of communication skills. The methodologies of manual communication, fingerspelling, and combinations of those two systems were not productive for her. She did not learn to read meaningfully. However, her art talent continued to give her satisfaction and became a source of income as well. Her paintings seem to come from an innate talent, developed primarily through her own intuition and instincts. K. lived with her parents for several years. Ultimately, she married a man who had profound hearing loss and vision deficits in the range of legally blind and was employed until government programs were reduced. She continues to benefit from a semi-sheltered environment. A family member reported that she is happy and well-adjusted.

Children with Significant Behavioral Differences

We make no claim of being professionally prepared in dealing with children who have significant behavior disorders, previously referred to as having severe emotional disturbances. Nevertheless, we would be remiss if the available information about others' experiences with such children and use of the Association Method of instruction was not at least recorded.

The McGinnis Association Method was used at St. Paul's Special School, Dublin, Ireland, for a number of years in the 1970s. St. Paul's is a partially residential school for boys and girls between three and twelve years of age who have demonstrated limitations and behaviors which led to a diagnosis of emotional disturbance. Diagnoses were made through the team approach and placement of children in the school was based on the team's recommendations. Where children lived, the severity of their problems, along with home and family factors determined whether or not they would be residential or day pupils.

The staff of St. Paul's School consisted of a principal, six teachers, two part-time speech therapists, eleven nurses, an occupational therapist, a play therapist, a psychologist, and a psychiatrist. In addition, there was a staff that provided meals and related services. Additional medical services were available on the basis of need.

The children whose educational management

ultimately included instruction based on the principles of the Association Method had already experienced a two-year program of a wide variety of activities. A considerable amount of conditioning (using candies) was used to alter the children's behaviors.

At first, the children were described as being "very rejecting of people." Gradually, they became more affectionate. In the mornings, children did structured work. In the afternoons, they worked on crafts and other handiwork and participated in psychomotor activities.

One portion of the Association Method was used earlier and in a different manner from that suggested by McGinnis: present progressive concepts and language were used in a less structured manner in an effort to stimulate and motivate the children to relate to the teacher and to develop an imitative behavior. Teachers demonstrated and spoke—"I am jumping," "I am clapping," "I am hopping," and so on—as a part of the beginning work. The children were brought into the actions by gentle coercion. Such periods of instruction were lengthy enough to provide the desired stimulation and motivation but not so long as to allow fatigue to develop. The balance of the morning program consisted of straightforward Association Method procedures. Levels dealing with teaching phonemes, cross drills/syllable drills, words, sentences, questions, and stories followed in the sequential order designated by the procedures. Children advanced from one level to the next as they established the desired skills in oral and written language. Some of the children had major problems related to apraxia; others demonstrated problems in memory for sequencing. Most of the children demonstrated reduced comprehension of even nonverbal tasks. According to the principal of St. Paul's at that time, such problems gradually became less and less significant.

Certain modifications were made at one stage of teaching noun vocabulary through use of the cross drill/syllable drill. Rather than using the lengthy syllable drill devised by McGinnis, a shorter form was used at St. Paul's. After the children had mastered the desired skills with single phonemes and could apply their skills for code-breaking, the short form noun drill was used for teaching vocabulary, primarily nouns. Two colors were used in the short form of the drill. The short form is illustrated below:

    b

    b oa – written in two colors

    b oa t – alternating colors for sounds in the word

    b oa t – written in one color

The temporal rate was slower than normal and both broken and blended forms of speech were used.

The Association Method was chosen as an approach to teaching certain children at St. Paul's Special School because of several factors: (1) its structured format, (2) its gradual increase in incremental elements of language for increasing memory for sequences, and (3) its multisensory aspects for teaching and learning. In addition, some of the children were observed to be reading, that is, calling the words in the Lady Bird books (a series of readers used widely in England and Ireland at that time), but did not demonstrate comprehension of the words they were able to say. The language structure of the Association Method was used to teach comprehension of language concepts and later used again with the Lady Bird books.

Of the four children who had progressed through a major portion of the language units of the Association Method, the following prognoses were stated: (1) an eleven-year-old boy was to be placed in a class for boys who were hard-of-hearing and/or aphasic at a boys' school for the deaf, (2) a ten-year-old boy's autism was considered to be too great for him to be able to function well out of the type of environment St. Paul's provided; he was borderline psychotic, (3) one twelve-year-old boy "was a complete write-off," (4) the future of another eleven-year-old boy was a "big question mark." No current information is available on the program at St. Paul's.

The recommendations of St. Paul's teaching staff regarding the use of the Association Method included several items: (1) that three years of conditioning activities be used before implementing the procedures, (2) that written work be deleted with the very young children with emotional disturbances because of their poor fine motor coordination and the probability of more frustration developing because of their poor achievement in writing skills, and (3) that one criterion for selecting children with whom to use the Association Method be that the child not exhibit obsessional behaviors.

Although limited, the effectiveness of the Association Method with the children at St. Paul's Special School can be attributed to several factors: (1) a compassionate staff committed to doing the most they could for the children in their care, (2) a stable staff with a minimum of teacher changes year to year, and (3) the staff's commitment to implementing a program and continuing its use over a long enough period of time to determine its usefulness and effectiveness.

With Developmental Disabilities

In the case of H., described earlier, mental retardation, currently referred to as developmental disability, was not the primary factor which hampered his acquisition of language and speech despite the diagnoses early evaluators gave. His performance on certain standardized tests simulated that of a child with mental retardation because of the unintelligible speech and the limitations of tests of that era. In this era, his diagnosis probably would be that of severe oral apraxia/childhood apraxia of speech. At the same time, there are no doubt other children whose performances have simulated the characteristics of aphasia/language disorders when in time, the primary factor related to delayed language and speech development was more appropriately identified as generalized mental retardation or developmental disability.

One boy, age four, presented a mixture of syndromes—aphasia/language disorder, moderate hearing loss, mental retardation/developmental disability, and major visual impairment. Over a two-year period of time, his language and speech developed slowly but steadily. Individualized professional help emphasized whole word, sentence, and question language appropriate for the typical child and for a child with measures of developmental disability. Some time later, the boy was enrolled in a day program where he was taught through the Association Method, supplemented to some extent with a variety of educational activities and instruction. When last heard from at age ten, the boy was "making progress slowly." His speech was intelligible and he had command of language adequate to daily needs. His written skills for the language he was taught were satisfactory.

L.'s story was somewhat different. A number of professionals were in agreement that, at two and three years of age, her major problem was that of receptive aphasia. Her hearing was measured in clinical audiological assessments available at the time and described as being within normal limits. She attended nursery and kindergarten settings during a two-year period of time.

At six years of age, L. was enrolled full-time in a private day program where she was taught through the Association Method procedures, supplemented by a minimum of two hours of work at home daily. The additional two hours of daily home program was a requirement of the school she attended. Upon leaving that setting because of a family move, L. demonstrated good use of the skills required in the Association Method program. She demonstrated comprehension and use of concepts of the second unit of the language and additional language related to description and time concepts. Her speech for the material she had been taught in the structured instructional program was good. Her speech in spontaneous conversation was less refined but intelligible. She was able to read and write sentences and questions related to her "learned material." The structure of her language in conversation reflected many of the characteristics associated with language of young children.

None of the above would seem so remarkable except for L.'s performance on the Hiskey-Nebraska Test of Learning Aptitude. She achieved the following age ratings on the test: Bead Patterns, 3–0; Memory for Color, 4–0; Picture Identification, 3–0, Picture Association, 3–0; Paper Folding, 3–6; Visual Attention Span, 4–0; Block Patterns, 3–0; Completion of Drawings, 3–0. Her CA was 7–7; her Hearing MA was 3–0.

The fact that L. achieved the academic skills as indicated, while at the same time demonstrating functioning almost four years below her chronological age on tasks of the Hiskey-Nebraska Test, is in itself remarkable. The concentrated efforts, the structured management of behavior, the unrelenting work of her parents and teachers suggest the measures of the accomplishments that can be attained under designated circumstances.

To our knowledge, no systematic attempt to use the Association Method with children whose sole disability is developmental has been undertaken. However, there are reasons to believe that such efforts could be productive and useful for such children. We base this belief on our knowledge of its effectiveness with some children with Down's Syndrome.

Implications for Academic Performance

While a major focus here is on achieving adequate oral skills for communication purposes, the influence of severe articulation disorders on later reading and academic skills cannot be ignored. Reading is viewed as transferring oral language into another symbol system which is written. Success in reading is highly correlated to competence in oral communication. Thus, an inadequate oral communication system is seen as an obstacle to the development of reading and other academic skills. In addition to the expected motor difficulties due to apraxia, poorer auditory perception and auditory sequencing abilities were noted by Yoss and Darley (1974). In light of the related deficits, it is important for speech-language pathologists who engage in therapy with those diagnosed with childhood apraxia of speech to provide the most efficacious methods of remediation available. In any case, perhaps J.S.'s progress and achievements can serve as encouragement for others to try these methods.

Additional Follow-Up Information

By sending a questionnaire to individuals (and/or their parents) who had been enrolled in the school between 1962 and 1981, follow-up information was collected. Ninety-seven questionnaires were sent. Six questionnaires were returned indicating the addressee had moved with no forwarding address. On seventeen others, who did not return the questionnaires, more current information was obtained through a variety of sources. Forty-three questionnaires were returned. A summary of some of the data from the questionnaire follows:

Graduated from college/university	2
Graduated from junior college	3
Graduated from high school and attending college/university	5
Graduated from high school only (1 on basis of social promotion)	18
Attending a junior college	1
Attending a state residential school for the deaf	4
Still in elementary school	9
Still in high school	4

Dropped out of:	Number	Reason for leaving:
College	3	Did not know what they wanted to do
10th grade	2	Subjects not interesting
8th grade	2	Subjects uninteresting; too difficult
7th grade	1	No reasons given
6th grade	1	Did not like learning sign language at school for deaf
3rd grade	1	Overage; content of program inadequate to needs

A variety of subjects were described as "difficult": math, history, science. Some reported helpful teachers; others reported teachers "not interested in helping." The volume of work, homework, and abstractness of the academic material reportedly influenced how well or poorly the children did in school.

Many of the children in the population surveyed were children who had difficulties as a result of rubella and/or Rh factor. Others were suspected of having had rubella but were products of seemingly normal pregnancies. Almost all of them had the behaviors Eisenson, Hardy, and McGinnis associated with "developmental aphasia"/language disorders. All got their start through the use of the Association Method.

Follow up research of children enrolled in the school in later years is underway and will be reported in subsequent editions.

Information provided in this chapter indicates that the McGinnis Association Method and the DuBard Association Method® are effective instructional procedures for children with a variety of disabilities. The earlier instruction begins, the shorter time period of multisensory instruction is required to help a child learn to learn. The more failure a child experiences before having some success, the more difficult it is to begin successful experiences. Adjustments to the program should be made cautiously and should be well documented. Documentation of results according to group research design (subjects and controls) is very difficult to obtain; however, there are many single subject research/clinical experiences that support the effectiveness of multisensory, structured instruction.

Epilogue

A great deal has been said about deficits for learning language and speech as observed in some children with presumed central nervous system dysfunction. Even more was said about specific techniques of the DuBard Association Method® which can be effective in reducing those deficits thus enabling children to make language and speech (and reading) useful in their environments. Other facets of development and efforts to improve weaknesses are vital as well. To be specific, the development of gross motor and fine motor skills should not be overlooked. Indeed, major efforts should be made to achieve that goal.

The preceding pages have dealt, also, with the theories, principles, techniques, and implementation of an instructional program designed to help the child with language-speech disorders and/or hearing loss develop functional communication abilities. One widespread criticism of these multisensory procedures has been that they result in the child's speech being stilted. This criticism is not justifiable, but stilted speech can occur if the teacher does not *devise ways for language to become a living tool for the child*, to become communication in its truest form. Unless the teacher and parents seize upon even minute episodes and events to make the child aware of the significance of the instructional program in relation to communication, a maximum level of functional communication might not be achieved. Unless children realize how they can use what they learn, one would indeed have to question the merit of the teaching technique. At the same time, some children with language disorders can have a volume of verbal output which belies their underlying language disorder. This seems to be particularly true in students diagnosed with dyslexia or reading disabilities and whose oral language skills have not been evaluated in depth. Speech-language pathologists, teachers, and parents should be aware that volume and quality of language should not be equated, and subtle pragmatic and semantic differences can be very significant.

Parental responsibilities involve reinforcement work (after the teacher has laid the foundation for oral and written communication) as well as appropriate behavioral and environmental management. Without this support and participation at home, progress will be less than desired. How the teacher creates personal interaction with the child and makes the language instruction come to life for the child may be two of the most important aspects of teaching children with language disorders. These factors are important in any educational program, but they are crucial in teaching the child with severe communication disorders and academic challenges.

Unless the teacher *seizes opportunities to make language instruction functional* for the child and devotes the necessary energy, effort, compassion, and love to make language a living experience in the child's life, no technique or method will be as effective as it could be. This kind of teaching is not easily accomplished. To give of oneself to such an extent can be very demanding, but if we do not try, why are we here?

APPENDIX

A

Phonetics and Northampton Symbols

GENERAL COMMENTS

Although one may be armed with a theoretical background and basic knowledge of phonetics, in order to be an effective teacher of speech and for the child to become an effective learner of speech, there are aspects of the teaching-learning process which go far beyond textbook knowledge and theoretical frames of reference. The child who learns to talk naturally, presumably, will have had good environmental models from which to learn. The acquisition of language and speech for such children is seemingly effortless. With other children, the tasks are not achieved so simply or so automatically.

There are volumes written on the topics of speaking, of speech delivery, and speech in relation to dramatics. The tasks in teaching children who are deaf or hard of hearing, language disordered, and some children with severe articulation disorders are quite another matter—both for the teacher and for the child. It is neither automatic nor effortless. On the basis of new information and analyses of speech disorders, some errors once considered as functional may very well be due to apraxia. Some of the professional literature suggests the possibility that childhood apraxia of speech (CAS) may be a more appropriate diagnosis for children whose speech is characterized by such multiplicity of articulation errors that their efforts are unintelligible.

The information which follows is based on class instructions from the late S. Richard Silverman in 1960, Central Institute for the Deaf, St. Louis, Missouri. These details appear also in Speech and Deafness (Calvert and Silverman 1975).

AVENUES OF LEARNING

Few of us are aware of how we learn whatever we learn. Although most of us take learning for granted, thought and analysis of the matter can help one determine which avenue of learning seems to be primary. The primary avenues for learning, as we are concerned with it here, include the auditory, visual, tactile, and motor-kinesthetic systems.

The child with typical hearing learns to speak by primarily using the auditory system. However, there can be little question but that other systems may well be vital supports for the process. The motor theory of speech perception is based on the role of the kinesthetic system in speech perception and ease of development (Lane 1965; Galantucci, Fowler and Turvey 2006). See chapter 5.

In teaching children with hearing impairments, auditory imperceptions, and severe articulation disorders, as well as those with specific learning disabilities/dyslexia, as many systems as possible should be utilized in order to provide the child with as much information about production as is possible. The speech disorders of children whose responses to auditory stimuli in environmental and clinical assessments demonstrate no weaknesses in auditory acuity indicate that even they need additional information related to learning speech and communication without depending on the auditory system as the primary avenue for learning. With such children, and those with peripheral hearing loss, the auditory system should be strengthened and used to maximum ability. However, other systems, that is, visual, tactile, and motor-kinesthetic, can add to the volume of information which can be useful for the child.

Some phonemes (speech sounds) have more information available through visual, tactile, and motor-kinesthetic systems than others. Most speech sounds can have such additional information available if the teacher is aware of which systems can be useful and if those avenues are used for teaching-learning to maximum advantage. However, it may be that little or no information about production of speech sounds and speech, in general, can be available to the child if the teacher (1) does not know which avenues can be helpful, (2) does not know how to use those avenues to best advantage without exaggerating to the point of distorting the information, (3) does not use articulators properly for high-quality enunciation and diction, (4) does not use jaw action properly, which sometimes includes using jaw action cautiously, (5) does not provide tactile cues which help most children regardless of whether or not we as teachers understand exactly how it helps, and (6) does not aid the child in transforming that information into a motor-kinesthetic aid, a self-internalizing of what has been heard, seen, and felt from the teacher's productions.

MULTISENSORY APPROACH

Multisensory experiences are plentiful in our learning of many activities. For the child with auditory imperceptions, a hearing loss, a language disorder, dyslexia, or one who has severely impaired articulation functioning stemming from any other source, use of as many channels, or sensory modalities, as is possible in teaching-learning can be beneficial.

Auditory Avenue

Regardless of the limitations of the child's auditory system, every effort should be made to utilize it. If the benefit of amplification can be established, it should be used, even though one should remember that merely hearing a sound or hearing speech is only a part of the process involved in understanding it. In addition, teachers need to remember that the auditory system cannot be considered the primary one for teaching-learning for the children being discussed herein.

Visual Avenue

Just as the auditory system may not be completely reliable as a primary avenue for teaching and learning, the visual system can have limitations as well. Nevertheless, allowing the child to become aware of the shape of the mouth, proper amounts of jaw action in some instances, and tongue placement can be beneficial in the teaching-learning process. The teacher-clinician's model stimulus should provide a maximum amount of information through the visual avenue by accentuating certain aspects of production without creating distortions through exaggeration.

Tactile Avenue

There are some professionals who are reluctant, even adamantly opposed, to utilizing tactile clues in teaching while others support the decision to regard the tactile sense as valuable in teaching and learning. Inability to explain why the tactile aspect is helpful or to understand its value should not be a factor which results in denying children some assistance in their learning tasks. Even if a child has hearing acuity within the normal limits, tactile clues can be helpful, and their proper use is recommended.

Motor-Kinesthetic Avenue (Kinesthetic: Calvert and Silverman 1975)

Often children are able to transfer information gained through the other avenues of learning into their own articulatory acts in order to gain good production. In essence, they internalize for their own use the information about the production of sounds which they are able to get from the teacher-clinician. What they have heard, seen, felt by touch, and felt through their own acts and movement of articulators is integrated while the teacher-clinician serves as the monitor for the acoustic properties of the productions. In addition, according to the motor theory of speech perception (Lane 1965), the motor act, the proprioceptive act, aids in recalling what is necessary to achieve a given production. Its potential role and beneficial aspects should not be ignored or neglected.

The following are additional suggestions which can prove to be helpful in teaching and helping the child develop the best quality of production of speech sounds.

   1. *Do not do anything that you do not want the child to imitate.* Children whose speech acquisition is achieved through such specialized instruction and whose instruction is based on the imitative process are inclined to imitate every move or motion the teacher-clinician makes during the instructional work. Being aware of the fact that the therapist seeks his/her imitative role but not being aware of which aspects of the therapist's actions are the most crucial, the child may imitate such movements as inadvertent head movement, hand gestures, or eye movements. If one is a careful observer, the child's unusual motions or acts during imitative production can be noted. The "extra" acts, those unrelated to speech, can usually be found to be based on some unneeded motions or mannerisms of the teacher-clinician.

2. "Get set, go." This command can help students who are inserting neutral vowel sounds before the target sound is reached. *By getting the mouth shaped and the articulators in place before phonating is begun,* the insertion of the neutral vowel can be reduced or avoided. This is especially important with production of single component vowels to avoid diphthongizing them. *It is equally important to stop phonating once its role is completed.* Careful placement of articulators and proper timing in phonation will help avoid such speech patterns as "caut" or "cuat" for cat.

3. Avoid excessive jaw action in producing such phonemes as /p/, /t/, /k/, /d/, /g/, and others. It is equally important to monitor carefully the amount of jaw widening used in the stimulus the child is to imitate. Otherwise, the child could imitate the jaw widening aspect more than is needed or desired for high-quality production.

4. A cardinal principle which can lead to better quality of production of vowel sounds is to try to convey to children the idea that with the tongue tip down at the base of the lower front teeth, the sound produced will be of the best quality. As speed in continuous speech is gained, the quality of their communication will be enhanced if they have learned proper production of isolated sounds and then combine them into syllables and words.

Avenues of teaching-learning are indicated in the charted information on the following pages.

NORTHAMPTON SYMBOLS
(Yale Chart Spellings)

Teaching-Learning Avenues		*Rating Codes*	
Key: A:	Auditory	+	= good
V:	Visual	-	= poor
T:	Tactile	±	= mixed value for teaching
M-K:	Motor-Kinesthetic		

Primary Spelling Symbols	*Key Words*	*Secondary Spelling Symbols*	*Exceptional Spellings*	*Teaching Learning Avenues*	*Production*
Consonants					
p	pie apple cup			A: - V: + T: + M-K: +	Lips closed; slight air pressure built up; a light puff of air is exploded by sudden parting of the lips.
b	boy about tub			A: ± V: + T: + M-K: +	Lips closed; slight air pressure built up; voice is added as a light puff of air is exploded by the sudden parting of the lips, a voiced/p/.
t	tie butter cut		bt (debt) th (Thomas)	A: - V: ± T: + M-K: +	Teeth are parted slightly; tongue tip is placed against the alveolar ridge; air pressure is built up; a light puff of air is exploded by suddenly dropping the tongue.
d	dog adore bird			A: ± V: ± T: + M-K: +	Teeth parted slightly; the tongue tip is placed against the alveolar ridge; air pressure is built up; voice is added as a light puff of air is exploded by suddenly dropping the tongue; a voiced /t/.
k	key basket book	c (can) ck (check)	ch (chorus) (Christmas)	A: - V: ± T: ± M-K: +	Tongue tip at the base of the lower teeth; the back of the tongue rises to contact the velum; air pressure is built up; the air pressure is released by the sudden dropping of the tongue. Exact point of contact between the tongue and velum is influenced by the vowel that follows the /k/ sound in a word.
g or g	go began bug			A: ± V: ± T: ± M-K: +	Tongue tip at base of lower teeth; the back of the tongue rises to contact the velum; air pressure is built up; voice is added as air pressure is released by suddenly dropping the tongue; a voiced /k/. Exact point of contact between tongue and velum is influenced by the vowel that follows /g/.

Primary Spelling Symbols	Key Words	Secondary Spelling Symbols	Exceptional Spellings	Teaching Learning Avenues	Production
f	foot coffee cuff	ph (phone) (elephant)	gh (laugh)	A: - V: + T: + M-K: +	Lower lip approximates the upper incisors; friction is created as air is emitted between the teeth and lip.
v	vine seven have			A: ± V: + T: + M-K: +	Lower lip approximates the upper incisors; voice is added. Friction is created as air stream is emitted between the teeth and lip. There is a greater amount of lip-teeth tension for /v/, a voiced /f/.
th	think anything bath			A: - V: + T: + M-K: +	Tongue blade in a broad, relaxed manner approximates the upper teeth; the tongue tip usually protrudes slightly between the teeth; the air stream passes between the tongue and teeth.
th	that leather bathe			A: ± V: + T: + M-K: +	Tongue position as for /th/; voice is added as air stream passes from the mouth.
s	son asked bus	ce (cent) ci (city) cy(cycle) or c(e) c(i) c(y)	sc (scent) ps (pseudo)	A: - V: ± T: ± M-K: -	1. Tongue tip at base of lower teeth; air flows through a small aperture and out of the oral cavity, producing the acoustic properties of /s/. 2. Tongue is against the alveolar ridge; air flows out producing the desired acoustic properties. Try to match the desired acoustic properties of /s/ without teaching placement. If teaching placement is necessary, teach tongue tip at base of teeth, as in No.1.
s	easy is	z (zebra)		A: ± V: ± T: ± M-K: -	Tongue in respective desired position as for /s/. With properties of a good /s/, add voice to get /z/.
sh	shoe ashen bush		ti (nation) ci (special) ce (ocean) ch (Chicago) su-(sugar)	A: - V: + T: + M-K: +	Lips slightly rounded-squared, and protruded; the tongue is broadened to touch the molars on each side; the tongue blade approximates sides of alveolar ridge; an aperture larger than for /s/ is formed down the middle of the tongue. Air is forced down the aperture; sound is produced as the air passes through the aperture.

Primary Spelling Symbols	Key Words	Secondary Spelling Symbols	Exceptional Spellings	Teaching Learning Avenues	Production
zh	measure beige		si (vision)	A: ± V: + T: + M-K: ±	Lip and tongue positions are the same as for /sh/. Voice is added as air passes through the aperture.

Note: zh is not an English spelling pattern but is used to indicate to the child that production is similar to sh with voicing added.

Primary Spelling Symbols	Key Words	Secondary Spelling Symbols	Exceptional Spellings	Teaching Learning Avenues	Production
ch	chair luncheon church	tch (watch)	tion (mention) c (cello) ture (furniture)	A: - V: + T: + M-K: +	Lips slightly rounded; the tongue is broadened along alveolar ridge touching molars on each side; air pressure is built up, and exploded by suddenly dropping the tongue and jaw; exploded /sh/.
j	jump enjoy	ge-(gem) -ge (rage) -dge (dodge) g-²	soldier gradual exaggerate	A: ± V: ± T: ± M-K: ±	Close jaw slightly; lips are slightly rounded; the tongue is broadened along alveolar ridge touching molars on each side; air pressure is built up, and voice is added as the air pressure is exploded by suddenly dropping the tongue and jaw; voiced /ch/.
h or h̶	hat doghouse		wh (who)	A: - V: ± T: ± M-K: ±	A light flow of air is emitted from the mouth. The position of the lips and tongue and degree of mouth opening will be influenced by the vowel that follows /h/. There is no single position of the articulators for the /h/.
wh	what anywhere			A: - V: + T: + M-K: +	Lips slightly rounded and protruded; tongue tip is down, or free floating; air flows over the contour of the tongue and out of mouth

Spelling Patterns

Note: *qu and x are not phonemes.* They are spelling patterns represented by the phonemes noted.

Primary Spelling Symbols	Key Words	Secondary Spelling Symbols	Exceptional Spellings	Teaching Learning Avenues	Production
kwh qu	quick			See /k/ /wh/	The qu has no sound of its own. It has a combination of /k/ and /wh/ sounds.
ks¹ x	box rocks			Same as for /k/ + /s/	The x has no sound of its own. It has a combination of the /k/ and /s/ sounds. Back of the tongue is humped up against the palate; sides of the tongue are in contact with the upper side teeth; suction occurs between the palate and tongue. Air explodes through a central aperture formed by the tip of the tongue in light contact with lower front teeth.

Primary Spelling Symbols	Key Words	Secondary Spelling Symbols	Exceptional Spellings	Teaching Learning Avenues	Production
Nasals					
m	man summer ham		mb (comb) mn (column)	A: ± V: + T: ± M-K: ±	Lips are closed lightly; teeth slightly parted; tongue in neutral position velopharyngeal port is open; voiced breath stream is emitted through the nasal cavity.
n	nose annoy can	kn (knee)	gn (sign) pn (pneu- monia)	A: + V: ± T: ± M-K: ±	Tongue is in the position as for /t/ and/or /n/ with the tip against the alveolar ridge; the velopharyngeal port is open; voiced air stream is emitted through the nasal cavity.
ng	song		n = ng in thank, bank, etc.	A: ± V: - T: ± M-K: ±	Tongue tip is down at back of lower teeth; the back of the tongue rises to contact the velum; the velopharyngeal port is open and voice is emitted through the nasal cavity.
Semi-vowels					
l	look follow ball battle			A: ± V: + T: ± M-K: +	Tongue blade is broad, fitted lightly against the alveolar ridge; voice flows around the tongue and out.
r (fricative) *or* r-	ran arise	wr (wrong)		A: ± V: - T: ± M-K: ±	Mouth is in a neutral position; the corners of the lips may be slightly tense; sides of the tongue blade contact the molars on each side; tongue tip is rolled up and back toward the hard palate; voice flows over the tongue.
y *or* y-	yet vineyard			A: ± V: ± T: ± M-K: ±	Tongue tip is down; the sides of the tongue blade touch the molars on each side; a small aperture is formed down the middle of the tongue; voice passes through this aperture and friction is produced; the sound is essentially the same as the vowel sound in feet.
w	was away			A: ± V: + T: + M-K: +	Lips rounded and slightly protruded; the lip position is held only momentarily and voice is emitted just before the lips move to the position for the next sound.

Primary Spelling Symbols	Key Words	Secondary Spelling Symbols	Exceptional Spellings	Teaching Learning Avenues	Production
Vowels					
oō	tōo boōt		ou (soup) ue (blue) oe (shoe) ew (flew) o (do) wo (two) ough (through) ui (fruit)	A: + V: + T: ± M-K: +	Lips are slightly rounded; tongue tip is at the base of the lower teeth; the back of the tongue is high; a very small aperture is formed down the middle of the tongue; voice is emitted through this aperture.
oŏ	boŏk	-ŭ- (put)	ou (could, would, should)	A: + V: + T: ± M-K: +	The lips should be slightly, but less rounded than for /oō/. Jaw begins to open, creating a widening on the vertical axis. The back of the tongue is relatively high, low in front; tongue tip is at the base of the lower teeth.
aw	awful saw	au (caught)	ough (bought) ar (quart) al (ball)	A: + V: + T: + M-K: +	Tongue elevation is low, nearing the floor of the mouth; lips are rounded; mouth is slightly more open than for /oō/. The tongue is relaxed.
-o-	hot			A: + V: + T: + M-K: +	Almost no elevation of the tongue; the mouth is open slightly; lips are not as rounded as for /aw/; phonation may be of shorter duration than for /aw/.
ee	feet see	ēa (meat) -e (me)	i-e (police) ei (receive) ey (key) ie (piece)	A: + V: ± T: ± M-K: ±	Most forward and highest point for the tongue that is possible; a difficult sound to get; tongue tip is at the base of lower front teeth; front part of the tongue blade is high; sides of tongue are against the molars; corners of the mouth are drawn back, as if in a smile. Slight space between the upper and lower teeth.
-i-	it hit	-ȳ (bicȳcle)		A: + V: ± T: ± M-K: ±	Front of the tongue blade is high. Jaw begins to open slightly. Tongue forms an aperture slightly larger than for /ee/ because it is lowered and the jaw is opened slightly; tongue tip is at or near the base of the lower front teeth.

Primary Spelling Symbols	Key Words	Secondary Spelling Symbols	Exceptional Spellings	Teaching Learning Avenues	Production
-e-	egg leg	ea (bread)	ai (said)	A: + V: ± T: ± M-K: ±	Tongue contour is slightly lower than for /-i-/; lips are more relaxed than for /-i-/. The jaw opening is slightly more than for /-i-/.
-a-	cat		ai (plaid)	A: + V: + T: ± M-K: +	Slight arching of the tongue blade in the middle; edges of tongue blade may come in contact with the upper molars. The tip of the tongue is at the base of the lower front teeth. Jaw is lower; mouth is open more.
a(r); ar	car			A: + V: + T: + M-K: +	General American vowelized *r* component is deemphasized in initial teaching; tongue is low and there is very little arching or curvature. The mouth is as open as it gets to be in speech. Easy relaxed phonation deemphasizing vowelized *r* common in some regions; for ease of teaching /-o-/ can be helpful until child is able to add the /r/ component.
ur	urn turn fur	er (her) ir (bird) or (word) ar (bear) *or* -er (her) -ir (bird) -or (word) -ar (bear)	ol (colonel)	A: + V: + T: ± M-K: ±	Reasonable amount of tension in lips and tongue must be present. If not, production will be *uh* instead of *ur*. The sides of the tongue touch the molars. The tongue contour influences acoustic properties. There is a slight rounding and protrusion of the lips. Voice is added; not the same sound as the consonant, fricative /r/ as in red.
-u-	under gum cut		o (mother) o-e (come, love) ou (tough) -a (soda)	A: + V: + T: + M-K: +	Sensation of production is in the middle of mouth; neutral sound, in that it is in the middle; is often an unstressed sound. Tongue is as flat as it will ever be in speech production. Tongue is a straight line. Tongue tip is at the base of the lower front teeth.
a-e	cake game	ai (paid) ay (pay)	ey (they) eigh (eight) ei (rein) et (ballet)	A: ± V: + T: + M-K: +	All diphthongs have a radical and a glide, two distinct components. Low front radical plus *y* glide; *y* glide is approximately /ee/ as in *feet*.

Primary Spelling Symbols	Key Words	Secondary Spelling Symbols	Exceptional Spellings	Teaching Learning Avenues	Production
ou	mouth	ow (cow)	ough (bough)	A: ± V: + T: + M-K: +	Diphthong: mid-back radical plus rounded *w* glide. *W* glide is an approximate /o͞o/ or /w/ sound.
i-e	like tie	igh (light) ý (sky)	i (mind, child)	A: ± V: + T: + M-K: +	Mid-back, wide radical close to *ah* sound plus high front *y* glide.
oi	oil boil	oy (boy)		A: ± V: + T: + M-K: +	Low, back, round radical plus high front round *y* glide.
o-e	home hope	oa (boat) ow (bow) -o (so)	ew (sew) ough (though) o (comb)	A: ± V: + T: + M-K: +	Mid-back round radical plus high back round *w* glide.
u-e	use perfume	ew (few)	eau (beautiful)	A: ± V: + T: + M-K: +	High, front, round radical plus high back round *w* glide.

APPENDIX

B

Sample Content of a Child's Book

In the pure form of the method, once cross drills have been introduced, drop drills are usually discontinued. However, research in the area of dyslexia indicates a benefit in continued practice in decoding nonsense syllables. Therefore, for that population, decoding drop drills should be continued. No phoneme should be used in a cross drill until after it has been taught in isolation first.

Multiple colors are used in the child's book at the phoneme level when it is being developed. Two colors only are used in this sample. Color differentiation in the child's book is discontinued when the child is capable of writing the stories and questions in the book independently.

In developing a book with a child, one should write on the front side of the pages only until instruction begins at the repetitive sentence level. Thus, at the drop-drill level, the child reads the drill, turns the page, and says it from the picture cue.

Additional sections for the correlative program may be designed according to the child's needs and the teacher's desires.

FIRST UNIT OF LANGUAGE

Phonemes
Drop Drills
Syllable Drills (Cross Drills)
Noun Vocabulary

david's book

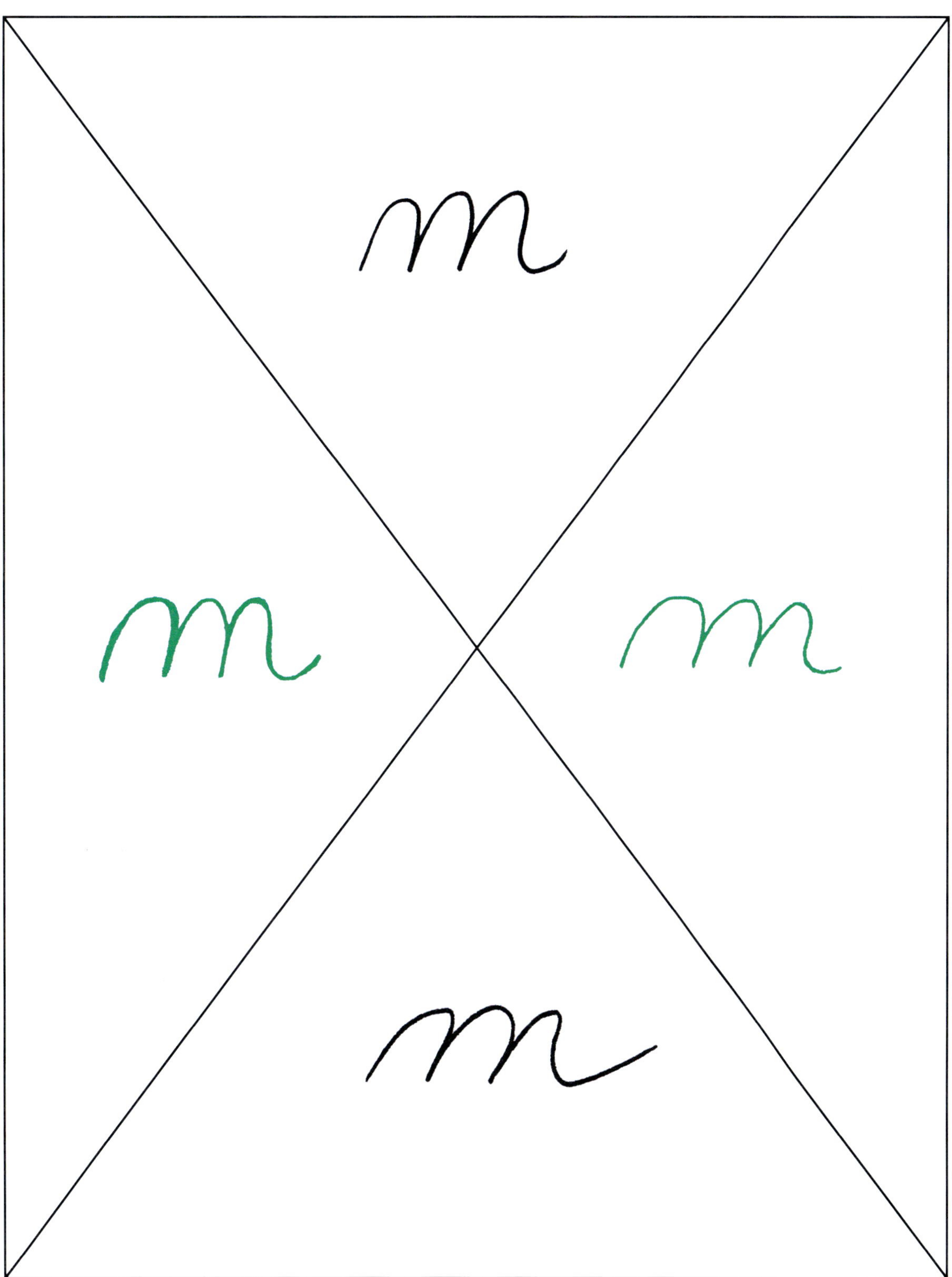

PLEASE NOTE:

Multiple colors are used in an actual child's book at the phoneme level.

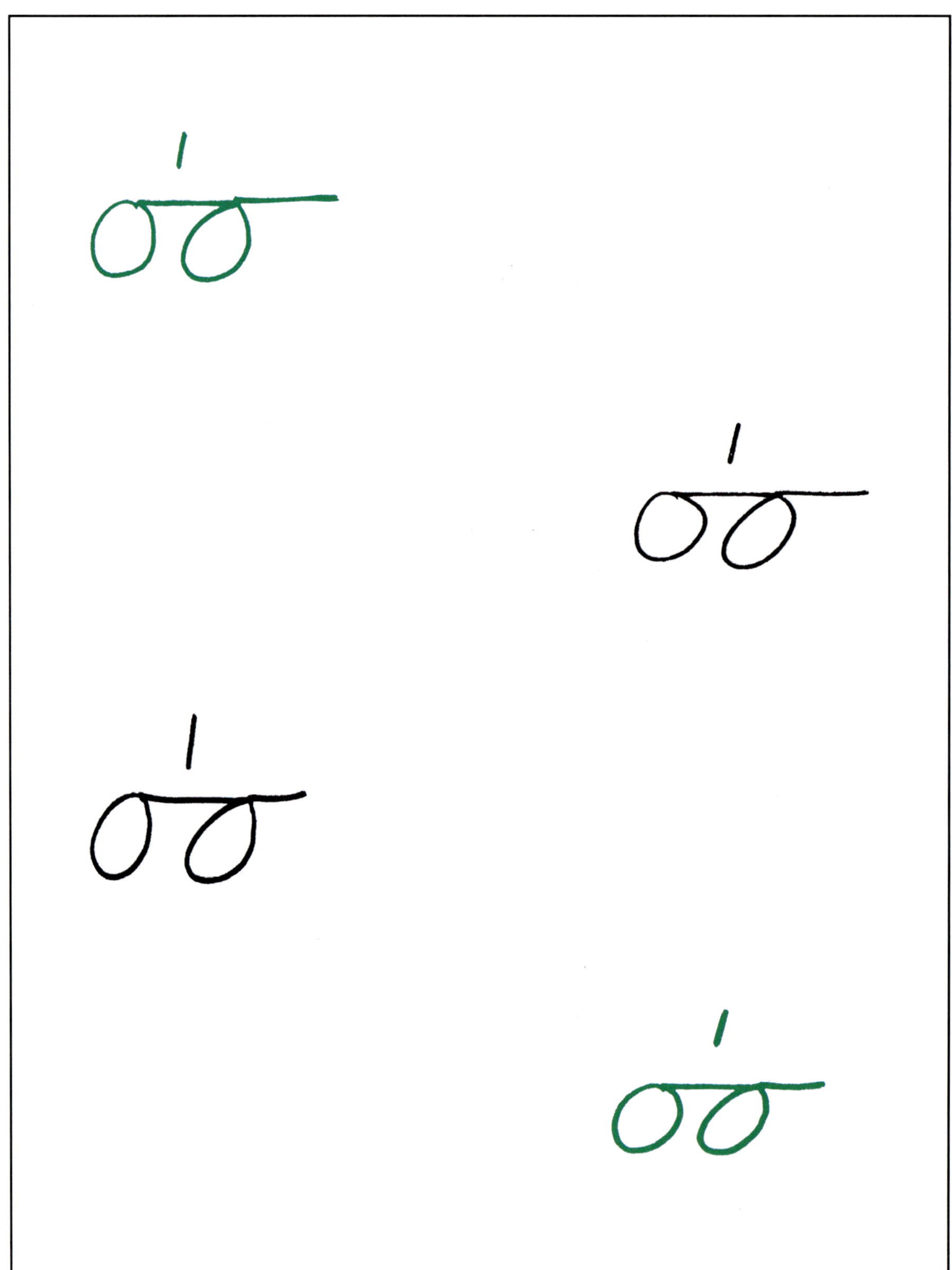

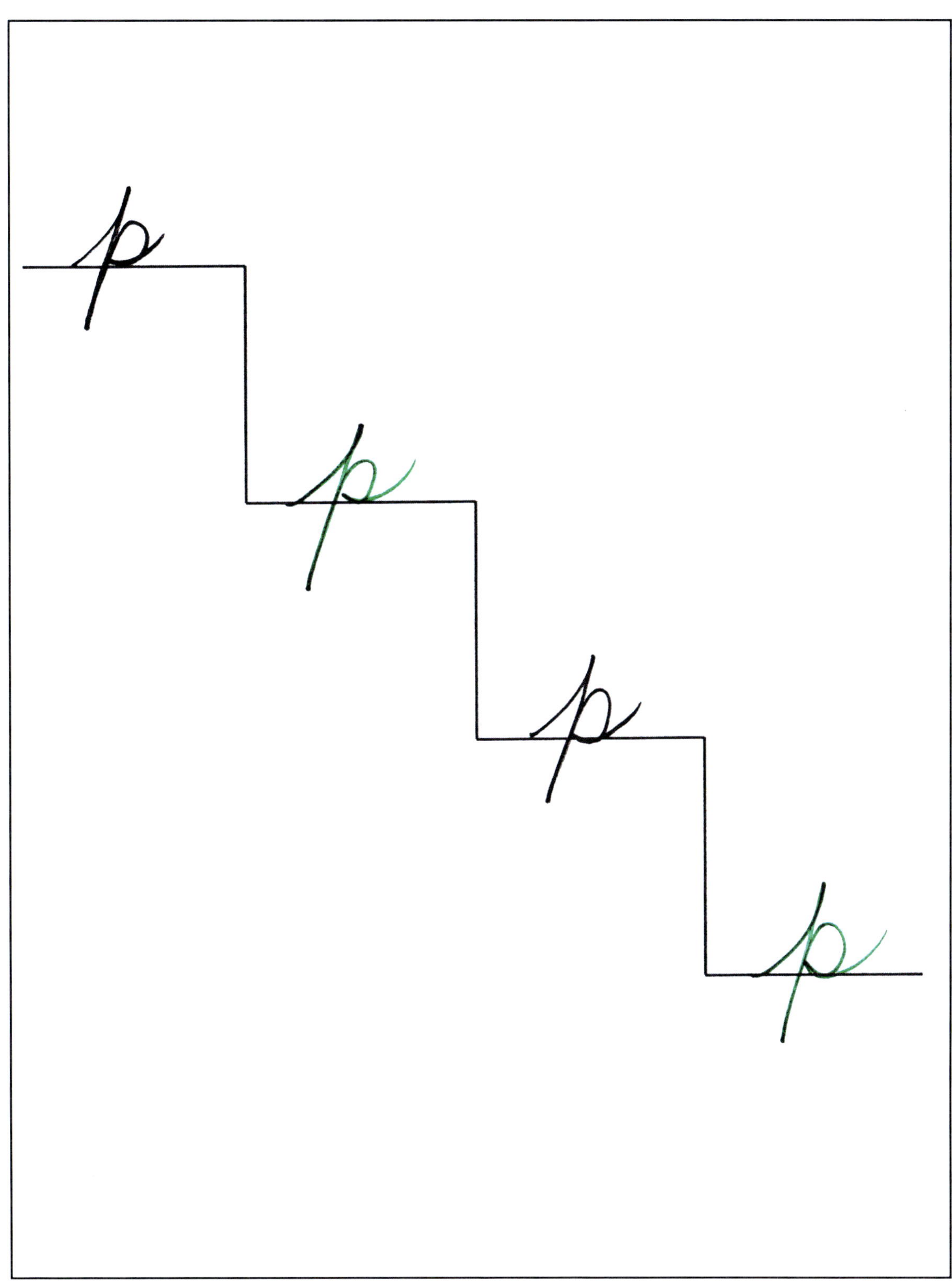

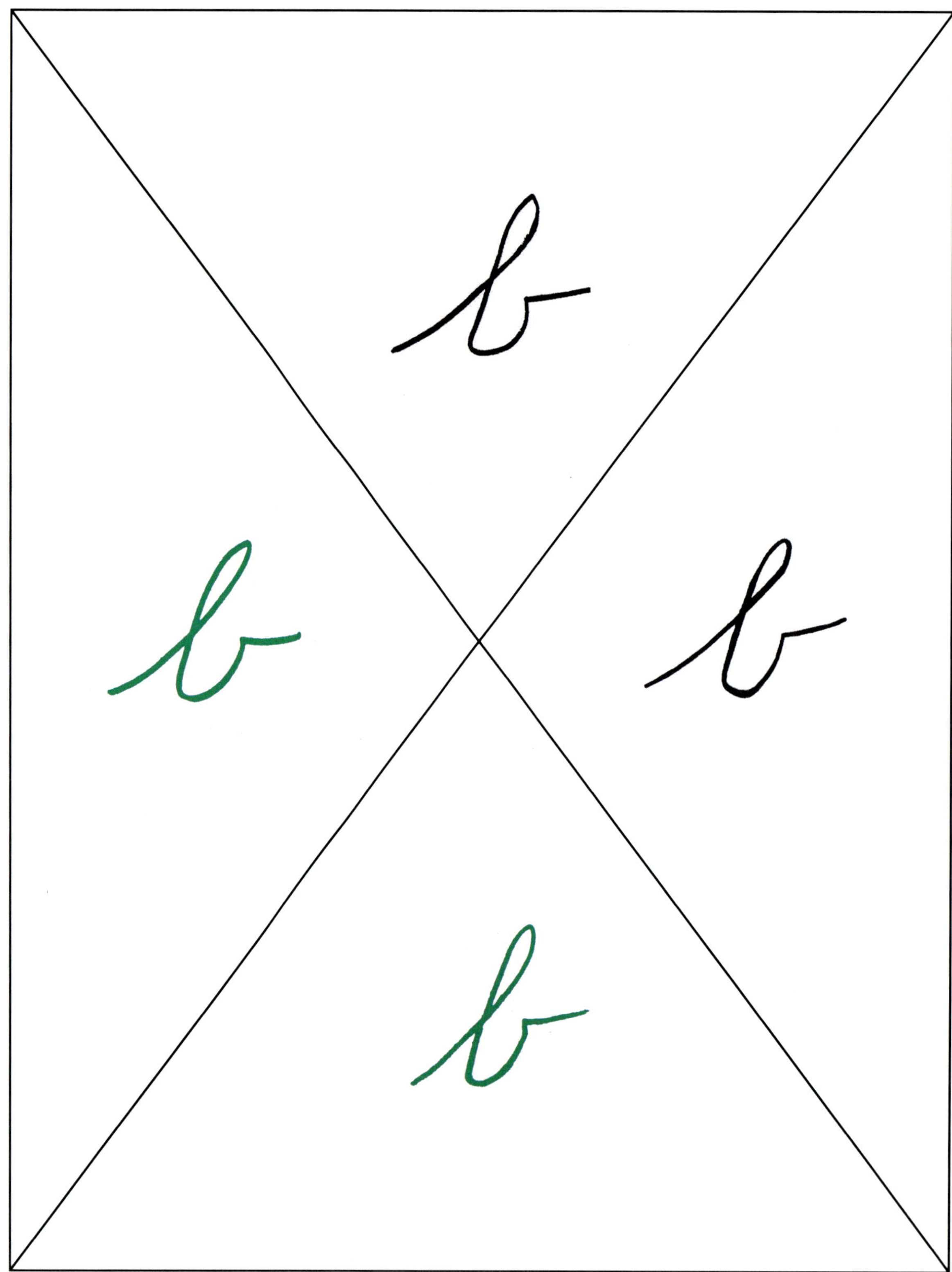

Pictures are not used for children who have dyslexia or for general education instruction.

mee

mee

mee

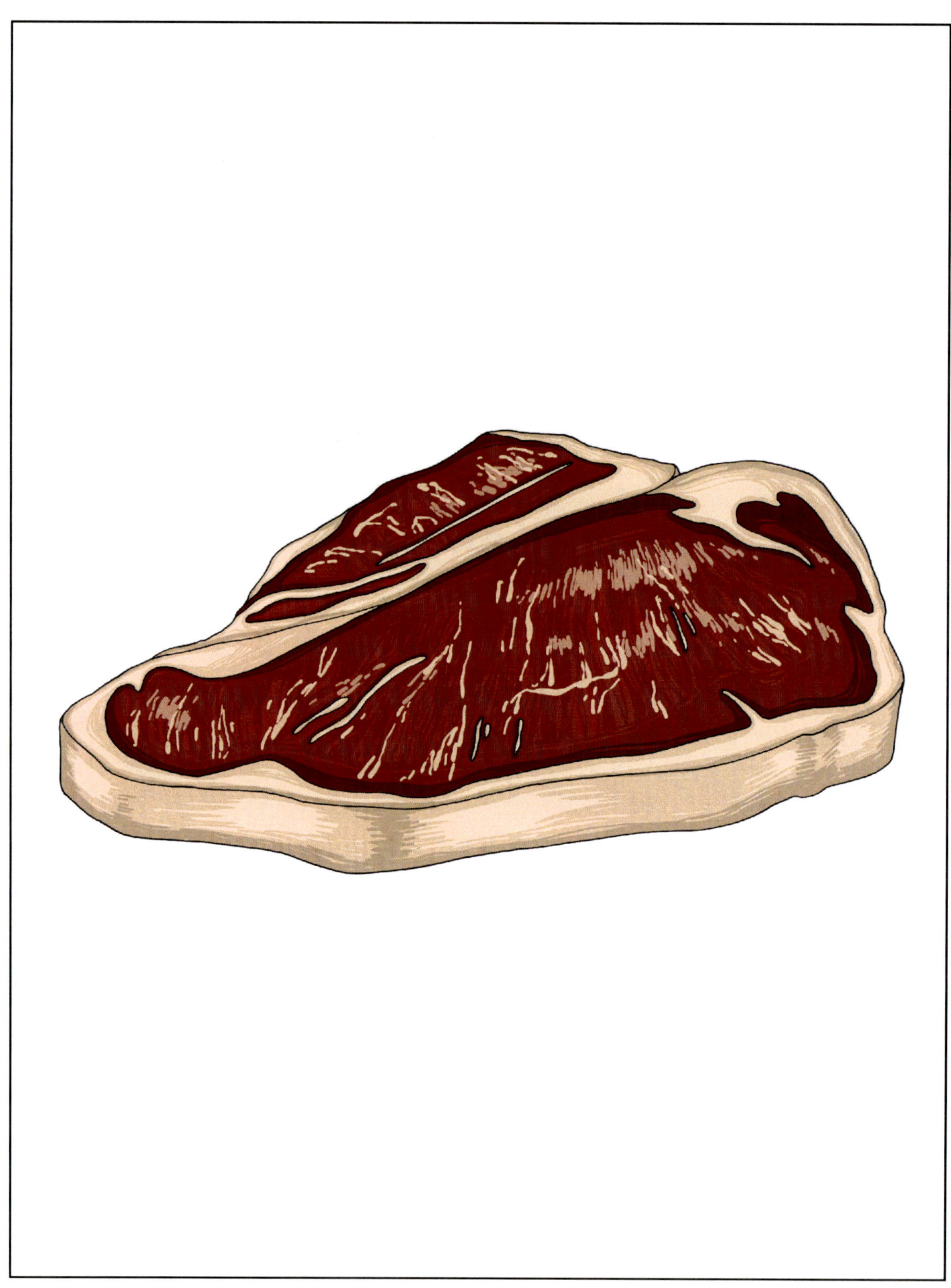

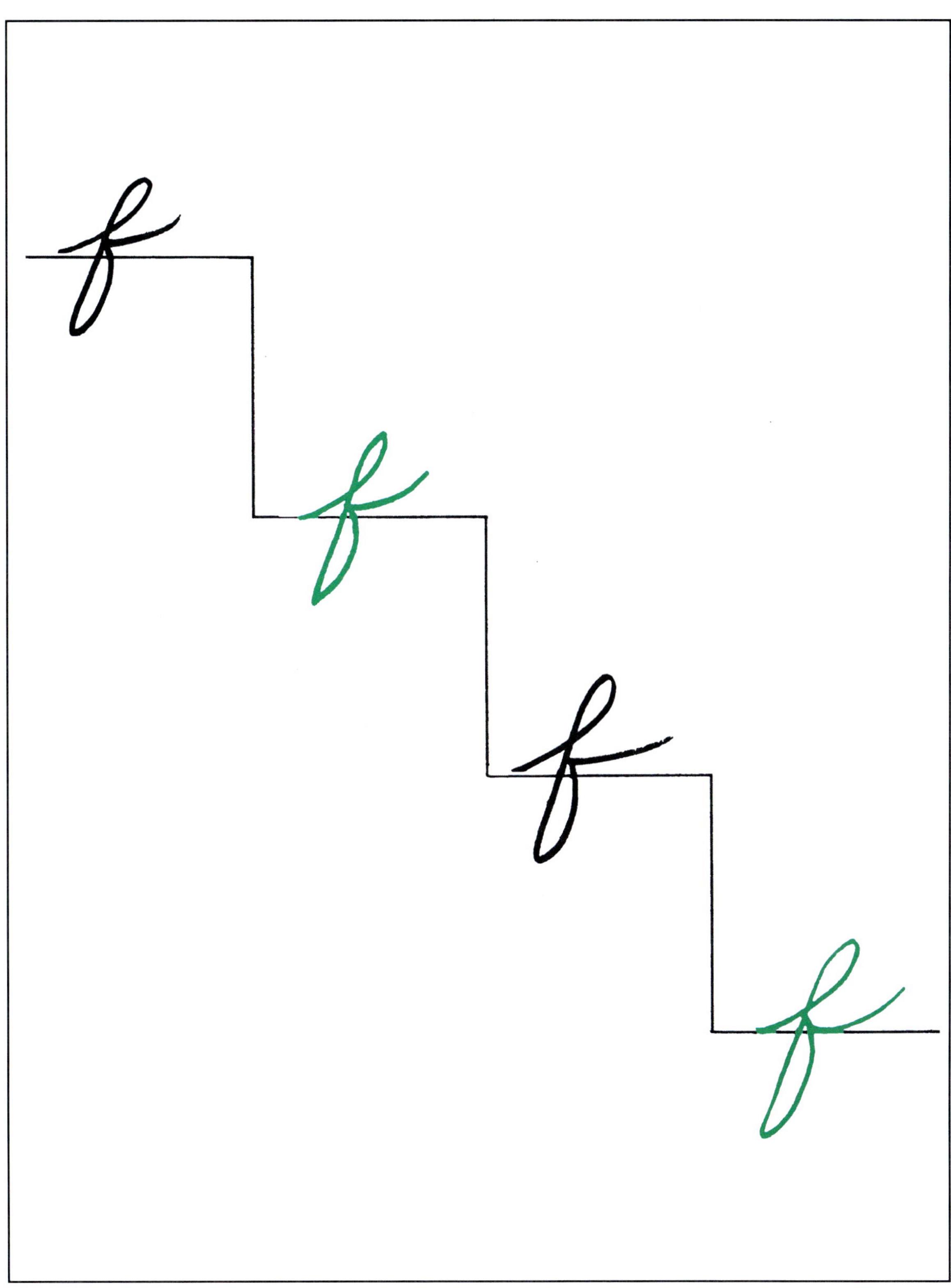

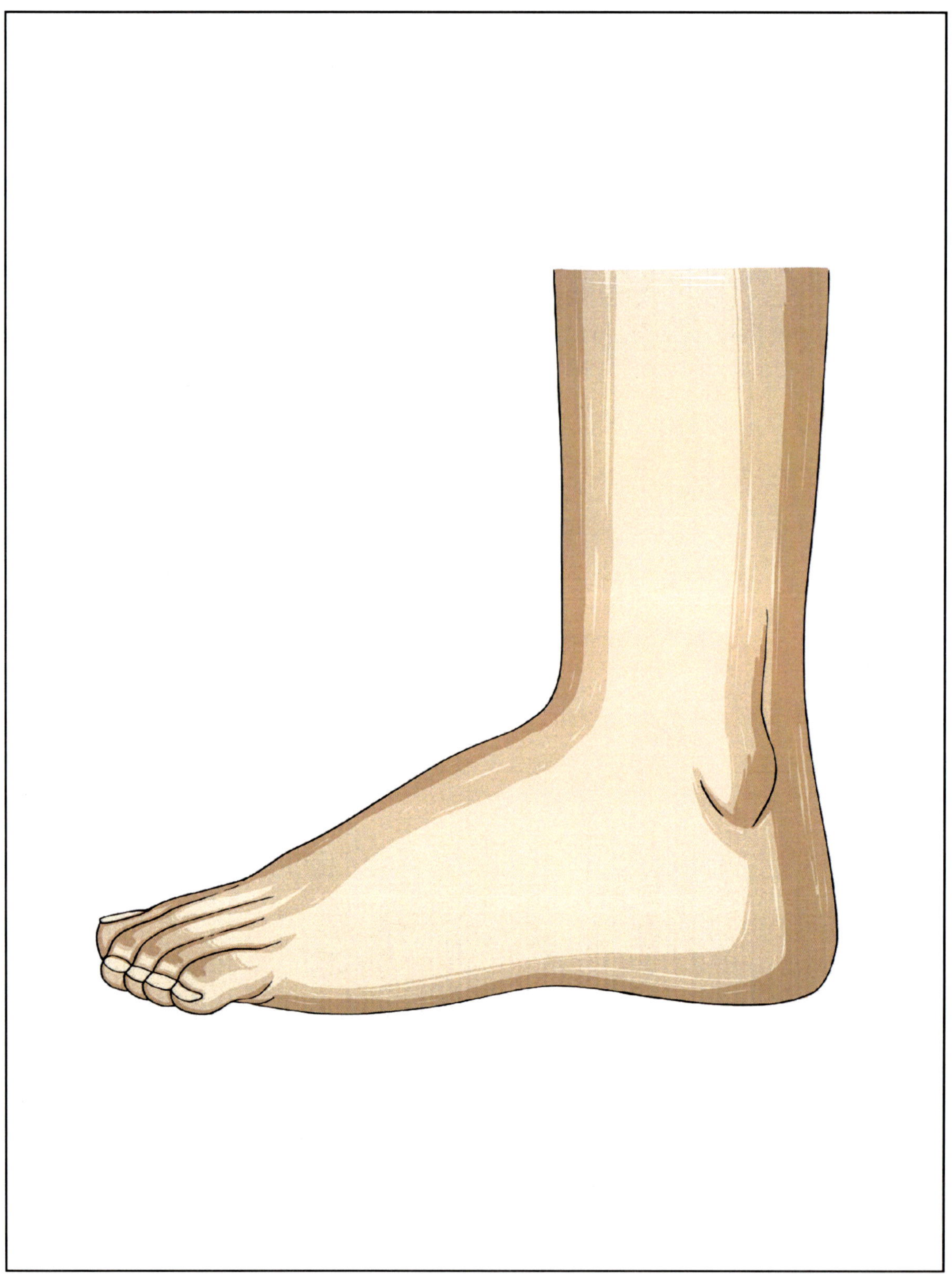

ti-e

ti-e

ti-e

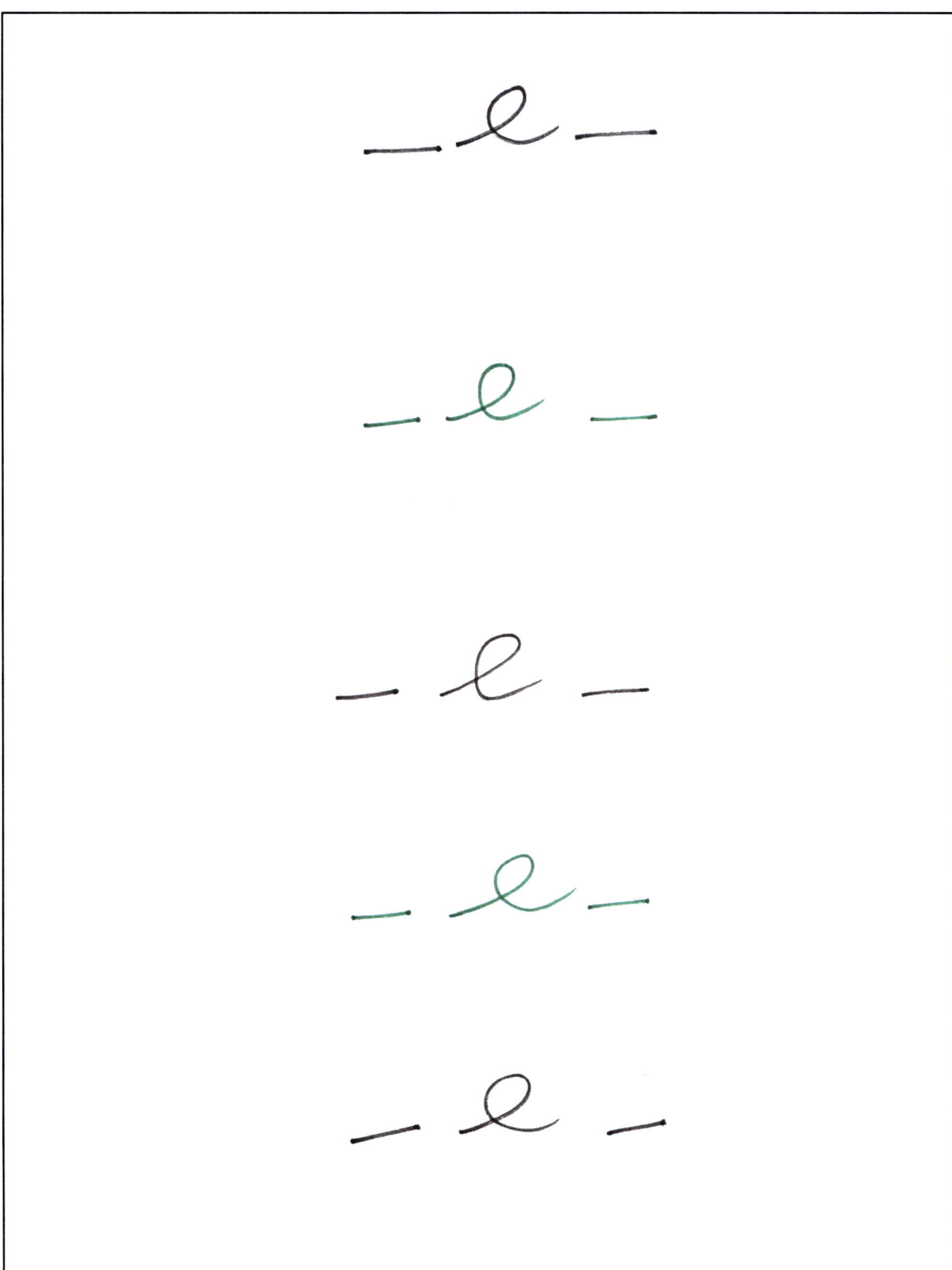

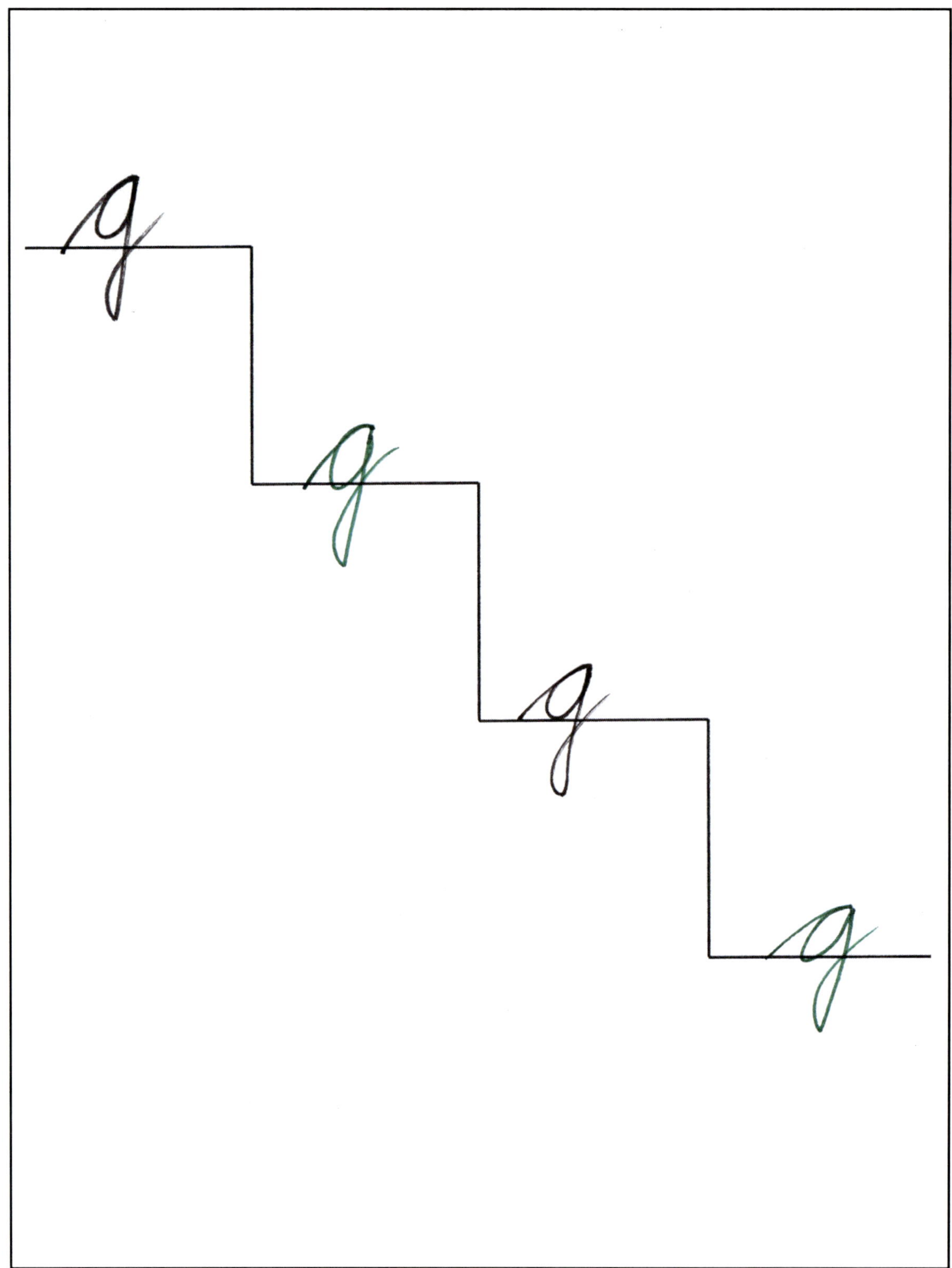

PLEASE NOTE:

Drop drills of the VC pattern, such as -eg (egg), oul (owl), should be utilized. Phonemes are always taught in isolation before they are applied in drop drills. Only the written symbols are used for students with learning disabilities/ dyslexia. Pictures are deleted.

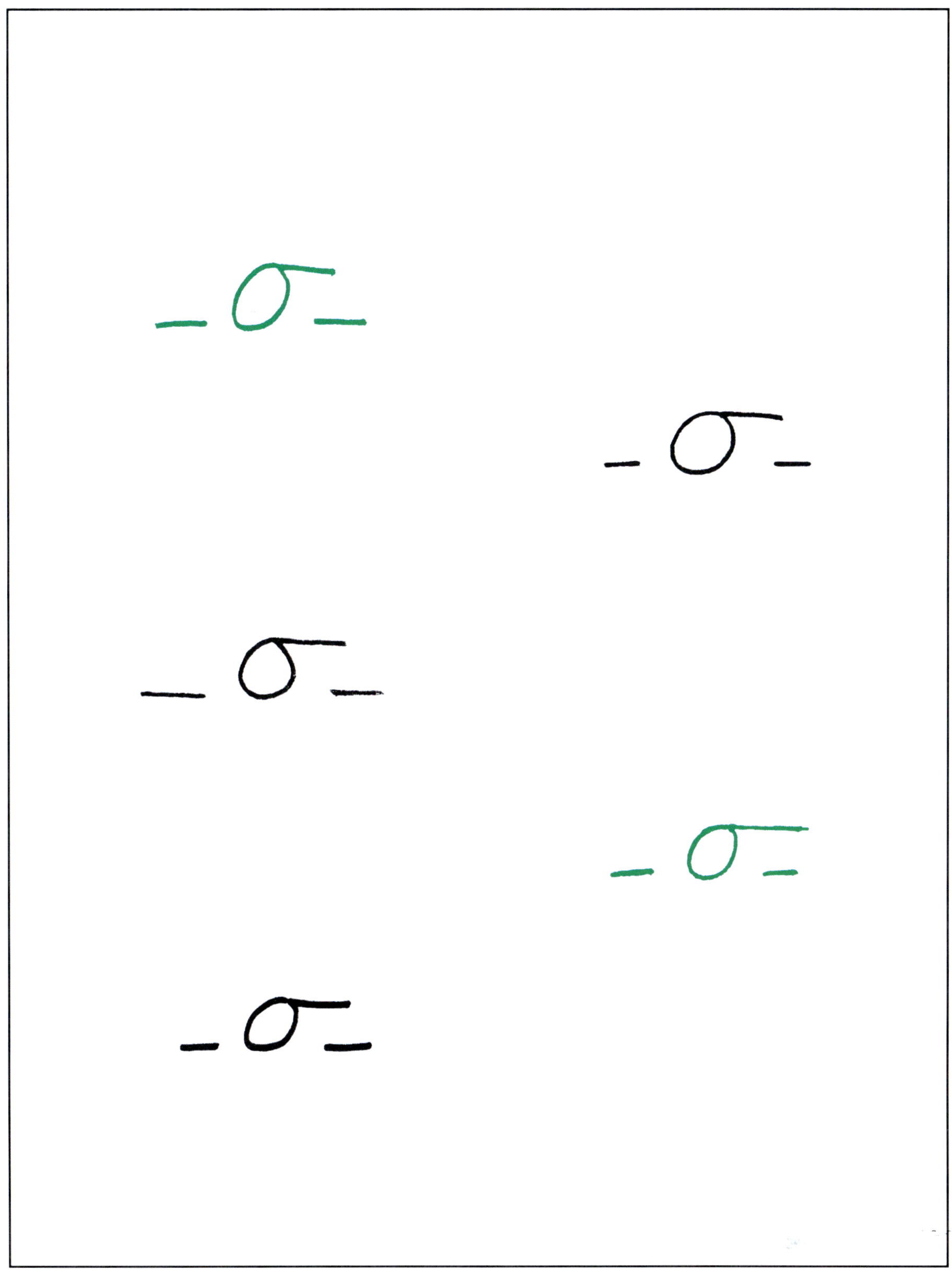

pie

arm

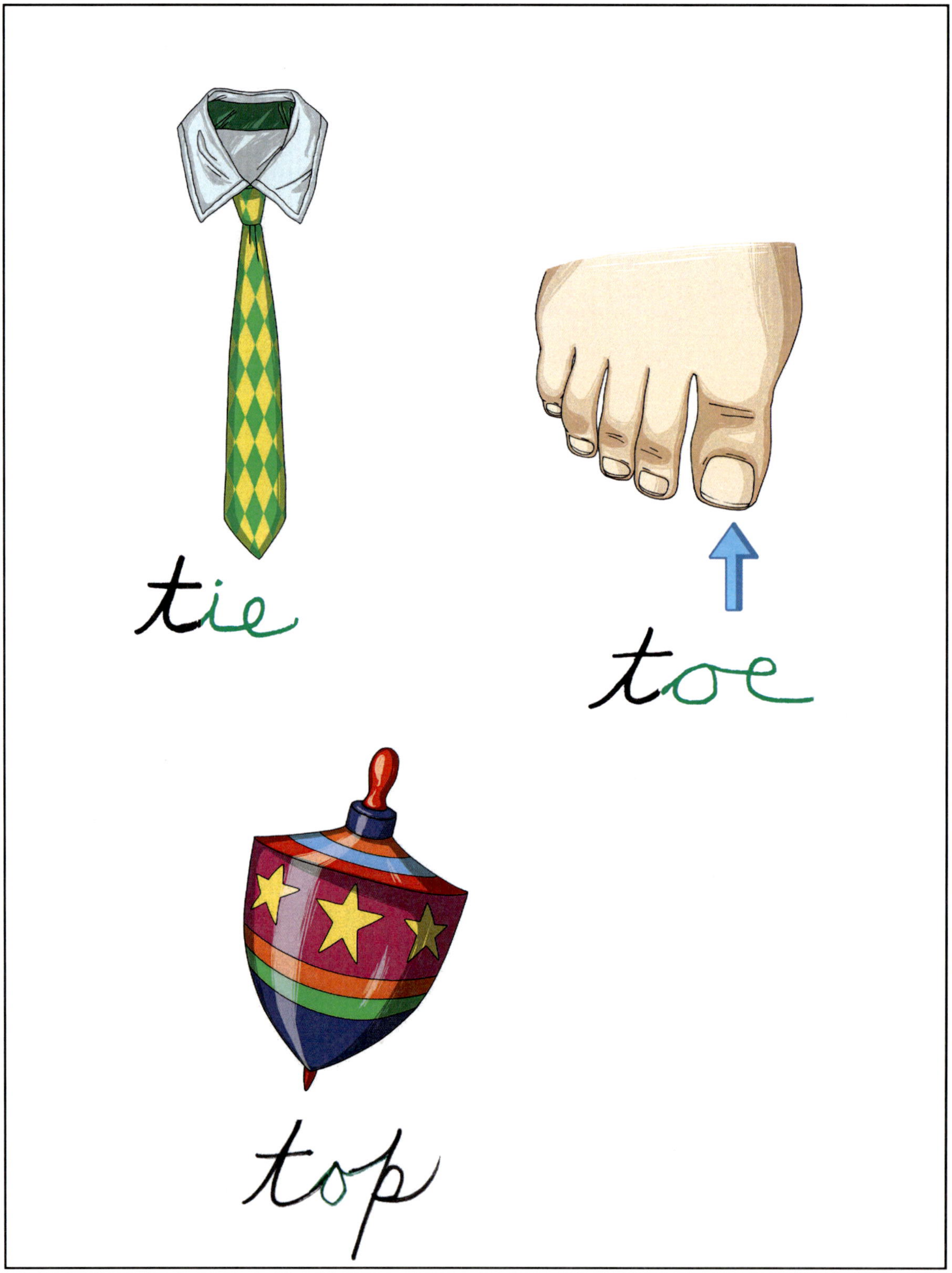

tie
toe
top

kee   céa   ckéa

kou   ców   cków

ka–   ca–   cka–

ko–   co–   co–

cow
key
cap

meat
moon
mop

SECOND UNIT OF LANGUAGE

Repetitive sentences; questions
Repetitive sentences with numbers; 'how many' questions
Animal stories; questions
Inanimate object stories; questions
Personal stories; questions
Preposition sentences; questions
Preposition round-up stories; questions
Descriptive stories; questions
Present progressive sentences; questions
Present progressive round-up stories; questions

what do you see?

I see a .

I see a .

I see a .

I see a .

I see a .

I see a .

I see a .

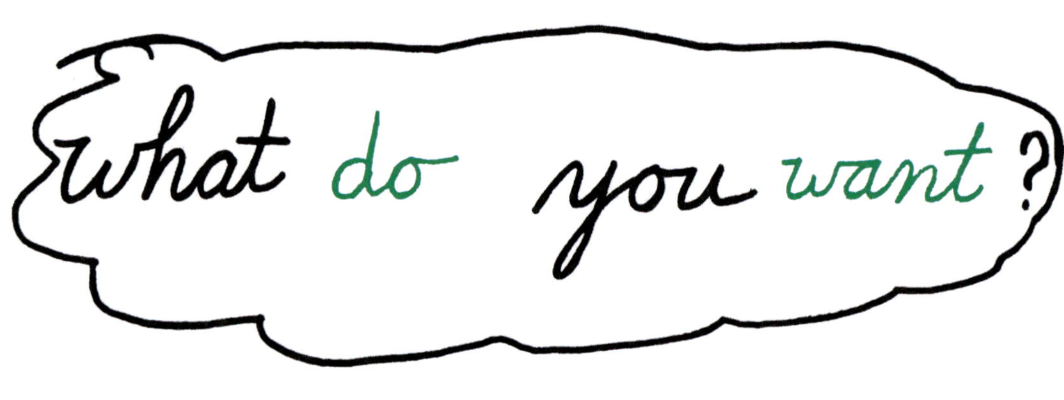
what do you want ?

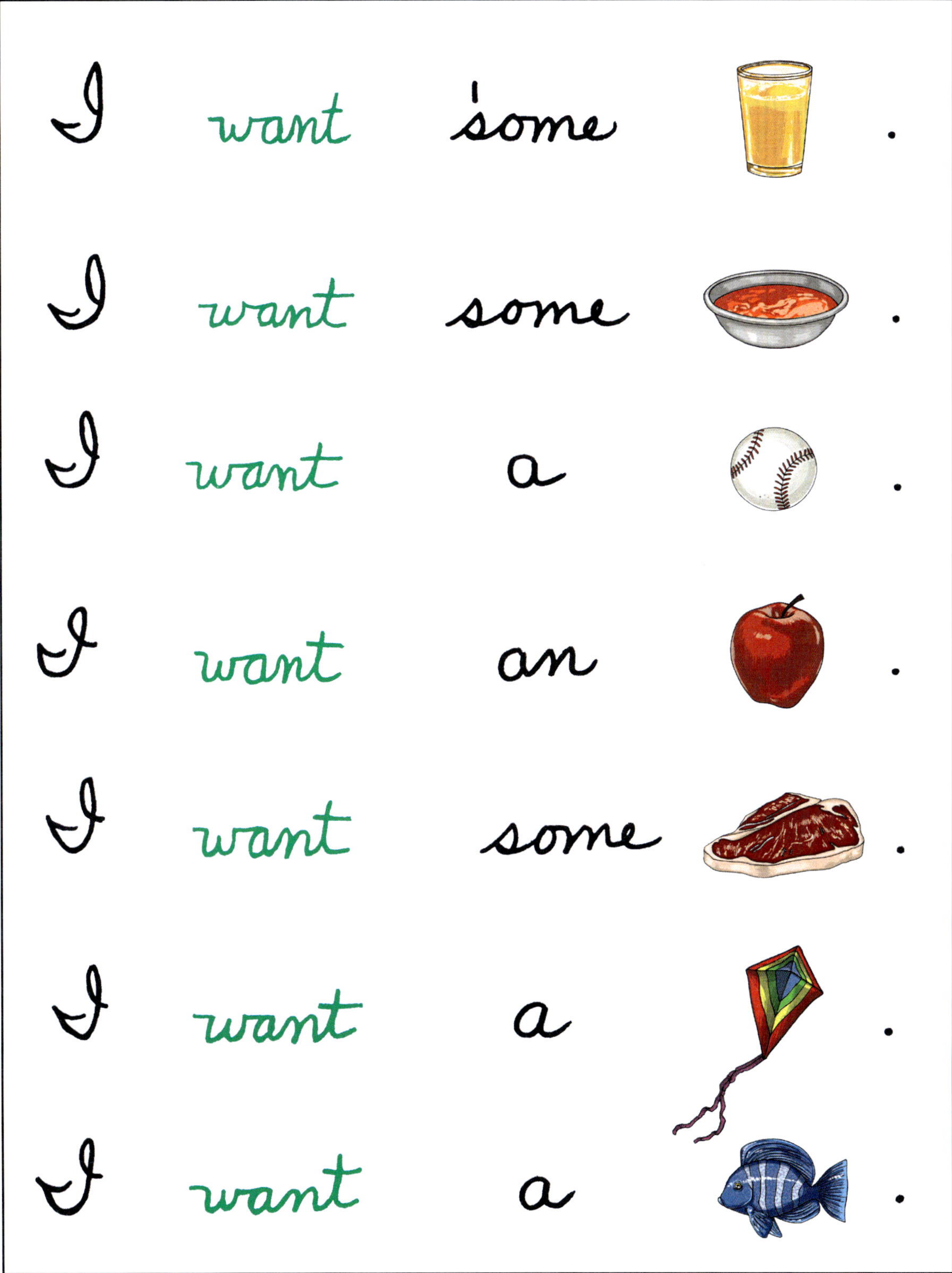

I want some .
I want some .
I want a .
I want an .
I want some .
I want a .
I want a .

what is this?

this is a .

this is a .

this is some .

this is an .

this is a .

this is some .

this is an .

how many boats is this?

how many cars did you see?

how many dogs does john have?

how many apples do you see?

how many shirts do you have?

how many bells do you want?

this is one boat.
I saw two cars.
john has five dogs.
I see one apple.
I have three shirts.
I want four bells.

what is this²¹ ?

how many caps do
you want?

how many boys² did
you see?

what do you have?

what do you see?

how many cups¹

does² mama have?

this is an egg.
I want eight caps.
I saw six boys.
I have some teeth.
I see a coat.
mama has one cup.

The *noun page format,* as illustrated on the following pages, is *used when all phonemes are represented in the child's book in cross drills.* As appropriate for 3- and 4-phoneme monosyllabic words, cross drills continue to be used for *board instruction.* The picture and the word *only* are placed in the *child's book.* Words with different beginning phonemes may be placed on the same page.

Whole-word vocabulary instruction of multisyllabic words (banana) also takes place at the board. The picture and the word are placed in the book in the next available space.

Only the word, without a picture, is placed in the book for the child with dyslexia/specific learning disabilities.

thumb
hose
house
ant
deer

flag
fence
ruler
glasses
banana

NOTE:
Students typically learn 4-phoneme monosyllabic words and more advanced vocabulary while simultaneously learning animal stories.

what *is* this?

how many ears *does* a cat *have*?

how many eyes *does* a cat *have*?

does a cat *have* a mouth?

how many feet *does* a cat *have*?

(LEVEL 1 ANIMAL STORY)

PLEASE NOTE:

'Yes' and/or 'no' are added in the left margin as appropriate as questions are introduced.

what is this?
does a horse have a tail?
does a horse have a mane?
how many legs does a horse have?
how many ears does a horse have?

(LEVEL 1 ANIMAL STORY)

this *is* a horse.

a horse *has* a tail.

a horse *has* a mane.

a horse *has* four legs.

a horse *has* two ears.

what is this?
does a fish have a mouth?
does a fish have a tail?
does a fish have fins?
does a fish have feet?
can a fish swim?
can a fish walk?

(LEVEL 2 ANIMAL STORY)

this is a fish.

a fish has a mouth.

a fish has a tail .

a fish has fins .

a fish has no feet.

a fish can swim.

a fish cannot walk.

what is this?

does a deer have antlers?

how many hooves does a deer have?

what kind of tail does a deer have?

can a deer run?

can a deer fly?

(LEVEL 3 ANIMAL STORY)

PLEASE NOTE:

'Yes' and/or 'no' are added in the left margin as appropriate as questions are introduced. Numbers are used on new vocabulary. It is the teacher's choice to use/not use on familiar vocabulary.

what is this?
what kind of ears
does a rabbit have?
what kind of tail
does a rabbit have?
does a rabbit have
whiskers?
can a rabbit hop?
can a rabbit swim?
what is a rabbit
covered with?

(LEVEL 4 ANIMAL STORY)

this is a rabbit.

a rabbit has long ears.

a rabbit has a short tail.

a rabbit has whiskers.

a rabbit can hop.

a rabbit cannot swim.

a rabbit is covered with fur.

what is this?
what color is it?
does it have doors?
does it have windows?
does it have walls?
does it have rooms?
does it have a roof?

this is a house.
it is white.
it has doors.
it has windows.
it has walls.
it has rooms.
it has a roof.

what is this?
does it have doors?
does it have windows?
does it have lights?
does it have bumpers?
what color is it?

PLEASE NOTE:

1's and 2's continue to be applied to new vocabulary in stories.

who are you?
what are you?
what color hair do
    you have?
what color eyes do
    you have?

---

what is your name?
what are you?
what color is your hair?
what color are your eyes?

I am Ricky.
I am a boy.
I have black hair.
I have brown eyes.

---

my name is Ricky.
I am a boy.
my hair is black.
my eyes are brown.

who *is* this?
what *is* she?
what color eyes *does* she *have*?
what color hair *does* she *have*?

---

who *is* this?
what *is* she?
what color *are* her eyes?
what color *is* her hair?

this *is* Wendy.
she *is* a girl.
she *has* blue eyes.
she *has* blond hair.

---

this *is* Wendy.
she *is* a girl.
her eyes *are* blue.
her hair *is* blond.

who *is* this?
what *is* he?
what color eyes *does* he have?
what color hair *does* he have?

---

who *is* this?
what *is* he?
what color *are* his eyes?
what color *is* his hair?

this *is* Jeff.
he *is* a boy.
he *has* brown eyes.
he *has* brown hair.

---

this *is* Jeff.
he *is* a boy.
his eyes *are* brown.
his hair *is* brown.

where is the duck?

the duck *is on* the table.

where *is* the giraffe?

the giraffe *is in* the soup.

where is the cat?

the cat is under the
chair.

where is the paintbrush?

where is the jump rope?

where is the suitcase?

where are the seals?

where is the lawn
mower?

where is the mechanic?

the paintbrush is in the box.

the jump rope is on the sidewalk.

the suitcase is under the bed.

the seals are on the rocks.

the lawn mower is in the garage.

the mechanic is under the truck.

Where are Mother, Sue, and Amy?
  (Who is in the kitchen?)
Where is Sue?
  (Who is between Mother and Amy?)

Where are two cake pans?
(What is on the cabinet?)
(How many cake pans are on
      the cabinet?)
Where are two eggs?
  (What is by one pan?)
  (How many eggs are by one pan?)
Where is a cup?
  (What is in front of the box?)
Where is the box?
  (What is behind the cup?)
Where is some cake mix?
  (What is in the box?)

Mother, Sue, and Amy are in the kitchen.
Sue is between Mother and Amy.

Two cake pans are on the cabinet.
Two eggs are by one pan.
A cup is in front of the box.
The box is behind the cup.
Some cake mix is in the box.

What kind of room *is* this?

What color *is* the sofa?

Where *is* it?

What color *are* they?

Where *are* four pictures?
(What *is on* one wall?)

Where *is* a mirror?
(What *is on* the other wall?)

What color *is* the carpet?

This is a living room.
The sofa is white.
It is between two chairs.
They are blue.
Four pictures are on one wall.
A mirror is on the other wall.
The carpet is beige.

what *is* this?
what color *are* the walls?
what else *is* green?
where *are* three towels?
(How many towels *are on* the towel bar?)
what color *is* one towel?
what color *is* another towel?
what color *is* the other towel?
where *are* some yellow flowers?

This *is* a bathroom.
The walls *are* light green.
The carpet *is* light green, too.
Three towels *are on* the towel bar.
One towel *is* light green.
Another towel *is* dark green.
The other towel *is* yellow.
Some yellow flowers *are on* the cabinet.

What is the boy doing?

The boy *is* running.

What are Andrew and Lisa doing ?

Andrew and Lisa are jumping.

What are the dog and cat doing?

The dog and cat *are* sleep*ing*.

what *is* the girl doing?

The girl *is blowing* the horn.

What is the boy doing?

The boy is jumping over the fence.

Where *is* the family?
(Who *is* in the den?)
What *is* Mother doing?
(Who *is* knitt*ing* [a sweater]?)
(What *is* Mother knitt*ing*?
What *is* Father do*ing*?
(What *is* Father read*ing*?)
(Who *is* read*ing* [the newspaper]?
What *are* the children do*ing*?
(Where *are* the children play*ing*?)
What *is* Peter do*ing*?
(Where *is* Peter putt*ing* his blocks?)
What *is* Mary do*ing*?
(Who *is* play*ing* with her dolls?)
What *is* Bob doing?
(Who *is* bounc*ing* a ball?)
What *is* **Ruff** do*ing*?

The family is in the den.
Mother is knitting a sweater.
Father is reading the news-
paper.
The children are playing on the
floor.
Peter is putting his blocks in a box.
Mary is playing with her dolls.
Bob is bouncing a ball.
Ruff is barking at him.

THIRD UNIT OF LANGUAGE

Past tense instruction sentences; questions
Experience stories; future tense
Sequence stories; questions

What did the girl do?

The girl fell.

What *did* the rope *do?*

The rope *broke*.

What *did* the flowers *do* ?

The flowers died.

What *did* someone *do* ?

Someone opened the door.

What *did* Joseph *do*?

Joseph kicked the football.

What did Brad do?

Brad *fell* on the grass.

Where will we go tomorrow?
How will we go?
Who will drive the minibus?
What will we take for our picnic lunch?
What will Mrs. Jones bring for dessert?
What will we do?
What will we play on?
Will we go swimming?

EXPERIENCE STORY: FUTURE TENSE LANGUAGE

Our Picnic

Tomorrow we will go to the park for a picnic. We will go in the Jones family's minibus. Mrs. Jones will drive it.

We will take sandwiches, drinks and chips for our picnic lunch. Mrs. Jones will bring us a surprise for dessert.

We will play on the swings and seesaws. We will climb on the monkey bars and play ball, too. We will not go swimming.

NOTE:

Only the past tense story goes in the child's book.

What did we do yesterday?
Where did we go yesterday?
How did we go to the park?
Who drove the minibus?
What did we take for our picnic lunch?
What did Mrs. Jones bring for dessert?
What was the surprise?
What did we do?
What did we play on?
What did we climb on?
Did we go swimming?
What happened to Don?
Did it hurt him?
What kind of time did we have?
When will we go on another outing?

EXPERIENCE STORY: CONVERTED TO PAST TENSE LANGUAGE

Our Picnic

Yesterday we went to the park for a picnic. We went in the Jones family's minibus. Mrs. Jones drove it.

We took sandwiches, drinks, and chips for our picnic lunch. Mrs. Jones brought us a surprise for dessert.

We played on the swings and seesaws. We climbed on the monkey bars and played ball, too. We did not go swimming. Don fell off of the seesaw but it did not hurt him.

We had a great time! Maybe we will go on another outing sometime.

What did Bill want to do?
What did he do first?
What did he get to cut the boards?
How many pieces did he cut for the floor?
How many pieces did he cut for the sides?
How many pieces did he cut for the roof?
What did Bill do with the pieces?
When did Bill get a surprise?
What was the surprise?
Why couldn't the birds get inside?
What did Bill forget to do?
What do you think Bill did next?

PAST TENSE SEQUENCE STORY OR IMAGINATION STORY

Bill's Birdhouse

Bill wanted to make a birdhouse. First, he found some boards. He got a saw to cut the boards. He cut one piece for the floor. He cut four pieces for the sides. He cut two pieces for the roof.

Later, Bill got his hammer and some nails. He nailed the pieces together. He got a big surprise when he finished. The birds could not get inside because he forgot to cut a hole in one side for them.

What do you think Bill did next?

What did Kim want to do one day?
What did she tell her mother?
What did she ask her mother
  to do?
What did Kim's mother do?
Where did Kim mix the butter
and sugar?
What did she do next?
What did she add after that?
When did Kim put the cake
batter in the greased pan?
How long did Kim bake
the cake?
Where did Kim bake the cake?
Why was Kim's father proud
of her?
Who was Kim proud of?
Why was Kim proud?

IMAGINATION STORY

Kim's Cake

One day Kim wanted to make a cake. She told her mother and asked her to help her. Kim's mother got the things for the cake.

Kim mixed the butter and sugar in the mixer. Next, she added four eggs and some vanilla. After that, she added the milk and the flour, salt and soda. When everything was mixed together well, Kim put the cake batter in a greased pan. Kim baked the cake in the oven for 50 minutes.

Kim's father was proud of Kim because she made such a good cake. Kim was proud of herself, too.

APPENDIX

C

Additional Vocabulary and Sample Drills

The following vocabulary words are suggested as appropriate for increasing the phonetic composition of the first unit of language. *The grouping of vocabulary in this section is done according to the number of phonemes in the words: 2-, 3-, 4-phonemes, etc.* The simplicity or complexity of the spelling patterns also was considered in organizing the groups. (Corresponding word cards and picture materials are available. See Appendix F). Other words may be chosen to satisfy individual needs, to reflect geographic regions, and to discuss seasonal and special events.

DUBARD SCHOOL FOR LANGUAGE DISORDERS VOCABULARY LIST

CV/VC Group 1:

arm	cow	ice	saw	toy	**OTHER**
bee	ear (vv)	jar	shoe		zoo
bow	egg	key	tea		
boy	eye (v)	owl	tie		
car	hoe	pie	toe		

CVC Group 2:

bag	cake	fish	hat	moth	sack	teeth
ball	cat	food	hose	net	shell	top
bike	cup	girl	leaf	nose	soap	
bird	duck	goat	log	peach	sun	
bowl	feet	ham	map	pin	tape	
OTHER:	coat	gate	man			

CVC Group 3:

bat	bone	coke	farm	lock	pen	ship
barn	book	dog	goose	meat	pig	shirt
bed	bus	doll	house	moon	rose	
bell	cane	dime	kite	mouth	seal	
boat	cap	face	lake	pan	sock	
OTHER:	fan	rug				

CVC/CVV Group 4

beach	cheese	foot	jet	moose	rain	thumb
bear	chin	hair	lamb	phone	rope	tooth
boot	deer	hook	leg	pot	sheep	web
can	fire	jam	match	rake	soup	
OTHER:	gum	gun	mop	pipe		

CVC/VCC/CCV/CVV Group 5:

ant	bug	door	juice	nurse	star	whale
apple	chair	fawn	knife	pear	tire	wheel
axe	comb	heel	light	ring	tree	vase
beet	cone	judge	mouse	safe	wave	
OTHER:	peas					

ADDITIONAL VOCABULARY:

NUMERALS

one	four	seven	ten
two	five	eight	
three	six	nine	

COLORS

black	green	red
blue	orange	white
brown	pink	yellow
gray	purple	

CVCC/CCVC Group 6

beans	clock	flag	hand	nuts	spoon
belt	clown	fence	lamp	plane	stool
box	crown	fox	lips	sand	swan
bread	desk	frog	milk	slide	thread
chest	drum	glass	nest	snake	train
OTHER:	broom	chalk	dress	floor	

CVCV/CVCVCV, ETC. GROUP 7:

baby	butter	flower	pencil	scissors	water
banana	candy	glasses	rabbit	table	window
basket	coffee	ladder	rocket	tee vee (t.v.)	
bucket	cookie	paper	ruler	tissue	
OTHER:	bunny	jello	jelly	letter	napkin
	pants (CVCCC)				

bawl   baul   baul

bel   beal   beal

bal   bal   bal

bu_el   bewl   bewl

bawlt   bault   bault

belt   bealt   bealt

balt   balt   balt

bu_elt   bewlt   bewlt

belt

NOTE:

Underlining denotes alternating colors.

rum   wrum   wrum
ra_em   wraim   wraym
ri_em   wrym   wrighm
ro_em   wroam   wroum

drum   dwrum   dwrum
dra_em   dwraim   dwraym
dri_em   dwrym   dwrighm
dro_em   dwroam   dwroum
                       drum

NOTE:

Underlining denotes alternating colors.

A P P E N D I X

D

Sample Stories

Animal Stories
Inanimate Object Stories
Calendar Stories
Oral Spelling
Expanded Personal Stories
Preposition Round-up Stories
Descriptive Stories
Present Progressive Round-up Stories
Past Tense Stories
Experience Stories
Imagination Stories

ANIMAL STORIES

Suggestions for content are listed below; choice of content is left to the teacher's discretion based on the needs of the child or group.

Animal	Possible Vocabulary	Language Concepts	Number Concepts
cat	feet, eyes, mouth, ears, nose	long (tail) short (ears)	two four
dog	choose from above		make appropriate for the specific animal
horse	choose from above		
cow	choose from above, plus horns, ears		
bird	wings, beak, claws	sharp (claws) can fly covered with feathers	
owl	ears, eyes, wings, beak, feathers	can fly covered with feathers	
duck	bill, wings, webbed feet	can fly/walk/swim/run covered with feathers	

Animal	Possible Vocabulary	Language Concepts	Number Concepts
goat	ears, legs, horns	can walk/run cannot fly/swim covered with hair	
mouse	ears, feet, mouth, nose, whiskers	little (ears) long (tail) can run, climb cannot fly/swim covered with hair	
rabbit	ears, tail, nose, whiskers, mouth	long (ears) short (tail) can hop/run cannot fly/swim covered with fur	
squirrel	tail, claws	long, bushy (tail) sharp (claws) short/little (ears) can climb/jump cannot swim/fly covered with fur	
fish	fins, mouth, eyes, gills no feet	can swim/jump cannot walk	
elephant	trunk	is gray big, floppy (ears) long (trunk) little (tail) can walk/swim	
giraffe	spots	long (neck) long (legs) short (mane) short (horns) has no voice	
deer	any appropriate vocabulary used previously; antlers rather than horns may be appropriate in certain instances		
zebra	new vocabulary: stripes, appropriate previously taught vocabulary or concepts may be used		
lion		bushy (mane)	
frog	wide mouth (use determined by the picture used in teaching) covered with skin		
lamb	choose from previously taught vocabulary and concepts		

Animal	Possible Vocabulary	Language Concepts	Number Concepts
sheep			
grasshopper	if circumstances happen to set the stage for using it, feelers in lieu of antennae		

In the following sample animal stories the use of question language is illustrated as well as how to expand vocabulary and concepts. Four levels of animal stories (with corresponding questions) are taught.

Level I.
Four- or five-line story primarily incorporating previously learned vocabulary.

Sample:

what is this?	this is a dog.
has a dog a mouth? (does a dog have a mouth?)	*(yes,) a dog has a mouth.
has a dog a nose? (does a dog...?)	(yes,) a dog has a nose.
how many eyes has a dog? (how many eyes does a dog have?)	a dog has two eyes.
how many ears has a dog? (how many ears does a dog have?)	a dog has two ears.

Notes: Based on the competencies of the children in the class, the teacher will decide whether to teach the "has" or the "does" question.

""Yes" and "no" are not part of the original story content. "Yes" and "no" for affirmation and negation are used only after the introduction of the question language and are written in the child's book in pencil. Writing these items in pencil is a visual cue to the child that this language is treated differently than the rest. Parentheses are not placed in the child's book. Parentheses are used in these examples as a reminder to the therapist to add "yes" and "no" after questions have been introduced.

Level II.
Addition of can/cannot and concept of negation to the Level I story.

Sample:

what is this?	this is a fish.
does a fish have a mouth?	(yes,) a fish has a mouth.
does a fish have fins?	(yes,) a fish has fins.
does a fish have feet?	(no,) a fish has no feet.
can a fish swim?	(yes,) a fish can swim.
can a fish walk?	(no,) a fish cannot walk.

Level III.
Addition of adjectives to the preceding levels.

Sample:

what is this?	this is a turtle.
how many feet does a turtle have?	a turtle has four feet.
how many eyes does a turtle have?	a turtle has two eyes.
what kind of tail does a turtle have?	a turtle has a short tail.
does a turtle have a shell?	(yes,) a turtle has a shell.
does a turtle have ears?	(no,) a turtle has no ears.
can a turtle crawl?	(yes,) a turtle can crawl.
can a turtle walk?	(yes,) a turtle can walk.
can a turtle run?	(no,) a turtle cannot run.

Level IV.
The concept of "is covered with" is added to the material of the previous levels.

Sample:

what is this?	this is a squirrel.
how many eyes does a squirrel have?	a squirrel has two eyes.
how many feet does a squirrel have?	a squirrel has four feet.
does a squirrel have whiskers?	(yes,) a squirrel has whiskers.
what kind of tail does a squirrel have?	a squirrel has a bushy tail.
what kind of claws does a squirrel have?	a squirrel has sharp claws.
can a squirrel climb?	(yes,) a squirrel can climb.
what is a squirrel covered with?	a squirrel is covered with fur.

INANIMATE OBJECT STORIES

Suggested Items	Possible Vocabulary
wagon	handle, wheels, bed
bike	handle bars, two pedals, seat, fenders
car	windows, tires, doors, fenders, windshield
dress	any vocabulary related to the item pictured or shown
sweater	same criteria as for dress
coat	same criteria as for above items

Sample stories follow.

Example of *board instruction* for the *first* inanimate story. The story is written in the child's book in the usual manner. Subsequent stories are written with 'it' used in the initial presentation. Questions are introduced when the story has been mastered.

this is a dress.

    it

~~a dress~~ has a collar.

    it

~~a dress~~ has sleeves.

    it

~~a dress~~ has a belt.

    it

~~a dress~~ has buttons.

what is this?	this is a bike.
does it have a seat?	(yes,) it has a seat.
does it have handle bars?	(yes,) it has handle bars.
how many fenders does it have?	it has two fenders.
how many pedals does it have?	it has two pedals.
how many wheels does it have?	it has two wheels.

what is this?	this is a clock.
does it have a face?	(yes,) it has a face.
does it have numbers?	(yes,) it has numbers.
what kind of hand does it have?	it has a long hand.
what kind of hand does it have?	it has a short hand.

CALENDAR AND RELATED STORIES

(Also see chapter 7.)

After children learn the names of days and months, a sample story like the following can be used.

this is a calendar.

it has days.

it has weeks.

it has months.

the months are ...

the days are ...

Questions should be taught about this story.

Seasons

A year has twelve months. The months are January, February, March, April, May, June, July, August, September, October, November, and December.

A year has four seasons. The seasons are winter, spring, summer, and autumn. Autumn is called fall, too.

December, January, and February are months of the winter season. March, April, and May are months of the spring season. June, July, and August are months of the summer season. September, October, and November are months of the autumn season.

The weather is colder in winter than in autumn. Sometimes it snows during the winter season. Sometimes we have a warm spell after the weather becomes cold. Winter is a dreary season. Some trees are bare. Sometimes the sky is dark during the day. The sky gets dark early at night also.

Holidays or Special Days

Columbus Day

October 12 is Columbus Day. Columbus was a sailor. He had three ships. One ship was called the Nina. Another ship was called the Pinta. The other ship was called the Santa Maria.

In 1492, Columbus and his men crossed the Atlantic Ocean. The trip took almost three months. They landed on October 12 in America.

Halloween

On Halloween children wear costumes so no one can tell who they are. They go trick or treating, and people give them candy.

The jack-o-lantern is a symbol of Halloween. It is made by cutting a face in a pumpkin.

TEACHING THE ALPHABET (LETTER NAMES) TO CHILDREN WITH SEVERE COMMUNICATION DISORDERS

Oral spelling may begin at the level of personal stories, if desired. Teaching the alphabet (letter names) is necessary for teaching the child oral spelling. The names of the letters of the alphabet may be taught as suggested in McGinnis (1963).

a = a-e; b = bee; c = see; d = dee; e = ee; f = -ef; g = jee; h = a-ech; i = i-e; j = ja-e; k = ka-e; l = -el; m = -em; n = -en; o = o-e; p = pee; q = ku-e; r = ar; s = es; t = tee; u = u-e; v = vee; w = du bl u-e; x = eks; y = wi-e; z = zee

EXPANDED PERSONAL STORIES: LEVELS, ORGANIZATION AND SAMPLES

Expanded: Level 1

Use 4 lines from basic stories and add:

1. Articles of clothing
    (Examples: shirt, pants, skirt, dress, jacket, sweater, shoes, boots, sandals, belt)
2. Single colors to describe clothing
    (Example: blue shirt)
3. Use only one sentence to describe an article of clothing
4. Stories should be no more than 7 lines

Sample:

who is this?	who is this?
this is Joe.	this is Joe.
what is he?	what is he?
he is a man.	he is a man.
what color hair does he have?	what color is his hair?
he has brown hair.	his hair is brown.
what color eyes does he have?	what color are his eyes?
he has brown eyes.	his eyes are brown.
what color shirt does he have on?	what color is his shirt?
he has on a red shirt.	his shirt is red.
what color pants does he have on?	what color are his pants?
he has on black pants.	his pants are black.
what color belt does he have on?	what color is his belt?
he has on a black belt.	his belt is black.

Expanded: Level 2
Use all content included in previous levels and add:
1. Solid plus single color to describe clothing
   (Example: solid blue shirt)
2. More than one sentence to describe one article of clothing
   (Example: she has on a solid blue shirt. it has long sleeves.)
3. Stories should be 7-8 lines

Sample:

who is this?
    this is Becky.
what is she?
    she is a lady.
what color eyes does she have?
    she has blue eyes.
what color hair does she have?
    she has red hair.
what color sweater does she have on?
what kind of sweater does she have on?
    she has on a solid red sweater.
how many buttons does it have?
    it has five buttons.
what color skirt does she have on?
what kind of skirt does she have on?
    she has on a solid black skirt.
what color boots does she have on?
    she has on black boots.

who is this?
    this is Becky.
what is she?
    she is a lady.
what color are her eyes?
    her eyes are blue.
what color is her hair?
    her hair is red.
what color is her sweater?
    her sweater is solid red.
how many buttons does it have?
    it has five buttons.
what color is her skirt?
    her skirt is solid black.
what color are her boots?
    her boots are black.

Expanded: Level 3
Use all content included in previous levels and add:
1. Patterns: checked (2 colors), plaid (1-3 colors), striped (2-3 colors), flowered (2-3 colors), polka-dotted (2-3 colors), print (2-3 colors) NOTE: these patterns are taught over several stories
2. Name the dominant colors
3. Use 2 or 3 sentences with "it" after naming the clothing item
   (Example: she has on a pink and white flowered sweater. it has long sleeves. it has four buttons.)
4. Use the negative (does not have) when an expected part is missing
   (Example: sleeves and collar would be expected parts of a shirt)
5. For pants/slacks/overalls, use "they" rather than "it"
6. More advanced vocabulary should be included
   (Examples: sweatshirt, sweatpants, overalls, suit, jumper, turtleneck, stockings, tee shirt, jacket, raincoat, necklace, bracelet, earrings, watch, flip flops, vest, zipper, hood, etc.)
7. Stories should be 8-9 lines (can delete sentences about hair and eyes to include more content about clothing)

Sample:

who is this?
    this is Charlie.
what is he?
    he is a boy.
what color hair does he have?
    he has blond hair.
what color eyes does he have?
    he has brown eyes.
what color sweatshirt does he have on?
what kind of sweatshirt does he have on?
    he has on a blue and white striped sweatshirt.

who is this?
    this is Charlie.
what is he?
    he is a boy.
what color is his hair?
    his hair is blond.
what color are his eyes?
    his eyes are brown.
what color is his sweatshirt?
    his sweatshirt is blue and white striped.
does it have sleeves?

does it have sleeves?
    (no,) it does not have sleeves.
does it have a hood?
    (yes,) it has a hood.
what color sweatpants does he have on?
what kind of sweatpants does he have on?
    he has on solid blue sweatpants.
what color tennis shoes does he have on?
    he has on white tennis shoes.

    (no,) it does not have sleeves.
does it have a hood?
    (yes,) it has a hood.
what color are his sweatpants?
    his sweatpants are solid blue.
what color are his tennis shoes?
    his tennis shoes are white.

Expanded: Level 4
Use all content included in previous levels and add:
1. Use "it" to identify more than one item of clothing
   (Example: he has on a dark green shirt. it has a collar. he has on a brown corduroy vest. it has three buttons.)
2. Add types of materials
   (Examples: denim, leather, corduroy, etc.)
3. Use color variations
   (Example: light blue)
4. Avoid using type of material and color variation in the same sentence
5. Stories should be 8-9 lines (can delete sentences about hair and eyes to include more content about clothing)

Sample:
who is this?
    this is Jane.
what is she?
    she is a girl.
what color blouse does she have on?
what kind of blouse does she have on?
    she has on a dark blue and white print blouse.
what kind of sleeves does it have?
    it has long sleeves.
what color vest does she have on?
    she has on a light blue vest.
how many buttons does it have?
    it has three buttons.
what color pants does she have on?
what kind of pants does she have on?
    she has on brown corduroy pants.
how many pockets do they have?
    they have two pockets.
what color loafers does she have on?
what kind of loafers does she have on?
    she has on solid brown loafers.

who is this?
    this is Jane.
what is she?
    she is a girl.
what color is her blouse?
    her blouse is dark blue and white print.
what kind of sleeves does it have?
    it has long sleeves.
what color is her vest?
    her vest is light blue.
how many buttons does it have?
    it has three buttons.
what color are her pants?
    her pants are brown corduroy.
how many pockets do they have?
    they have two pockets.
what color are her loafers?
    her loafers are solid brown.

ROUND-UP STORIES USING PREPOSITIONS

Questions used after teaching the story	Story
Where are the children?	The children are in the playroom.
Where is Sally?	Sally is on the sofa.
What does Sally have?	Sally has a teddy bear, a cat, and a duck.
Where is Jim?	Jim is on the floor.
What does he have?	He has a truck and a wagon.

Where is Sue?

What does she have?

Sue is by the dollhouse.

She has the doll furniture.

Who is on the sofa?

Who has a teddy bear . . . ?

Who is on the floor?

Who has a truck . . . ?

Who is by the dollhouse?

Who has the doll furniture?

Optional questions which are appropriate but less expanding may be used as secondary questioning for double-checking and variety.

Where are Mary and Betty?

Where is Mary?

Where is Betty?

Where are two doll buggies?

Who has the girls' dolls?

Mary and Betty are outside.

Mary is on the rug.

Betty is on the other rug.

Two doll buggies are on the grass.

Spot and Ruff have the girls' dolls.

Where are Bob and Betsy?

Where is a sand pail?

What does Betsy have?
  (How many seashells does Betsy have?)

Who has one seashell?
  (How many seashells does Bob have?)

Where are five sheep?
  (How many sheep are in the grass?)

Bob and Betsy are on the bench.

A sand pail is between Bob and Betsy.

Betsy has two seashells.

Bob has one seashell.

Five sheep are in the grass.

SAMPLE DESCRIPTIVE STORIES

This is a kitchen.
The refrigerator, dishwasher, and oven are white.
A microwave oven is on the counter.
A mixer is on the counter, too.
Four mugs are on a tray.
It is by the sink.
A window is over the sink.

This is a dining room.
Four chairs are around the table.
A bowl of fruit is on the table.
A lamp is over the table.
Some dishes and some other things are in the china cabinet.
It is between two plants.

At the round-up and descriptive story levels, the primary question language for sentences containing prepositions will be "Where....?" Multiple questions of varying forms should be used at this level for each appropriate sentence. These could include: "What...?", "What color...?", "How many...?", and so on.

PRESENT PROGRESSIVE ROUND-UP STORIES

The children are playing outside.
Jason is holding a bat.
Abbie is throwing the ball.
Ruff is jumping up and down.
Debbie is sitting on the grass.
She is holding a teddy bear.
Tiger is standing by Ann.

Note: The primary question for present progressive stories is: What is/are _____ doing?

PAST TENSE STORIES

Stimulus: Series of three pictures in sequence

Father and the children went to the zoo one Saturday. They looked at all of the animals. Sally pointed to the giraffe. Jane told Father, "Look at the giraffe." Two zebras watched Bill feed the elephants. Jane told Bill, "Look at the giraffe." Bill turned his head to look at the giraffe. When he turned his head, the elephant snatched the whole bag of peanuts away from him. Some of them spilled on the ground. Bill was very surprised by the elephant. He never saw what the giraffe was doing.

Stimulus: A single picture

Father sent David to the apple tree to pick the apples. David took a basket and a bucket to put the apples in. David filled the basket with apples. Two more apples are on the grass by the basket. David is holding the empty bucket and reaching for an apple off the tree. David's dog, Mutt, is jumping up and down.

Questions which will use the new verb concepts should be taught about the story.

Note: The primary question for past tense stories is: What did _____ do?

SAMPLE EXPERIENCE STORIES
(Same topic written on three levels of difficulty)

Lower Level

Before the activity:

we will make cookies.
we will mix the rice krispies, sugar, and peanut butter.
we will put the cookies on a pan.
we will eat the cookies at snack time.

Instruction at the board after the activity:

    made
we ~~will make~~ cookies.
    mixed
we ~~will mix~~ the rice krispies, sugar, and peanut butter.
    put
we ~~will put~~ the cookies on a pan.
    ate
we ~~will eat~~ the cookies at snack time.

Intermediate Level

Before the activity:

we will make cookies.
we will mix rice krispies and coconut.
maureen will stir the syrup, brown sugar, peanut butter, and vanilla.
we will mix all of the things together.
we will wait for it to cool.
we will shape the cookies on the pan.
we will eat the cookies at snack time.

Story changed to past tense language after the activity:

we made cookies.
we mixed rice krispies and coconut.
maureen stirred the syrup, brown sugar, peanut butter, and vanilla.
we mixed all of the things together.
we waited for it to cool.
we shaped the cookies on the pan.
we ate the cookies at snack time.

Upper Level

Before the activity:

We will make Rice Krispie cookies at 10 o'clock.
First, we will read the recipe.
Christy will measure four cups of Rice Krispies.
Trey will measure one cup of coconut.
They will mix the Rice Krispies and coconut.
Next, Aphelia will measure the Karo syrup and brown sugar.
She will pour them into a pot.
James will measure the peanut butter and vanilla.
He will pour them into the pot.
Olivia will cook and stir the ingredients.
After that, she will mix all of the ingredients together.
We will wait for the mixture to cool.
When it is cool, Ashley and Anita will shape the cookies on the pan.
After lunch, we will eat the cookies.
We will share our cookies with the other children.

After the activity:

We made Rice Krispie cookies at 10 o'clock.
First, we read the recipe.
Christy measured four cups of Rice Krispies.
Trey measured one cup of coconut.
They mixed the Rice Krispies and coconut.
Next, Aphelia measured the Karo syrup and brown sugar.
She poured them into a pot.
James measured the peanut butter and vanilla.
He poured them into the pot.
Olivia cooked and stirred the ingredients.
After that, she mixed all of the ingredients together.
We waited for the mixture to cool.

When it was cool, Ashley and Anita shaped the cookies on the pan.
    After lunch, we ate the cookies.
    We shared our cookies with the other children.

At each story level, appropriate questions would be used with both forms of the story.
Traditional paragraph format may be used at the teacher's discretion, especially at the upper level.

IMAGINATION STORIES

Single picture stimulus:

One day Amy and her dog, Penny, were playing outside. The day before it had rained and the ground was wet. Penny walked through a mud puddle when Amy was not looking. When they went into the kitchen, Penny's muddy feet made dirty tracks on the kitchen floor. Amy was afraid her mother would be angry so she got a sponge and cleaned Penny's feet. After that, she cleaned the floor. Mother will be proud of Amy because she was helpful.

Five neighborhood boys were on the Eagles baseball team. One afternoon they practiced until six o'clock. When they stopped practicing they were hungry and thirsty, so they went to Tom's house to get something to eat.
When they got inside, they dropped the bat and catcher's mask on the floor. Tom found some milk in the refrigerator and poured a glassful for each boy. Before Dick could drink all of his, he and Bob started pushing each other and some of Dick's milk spilled on the floor. His cap fell on the floor, too.
Jim jumped up and down because he was so happy; he had hit a home run. While he was jumping he stepped on Bill's shoelace and it came untied. Bill put his glove on the floor, sat down, and tied his shoelace.
After Tom drank his milk, he wanted some water. While he was getting some water he heard his mother drive into the carport. He yelled to the boys to stop pushing each other, clean the floor, and pick up the baseball things off the floor.

A story of this length might constitute several lessons. Dividing a story for several instructional sessions would be done on the basis of circumstances, teacher's judgment, and various needs.

APPENDIX

E

Sample Instructional Program: Learning Disabilities/Dyslexia

J.G. was the first student with dyslexia/specific learning disabilities in reading who was enrolled at the School for Children with Language Disorders (now known as the DuBard School for Language Disorders). He was enrolled from 1973-75 and is described in the case histories (pp. 151-152). The format for his instructional program was essentially the same as that used for children with receptive-expressive language disorders but was modified as appropriate. At times there were temptations to take shortcuts in the early stages. When this was done, it always proved to have been a mistake and invariably it was necessary to go back and bring him through the previously omitted work. Teachers who have used the procedures with groups have stressed the necessity of using the procedures as a full multisensory approach rather than eliminating aspects of the procedures. The need for overlearning to take place is as crucial for those who have learning disabilities or who are learning different as it is for those who have oral language disorders. It has been noted also that the basic word list in Appendix C correlates well with several basal reading programs and some linguistic programs.

J.G.'s program utilized cursive writing throughout his first year of instruction. Color differentiation was made through the cross-drill/syllable-drill instruction and until he demonstrated ability to break the code of written words easily without the color differentiation. For the sake of convenience, however, the program illustrated here is in manuscript. It is urged that instruction utilize cursive writing, however.

SEQUENTIAL CONTENT OF J.G.'S PROGRAM

Book I

First Phonemes: m, -o-, b, ee, t, o-e

First Drop Drills: bo-e,
> followed by the material which included phonemes and drop drills intermittently prior to instruction of cross drills/syllable drills.

f, mee, p, -a-, ma-, o͞o[1], d, i-e, fo͞o[1], k, -i-, do-, l, -e-, a-e, le-, g, -u-

Cross Drills

bo-e	boa	bŏw[2]
ba-	ba-	ba-
bee	bĕa[1]	bĕa[1]
be-	bĕa[2]	bĕa[2]

Potential Vocabulary from above drill: bow, bat, bee, boat, bed, bean, bag

Additional phonemes taught in isolation concurrently: aw, l, o͞o[2], th

bur	bir	ber	bird
baw	baw	bau	ball
bi-e	bigh	bȳ[2]	bike
boi	boy	boy	boy
bŏo[2]	bŭ-[2]	bŭ-[2]	bŏok[2]

Potential Vocabulary from above drill: bird, ball, bike, boy, book

It should be noted here that J.G.'s cross drills consisted of only four lines when instruction was begun. As additional words were taught through drills at the board, the new line was added in his book as a part of the record. This was done in the interest of saving time and material. Adding the additional lines which were used for practice did not jeopardize his progress or confuse him.

mo-	mo-	mo-
mee	m$\overset{1}{e}$a	m$\overset{1}{e}$a
m$\overset{1}{o}$o	m$\overset{1}{o}$o	m$\overset{1}{o}$o
ma-	ma-	ma-
mou	m$\overset{1}{o}$w	m$\overset{1}{o}$w

Potential Vocabulary from above drill: mop, moon, mouth, meat, man, moth

Additional phonemes taught in isolation concurrently: $\overset{1}{s}$, n, $\overset{2}{s}$, th, wh

$\overset{1}{s}$aw	$\overset{1}{s}$au	$\overset{1}{s}$au
$\overset{1}{s}$u-	$\overset{1}{s}$u-	$\overset{1}{s}$u-
$\overset{1}{s}\overset{2}{o}$o	$\overset{1}{s}\overset{2}{o}$o	$\overset{1}{s}\overset{2}{o}$o
$\overset{1}{s}$o-e	$\overset{1}{s}$oa	$\overset{1}{s}\overset{2}{o}$w
$\overset{1}{s}$ee	$\overset{1}{s}\overset{1}{e}$a	$\overset{1}{s}\overset{1}{e}$a
$\overset{1}{s}$o-	$\overset{1}{s}$o-	$\overset{1}{s}$o-

Potential Vocabulary from above drill: $\overset{1}{s}$aw, $\overset{1}{s}$un, $\overset{1}{s}\overset{1}{e}$al, $\overset{1}{s}$ock, $\overset{1}{s}$oap. Secondary spellings, ce, ci, cy, may be used in the second and third columns as desired.

Additional phonemes: ar, ou

tee	t$\overset{1}{e}$a	t$\overset{1}{e}$a
ti-e	tigh	t$\overset{2}{y}$
to-	to-	to-
t$\overset{1}{o}$o	t$\overset{1}{o}$o	t$\overset{1}{o}$o
toi	toy	toy

Potential Vocabulary from above drill: t$\overset{1}{e}$a, tie, toy, tee$\overset{1}{t}$h, tire, top

Because of the specific phonetic composition, some words were taught in a *single line cross drill* in two-color arrangement. Care was taken to make sure that adequate written practice was given to insure mastery.

Drill			*Noun Vocabulary*
arm	arm	arm	arm
-e$\underset{1}{g}$	e$\overset{2}{a}$g	e$\overset{2}{a}$g	egg
i-e$\overset{1}{s}$	ighce	-$\overset{2}{y}$ci	ice
eeur	eair	ear	ear
	or:		
-iur	-iur	-$\overset{1}{y}$ar	ear
(if local pronunciation dictates it)			
i-e	igh	-$\overset{2}{y}$	eye

Repetitive Sentences with the appropriate question on the facing page were then introduced.

I see a (noun).
this is a (noun).

Phonemes: y-, w, h, ur

Cross Drills

gu-	gu-	gu-
go-e	goa	g$\overset{2}{o}$w
g$\overset{1}{o}$o	g$\overset{1}{o}$o	g$\overset{1}{o}$o
ga-e	gai	gay
gur	gir	ger

Potential Noun Vocabulary: gun, goat, girl, g$\overset{1}{o}\overset{1}{o}$se

kar	car	ckar
kou	c$\overset{1}{o}$w	ck$\overset{1}{o}$w
kee	c$\overset{1}{e}$a	ck$\overset{1}{e}$a
ka-e	cai	ckay
ko-e	coa	ck$\overset{2}{o}$w
ki-e	kigh	ck$\overset{2}{y}$

Potential Noun Vocabulary: car, c$\overset{1}{o}$w, key, cake, coat, coke, kite

Additional phonemes taught in isolation concurrently: v, j, sh, ng, r

Repetitive Sentence-Question Pages

I want a _____.
I have a/an/some _____.

Additional phonemes taught in isolation concurrently: r, ch, u-e, and the letter x as having the sounds of k$\overset{1}{s}$.

Cross Drills

shi-	sh$\overset{1}{y}$	sh$\overset{1}{y}$
shur	shir	sher
sh$\overset{1}{o}$o	sh$\overset{1}{o}$o	sh$\overset{1}{o}$o
shee	sh$\overset{1}{e}$a	sh$\overset{1}{e}$a

Potential Vocabulary from the above drill: ship, shoe, shirt, sheep

ro-e	wroa	wr$\overset{2}{o}$w
ra-e	wrai	wray
ree	wr$\overset{1}{e}$a	wr$\overset{1}{e}$a

Potential Vocabulary from the above drill: rope, wreath

do-	do-	do-
du-	du-	du-
di-e	digh	dy̆²
dee	dĕa¹	dĕa¹
do-e	doa	dŏw²

Potential Vocabulary from the above drill: doll, duck, dime, deer, door

cha-	cha-	cha-
chee	chĕa¹	chĕa¹
chŏo¹	chŏo¹	chŏo¹

Potential Vocabulary from the above drill: chair, cheese

Secondary spelling, tch, may be used in the second and third columns.

lo-	lo-	lo-
li-e	ligh	ly̆²
la-	la-	la-
la-e	lai	lay
le-	lĕa²	lĕa²

Potential Vocabulary from the above drill: lock, light, lamb, lake, leg

no-e	knoa	knŏw²
ni-e	knigh	kny̆²
nee	knĕa¹	knĕa¹

Potential Vocabulary from the above drill: nose, knife, knee

pi-e	pigh	py̆²
pa-	pa-	pa-
pe-	pĕa²	pĕa²
pi-	py̆¹	py̆¹

Potential Vocabulary from the above drill: pie, pipe, pan, pen, pin

fŏo²	phŭ²-	phŭ²-
far	phar	phar
fee	phĕa¹	phĕa¹
fi-	phi-	phi-
fo-e	phoa	phŏw²

Potential Vocabulary from the above drill: foot, farm, feet, fish, phone

ho-e	hoa	hŏw²
hou	hŏw¹	hŏw¹
haw	hau	hau
hee	hĕa¹	hĕa¹
ha-	ha-	ha-

Potential Vocabulary from the above drill: hoe, house, hair, hat

As more vocabulary was taught it was always incorporated into use in sentences and questions. In addition, the same vocabulary was used in different types of sentences to provide additional experience in code-breaking and to avoid the chance that sentences had been memorized on an auditory memory basis. Colors and numbers were taught as single words and later incorporated into sentences and stories. After the previously cited vocabulary, repetitive sentences, questions and supplementary work were completed and J.G. could read and write the material, stories of the following type were introduced. The teacher did not use pictures until J.G. had mastered the code-breaking skills for reading.

I. Nine animal stories and questions as designed by McGinnis for the procedures.

II. Stories with questions that gave more variety and less predictability for the child who had no difficulties in auditory comprehension of language. Example:

> mark went to a farm.
> he saw three cows.
> he saw four ducks.
> he saw two goats.
> he found some eggs.
> he had lots of fun.

III. One inanimate object story

IV. Expanded stories

> the boy ate some cake.
> it was warm.
> it was good.

> sam found a duck.
> the duck was not big.
> it was lost.

> mike has a fish.
> he got it at the pet shop.
> the fish is in a bowl.

> Tom saw a nest.
> the nest was in a bush.
> the nest was made of straw and sticks.
> three eggs were in the nest.

> Tim has a bug.
> he found it in his yard.
> it is not big.

it has six legs.
Tim put it in a jar.

Shep is a big, brown dog.
he is a farm dog.
he has long hair.
he has a loud bark.
he barks at the cows and sheep.

Expanded Program

I.   Preposition language for reading and writing
      was included.
II.   Present progressive, future and past tense
      concepts were taught within the context of
      stories.
III. J.G.'s program included some of each of the
      types of stories designed for use with children
      with receptive-expressive language disorders.
      He progressed through the levels of stories
      more rapidly than they because he did not
      have difficulties with comprehension of oral
      language.

During J.G.'s second year of enrollment two texts of a pre-primer type, which had excellent pictures, were used. The content had been rewritten for use in the school. The stories had been prepared in a commercial cursive type. J.G.'s teacher prepared and used factual stories related to science and social studies. During the last nine months of his enrollment, J.G.'s instructional program included the use of commercially available readers with accompanying workbooks.

SAM STORIES

McGinnis' program utilized story work in the ways discussed earlier. They were developed with controls placed on the particular verb tense that was being focused upon in the child's instructional language program. Controls were placed on the length of the story, as well, because of the poor memory skills of the children. A great deal of checking and double-checking on the children's comprehension was necessary. Pictorial materials were used extensively as an aid to determining that the child had an adequate understanding of the relationship between the linguistic component and the item/object/person or action which the linguistic component represented. Needless to say, it was necessarily a slow process, but in the long run it was justifiable.

In essence, the initial population enrolled in the DuBard School for Language Disorders was like that of McGinnis' population. In addition, as a newcomer to the work, DuBard concluded that it was appropriate to adhere closely to the plan and manner of implementing that plan until a measure of security had been gained in the whole undertaking. *We still hold the view that it is important to have command of the basics before it is appropriate and safe to start modifications.* Any number of analogies could be presented which support that viewpoint. However, it will be the reader's opportunity to give some thought to the idea.

Even by the late 1960s there were few appropriate language tests. There were few, if any, special services in schools for children who did not follow the usual learning patterns. The programs available were programs which addressed aspects of developmental disabilities. There were few professionals aware of language programs; only a few more were becoming aware of a group of children who were ultimately viewed as learning disabled. The relationship between the learning difficulties and language deficiencies had not been a part of the growth in knowledge and/or awareness about some aspects of learning which were important in teaching children. A number of children who were "in trouble" as far as learning was concerned began to show up on the scene for evaluations at the school. In analyzing the skills and weaknesses of those children, we observed that they demonstrated the same weaknesses as the other children who were more severely disabled and who were enrolled. The major strength of the "new" population was that they had learned to talk, seemed to be "O.K.," and had entered general education schools. The pitfall was that they did not progress and succeed in a manner which was expected. In short, they were smart but they did not learn in the instructional programs available to them. It was with such a population of children enrolled that the Sam Stories arose.

The beginning work for the population of children described above was according to the plan as designed by McGinnis. Teaching the sound-symbol relationships as designed in McGinnis' work was crucial to teaching the code-breaking skills for the reading process. The significance of that level of work for speech skills was minimal. Some of those who had demonstrated speech difficulties in earlier years had received speech therapy and had been dismissed from their respective speech therapy programs. Others "talked a little funny" in terms of some of their expressions and/or in trying to use multisyllabic words; others did not demonstrate articulation errors. They demonstrated much higher levels of comprehending/understanding basic language than did the very early populations and did not require the use of picture material as much. In fact, it was observed that after some skills with the code-breaking process had been achieved by the children, using pictures simultaneously with the linguistic units was detrimental to progress. If they saw the picture, they were not inclined to really break the linguistic code of the word. Thus, changes were made.

For the children described above, their programs progressed rather rapidly through the sequential language levels. Concepts and language structure of the sentence and question forms for the basic sentences, animal stories, personal stories, and preposition work went smoothly. The goals always emphasized reading and writing of the language. There came a time when there was a desire to see how those children would respond and achieve with language that expanded tenses, concepts, and vocabulary that was not taught in the structured format. Thus, the advent of the Sam Stories.

The first Sam Story was developed spontaneously with the child. The phonetic composition of the words used were VC/CV or CVC so that the child would apply the skills he had acquired in the more structured work without risking overloading the requirements made of him. The child responded well, as had been expected, and he became excited about the new format of things and very quickly asked for another story. As might be expected, the stories became known as Sam Stories simply because the first name used for the main character was Sam.

The following are some of the initial Sam Stories which led to developing a whole new section in the curriculum. In each case, the story was presented one line at a time and the question forms were used after the child had read the story. (Numerals were used to indicate voicing or no voicing on specific consonants and vowels, but they are not shown here.)

---

what is sam?
how old is he?
how many sisters does he have?
what do they have?
what is the pet?

what does sam have?
what is his name?
where does tim live?
who likes to play?

when does sam feed tim?
when does sam play with tim?
who walks on the floor?
who is a good pet for sam?

who is sam's friend?
where does he live?
who walks to school?
who is their teacher?
what do they have at school?

when was jack's birthday?
who went to jack's house?
what did he give jack?
what was it?
what did they eat?

what did jack like?
who put dirt in the truck?
where did they push it?
what did they have?

sam is a boy.
he is nine years old.
he has three sisters.
they have a pet.
the pet is a turtle.

sam has a pet turtle.
his name is tim.
tim lives in sam's room.
sam and tim like to play.

sam feeds tim in the morning.
after school, sam plays with tim.
tim walks on the floor.
tim is a good pet for sam.

jack is sam's friend.
he lives next door.
jack and sam walk to school.
miss ward is their teacher.
they have fun at school.

friday was jack's birthday.
sam went to jack's house.
he gave jack a present.
it was a red dump truck.
they ate some cake and ice cream.

jack liked his new truck.
jack and sam put dirt in the truck.
they pushed it on the sidewalk.
they had a good time.

what did the mailman bring to sam one day?	one day, the mailman brought a box to sam.
was sam surprised?	sam was surprised.
what did he do?	he looked at the box.
was it very long?	it was very long.
did sam know what was in the box?	sam did not know what was in the box.
who opened the box?	sam opened the box.
what did he do?	he took out some paper.
what did he see?	he saw a shiny new rod and reel.
was sam very happy?	sam was very happy.
what did he want to do?	he wanted to go fishing right away.
who woke up early on saturday?	sam woke up early on saturday.
where were he and dad going?	he and dad were going fishing.
what did they do first?	first, they ate breakfast.
what did they do next?	next, they got the rod and reel and tackle box.
what did they do then?	then sam and dad drove to the lake.

Because these stories were effective with the children, we developed more Sam Stories. They were used in a sequential manner to provide continuity of themes from story to story and to expand the concepts in the written form in any way feasible so long as the child's progress was not jeopardized and/or frustration did not develop. The primary control used in developing the stories was that they were kept at a length of four to six lines. This decision was based on the idea that it is better to have many experiences rather than one experience over and over as would be the case in trying to work through a story that was too lengthy.

NOUN VOCABULARY ORGANIZATION FOR STUDENTS WITH DYSLEXIA

In recent years as increasing numbers of children with dyslexia or less than optimum reading skills have been served utilizing the DuBard Association Method®, adjustments have been made to the curriculum to enhance their instructional program. One of those changes has been to organize the vocabulary, as listed in Appendix C, according to spelling patterns. The following list is provided for use with those students. Note: *May teach in same cross drill if the student can handle. This applies to all vocabulary in parentheses.. Speech may demand order of presentation to vary. The teacher or therapist may teach across groups for spelling/speech needs.

NOUN VOCABULARY

Group 1 - CV/VC	Group 2 - CVC	Group 3 - CVC	Group 4 - CVC/CVV	Group 5 - CVC/VCC/CVV
arm	bag (bug)*	bat (boot, beet, boat)	can	ant
bee	cat (kite)	bed (bird)	chin	ax
car	cup (cap)	bus	jam	bug (bag)
egg	duck	cap (cup)	jet	judge
hoe	fish	lock (lake)	lamb	ring
jar	ham	pan (pen, pin)	leg (log)	
pie	hat	pen (pan, pin)	match	cone (can, cane)
saw	log (leg)	pig	pot	knife
tie	map	ship (sheep)	thumb	safe
toe	moth (mouth)	sock (sack)	web	vase
	net			wave
bow	pin (pan, pen)	bone (barn)	phone (fawn)	whale (wheel)
boy	sack (sock)	cane (can, cone)	rake	
cow	sun	coke (cake)	rope	beet (bat, boat, boot)
owl	top (tape)	dime		fawn (phone)
tea		face	beach	heel
toy	bike (book)	kite (cat)	boot (bat, boat, beet)	juice
	cake (coke)	lake (lock)	cheese	light
ice	hose	rose	foot (feet)	mouse (moose)
key	nose		hook	tree
shoe	tape (top)	boat (bat, boot, beet)	moose (mouse)	wheel (whale)
		book (bike)	rain	
ear	ball (bowl, bell)	dog	soup (soap)	chair
eye	bowl (ball, bell)	goose	sheep (ship)	door (deer)
	feet (foot)	house	tooth (teeth)	nurse
	food	meat		pear
	goat	moon	bear	star
	leaf	mouth (moth)	deer	tire
	peach	seal	fire	
	soap (soup)		hair	apple
	teeth (tooth)	barn (bone)		comb
		farm		
	bird (bed)	shirt		
	girl			
		bell (ball, bowl)		
	shell	doll		

APPENDIX

F

Related DuBard Association Method® Materials

The DuBard Association Method® has been implemented for decades utilizing teacher-made materials and other materials which professionals have adapted for this phonetic, multisensory instruction. In recent years, for ease of implementation, the following materials have been developed:

1. Manuscript Cards (4x6, 282 phoneme, drop drill, noun vocabulary cards)
2. Noun Picture Cards (4x6, 191 color picture cards)
3. Noun Picture Cards (8 1/2 x 11, 191 color picture cards--enlarged for large group instruction)
4. Noun Picture Vocabulary Stickers
5. Drop Drill Flipbook
6. Drop Drill Practice Book

The materials listed above, and this textbook, are available through:

Barnes and Noble Bookstore
The University of Southern Mississippi
118 College Drive #5062
Hattiesburg, MS 39406-0001
Phone: 601.266.4381
Fax: 601.266.4355
www.usm.edu/bookstore

Items 1 - 3 above and this textbook are available through:

Pro-Ed, Inc.
8700 Shoal Creek Boulevard
Austin, TX 78757-6897
Phone: 1.800.897.3202
Fax: 1.800.397.7633
E-mail: info@proedinc
www.proedinc.com

DuBard Association Method® IEP and General Objectives (Curriculum) checklists are available to schools through:

Language Learning Aptitudes, Inc.
1102 Sandalwood Drive
Hattiesburg, MS 39402

or contact

DuBard School for Language Disorders
The University of Southern Mississippi
118 College Dr. #5215
Hattiesburg, MS 39406-0001
Phone 601.266.5223
Email dubard@usm.edu
www.usm.edu/dubard
Additional materials are in the planning stages.

For maximum effectiveness, it is recommended that the materials cited be used by professionals who have had intensive preparation in the DuBard Association Method® or by parents who are utilizing them for home reinforcement activities under the guidance of a professional.

It is recommended that professionals receive intensive preparation prior to implementing the DuBard Association Method®. See the website of the International Multisensory Structured Language Education Council (IMSLEC) www.imslec.org for recommended national professional development standards at the teaching and therapy levels.

A P P E N D I X

G

Professionals and Sites Using the DuBard Association Method®

A registry of professionals and sites using the DuBard Association Method® is maintained at the DuBard School for Language Disorders at The University of Southern Mississippi. For information, contact:

DuBard School for Language Disorders
The University of Southern Mississippi
118 College Dr. #5215
Hattiesburg, MS 39406-0001
Phone 601.266.5223
Fax 601.266.6763
Email dubard@usm.edu
www.usm.edu/dubard

Bibliography

Aaron, P., Joshi, M. and Quatroche, D. 2008. *Becoming a professional reading teacher.* Baltimore: Paul H. Brookes Publishing Co, Inc.

Albritton, E. 1985. *Performance of three groups of subjects on the Hiskey-Nebraska Test of Learning Aptitude.* (Unpublished study), University of Arkansas, Little Rock.

Alloway, T.P. 2009. Working memory, but not IQ, predicts subsequent learning in children with learning difficulties. *European Journal of Psychological Assessment* 25(2):92–98.

Alloway, T.P. and Alloway, R.C. 2010. Investigating the predictive roles of working memory and IQ in academic attainment. *Journal of Experimental Child Psychology* 106:20-29.

Alloway, T.P., Gathercole, S.E., Adams, A.M., Willis, C., Eaglen, R. and Lamont, E. 2005. Working memory and other cognitive skills as predictors of progress toward early learning goals at school entry. *British Journal of Developmental Psychology* 23:417-426.

Alloway, T.P., Gathercole, S.E., Kirkwood, H. and Elliott, J. 2009. The Working Memory Rating Scale: A classroom-based behavioral assessment of working memory. *Learning and Individual Differences* 19:242-245.

American Academy of Ophthalmology. 1992. *Learning disabilities, dyslexia, and vision.* A Policy Statement of the American Academy of Pediatrics, American Association for Pediatric Ophthalmology and Strabismus, and American Academy of Ophthalmology. San Francisco, CA.

________. 2009. *Learning disabilities, dyslexia, and vision.* A Joint Statement of the American Academy of Pediatrics, American Academy of Ophthalmology, American Association for Pediatric Ophthalmology and Strabismus, and American Association of Certified Orthoptists. San Francisco, CA. Retrieved July 21, 2011 from http://www.aao.org/about/policy/upload/Learning-Disabilities-Dyslexia-Vision-2009.pdf

American Speech-Language-Hearing Association. 1992 (February). *Issues in central auditory processing disorders: A report from the ASHA ad hoc committee on central auditory processing.* Symposium on Central Auditory Processing Disorders, Orlando, FL.

________. 1993. *Definitions of communication disorders and variations* [Relevant Paper]. Available from www.asha.org/policy.

________. Task Force on Central Auditory Processing Consensus Development. 1996. Central auditory processing: Current status of research and implications for clinical practice. *American Journal of Audiology* 5:41-52.

________. 1997-2011. *What are some signs or symptoms of a language-based learning disability?* Retrieved April 17, 2008 from http://www.asha.org/public/speech/disorders/language-based-learning-disabilities.htm

________. 1997-2011. *How does your child hear and talk?* Retrieved July 17, 2011 from http://www.asha.org/public/speech/development/chart.htm

________. 1997-2011. *Incidence and prevalence of communication disorders and hearing loss in children – 2008 ed.* Retrieved September 29, 2011 from http://www.asha.org/research/reports/children

________. 1997-2011. *Speech-language pathologists: Language experts and literacy resource.* Retrieved November 12, 2011 from http://www.asha.org/publications/literacy

________. 2005. *(Central) auditory processing disorders* [Technical Report]. Available from www.asha.org/policy

________. 2007. *Childhood apraxia of speech* [Technical report]. Available from www.asha.org/policy

Aram, D. and Hall, N.E. 1989. Longitudinal follow-up of children with preschool communication disorders: Treatment implications. *Journal of Communication Disorders* 13:159-170.

Armbruster, B.B., Lehr, F., and Osborn, J. 2001. *Put reading first: The research building blocks for teaching children to read kindergarten through grade three.* Jessup, MD: National Institute for Literacy.

Aten, J., and Davis, J. 1968. Disturbances in the perception of auditory sequence in children with minimal cerebral dysfunction. *Journal of Speech and Hearing Research* 11:236–45.

Attneave, F. 1959. *Applications of information theory to psychology.* New York: Henry Holt.

Baddeley, A. 2000. The episodic buffer: A new component of working memory? *Trends in Cognitive Sciences* 4:417-423.

Baddeley, A., Gathercole, S., and Papagno, C. 1998. The phonological loop as a language learning device. *Psychological Review* 105:158-173.

Baddeley A.D., and Hitch G. 1974. Working memory. In G. Bower Ed., *The Psychology of Learning and Motivation* 8:47–90.

Ballard, K.J., Granier, J.P. and Robin, D.A. 2000. Understanding the nature of apraxia of speech: Theory, analysis, and treatment. *Aphasiology* 14(10):969-995.

Bannatyne, A. 1973. *Reading: An auditory-vocal process.* San Rafael, CA: Academic Therapy Publications.

Bar, M. 2007. The proactive brain: using analogies and associations to generate predictions. *Trends in Cognitive Sciences* 11(7):280-289.

Barry, H. 1961. *The young aphasic child.* Washington, DC: The A. G. Bell Association for the Deaf.

Bashir, A. S. and Scavuzzo, A. 1992. Children with language disorders: Natural history and academic success. *Journal of Learning Disabilities* 25:53-65.

Battle, D.E. 2002. Language development and disorders in culturally and linguistically diverse children. In D. K. Bernstein and E. Tiegerman-Farber, Eds. *Language and communication disorders in children, 5th ed.* Boston: Allyn and Bacon.

Beery, K. 1997. *Test of Visual-Motor Integration (VMI).* Parsippany, NJ: Modern Curriculum Press.

Beery, K.E., Buktenica, N.A., and Beery, N.A. 2010. *Beery-Buktenica Developmental Test of Visual-Motor Integration – 6th ed. (Beery VMI).* Austin, TX: Pro-Ed, Inc.

Bellis, T.J. 2003. *Assessment and management of central auditory processing disorders in the educational setting: From science to practice, 2nd ed.* Delmar, NY: Thomson Learning.

________. 1997-2011. *Auditory processing disorders (APD) in children.* ASHA. Retrieved August 25, 2011 from http://www.asha.org/public/hearing/Understanding-Auditory-Processing-Disorders-in-Children

________. 1997-2011. *Understanding auditory processing disorders in children.* ASHA. Retrieved February 17, 2010 from http://www.asha.org/public/hearing/disorders/understand-apd-child.htm

Bender, R. 1968. Teaching the non-verbal child. *Volta Review* 70(7):537–48.

Bernstein, D.K., and Tiegerman-Farber, E. (Eds.). 2002. *Language and communication disorders in children, 5th ed.* Boston: Allyn and Bacon.

Berry, V. 2000. *Central auditory processing: Identification and management.* Hattiesburg, Mississippi: 3rd Annual DuBard Symposium: Dyslexia and Related Disorders.

Birsh, J.R. (Ed.). 2002. *Multisensory teaching of basic language skills.* Baltimore, MD: Paul H. Brookes Publishing Co., Inc.

________. 2011. *Multisensory teaching of basic language skills, 3rd ed.* Baltimore, MD: Paul H. Brookes Publishing Co., Inc.

blend. 2011. In *Merriam-Webster.com.* Retrieved November 5, 2011, from http://www.merriamwebster.com/dictionary/blend

Bloodstein, O. 1979. *Speech pathology: An introduction.* Boston: Houghton Mifflin Co.

Bockmiller, P., and Coley, J. 1981. A survey of methods, materials, and teacher preparation among teachers of reading to the hearing impaired. *Reading Teacher* 34:526–29.

Boudreau, D. and Costanza-Smith, A. 2011. Assessment and treatment of working memory deficits in school-age children: The role of the speech-language pathologist. *Language, Speech and Hearing Services in the Schools* 42:152-166.

Bowerman, M. 1988. Discussion summary-development of concepts underlying language. In R. Schiefel-Busch and L. Lloyd, Eds., *Language perceptives-acquisition, retardation and intervention*. Austin, TX: Pro-Ed.

Bracken, B.A. and McCallum, R.S. 2005. *Universal Nonverbal Intelligence Test (UNIT)*. Austin, TX: Pro-Ed, Inc.

Bradley, D.P. 1989. A systematic multiphonemic approach to articulation treatment. In P.W. Newman, G.M. Low, N.A. Creaghead, and W.A. Secord, Eds., *Assessment and remediation of articulatory and phonological disorders*, 305–22. Columbus, OH: Charles E. Merrill Publishing Co.

Brown, L., Sherbenon, R. and Johnsen, S. 1997. *Test of Nonverbal Intelligence-3rd ed. (TONI-3)*. Austin: Pro-Ed.

________. 2010. *Test of Nonverbal Intelligence-4th ed. (TONI-4)*. Austin: Pro-Ed.

Brown, V., Hammill, D., and Wiederholt, J. 1986. *Test of Reading Comprehension (TORC)*. Austin: Pro-Ed.

Brown, V.L., Wiederholt, J.L. and Hammill, D.D. 2009. *Test of Reading Comprehension-4th ed. (TORC-4)*. Austin: Pro-Ed.

Calvert, D. 1986. *Descriptive phonetics*. New York: Thieme-Stratton.

Calvert, D., and Silverman, R. 1983. *Speech and deafness*. Washington, DC: The A. G. Bell Association for the Deaf.

Carrow, E. 1973. *Test of Auditory Comprehension of Language*. Austin, TX: Learning Concepts.

Carrow-Woolfolk, E. 1985. *Test of Auditory Comprehension of Language-Revised (TACL-R)*. Allen, TX: DLM Teaching Resources.

________. 1999. *Test of Auditory Comprehension of Language-3rd ed. (TACL-3)*. Austin, TX: Pro-Ed.

________. 1995. *Oral and Written Language Scales (OWLS)*. Circle Pines, MN: American Guidance Service, Inc.

Carrow-Woolfolk, E., and Lynch, J.I. 1982. *An integrative approach to language disorders in children*. New York: Grune and Stratton.

Carrow-Woolfolk, E., and Williams, K.T. 2011. *Oral and Written Language Scales, 2nd ed. (OWLS-II)*. Torrance, CA: Western Psychological Services.

Catts, H.W. 1989. Defining dyslexia as a developmental language disorder. *Annals of Dyslexia* 39:50–64.

________. 1996. Defining dyslexia as a developmental language disorder: An expanded view. *Topics in Language Disorders* 16(2):14–29.

________. 1997. Early identification of language-based reading disabilities. *Language, Speech, and Hearing Services in Schools* 28:86–89.

Chapel Hill Training Outreach Project, Inc. 2003. *Learning Accomplishment Profile - 3rd ed. (LAP-3)*. Lewisville, NC: Kaplan Early Learning Company.

Chermak, G. 1992. *Central auditory processing disorders (CAPD): Key concepts and clinical consideration*. Paper presented at American Speech-Language-Hearing Association Conference on Central Auditory Processing Disorders, Orlando.

Chermak, G.D., Hall, J.W., III, Musiek, F.E. 1999. Differential diagnosis and management of central auditory processing disorder and attention deficit hyperactivity disorder. *Journal of the American Academy of Audiology* 10(6):289–303.

Colarusso, R. and Hammill, D. 1996. *Motor-Free Visual Perception Test – Revised (MVPT-R)*. Novato, CA: Academic Therapy Publications.

________. 2002. *Motor-Free Visual Perception Test – 3rd ed. (MVPT-3)*. Austin, TX: Pro-Ed, Inc.

Cole, P., and Wood, M.L. 1978. Differential diagnosis. In F.N. Martin, Ed., *Pediatric audiology*, 265–305. Englewood Cliffs, NJ: Prentice-Hall, Inc.

Coley, J., and Bockmiller, P. 1980. Teaching reading to the deaf: An examination of teacher preparedness and practices. *American Annals of the Deaf* 125:909–915.

Cornett, D. 2010. *Effective intervention across disabilities: Use of phonetic, multisensory language instruction*. Poster session presented at the American Speech-Language-Hearing Association Convention, Philadelphia.

Conway, C.M., Baurnschmidt, A., Huang, S. and Pisoni, D.B. 2010. Implicit statistical learning in language processing: Word predictability is the key. *Cognition* 114(3):356–371.

Costello, J.M. 1984. *Speech disorders in children*. San Diego, CA: College-Hill Press.

Cox, A.R. 1984. *Foundations for literacy: Structures and techniques for multisensory teaching of basic written English language skills (Rev. ed.)*. Cambridge, MA: EPS/School Specialty, Inc.

Cullum, A. 1978. *The geranium on the window sill just died, but teacher, you went right on*. New York: Quist.

Curtis, J.F. 1956. Disorders of articulation. In W. Johnson, S.F. Brown, J.F. Curtis, C.W. Edney, and J. Keaster, Eds., *Speech handicapped school children*, Rev. ed., 92–153. New York: Harper and Brothers.

Darley, F., Aronson, A.E., and Brown, J.R. 1975. *Motor speech disorders*. Philadelphia: W. B. Saunders.

Davis, H. 1952. Information theory: 3. Applications of information theory to hearing research. *Journal of Speech and Hearing Disorders* 17:189–97.

Davis, H., and Silverman, S.R. (Eds.). 1970. *Hearing and deafness*. New York: Holt, Rinehart, and Winston.

DeBonis, D.A. and Moncrieff, D. 2008. Auditory processing disorders: An update for speech-language pathologists. *American Journal of Speech-Language Pathology* 17:4-18.

DeHirsch, K. 1967. Differential diagnosis between aphasic and schizophrenic language in children. *Journal of Speech and Hearing Disorders* 32(2):3–9.

DeRenzi, E., Pieczuro, A., and Vignolo, L.A. 1966. Oral apraxia and aphasia. *Cortex* 2:50–73.

Deuel RK. 1995. Developmental dysgraphia and motor-skills disorders. *Journal of Child Neurology* 10:S6–S8.

DuBard, E. 1962. A deaf child who did not learn. *Volta Review*. Washington DC: The A.G. Bell Association for the Deaf.

_________. 1967. *Analysis of the Association Method for teaching aphasic children in relation to information theory and motor theory of speech perception*. (Unpublished Ph.D. dissertation). University of Southern Mississippi, Hattiesburg.

_________. 1983. *Teaching aphasics and other language-deficient children. 3rd ed.* Jackson, MS: University Press of Mississippi.

DuBard, N.E. and Martin, M.K. 2000. *Teaching language-deficient children*. Cambridge, MA: Educators Publishing Service, Inc.

Dunn, L.M., and Dunn, L.M. 1981. *Peabody Picture Vocabulary Test-Revised*. Circle Pines, MN: American Guidance Service.

Early, G.H. 1973. The case for cursive writing. *Academic Therapy* 9(1):105–8.

Early, G.H., Nelson, P.A., Kleber, D.J., Tregoob, M., Huffman, E. and Cass, C. 1976. Cursive handwriting, reading, and spelling achievement. *Academic Therapy* 12(1):67-74.

Ehrler, D.J. and McGhee, R.L. 2008. *Primary Test of Nonverbal Intelligence (P-TONI)*. Austin, TX: Pro-Ed, Inc.

Eisenson, J. 1968. Developmental aphasia: A speculative view with therapeutic implications. *Journal of Speech and Hearing Disorders* 33(1):3–13.

_________. 1972. *Aphasia in children*. New York: Harper and Row.

_________. 1984. *Aphasia and related disorders in children. 2nd ed.* New York: Harper and Row.

Eisenson, J., and Ogilvie, M. 1977. *Speech correction in the schools. 4th ed.* New York: Macmillan.

Elliot, R.N., Powers, A.R., and Funderburg, R.S. 1988. Learning disabled hearing impaired students: Teacher survey. *Volta Review* 90:277-278.

Ellis Weismer, S. and Hesketh, L.J. 1996. Lexical learning by children with specific language impairment: Effects of linguistic input presented at varying speaking rates. *Journal of Speech and Hearing Research* 39:177-190.

Fadiga, L., Craighero, L., Buccino, G., and Rizzolatti, G. 2002. Speech listening specifically modulates the excitability of tongue muscles: a TMS study. *European Journal of Neuroscience* 15(2):399-402.

Ferre, J. 2007, August 14. Understanding intervention for (C)APD: As easy as A-B-C. *The ASHA Leader.*

Fey, M.E. 1999. Speech-language pathology and the early identification and prevention of reading disabilities. *Perspectives* 25(1):13–17.

Fitzgerald, E. 1963. *Straight language for the deaf.* Washington, DC: Volta Bureau.

Fletcher, H. 1953. *Speech and hearing in communication*. New York: D. Van Nostrand Company.

Floel, A., Ellger, T., Bretenstein, C., Knecht, S. 2003. Language perception activates the hand motor cortex: implications for motor theories of speech perception. *European Journal of Neuroscience* 18:704-708.

Franke, K. 1948. The deaf in post-war Germany. *Volta Review*, June issue.

Friel-Patti, S. 1999. Clinical decision-making in the assessment and intervention of central auditory processing disorders. *Language, Speech, and Hearing Services in Schools* 30:345-352.

Fudala, J.B. 2000. *Arizona Articulation Proficiency Scale. 3rd ed.* Los Angeles: Western Psychological Services.

Fudala, J.B., and Reynolds, W.M. 1989. *Arizona Articulation Proficiency Scale. 2nd ed.* Los Angeles: Western Psychological Services.

_________. 1994. *Arizona Articulation Proficiency Scale. 3rd ed. (AAPS-3).* Los Angeles: Western Psychological Services.

Gallantuci, B., Fowler, C.A., and Turvey, M.T. 2006. The motor theory of speech perception reviewed. *Psychonomic Bulletin & Review* 13:361-377.

Gallaudet Research Institute. 1996. *Stanford Achievement Test, 9th ed., Form S, Norms Booklet for Deaf and Hard-of-Hearing Students.* (Including Conversions of Raw Score to Scaled Score & Grade Equivalent and Age-based Percentile Ranks for Deaf and Hard-of-Hearing Students.) Washington, DC: Gallaudet University.

Gardner, M. 1996. *Test of Auditory Perceptual Skills– Revised (TAPS-R).* Hydesville, CA: Psychological and Educational Publications, Inc.

Geers, A., Tobey, E., Moog, J., and Brenner, C. 2008. Long-term outcomes of cochlear implantation in the preschool years: From elementary grades to high school. *International Journal of Audiology* 47(Suppl. 2):S21-S30.

Geers, A.E. and Lane, H.S. 1984. *Central Institute for the Deaf Preschool Performance Scale (CID-PPS).* Wood Dale, IL: Stoelting Co.

Gillam, R.B. 1997. Putting memory to work in language intervention: Implications for practitioners. *Topics in Language Disorders* 18:72-79.

Gillingham, A. and Stillman, B.W. 1997. *The Gillingham manual.* Cambridge, MA: EPS/School Specialty, Inc.

Gray, B., and Ryan, B. 1973. *A language program for the non-language child.* Champaign, IL: Research Press.

Griffiths, P. 1972. *Developmental aphasia: An introduction.* London: Invalid Children Aid Association.

Guardino, C.A.2008. Identification and placement for deaf students with multiple disabilities: Choosing the path less followed. *American Annals of the Deaf* 153(1):55-64.

Hall, P.K., Jordan, L.S. and Robin, D.A. 1993. *Developmental apraxia of speech: Theory and clinical practice.* Austin, TX: Pro-Ed, Inc.

Hammermeister, F.K., and Israelite, N.K. 1983. Reading instruction for the hearing impaired: An integrated language arts approach. *Volta Review* 85(3):136–148.

Hammill, D.D., and Larsen, S.C. 1978. The effectiveness of psycholinguistic training: A reaffirmation of position. *Exceptional Child* 44:402–17.

________. 2009. *Test of Written Language-4 (TOWL-4).* Austin, TX: Pro-Ed, Inc.

Hammill, D.D., Mather, N. and Roberts, R. 2001. *Illinois Test of Psycholinguistic Abilities-3 (ITPA-3).* Austin, TX: Pro-Ed, Inc.

Hammill, J.R. (Ed.). 1988. *Teaching aphasic children: The instructional methods of Barry and McGinnis.* Austin, TX: Pro-Ed, Inc.

Hardy, W.G. 1965. On language disorders in young children: A reorganization of thinking. *Journal of Speech and Hearing Disorders* 30(1):16.

Harris, K., Bastian, J., and Liberman, A.M. 1961. Mimicry and the perception of a phonemic contrast indicated by silent interval: Electromyographic and acoustic measures. *Journal of Acoustic Society of America* 33:842.

Hartfield, F.M. 1981. Analysis and remediation of aphasia in the USSR: The contribution of A.R. Luria. *Journal of Speech and Hearing Disorders* 46:338–47.

Head, H. 1963. *Aphasia and kindred disorders of speech*, II. New York: Hafner Publishing Company.

Hegde, M.N. and Maul, C.A. 2006. *Language disorders in children: An evidence-based approach to assessment and treatment.* Boston: Pearson Education, Inc.

Henderson, E.H., Coulter, B., Templeton, S., Thomas, J.A.M. 1987a. *Spelling, B.* Boston: Houghton Mifflin Company.

________. 1987b. *Spelling, C.* Boston: Houghton Mifflin Company.

Heyman, E. 1977. Cursive writing begins with chalk. *Teaching Exceptional Children* 4:106–9.

Hier, D.C., Lemay, M., Rosenberger, P.B., and Perlo, V.P. 1978. Developmental dyslexia: Evidence for a subgroup of reversal of cerebral asymmetry. *Archives of Neurology* 35:90-92.

Hirsh, I.J. 1967. Information processing in input channels for speech and language: The significance of serial order of stimuli. In C.H. Millikan and F. L. Darley, Eds., *Brain mechanisms underlying speech and language.* New York: Grune and Stratton.

Hirsh, I.J., and Fraisse, P. 1964–65. *Central Institute for the Deaf periodic progress reports.* St. Louis, MO: Central Institute for the Deaf.

Hiskey, M.S. 1966. *Hiskey-Nebraska Test of Learning Aptitude.* Lincoln, NE: Union College Press.

Hockett, C. 1960. The origin of speech. *Scientific American* 203:88–95.

Hoyt, C.S. 1999. Visual training and reading. *American Orthoptic Journal* 49:23–25.

Hurst, C.G., Jr., Black, J.W., and Singh, S. 1966. Self-administered procedures in changing pronunciation dialect. *Journal of Speech and Hearing Research* 9(2):248–52.

Individuals with Disabilities Education Act. 2004. U.S. Department of Education. Retrieved July 18, 2011 from http://IDEA.ed.gov

International Dyslexia Association. 2002. *Definition of dyslexia.* Retrieved October 30, 2011 from http://www.interdys.org/FAQ.htm

International Multisensory Structured Language Education Council (IMSLEC). 1995. *Content and Principles of Instruction.* www.imslec.org

Irwin, J., and Marge, M. 1972. *Principles of childhood language disabilities.* New York: Appleton-Century, Crofts.

Jaffe, M.B. 1984. *Neurological impairment of speech production: Assessment and treatment.* In J. Costello, Ed., Speech disorders in children. San Diego: College-Hill Press.

Jerger, J. and Musiek, F. 2002. On the diagnosis of auditory processing disorder: A reply to "Clinical and research concerns regarding Jerger & Musiek (2000) APD recommendations. *Audiology Today* 14(2):19-21.

Johnson, D., and Myklebust, H. 1967. *Learning disabilities: Educational principles and practices.* New York: Grune Stratton.

Johnson, W., Brown, S.F., Curtis, J.F., Edney, C.W., and Keaster, J., (Eds.). 1956. *Speech handicapped school children. Rev. ed.* New York: Harper and Brothers.

Johnston, K.L. 1980. Auditory processing disorders in aphasic adults: Diagnosis and treatment. In P. Levinson and C. Sloan, Eds., *Auditory processing and language*, 163–88. New York: Grune and Stratton.

Joshi, R.M., Binks, E., Graham, L., Ocker-Dean, E., Smith, D.L., and Boulware-Gooden, R. 2009. Do textbooks used in university reading education courses conform to the instructional recommendations of the National Reading Panel? *Journal of Learning Disabilities* 42:458.

Just, M. and Carpenter, P. 1992. A capacity theory of comprehension: Individual differences in working memory. *Psychological Review* 99:122-149.

Kamhi, A.G. 1998. Trying to make sense of developmental language disorders. *Language, Speech and Hearing Services in the Schools* 29:35-44.

Katz, J. 1983. Phonemic synthesis, perspectives on central auditory processing, central auditory processing disorders. In E. Lasky and J. Katz, Eds., *Central auditory processing disorders: Problems of speech, language and learning*, 269–95. Austin, TX: Pro-Ed.

________. (Ed.). 1985. *Management of auditory problems: Handbook of clinical audiology. 3rd ed.* New York: Thieme-Stratton.

Katz, J., Johnson, C.D., Tillery, K.L., Bradham, T., Brandner, S., Delagrange, T.N., Ferre, J.M., King, J.M., Kossover-Wechter, D., Lucker, J.R., Medwetsky, L., Saul, R.S., Rosenberg, G.G., and Stecker, N.A. 2002. *Clinical and Research Concerns - Regarding Jerger & Musiek (2000) APD Recommendations.* Retrieved July 26, 2011 from http://www.audiologyonline.com/articles/article_detail.asp?article_id=341

Katz, J., Stecker, N., and Henderson, D. 1992. *Central auditory disorders.* Baltimore, MD: Mosby Yearbook.

Kaufman, N. 2008. *Childhood apraxia of speech.* Retrieved November 17, 2011 from http://kidspeech.com/resources/printable-information.html

Kessler, J.W. 1966. *Psychopathology of childhood.* Englewood Cliffs, NJ: Prentice-Hall, Inc.

King, C., and Quigley, S.P. 1985. *Reading and deafness.* San Diego, CA: College-Hill Press.

Kinsey, A.C., Pomeroy, W.B., Martin, C.E., and Gebhard, P.H. 1953. *Sexual behavior in the human female.* Philadelphia: W.B. Saunders.

Kirby, A.M. 1965. *A manual for use with the Association Method.* Randolph, MA: Boston School for the Deaf.

Kirk, S.A., McCarthy, J.J., and Kirk, W.D. 1968. *Illinois Test of Psycholinguistic Abilities.* Urbana: Illinois Press.

Koch, D.B., McGee, T.J., Bradlow, A.R. and Kraus, N. 1999. Acoustic-phonetic approach toward understanding neural processes and speech perception. *Journal of the American Academy of Audiology* 10(6):304–318.

Lahey, M. 1990. Who shall be called language disordered? Some reflections and one perspective. *Journal of Speech and Hearing Disorders* 55:612-620.

Lake, O.D. 1980. Syntax and sequential memory in hearing impaired children. In H. Reynolds and C. Williams, Eds., *Proceedings of the Gallaudet conference on reading in relation to deafness*, 193–212. Washington, DC: Gallaudet College.

Lane, H. 1965. The motor theory of speech perception: A critical review. *Psychological Review* 82(4):275–309.

Lane, H., and Baker, D. 1974. Reading achievement of the deaf: Another look. *Volta Review* 76:489–99.

Larsen, S. and Hammill, D. 1994. *Test of Written Spelling-3rd ed. (TWS-3).* Austin: Pro-Ed.

Larsen, S., Hammill, D., and Moats, L. 1999. *Test of Written Spelling-4th ed. (TWS-4).* Austin: Pro-Ed.

LaSasso, C. 1978. National survey of materials and procedures used to teach reading to hearing impaired children. *American Annals of the Deaf* 123:22–30.

Lasky, E., and Katz, J. 1983. Perceptives on central auditory processing. In E. Lasky and J. Katz, Eds., *Central auditory processing disorders: problems in speech, language and learning,* 3–9. Austin, TX: Pro-Ed.

Laurent Clerc National Deaf Education Center Gallaudet University. 1995-2011. *Deaf students with disabilities.* Retrieved July 17, 2011 from http://www.gallaudet.edu/clerc_center/information_and_resources

Leonard, C. M., Eckert, M. A., Given, B. K., Berninger, V. W., and Eden, G. F. 2006. Individual differences in anatomy predict reading and oral language deficits. *Brain* 129(12):3329-3342.

Levinson, P., and Sloan, C., (Eds.). 1980. *Auditory processing and language.* New York: Grune and Stratton.

Liberman, A.M. 1957. Some results of research on speech perception. *Journal of Acoustical Society of America* 80:117–23.

________. 1961. The discrimination of relative onset time of the components of certain speech and non-speech patterns. *Journal of Experimental Psychology* 61:379–88.

________. 1962. A motor theory of speech perception. *Proceedings of the speech communications seminar.* Stockholm, Sweden: Royal Institute of Technology.

Liberman, A.M., Cooper, F.S., Shankweiler, D.P. and Studdert-Kennedy, M. 1967. Perception of the speech code. *Psychological Review* 74:431–61.

Liberman, A.M., Delattre, P., and Cooper, F.S. 1952. The role of selected stimulus variables in the perception of the unvoiced stop consonants. *American Journal of Psychology* 65:497–516.

Liberman, A.M., Harris, K.S., Eimas, P., Lisker, L., and Bastian, J. 1961. An effect of learning on speech perception: The discrimination of durations of silence with and without phonemic significance. *Language and Speech* 4:175–95.

Liberman, A.M., and Mattingly, I.G. 1985. The motor theory of speech perception revised. *Cognition* 21:1-36.

Liberman, I.Y., Shankweiler, D., Liberman, A.M., Fowler, C., and Fischer, F.S. 1977. Phonetic segmentation and recoding in the beginning reader. In A.S. Reber and D. Scarborough, Eds. *Reading theory and practice.* Hillsdale, NJ: Erlbaum Associates.

Lichenstein, E. 1983. *The relationship between reading processes and English skills of deaf students.* Rochester, NY: National Technical Institute for the Deaf.

________. 1984. Deaf working memory processes and English language skills. In D. Martin, Ed., *International symposium on cognitive education and deafness: Working papers* 2, 331–60. Washington DC: Gallaudet College.

Lindamood, C. and Lindamood, P. 1979. *Lindamood Auditory Conceptualization Test-Revised.* Austin: Pro-Ed.

Lindamood, P.C. and Lindamood, P. 2004. *Lindamood Auditory Conceptualization Test-3rd ed. (LAC-3).* Austin: Pro-Ed.

Ling, D. 1976. *Speech and the hearing impaired child: Theory and practice.* Washington, DC: The A.G. Bell Association for the Deaf.

Ling, D., and Ling, A. 1978. *Aural habilitation: The foundations of verbal learning in hearing impaired children.* Washington, DC: The A.G. Bell Association for the Deaf.

Lipstreu, B.L., and Johnson, M.K. 1988. Teaching time using the whole clock method. *Teaching Exceptional Children* (Spring):10–12.

Loewe, A. 1979. The historical development of oral education. A paper presented at the *Symposium on Oral Education,* St. Michielsgestel, The Netherlands, November 25-December 1.

Lowe, A.D. and Campbell, R.A. 1965. Temporal discrimination in aphasoid and normal children. *Journal of Speech and Hearing Research* 8:313-314.

Luckner, J.L. and Handley, C.M. 2008. A summary of the reading comprehension research undertaken with students who are deaf or hard of hearing. *American Annals of the Deaf* 153(1):6-36.

Luria, A.R. 1966. *The higher cortical functions of man.* New York: Basic Books.

________. 1970. *Traumatic aphasia: Its syndromes, psychology and treatment.* The Hague: Mouton.

Maas, E., Robin, D.A., Hula, S.N.A., Wulf, G., Ballard, K.J., and Schmidt, R.A. 2008. Principles of motor learning in treatment of motor speech disorders. *American Journal of Speech-Language Pathology* 17:277-298.

Maisog, J.M., Einbinder, E.R., Flowers, D.L., Turkeltaub, P.E., and Eden, G.F. 2008. A meta-analysis of functional neuroimaging studies of dyslexia. *Annals of the New York Academy of Sciences* 1145:237-259.

Marschark, M., Sapere, P., Convertino, C.M., Mayer, C., Wauters, L., and Sarchet, T. 2009. Are deaf students' reading challenges really about reading? *American Annals of the Deaf* 154(4):357-370.

Martin, J.G. 1972. Rhythmic hierarchical versus serial structure in speech and other behavior. *Psychological Review* 79:487–509.

Martin, M.K. 1985. *Comparative studies of the use of cursive vs. manuscript characters in the teaching of young handicapped children.* (Unpublished Ph.D. dissertation). University College, National University of Ireland, Dublin.

________. 1987. A comparative study of the use of cursive versus manuscript characters in teaching profoundly hearing impaired children to recognise sounds and words. *Journal of the British Association of Teachers of the Deaf* 11:173–82.

________. 2005. *Efficacy of an intensive, multisensory therapy model for children challenged with developmental apraxia of speech.* Paper presented at the AcademyHealth Conference, Boston.

________. 2010. *Accessing success through the DuBard Association Method®.* Poster session presented at the Alexander Graham Bell Association for the Deaf and Hard of Hearing Convention, Orlando.

________. 2011. *Intervention for language-based learning differences: Three therapy models.* Paper presented at the International Dyslexia Association Conference, Chicago.

Martin, M.K. and Schraeder, M. 2010. *Efficacy of the DuBard Association Method® for childhood apraxia of speech.* Paper presented at the Childhood Apraxia of Speech Association of North America (CASANA) Convention, Pittsburgh.

Martin, N. and Brownell, R. 2005. *The Test of Auditory Processing Skills (TAPS-3).* East Moline, IL: LinguiSystems, Inc.

Massaro, D.W. and Chen, T.H. 2008. The motor theory of speech perception revisited. *Psychonomic Bulletin and Review* 15:453-457.

McCauley, J. and Fey, M.E. (Eds.). 2006. *Treatment of language disorders in children.* Baltimore: Paul H. Brookes Publishing Co., Inc.

McGinnis, M.A. 1939. *Congenital aphasia.* (Unpublished Master's thesis). Washington University, St. Louis.

________. 1963. *Aphasic children.* Washington, DC: The A.G. Bell Association for the Deaf.

McIntyre, C.S. and Pickering, J.S. (Eds.). 1995. *Clinical studies of multisensory structured language education.* Salem, OR: International Multisensory Structured Language Education Council (IMSLEC).

McIntyre, C.S. and Pickering, J.S. 2011 (November). *Language learning intervention research: Early childhood-grade 7.* Paper presented at the meeting of The International Dyslexia Association, Chicago.

McQueen, P.L. 1963. *McQueen integrated phonics. (Open Court Basic Readers).* Chicago: R.R. Donnelley and Sons and Company.

McReynolds, L.V. 1966. Operant conditioning for investigating speech sound discrimination in aphasic children. *Journal of Speech and Hearing Research* 9:519–28.

Mecham, M., Berko, M., Berko, F., and Palmer, M., (Eds.). 1966. *Appraisal of speech and hearing: Communication training in childhood brain damage.* Springfield IL: Charles C. Thomas.

Medwetsky, L. 2011. Spoken language processing model: Bridging auditory and language processing to guide assessment and intervention. *Language, Speech and Hearing Services in the Schools* 42:286-296.

Merzenich, M.M., Jenkins, W.M., Johnston, P., Schreiner, C., Miller, S.L., Tallal, P. 1996. Temporal processing deficits of language-learning impaired children ameliorated by training. *Science* 271 (5245):77–81.

Miller, G.A. 1951. *Language and communication.* New York: McGraw-Hill.

Moats, L.C. 1997. California reading initiative. *Perspectives* 23(1):1, 4–5.

Moats, L.C. 1999. *Teaching reading is rocket science.* Washington, DC: American Federation of Teachers.

Moats, L.C. 2000. *Speech to print.* Baltimore: Paul H. Brookes Publishing Co.

Monroe, M. 1932. *Children who cannot read.* Chicago: University of Chicago Press.

Montgomery, J.W. 2002. Understanding the language difficulties of children with specific language impairments: Does verbal working memory matter? *American Journal of Speech-Language Pathology* 11:77-91.

Moores, D.F. 1987. A new perspective on reading abilities of deaf students. *Education Forum* (Fall).

Mosheim, J. 2009. From sounds to symbols. *ADVANCE for Speech-Language Pathologists* 19(14):6.

Muma. J. 1978. *Language handbook.* Englewood Cliffs, NJ: Prentice-Hall.

Myklebust, H.R. 1954. *Auditory disorders in children.* New York: Grune and Stratton.

________. 1960. *The psychology of deafness.* New York: Grune and Stratton.

Myklebust, H.R., and Johnson, D. 1962. Dyslexia in children. *Exceptional Children* 29(1):14–25.

Nagarajan, S.S., Wang, X., Merzenich, M.M., Schreiner, C.E., Jenkins, W.M., Johnston, P.A., Miller, S.L., Byma, G., and Tallal, P. 1995. Modified speech for training language-based learning disabled children (LLDs). *Society for Neuroscience Abstracts* 21(1):173.

Nance, L. 1946. Differential diagnosis of aphasia in children. *Journal of Speech and Hearing Disorders* 11:219-223.

National Institute of Child Health and Human Development. 2000. *Report of the National Reading Panel. Teaching children to read: An evidence-based assessment of the scientific research literature on reading and its implications for reading instruction* (NIH Publication No. 00-4769). Washington, DC: U.S. Government Printing Office.

National Institutes of Health. 1998. *Reading and reading disabilities.* Retrieved October 1, 2003 from the National Institute of Child Health and Human Development http://www.readbygrade3.com/lyon.htm

National Institute of Neurological Diseases and Stroke (NINDS). 1968. Monograph #11. *Reading Forum.*

Newborg, J. 2004. *Battelle Developmental Inventory-2nd ed. (BDI-2).* Rolling Meadows, IL: Riverside Publishing Co., Inc.

Newborg, J., Stock, J.R. and Wnek, L. 1984. *Battelle Developmental Inventory (BDI).* Chicago: Riverside Publishing Co., Inc.

Newcomer, P.L., and Hammill, D.D. 1988. *Test of Language Development-2-Primary.* Austin, TX: Pro-Ed.

________. 1997. *Test of Language Development–Primary. 3rd ed. (TOLD-P:3).* Austin, TX: Pro-Ed.

________. 2008. *Test of Language Development–Primary. 4th ed. (TOLD-P:4).* Austin, TX: Pro-Ed.

Newman, P., Craighead, N.A., and Secord, W. 1985. *Assessment and remediation of articulatory and phonological disorders.* Columbus, OH: Charles E. Merrill Publishing Co.

Northern, J.L., and Downs, M.P. 1978. *Hearing in children. 2nd ed.* Baltimore: Williams and Wilkins.

________. 2002. *Hearing in children. 5th ed.* Baltimore: Lippincott Williams and Wilkins.

Ogden, P. 1979. *Experience and attitudes of oral deaf adults regarding oralism.* (Unpublished Ph.D. dissertation). University of Illinois, Urbana-Champaign.

Olsen, W.O. 1976. Acoustics and amplification in classrooms for the hearing impaired. In F.H. Bess, Ed., *Childhood deafness: Causation, assessment and management.* Baltimore, MD: Williams and Williams.

Orton Dyslexia Society. 1997. *Informed instruction for reading success: Foundations for teacher preparation.* A Position Paper of The Orton Dyslexia Society. Cambridge, MA.

Orton, J.L. 1966. The Orton-Gillingham approach. In J. Money, Ed., *The disabled reader: Education of the dyslexic child.* Baltimore: The John Hopkins Press.

Orton, S.T. 1937. *Reading, writing and speech problems in children.* New York: W.W. Norton & Co.

________. 1937. Reprint, 1989. *Reading, writing and speech problems in children.* Austin,TX: Pro-Ed.

Paul, R. 2007. *Language disorders from infancy through adolescence: Assessment and intervention.* New York: Elsevier.

Penfield, W., and Roberts, L. 1959. *Speech and brain mechanisms.* Princeton, NJ: Princeton Univ. Press.

Pickering, J.S. 1997. *Sequential English Education (SEE).* Dallas: The June Shelton School and Evaluation Center.

Pollack, B.J. 1997. Council for Exceptional Children. *Educating children who are deaf or hard of hearing: Additional learning problems.* Retrieved July 18, 2011, http://www.cec.sped.org

Poppen, R.J., Stark, J., Eisenson, J., Forrest, T., and Wertheim, G. 1969. Visual sequencing performance of aphasic children. *Journal of Speech and Hearing Disorders* 12(2):288–300.

Power-deFur, L. 2010, August 31. The educational relevance of communication disorders. *The ASHA Leader.*

Powers, A., Funderburg, R., and Elliott, R. 1986. *Learning disabled students: The state of the art.* Alexander G. Bell Association Convention, Chicago.

Preschool Performance Scale. 1984. St. Louis, MO: Central Institute for the Deaf.

Randall's Island Test-Revised. 1969. St. Louis, MO: Central Institute for the Deaf.

Reed, V.A. 2005. *An introduction to children with language disorders.* Boston: Pearson Education, Inc.

Reynolds, C.R. and Kamphaus, R.W. 2003. *Reynolds Intellectual Assessment Scales (RIAS).* Torrance, CA: Western Psychological Services.

Reynolds, G.S. 1968. *A primer of operant conditioning.* Atlanta: Scott Foresman.

Richard, G. 2004, March 30. Redefining auditory processing disorder: A speech-language pathologist's perspective. *The ASHA Leader.*

Richardson, E. and Dibenedetto, B. 1985. *Decoding Skills Test.* Los Angeles: Western Psychological Services.

Robertson, C. and Salter, W. 1997. *Phonological Awareness Test.* East Moline, IL: LinguiSystems, Inc.

________. 2007. *The Phonological Awareness Test-2 (PAT-2).* East Moline, IL: LinguiSystems, Inc.

Roeser, R.J. and Downs, M.P. 1981. *Auditory disorders in school children.* New York: Thieme-Stratton.

________. 2004. *Auditory disorders in school children-The law, identification, remediation 4th ed.* New York: Thieme-Stratton.

Rosenbek, J.C., McNeil, M.R., and Aronson, A.E., (Eds.). 1984. Apraxia of speech. San Diego, CA: College-Hill Press.

Rosenthal, W.S., and Eisenson, J. 1971. *Auditory threshold-duration functions in aphasic subjects. Implications for the interaction of linguistic and auditory processing in aphasics.* Paper presented at the American Speech and Hearing Association Convention, Chicago.

Ross, D. 2006. Mild and unilateral hearing loss in children. *Access Audiology* 5(2). Retrieved July 26, 2011 from http://www.asha.org/aud/articles/hearlosschild.htm

Samar, V.J. 1999. Identifying learning disabilities in the deaf population: The leap from Gibraltar. *NTID Research Bulletin* 4(1):1,3-5.

Sanders, D.A. 1977. *Auditory perception of speech.* Englewood Cliffs, NJ: Prentice-Hall, Inc.

Sanford, A.R. and Zelman, J.G. 1995. *Learning Accomplishment Profile (Rev. ed.).* Chapel Hill, NC: Chapel Hill Training Outreach Project.

Sattler, J. 1988. *Assessment of children. 3rd ed.* San Diego, CA: Jerome M. Sattler, Publisher.

________. 1994. *Assessment of children.* San Diego, CA: Jerome M. Sattler, Publisher.

Schein, J.D., and Delk, T.K. 1974. *The deaf population in the United States.* Silver Springs, MD: National Association of the Deaf.

Seal, N. 1974–75. *Language intervention program* (unpublished). Washington Parish Schools, Franklinton, LA.

Semel, E., Wiig, E.H. and Secord, W.A. 1995. *Clinical Evaluation of Language Fundamentals-3rd ed. (CELF-3).* Orlando: The Psychological Corporation.

________. 2003. *Clinical Evaluation of Language Fundamentals-4th ed. (CELF-4).* San Antonio, TX: Pearson.

________. 2004. *CELF-4 Screening Test.* San Antonio, TX: Pearson.

Serio, M. 1968. Cursive writing: An analytical approach. *Academic Therapy* 4(1):67–70.

Shaywitz, S. 2003. *Overcoming dyslexia.* New York: Vintage Books.

Shaywitz, S.E. and Shaywitz, B.A. 2007. September 04. The neurobiology of reading and dyslexia. *The ASHA Leader.*

________. 2008. Paying attention to reading: The neurobiology of reading and dyslexia. *Development and Psychopathology* 20:1329-1349.

Schmidt, R.A. and Lee, T.D. 2005. *Motor control and learning: A behavioral emphasis, 4th ed.* Champaign, IL: Human Kinetics.

Sheslow, D. and Adams, W. 2008. *Wide Range Assessment of Memory and Learning, 2nd ed. (WRAML-2).* Lutz, FL: PAR, Inc.

Shipley, K.G. and McAfee, J.G. 2004. *Assessment in speech-language pathology.* Clifton Park, NY: Delmar Learning.

Sices, L., Taylor, H.G., Freebairn, L., Hansen, A., Lewis, B. 2007. Relationship between speech-sound disorders and early literacy skills in preschool-age children: Impact of comorbid language impairment. *Journal of Developmental and Behavioral Pediatrics* 28:438-447.

Silverman, S.R. 1961-62. *Lectures at Central Institute for the Deaf,* St. Louis, MO. Typescript.

Skinder-Meredith, A. 2001. Differential diagnosis: Developmental apraxia of speech and phonologic delay. *Augmentative Communication News* 1:5-8.

Slingerland, B.H. 1971. *A multi-sensory approach to language arts for specific language disability children, Book 1.* Cambridge, MA: Educators Publishing Service, Inc.

________. 2008. *The Slingerland multisensory approach: A practical guide for teaching reading, writing, and spelling.* Bellevue, WA: Slingerland® Institute for Literacy.

Sloan, C. 1980a. Auditory processing disorders and language development. In P. Levinson and C. Sloan, Eds., *Auditory processing and language,* 101–115. New York: Grune and Stratton.

________. 1980b. Auditory processing disorders in children: Diagnosis and treatment. In P. Levinson and C. Sloan, Eds., *Auditory processing and language,* 117–133. New York: Grune and Stratton.

________. 1986. *Treating auditory processing difficulties in children.* San Diego, CA: College-Hill Press.

Snow, C.E., Scarborough, H.S. and Burns, M.S. 1999. What speech-language pathologists need to know about early reading. *Topics in Language Disorders*, 20(1):48–58.

Snyder, L.S. 1980. Have we prepared the language disordered child for school? *Topics in Language Disorders* 1:29–45.

Soukop, M. and Feinstein, S. 2007. Identification, assessment, and intervention strategies for deaf and hard of hearing students with learning disabilities. *American Annals of the Deaf* 152(1):56-62.

Spalding, R.B. 1990. *The writing road to reading.* New York: William Morrow & Co.

_______. 2003. *Writing road to reading: The Spalding method for teaching speech, spelling, writing and reading, 5th Rev. ed.,* Mary E. North, Ed. New York: HarperCollins Publishers, Inc.

Spalding, R.B., and Spalding, W.T. 1990. *The writing road to reading: A proven method of phonics for teaching children to read. 2nd ed.* New York: William Morrow and Company.

Spencer, P.E. and Marschark, M. 2010. *Evidence-based practice in educating deaf and hard-of-hearing students.* New York: Oxford University Press, Inc.

Stasio, J.T. 1976. Cursive and manuscript writing. *The Pointer* 1:54–56.

Stedman's Medical Dictionary 28th ed. 2006. New York: Lippincott Williams & Wilkins. Retrieved July 18, 2011 from http://dictionary.webmd.com/terms/differential-diagnosis

Stein, K., and Seligman, C. 1986. *Healing a hearing impaired child with a learning disorder.* Alexander G. Bell Association Convention, Chicago.

Steinberg, D.D. 1982. Overcoming linguistic limitations of hearing-impaired children through teaching written language. *Topics in Language Disorders* 2(3):17–28.

Stone, C.A., Silliman, E.R., Ehren, B.J. and Apel, K. (Eds.). 2004. *Handbook of language and literacy.* New York: The Guilford Press.

Strand, E.A. and Skinder, A. 1999. Treatment of developmental apraxia of speech: Integral stimulation methods. In A. Caruso and E. Strand, Eds., *Clinical management of motor speech disorders in children.* New York: Thieme.

Strand, E.A., Stoeckel, R. and Baas, B. 2006. Treatment of severe childhood apraxia of speech: A treatment efficacy study. *Journal of Medical Speech-Language Pathology* 14(4):297-307.

Sullivan, A. and Perigoe, C.B. 2004. The Association Method for children with hearing loss and special needs. *Volta Review* 104(4):339-348.

Tallal, P. 1980. Auditory processing disorders in children. In P. Levinson and C. Sloan, Eds., *Auditory processing and language,* 81–100. New York: Grune and Stratton.

Tallal, P., and Piercy, M. 1973a. Defects of nonverbal auditory perception in children with developmental aphasia. *Nature* 241:468–69.

_______. 1973b. Developmental aphasia: Impaired rate of nonverbal processing as a function of sensory modality. *Neuropsychologia* 11:389–98.

_______. 1974. Developmental aphasia: Rate of auditory processing and selective impairment of consonant perception. *Neuropsychologia* 12:83–93.

_______. 1975. Developmental aphasia: The perception of brief vowels and extended stop consonants. *Neuropsychologia* 13:69–74.

Tallal, P., Miller S.L., Bedi, G., Byma, G., Jenkins, W.M., Wang, X., Nagarajan, S.S., and Merzenich, M.M. 1995. Training with temporally modified speech results in dramatic improvements in speech perception and language comprehension. *Society for Neuroscience Abstracts* 21(1):173.

Tallal, P., Miller, S.L., Bedi, G., Byma, G., Jenkins, W.M., Wang, X., Nagarajan, S.S., Schreiner, C., Jenkins, W.M., and Merzenich, M.M. 1996. Language comprehension in language-learning impaired children improved with acoustically modified speech. *Science* 271(5245):81–84.

Thorndike, R.L., Hagen, E.P., and Sattler, J.M. 1986. *Stanford-Binet Intelligence Scale: 4th ed.* Chicago: The Riverside Publishing Co.

Tobey, E.A., Cullen, J.K., Gallagher, A.F., and Rampp, D.L. 1976. *Performance of children with auditory processing disorders on a dichotic stop-vowel identification task.* Paper presented at American Speech and Hearing Association Convention, Houston.

Town, C.H. 1967. Congenital aphasia. *Psychological Clinic* 5(6):167.

Travis, L.E., and Rasmus, B. 1931. The speech sound discrimination ability of cases with functional disorders of articulation. *Quarterly Journal of Speech* 17:217–26.

Trezek, B.J., Wang, Y., and Paul, P.V. 2010. *Reading and deafness–Theory, research and practice.* Clifton Park, NY: Delmar, Cengage Learning.

Trigg, K. 1990. *Use of the Association Method with Choctaw Indian children.* Choctaw Indian Reservation, Philadelphia, MS. Typescript.

U.S. Department of Education, National Center for Education Statistics. 2010. *Digest of Education Statistics,* 2009 (NCES 2010-013), Table 50.

Van Riper, C. 1972. *Speech correction principles and methods. 5th ed.* Englewood Cliffs, NJ: Prentice-Hall, Inc.

Van Uden, A. 1968. *A world of language, part I.* St. Michielsgestel, The Netherlands: Institute for the Deaf.

________. 1969. Johann Vatter, a German teacher of the deaf. *The Teacher of the Deaf.*

________. 1982. *Seminar in evaluating dyspraxic children* conducted at School for Children with Language Disorders, University of Southern Mississippi, Hattiesburg.

Velleman, S.L. 2003. *Childhood apraxia of speech resource guide.* Clifton Park, NY: Delmar Learning.

Vickery, K.S., Martin, M.K., Farrell, M. and Peterson, K. 2011. *Teaching the teachers: Effective models for colleges and universities.* Paper presented at the International Dyslexia Association Conference, Chicago.

Wagner, R., Torgesen, J., and Rashotte, C. 1999. *Comprehensive Test of Phonological Processing* (CTOPP). Austin, TX: Pro-Ed.

Walsh, K., Glaser, D. and Wilcox, D.D. 2006. *What education schools aren't teaching about reading and what elementary teachers aren't learning.* Washington, DC: National Council on Teacher Quality.

Watkins K.E., Strafella, A.P., and Paus, T. 2003. Seeing and hearing speech excites the motor system involved in speech production. *Neuropsychologia* 41:989-994.

Weaver, W. 1952. Information theory 1: Information theory to 1951, a non-technical review. *Journal of Speech and Hearing Disorders* 17(2):166–74.

Wechsler, D. 1974. *Wechsler Intelligence Scale for Children-Revised.* New York: The Psychological Corp.

________. 1991. *Wechsler Intelligence Scale for Children-3rd ed.* San Antonio: The Psychological Corporation.

________. 1992. *Wechsler Individual Achievement Test (WIAT).* San Antonio: The Psychological Corporation.

________. 2003. *Wechsler Intelligence Scale for Children-4th ed.* San Antonio: Pearson.

________. 2009. *Wechsler Individual Achievement Test®-III (WIAT®-III).* San Antonio: Pearson.

Weisenburg, T., and McBride, K. 1935. *Aphasia.* New York: The Commonwealth Fund.

Werker, J.F. 2000. Perceiving speech: A developmental perspective. *Journal of the Acoustical Society of America* 108: 2560.

West, R. (Ed.). 1960. *Childhood aphasia. Proceedings of the Institute on Childhood Aphasia.* Stanford, CA: National Society for Crippled Children and Adults.

Wiederholt, J. and Bryant, B. 1992. *Gray Oral Reading Test-3 (GORT-3).* Austin: Pro-Ed.

________. 2001. *Gray Oral Reading Test-4 (GORT-4).* Austin: Pro-Ed.

Wiley, S. and Moeller, M. 2007, January 23. Red flags for disabilities in children who are deaf/ hard of hearing. *The ASHA Leader.*

Wilson, B.A. 1988. *Wilson Reading System.* Millbury, MA: Wilson Language Training.

Wolf, M. and Denckla, M.B. 2005. *RAN/RAS: Rapid Automatized Naming and Rapid Alternating Stimulus Tests.* Austin, TX: Pro-Ed, Inc.

Wood, M.L. 1982. *Language disorders in school-age children.* Englewood Cliffs, NJ: Prentice-Hall, Inc.

Wood, N.E. 1964. *Delayed speech and language development.* Englewood Cliffs, NJ: Prentice-Hall, Inc.

Woodcock, R.W., McGrew, K.S., and Mather, N. 2001, 2007. *Woodcock-Johnson NU Tests of Achievement (WJ III®).* Rolling Meadows, IL: Riverside Publishing.

Yale, C.A. 1946. *Formation and development of elementary English sounds.* Northampton, MA: Clarke School for the Deaf.

Yeung, H., Scott, M., Gick, B., and Werker, J. 2008. Articulatory gestures influence the perception of speech. *Journal of the Acoustical Society of America* 124(4):2439-2439.

Yoss, D.A., and Darley, F.L. 1974. Developmental apraxia of speech in children with defective articulation. *Journal of Speech and Hearing Research* 17(3):399–416.

Young, E.H., and Hawk, S.S. 1955. *Moto-kinesthetic speech training.* Stanford, CA: Stanford University Press.

Index

A